PARTNERS IN DIALOGUE

Christianity and Other World Religions

ARNULF CAMPS

*Translated from the Dutch
by John Drury*

ORBIS BOOKS

Maryknoll, New York 10545

The Catholic Foreign Mission Society of America (Maryknoll) recruits and trains people for overseas missionary service. Through Orbis Books Maryknoll aims to foster the international dialogue that is essential to mission. The books published, however, reflect the opinions of their authors and are not meant to represent the official position of the Society.

Originally published in three volumes as *Christendom en godsdiensten der wereld: niéuwe in-zichten en nieuwe activiteiten*, copyright© 1976. Uitgeverij Bosch & Keuning n.v., Baarn, Netherlands; *De weg, de paden en de wegen: de Christelijke theologie en de concrete godsdien-sten*, copyright© 1977 Uitgeverij Bosch & Keuning n.v.; and *Geen doodlopende weg: lokale kerken in dialoog met hun omgeving*, copyright© 1978 Uitgeverij Ten Have bv, Baarn, Netherlands

Library of Congress Cataloging in Publication Data
Camps, Arnulf, 1925–
Partners in Dialogue

    "Originally published in three volumes as
Christendom en godsdiensten der wereld . . . De weg,
de paden en de wegen . . . Geen doodlopende weg"
—T.p. verso.
    1. Christianity and other religions. I. Title
BR127.C2513 1983   261.2   82-18798
ISBN 0-88344-378-3 (pbk.)

Contents

Preface

In older missiological works the word "dialogue" was not used. We had to wait for the post-colonial period of missions, the late fifties and the early sixties, before missiologists started to prefer the notion and the reality of dialogue above that of mission. Today the word and the necessity of dialogue is commonly accepted in all continents. This is an important development; but there is still quite some confusion. Even some slogans have come up: there are no longer missions, only dialogue is left! Or, we should reaffirm the missionary task of the churches and dialogue is just a kind of missionary method. Or, dialogue has to do only with cooperation in practical fields, not with truth! Or, dialogue is a comprehensive approach, a common striving after the fulness of salvation! When I started my missiological teaching at the Catholic University of Nijmegen, Holland, in 1963, I decided to concentrate my activities on an attempt to solve this problem. During all these years I have been lecturing on the theology of dialogue. The main results of that teaching were laid down in three books, which were published in Dutch in 1976, 1977, and 1978. The first book has a rather theoretical character. It treats various theological positions missiologists and theologians today take in the debate concerning dialogue and mission. It also contains a good deal of historical research, as in the past there have always been men and women of dialogue. The second book deals with practical dialogues in various religious and social situations. More than in the first book our own position will here be clarified. The third volume inquires after the results of the dialogue: does dialogue change the life of Christians and of Christian communities? Our answer is affirmative.

Now the three books are available in an English translation, and they are very well combined as three parts of one book. I am most grateful to Orbis Books for having accepted this result of so many years of research for translation. It is a wonderful translation, and I would like to congratulate the translator. For sure, his task was not easy. He has understood my intention—often expressed in long Dutch sentences—most clearly. He has even improved upon the text by dividing long paragraphs into smaller ones and by reediting the literature mentioned in the notes. He sometimes left out books and articles which will certainly not be available to English-speaking readers, and he often added literature in English written after 1978. I thank him for that.

Substantial changes have not been made by me. I think that the present text gives a good idea of the development of my ideas during the last nineteen years. I did not change in any substantial way my views. Just a few rather substantial corrections were made, but they are corrections, improvements of the original text.

I hope that through the good services of Orbis Books this dialogical missiology will stimulate discussion among Christians of all denominations. Above all I hope that this view on dialogue will be helpful to Christians of all continents to realize the fulness of salvation, which is in Christ Jesus, who is the Word of God spoken to men and women of all nations since the beginning of human history. The Word of God is in constant dialogue with people of whatever religion or ideology. As religious people we have the task to take part in this dialogue and we have to try to discover the fulness of God's Word. As I learned from my colleague Professor Dr. Piet Schoonenberg, we Christians have to enter this process humbly and patiently and above all gratefully as we have received so many treasures in Jesus Christ.

PART ONE

Christianity and Religions of the World: New Insights and New Activities

One might well spend a long time debating whether the title of Part One is apt. Judgments have always been passed on other religions from the stand-point of Christianity, but in the last twenty years in particular the subject has become very topical in the literature. The market has been flooded with titles dealing with the subject in one form or another: e.g., Christianity and other religions, Christian faith and the non-Christian religions, the relevance of Christian faith today, Meru and Golgotha, the Christian message in a non-Christian world, and so forth. Literature of this type is appearing in many languages and lands, and not least on the continents of Asia and Africa.

Here I have opted for a fairly traditional title, but underneath it lies a particular standpoint of my own. There is a great need for clarification and theological enlightenment in this area because the various standpoints are quite divergent. This part represents an attempt to reconcile them. It aims to show, not only that a dialogue with other religions is necessary and, from a Christian viewpoint, justified, but also that intramural Christian dialogue on the matter can come to a halt so that we may join together at last and begin the great dialogue.

For a long time Christianity in its many forms has not always recognized other religions as legitimate partners in a dialogue. In this part examples will be given of that fact. Suffice it to say here that Africa has been recognized as such a partner only very recently, and not just by Christianity alone. In the Greco-Roman ages the inhabitants of that continent were slaves. That con-tinued for centuries afterwards. The forces of Islam on the one hand and the

1

Western powers on the other scoured the coastal areas and penetrated the interior to some extent in their search for slaves. On the Christian side this process began in the fifteenth and sixteenth centuries, mainly in West Africa. On the Muslim side it began somewhat earlier and was concentrated in East Africa. The inhabitants of the dark continent were regarded as idolaters. They knew nothing of God, lived like wild animals, could not be trusted, and were thieves. Around the beginning of the eighteenth century the idea began to gain currency that the Africans were the accursed descendants of Ham (or Cham); the idea itself, of course, is unsound both ethnologically and exegetically. But at the time of Vatican I a group of missionaries proposed special prayers for Black Africa so that God might at last free it from the curse of Ham.[1]

St. Francis Xavier may stand as another example. With indomitable zeal he traversed East Africa, India, Malacca, the Moluccas, and Japan. He tried to convert as many people as possible in the shortest possible time because he was convinced that they would go to hell otherwise.[2] The underlying view was obviously a very pessimistic one about the chances for salvation in non-Christian religions. Further on in this book we shall see that there have always been exceptions among the Christian missionaries, but also that they definitely were exceptions. I shall try to impress upon my readers that we have not advanced much further and that we must go back deep into the Judeo-Christian tradition to arrive at a better approach—without, however, rendering mission work superfluous.

In this book I am writing about religions. Misunderstanding can readily crop up with regard to this topic. Theologically speaking, we find that there are countless definitions of religion. We can make a distinction between religions and folk-religions. We can also debate whether we should start with the original intentions of these religions and their founders or with the later forms that have arisen in the course of history. Furthermore, there is now a renewed search into their own sources going on in other religions.

Amid this multitude of problems I have opted for the following standpoint. I am writing a theological work. From the theological standpoint we can say that God has always communicated with humans from the very beginning, inviting them to enter into a dialogue with him. He is still doing that now. To this invitation human beings have always responded within social ties based on tribe or folk or group. It is this positive response that I call religion. Thus our first direct concern is not the institutional forms of religion as such, but rather the response of human beings to the vital questions of life and death posed by God's invitation. In its Declaration on the Relationship of the Church to Non-Christian Religions Vatican II had this to say on the matter: "Human beings look to the various religions for answers to those profound mysteries of the human condition which, today even as in olden times, deeply stir the human heart: What is a human being? What is the meaning and purpose of our life? What is goodness and what is sin? Where lies the path to true happiness? What is the truth about death, judgment, and retribution beyond the grave? What, finally, is that ultimate and unutterable mystery which engulfs our being, and whence we take our rise, and whither our journey leads us?"[3]

On the basis of this theological conception I intend to develop my ideas further, for I find in it a twofold basis for the possibility of dialogue. Firstly, there is a basis for a dialogue with other religions because they, too, recognize these questions and, as will become evident, are glad to enter into dialogue with Christians in their search for answers. Secondly, there is a basis for dialogue with human beings who hold other views of life which can hardly be called religions in the institutional sense, but which do seek to give answers to the same questions cited above: e.g., communism and humanism. For the sake of brevity I must limit my attention to the more religious philosophies of life; but my exposition is not unmindful of these latter human beings, and it may well serve as a start towards dialogue with them.

My starting point, then, is theological. However, that does not mean that I am restricting myself to a strictly religious terrain. I hope the reader will discover that this dialogue is of basic value both for a revitalized missiology and for a revitalized approach to the world and its current problems, however much one may wish to make a distinction between the two.

Insofar as missiology is concerned, my view is that an open and modern theology of religions is a sound basis for the solution of current problems such as efforts to find one's own proper way of being a church, one's own proper theology, one's own liturgy, one's own way of mission and service in the world, and so forth. Insofar as the approach to the world is concerned, I am convinced that the problems of the world are deeply bound up with the religious motivation of human beings, a motivation which they derive from their religious life. And when I say "problems of the world," I am referring to such problems as the following: the freedom of human beings, the quest for a new economic order, the humanization of life, cooperative effort for development and liberation. Thus our theologically oriented dialogue cuts in two directions.

I hope it will be clear from this study that those who are the heirs of Judeo-Christian revelation—and, to some extent at least, those who are heirs of the Muslim life of faith should be added here—have a distinctive task in today's world. Monotheistic religions represent a revolution in the religious thinking of humankind; with them something new began in human history. They offer us definite developmental values that are important for all of humanity and that we may pass on to people with different philosophies of life through open-hearted dialogue. Perhaps here we will discover our mission in this world.

To repeat myself once again, it is my opinion that this mission applies especially to Christians; but that in no way detracts from the mission that other monotheistic religions have.

1

The Causes of a Changing Outlook

From my Introduction it should be obvious that I am going to deal, not just with the worldwide religions, but with the religions of the world in general. Africa and the other continents with archaic religions also have a right to speak out. This fact will also be brought out clearly in this chapter, where I shall deal with the changing outlook and attitude evident between Christianity and other religions. As far as I can see, the causes are basically twofold: extra-ecclesial and intra-ecclesial.

EXTRA-ECCLESIAL FACTORS

First and foremost among the extra-ecclesial factors is the fact that our world is becoming more and more pluriform in the religious realm. In an earlier day the various religions were generally confined within a geographically limited area. Hinduism was at home on the Indian subcontinent, Buddhism in East and Southeast Asia, and Islam in the Middle East and North Africa primarily. That situation has changed completely. A great migration is in progress. Today we find many Turks, Moroccans, and Tunisians in Western Europe, even in the Netherlands. Buddhists, not too numerous in Holland, can be found in large numbers in England and Germany.

Besides the corporeal presence of human beings professing other religions, there is also a more spiritual presence. Through the modern communications media such as radio and television, they can reveal themselves in their otherness to us and thus become present to us. I do not believe that this is the beginning of a great world culture. With Paul Ricoeur I feel that the technological achievements of Western culture will become a universal reality—however much some voices are raised today expressing the undesirability of this outcome and the need for a well-adapted social technology in each of the various lands—but that the nature of other cultures, which includes their religious values, will remain intact.[4] On the other side of the coin, it is also true that Christianity has broken through its earlier geographical confinement and is now present in many different forms in practically all the countries of the world. So there is now a real chance for these religions to meet, and that opportunity is being seized. Zen meditation and Yoga sessions are no longer a strange sight in the West, and more and more literature is appearing: about other religions here in the West and about Christianity in other regions of the world.[5]

A second factor contributing to a changing outlook is the fact that within the various world religions we can detect a growing consideration for the world as a whole and a concomitant mission-mindedness. They have begun to take the path that Christianity and, to some extent, Islam set out upon earlier. One example in the case of the latter may suffice here. Since the eighteenth century the view has taken strong hold among Muslims that they possess the only rational religion which is fully suited to human nature; it has no mysteries and no superhuman obligations. This view has been spread far and wide from its beginnings on the old Indian subcontinent through such great thinkers as Shah Wali 'Ullah, Sir Sayyid Ahmad Khan, and Khalifa Abdul Hakim. Since this religion is so suited to human beings, it must be brought to all humans. This notion was adopted in the Ahmadiyya mission, which can be found now in the Netherlands and in many other Western lands as well as in Africa and Asia.[6]

In Hinduism, too, a more monotheistically oriented line of thought arose in the nineteenth century through its polemics with Anglican Christians. This led once again to a more universal outlook. There arose such movements as the Brahma Samaj and the Church of the New Dispensation, in which the person of Jesus of Nazareth in particular played a great role. This ultimately gave rise to the Ramakrishna mission, which now has more than a hundred centers in Europe and North America.[7]

Buddhism, too, has become quite active. Here I shall mention only two examples. The Buddhist mission for Germany operates out of Sri Lanka and has a training institute in Colombo. From the Netherlands Buddhism is propagated under the leadership of a monk from Thailand, and it has a temple in Waalwijk.[8]

A third extra-ecclesial factor of great importance is the collapse of the colonial system. This has led on the one hand to a revival of the old religions and cultures, and on the other to the demise of our old feeling of superiority. The collapse of the colonial system hardly needs to be proven here. We find colonies now only in a few areas in South Africa, the Caribbean, and Central America. The revival of the old religions and cultures is also a fact. Zaire is searching for authenticity, Tanzania for an African socialism, and Zambia for an African humanism. China has brought forth a new human being, and in Laos and Cambodia people are trying to do the same. Liberation theology and a few radical movements in Latin America point in the same direction.

In many places the old is coming back in a revitalized form. We even see new religions arising in lands that have never been colonies: Japan, for example. All this makes us Westerners a bit more modest, and as Christians we are being a bit more attentive to what is really finding expression in all this. It is not without reason that we are currently talking about local churches. They are now asserting themselves and we must reckon with them.[9]

A fourth factor contributing to the changing attitude between Christianity and the religions of the world is our changing image of what a human being is. Here again I can only allude to a few facets. Right now we are more oriented towards the other than we were before. The needs of the world are familiar to us; every day we see and hear more about them. Numerous agencies now exist to do something about those needs: e.g., the World Health Organization, the World Food Organization, UNESCO, Come Over the Bridge, A Guest at Table, Bread for the World, Cor Unum, and the various programs of the World Council of Churches.

There is a new turning of attention to the concrete living conditions of concrete human beings, and billions have been spent on them, though people may well question whether this help is basic enough in the long run. Human fellowship is not just a word any more, and a deeper change is also in process. Thinkers in the Third World, such as Che Guevara, Paulo Freire, Ivan Illich, and Mao Tse-Tung, have come forward with new images of the human being. There is need for a new dialogue between them and us, and a whole realm of thinking and doing lies before us. My impression is that Christianity is dealing with these things in a way that is still too anonymous and underground, considering that these things will decide and shape the world of a future day.[10]

Finally, I would like to mention one other factor. It is gaining recognition only slowly and hesitantly. For many years since World War II we have been occupied with the work of development and with cooperative ventures in this field. We have had to register many disappointments in this area, and many critical books have been written on the subject. Such, for example, was Gunnar Myrdal's *Asian Drama* (1968). Many new views and outlooks have also been put forth. There are now many models of development, but they are all under fire from critics. Even the traditional credibility of religions and ideologies as factors promoting development has been reduced to zero.

Today we stand at a new beginning. More recently we have been probing deeper and trying to find where the real forces for humanization and development lie. More and more people in the non-Western world are coming to the conviction that they must seek out and cultivate the native values in their own culture and religion that will ensure development in their own proper way. In this process people expect help from a more modest Christianity. Such a Christianity will divest itself of its Western garb and go back to its original source of inspiration. In dialogue with developmental values that are truly Judeo-Christian, it may then arrive at a suitable and basic solution to the problems we face.

If we wish to use a learned term, we may call this the maieutic art, the art of bringing development to birth; it is inextricably bound up with dialogue and always goes hand in hand with the latter. For example, one wonders whether the present-day situation in Indonesia has anything to do with the mystical inclination of the Javanese. One wonders about the fatalism in popular

Islam. Does the feeling that one is crushed under the omnipotence of God really have anything to do with authentic Islam? And people are also wondering now whether the plight of the rural inhabitants of Latin America has anything to do with their popular Catholicism, which tends to resign them to their hard lot. Here we have a whole new area for dialogue and mutual assistance.[11]

INTRA-ECCLESIAL FACTORS

For the sake of brevity we can perhaps trace all these factors back to one factor: the shift, at least in the Catholic Church, from monologue to dialogue. One can certainly maintain that from the age of Constantine to the era of Vatican II the Church was monologic in structure and mentality. This pattern was broken only by a few charismatic movements and by a few prophetic figures such as Cardinal Nicholas of Cusa. And when I refer to charismatic movements, I am thinking primarily of the movement set in motion by Francis of Assisi.

The new thing today is that it is the Church as a whole, and hence the hierarchy as well, that has accepted dialogue with the world as the basic principle and starting point. This is clear from the documents of Vatican II as well as from such papal encyclicals as *Pacem in terris, Eclesiam suam,* and *Populorum progressio.* It is also obvious from the erection of new organs of contact with the world, and hence with other religions. Three new secretariats have arisen: one to promote unity among Christians, one to promote dialogue with the non-Christian religions, and one to promote dialogue with nonbelievers. We have also seen the establishment of the Commission for Justice and Peace and the Council for the Laity.

It cannot be said that all these new organisms are functioning as well as they might, but they do point up a basic change in direction: i.e., a turning towards the world and towards greater openness, not just to talk to the world but also to listen to it in turn. The Church is no longer considered the People of God already perfectly realized. Instead it is the People of God on pilgrimage. In dialogue and cooperation with the world, other religions, and ideologies, it now seeks to shape the Kingdom of God in all its fullness. People no longer cling to the old attitude that there is no salvation outside the Church. The Catholic Church recognizes the ecclesial character of the other Churches, the authentic religious elements in non-Christian religions, and even positive values in various ideologies. God's salvific will is at work somehow outside Christianity and Judaism, and there we also find elements of divine revelation.

This changed outlook can be illustrated by citing various documents of Vatican II. Here I think it would be wisest for us to stick with the aforementioned conciliar declaration dealing with non-Christian religions *(Nostra aetate).* It makes many interesting points. For example, it says that the age-old primitive religions have a deeply religious sense; that in Hinduism people contemplate the divine mystery and express it through an inexhaustible wealth of myths and penetrating philosophical inquiry; that the Hindus seek release from the anguish of our condition through ascetical practices, deep meditation, or flight to God in trustful love. In Buddhism we find, according to the conciliar document, an acknowledgment of the radical insufficiency of this transient world. Buddhism teaches people a way to attain a state of absolute freedom or supreme enlightenment in a devout and confident spirit (NA 2).

The conciliar document speaks very positively about Islam (NA 3). It says that the Church looks on the Muslims with great respect. They worship the one God, the living, self-subsistent God who is merciful and almighty, who created heaven and earth, and who has spoken to human beings. The Church praises their wholehearted submission to God and their veneration of Jesus and Mary. In sharp contrast to the comments of the Church in earlier periods of controversy with Muslims, *Nostra aetate* also acknowledges that the Muslims prize the moral life and honor God through prayer, fasting, and almsgiving. Acknowledging the hostility that prevailed between the two religions in past centuries, the conciliar document urges all to forget the past, to strive for mutual understanding, and to make common cause in promoting the needs and rights of all human beings.

The next section of *Nostra aetate* (NA 4) deals with the Jewish religion in some detail. It openly acknowledges that the roots of Christianity lie in the people of the Old Testament. This common heritage must be preserved and studied by both parties. This will lead to mutual understanding and respect. The death of Jesus cannot be blamed on all the Jews living at the same time, nor on the Jews of today. In catechesis and preaching, Christians must be on the lookout for imprudent statements. The painful relations of the past must be energetically condemned and not allowed to crop up again.

With regard to other religions in general (NA 2), the Catholic Church rejects nothing that is true and holy in them. She has sincere respect for their ways of conduct and of life, their rules and teachings, which often reflect a ray of the Truth that enlightens all humans even though they may be at variance with what the Catholic Church itself teaches. The Catholic Church itself "proclaims and must ever proclaim Christ, 'the way, the truth, and the life' (John 14:6), in whom human beings find the fullness of religious life and in whom God has reconciled all things to Himself" (NA 2). The task proposed to the members of the Church is: "Prudently and lovingly, through dialogue and collaboration with the followers of other religions, and in witness of Christian faith and life, acknowledge, preserve, and promote the spiritual and moral goods found among these human beings, as well as the values in their society and culture" (NA 2).

If ever dialogue and cooperation for the sake of the world have been urged, they were certainly urged in this document. Dialogue is not an abstract game to be played with learned words; like the Church itself, dialogue is in the service of the world with all its concrete problems of today. This Church is the sacrament of the world. As a community of human fellowship, it stands as a symbol for the world; in the latter, too, the dialogic mode of existence must become a reality between human beings.

This dialogue is not just a new method or tactic. It is not a matter of self-gain, but a matter of sharing and communicating oneness and union. Through dialogue the other is to be given a chance to become himself even more. I shall return to this point later when I stress that dialogue must have a creative result. It must give birth to something new, to a *tertium quid,* to a distinctive and native way of being Christian within another culture or another religion. Perhaps this view offers us a way out of the present ecumenical impasse about which we are now hearing so much. In short, dialogue leads to pluriformity within Christianity.[12]

An indication of this can be seen in the self-affirmation we now see, particularly at the 1974 Synod of Bishops. The African bishops in particular have clearly settled accounts with what used to be called the theology of adaptation. According to that theology, Western Christianity stood as the norm; accommodations to the specific and distinctive reality of the non-Christian world were to be allowed only with regard to external, incidental, and accidental matters. Now the native bishops are pleading for an incarnational theology in which all the rich religions and cultural data of other human traditions are taken up into the Christian corpus of faith. They are pleading pointedly for a distinction between faith, which is perduring, and theology, liturgy, and catechesis. The latter are forms of ecclesial life, forms of service to the Church and the world, that can and must change in terms of different ages and cultures. Here too, then, we hear the summons to pluriformity within unity.[13]

I can conclude this chapter with the simple observation that many factors, both within and outside the Church, have contributed to the changed situation in which we now live. Today the relationship of Christianity to other religions is fundamentally different. Theologically speaking, we must set out on new pathways if we are to justify and explain this new approach. But before I tackle that task, I should like to enumerate some of the new phenomena which show that it is not simply a matter of new ideas shared by only a few thinkers, that instead much change has also been taking place in the realm of facts and deeds. There are new initiatives and new experiments. These, too, must be considered before we can explore the matter more deeply in theological terms.

2

New Forms of Dialogue and Contact

In this chapter I want to examine the new forms of dialogue and contact from three different sides. This will provide us with a specific formulation of the problem that will concern us in the next chapter.

A first set of new initiatives and experiments is to be found on the Catholic side. Here I am referring to the activities carried on by the Secretariat for Non-Christians in the Vatican. This secretariat focuses primarily on the religious human being in dialogue; it seeks to establish contact and dialogue on that level specifically. In the first phase of its existence, after it was established in 1964, the work of this secretariat consisted primarily in scholarly publications and scholarly contacts undertaken by its consultors scattered around the world. Examples of this are to be found in its *Bulletin*. At first, articles were published in French and English only; now they are published in a variety of languages. In them we find reports of the deliberations of consultors and views of others concerning dialogue. Later we also find guidelines for dialogue with various religions. Thus we find specific sets of guidelines for dialogue with Buddhism, Islam, Hinduism, and the African religions. The guidelines present a theoretical exposition of these religions and enumerate a series of points which can serve as the basis for dialogue.

What is envisioned here is a very specific notion of dialogue. The dialogue in question is not one regarding salvation. It is not designed to bring together the salvific values present in Christianity and other religions so that we might arrive at the sort of new, creative synthesis I mentioned in the previous chapter. Here dialogue remains a mutual conversation about religious experiences and the contents of one's faith in order to arrive at better mutual understanding and hence cooperative efforts. This method is then justified in a few more thoroughgoing studies: e.g., *Vers la rencontre des religions, suggestions pour le dialogue* (Vatican City, 1967); and *Religions, thèmes fondementaux pour une connaissance dialogique* (Rome, 1970). This might well be called a preliminary phase, which was under the direction of Paolo Cardinal Marella.

Another approach along the same lines began in 1973, when Sergio Cardinal Pignedoli became president of this secretariat and Msgr. Pietro Rossano its secretary. Henceforth emphasis was laid on meetings with non-Christians; many trips and dialogues took place. There were meetings in Thailand and Japan, in West and East Africa, in Indonesia and Malaysia, and finally in Tripoli (Lybia). Experts from various parts of the world were also invited to the secretariat. But when one reads the reports of these meetings, one gets the distinct impression that there is no desire at all to dialogue about salvation for fear of coming into conflict with the Congregation for the Evangelization of Peoples. There is a deliberate effort to maintain an artificial distinction between the two Vatican organisms. The secretariat restricts its attention to mutual religious understanding and the desire for cooperative ventures, which as yet have not been implemented in deeds.[14]

A second approach to our problem derives from the earlier International Missionary Council and the present-day Division for Dialogue of the World Council of Churches (Geneva). Two outstanding dissertations have now appeared on this subject, so that we now have an overall view of it from the first meeting of the International Missionary Council in Edinburgh in 1910 to the Uppsala meeting of the World Council of Churches in 1968.[15] Here again we find a distinctive line of development resulting in a specific standpoint or approach.

Obviously people involved on this side have been occupied with the problem for a longer time than those on the Catholic side. In the beginning the viewpoints were quite divergent. Some felt that they, as Christians, could not take the step over to dialogue; others, particularly the Anglo-Saxons and the Indian theologians, were quite willing to venture in that direction. The latter saw the step as a very wholesome and saving one. Then the bomb was dropped in Tambaram: Hendrik Kraemer's book entitled *The Christian Message in a Non-Christian World* (London, 1938). Following closely in the footsteps of Karl Barth, Kraemer judged that other religions as systems were merely human works, however great they might be on that level, and that they were efforts at self-deliverance. Over against them, and also over Christianity as an institution, he set Christian faith with its demand to renounce everything.

The book marked a critical juncture. It was not accepted by the Indian theologians. It also aroused much opposition in other non-Christian lands, where people felt that it nullified devotion to one's own traditions. However, the book also found wide acceptance, especially among theologians in Europe. It is my impression that neither the International Missionary Council nor the World Council of Churches has managed to get beyond this dilemma. They are still wrestling with the complex of theological problems posed by other religions. One also gets the feeling that people are trying to sidestep the problem by getting into concrete dialogues with representatives of other religions. Thus we see no theoretical expositions among Christians, but rather an emphasis on concrete encounters with human beings of another faith, as people now put it.

The striking fact is that the subject matter of these encounters has no relation whatsoever to the theological question concerning the salvific value of other religions, and hence to the theological justification of dialogue. Instead these encounters deal with problems between human beings. The first such encounter took place in Ajaltoun (Lebanon) in 1970, where Hindus, Buddhists, Christians, and Muslims met. But the clearest example of this particular development was the 1974 meeting in Colombo (Sri Lanka), where Jews were also present with the groups mentioned above. The memorandum of the meeting is indicative. Points for discussion and further consideration were to include the following: pluralism in the world; the differing interpretations of history; cooperative efforts on behalf of the human dignity of all persons; the awareness of living under the physical threat of death and annihilation by war or famine, exploitation or indoctrination; the problem of a world community threatened by underdevelopment; and the internal difficulties of the new nations. All this led to a series of concrete recommendations. But here again one must note that the theological problem of dialogue and the encounter of religions, and the relationship of that to mission, was not resolved.[16]

This contrast between the standpoints of the two sides already mentioned—i.e., the Secretariat for Non-Christian Religions on the Catholic side and the International Missionary Council of the World Council of Churches on the Protestant side—is particularly accentuated by a whole series of initiatives that have taken place on both national and international planes. It is surprising how many national and international congresses between different religions have taken place in recent years. Also surprising is the fact that most of them have a permanent character.

The history of these congresses goes back to the World's Parliament of Religions, which was held in Chicago in 1893. Representatives from practically all the religions of the world attended it. It was a great event, which made a deep impression on people of that day. The Catholic Church and other Churches participated fully in it. The report on the preparations for this congress and its actual proceedings takes up two thick volumes. It contains valuable material that has still not been utilized for further study and scholarly examination.[17]

It is impossible to summarize the 1,600 pages of this report here. One can say that the primary intention of this parliament was to provide those involved with positive enlightenment about religions. It was an exchange of data. But here we already glimpse the emergence of a theme that will recur in later congresses: i.e., compassion for the plight of one's fellow human beings. We find a speech on the responsibility of the Catholic Church for what was then called "the negro race." Others spoke about international arbitration, international justice and friendship, the brotherhood of human beings, and America's duties towards China. It was a long time before any such congress took place again, and no congress has been so universal; but these themes have come back again.

We cannot discuss all the congresses that have taken place. Some selection is necessary. But I would like to mention that the idea of a world parliament of religions has cropped up again in our day, and that from India there has been a proposal that the Pope act as chairman of such a meeting.

One important organization to be mentioned here is the Temple of Understanding, which held a first spiritual summit conference in Calcutta in 1968. Thomas Merton attended and was one of those who led the participants in prayer. Those attending included Hindus, Christians, Buddhists, Muslims, Jews, and followers of Confucius and Zoroaster. Sikhs and Bahaists also were present. The theme was the relevance of religions for the problems of the modern world. The speakers were conscious of the fact that the twentieth century poses challenges to human beings in various areas, and also new problems: e.g., the reality of science and technology, racism, the dangers of war, and the threat of armaments. Each religion sought to offer an answer to human beings and the world on the basis of its own inspiration and vision of God.

It is my impression that the participants at this conference dug deeper than those at the meetings of the World Council of Churches because they followed through. On the one hand they went to the core of their own religion and its relevance for the world; on the other hand they brought the varying views of their different religions into contact and comparison with each other. Also worth noting is the fact that the whole problematic was dealt with in greater detail than it had been in the meetings organized by the Secretariat for Non-Christians because the participants pushed on to the tasks of these human beings vis-à-vis the world. Here we come closer to the solution of one of the two basic sets of problems that will occupy our particular attention here: the intrinsic interweaving of religious motivation and its operativeness in the world. The other problem, which still persists and which I alluded to earlier, did not come under discussion: i.e., What precisely is a dialogue about salvation and what is the specific role of Christian values in this?[18]

A second conference of the Temple of Understanding was held in Geneva in 1970. There again we find the same outlook.[19] Here, too, we can say that some sought to bring the various religions to one denominator—always a hazardous undertaking—and that the participants came together to resolve the personal and collective problems of humanity. There was talk about mutual understanding, peace, justice, and brotherhood. A standing commission was appointed, but I have not been able to ascertain whether it has held further meetings. I only know that in 1971 a small-scale meeting was held at Harvard University among a group of scholars. They discussed the topic: religion in the seventies. A surprising number of Jewish people were invited to this conference. Perhaps large-scale conferences may come to seem impracticable and people will switch to more regional meetings.

A second major organization is the World Conference of Religions and Peace. Its chairman and guiding spirit is the archbishop of New Delhi, Angelo Fernandes. But we cannot forget the American, Homer A. Jack, who is the secretary-general of the organization and who, with his wife, has shouldered the burden of the work. He is in charge of the organization's headquarters in New York. The origin of this movement goes back to a national inter-religious conference on peace that was held in Washington in 1966. The 500 participants at that conference voted to explore the possibility of holding a World Inter-Religious Conference on Peace in 1967. This led to a preliminary international symposium of religions on peace, which was held in New Delhi in 1968.[20] Nine world religions met for five days and discussed the theme. Noteworthy is the fact that there was no trace of syncretism, about which some had been fearful. Profound differences in theology and culture were brought out in the open. The participants resolved to work for a truly international conference and even seconded the notion that they would have to establish regional sections. In itself the conference had a good impact on peaceful relations between the differing religions and peoples in India. Those involved saw very well that the absence of Africa and Latin America at the conference was a drawback.

All this led to an International Conference of Religions for Peace in Kyoto, Japan, in 1970.[21] It was truly an international meeting, at which Africans and Latin Americans were also present. The large participation of India and Japan was particularly noteworthy. Again there were many speeches; but the reports on disarmament, development, human rights, the Vietnam question, South Africa, the Middle East, young people, and peace activities predominated. Three position papers on disarmament, development, and human rights respectively had a strong impact on the proceedings. All the religions led a prayer service of their own. One got a clear picture of the direct involvement of the various religions in concrete world problems on the basis of their own sources of inspiration. Greatly contributing to this impression was Archbishop Helder Camara's introductory remarks on religion and the necessity for structural changes in today's world.

A second World Conference of Religions and Peace was held in Louvain in 1974.[22] Again people from every corner of the earth met, but this time a large number of representatives from international organizations were also present. The Vatican was represented by the Secretariat for Non-Believers. No big speeches or lectures were held. The work was conducted in committees. Topics included disarmament and security, economic development and human liberation, human rights and basic freedoms, the environment and human survival, religion and population problems, and the Declaration of the United Nations against religious intolerance. Separate working groups examined the role of religion in current issues concerning peace, in specific situations of conflict, in South Africa, and in educating people for peace. The participants also drew up the Louvain Declaration, which was signed by Buddhists, Christians, Confucianists, Hindus, Jains, Jews, Muslims, Shintoists, Sikhs, followers of Zoroaster, and others. The reports of the committees and the working groups are detailed and thoroughgoing. They have helped to raise the consciousness of the various religions with regard to these modern problems, even of those religions that are not by nature so oriented towards the world. Very practical proposals have been made.

In the meantime the conference has acquired the status of a nongovernmental organization in the United Nations and its organisms as well as in the Council of Europe. Thus it can participate in discussions held by various commissions in which the aforementioned topics are treated. A move towards regionalization is also noticeable. The international headquarters are in New York, and there are national bureaus in Japan, India, the United States, Europe as a whole, and Canada. Also interesting is the fact that the European working group has evinced the need to arrive at some spirituality for this world conference of religions. A core group has already met twice. It prepared a paper that is now being studied by the regional groups and that will certainly have an important place on the agenda of the third World Conference of Religions and Peace.

So here again we find a striving for interiority together with a desire to be actively effective in the world, and a concern for the relationship between both. This, too, is an interesting sign insofar as our formulation of the problem in this book is concerned. Here again I must note that the more difficult and delicate problems of a dialogue concerning salvation are not yet in sight.

Here I also want to mention a third organization: The World's Congress of Faiths. Actually this is a fairly old organization. It arose some forty years ago in England, where people from many different colonial areas and religions found themselves living together. All the meetings of this organization, which usually took place each year, were held in England. The objective of the organization makes it clear what people have in mind. They are not concerned with institutionalized religions as such but with faiths. This includes everyone who, on the basis of his or her view of life, feels they can contribute something to humanity and its well-being. In this case there is not such a clear and express orientation to the world as we find in the two organizations mentioned above. The emphasis is on an exchange of ideas, and there is no great urge to arrive at some world community sharing only one faith. This movement also has sections in other countries. The Dutch section, established in 1948, is known as the Wereldgesprek der Godsdiensten. This group is mainly interested in discussions concerned with specific topics. For example, it has examined religious education at the high-school level and prepared a bibliography of written and audio-visual materials. It has also considered the critical situation in the Middle East and the religious problems resulting from the emigration of large numbers from Surinam. It also sponsored the idea of setting up an educational center, and this led to the establishment of Interreligio in Rotterdam in 1972. Branch sections of the organization have also been established in Germany, Belgium, and India. The main purpose is to foster a better understanding and knowledge of religions, but there is also a desire to tackle the problems of the world.[23]

Of course other organizations of this sort have arisen in recent times and some of them are still active.[24] But I feel that my sketch of the three aforementioned organizations provides a good summary of the most important developments on the international level.

On the national level many initiatives have also taken place that deserve mention here, but they cannot all be considered here. India occupies a pre-eminent place in this regard. There the Catholic Church in particular has been very active under the direction of the Secretariat for Dialogue, which is fortunate to be under the vigorous leadership of Rev. Albert Nambiaparambil, C.M.I.[25] Underlying all his initiatives is the following conviction: "Since we live in close contact with people of other religions, the Church in India must involve itself in a dialogue with them. Inter-religious dialogue is the response of the Christian faith to God's saving presence in the religious traditions of humanity, and the expression of our hope and expectation of the fulfillment of all things in Christ."[26]

Here we have the first clear expression of the idea of a dialogue about salvation. That is why it is particularly important for us to explore the many experiments in India here in this book. We can say that dialogue with other religions began some ten years ago in India and that it was first viewed with suspicion. It was looked upon as a luxury to be indulged in by a few intellectuals, or inhabitants of ashrams, or small meditation groups. The great mass of Christians would first have to be educated for dialogue before they could undertake it on their own.

Pope Paul VI himself provided a good push in the right direction when he visited India in 1964. At that time he said that we must meet each other, not just as tourists but as pilgrims on the road seeking God, not just in stone buildings but in the hearts of human beings. Human beings and nations must meet each other as brothers and sisters, as children of God. In mutual friendship and understanding, and in holy fellowship, we must also begin to work together to build a communal future for the human race. At the 1968 Pastoral Council in India this thought was echoed, and it was also pointed out that the other religions of India have made a great contribution to the spiritual wealth of humanity. Forgiveness was asked for past negligences, and people looked towards mutual cooperation in the current crisis of modernization and secularization. A start has now been made in that direction, but one cannot say that the phenomenon has yet become general. Hence great attention has been focused on accompanying and helping the Christians of India in this new task. The episcopal commission for dialogue has also undertaken three steps: arranging "get-togethers" for dialogue, organizing inter-religious "live-togethers," and holding courses on Islam.

The "get-togethers" are regional affairs and last two or three days. They are study meetings which examine the nature of dialogue, its demands and difficulties, its risks and concrete possibilities. Leaders of other religions and nonbelievers are also present to offer their views about these questions and to share their vision of life with Christians. Concrete steps are proposed at the last of these meetings. Thus the aim of these meetings is primarily educational and informative. Greater awareness and a change of mentality are the goals sought.

The "live-togethers" go a step further. The first was held in 1973 in Benares between Hindus and Christians. Later gatherings included Muslims and Sikhs as well. The participants join together for prayer, meditation, and joint reflection on the religious realm. They share the same lifestyle and the expenses, considering such questions as the following: What does my religion mean to me? What is my attitude towards other religions? How do I feel about prayer, religious experience, and meditation in my own life? What about my religion and social concern for my neighbors? What are the challenges to my religion and how do I resist them? What hopes do I cherish? What crisis in values do I face? What concrete steps can we take to foster mutual unity and cooperation between believers?

Courses on Islam are necessary in India because more than sixty million Muslims still live there. They cannot be overlooked in the matter of dialogue. Special preparation is needed in this case, however, because of long-standing ignorance and bad relations. These courses are given jointly with the well-known Protestant institute, the Henry Martin Institute for Islamic Studies, in Hyderabad. The course lasts three days, providing information about Islam, discussing points of misunderstanding, and so forth. There are discussions with Muslim leaders. When possible, the participants also visit a mosque at the time for prayer.

So far ten such courses have been given in various parts of India. There have been five "get-togethers" and nine "live-togethers." Christians from other denominations participated in all of them, so that the activities also served an ecumenical purpose. The aim is to place responsibility for this new event in the hands of the local communities. There are now thirteen ashrams, fifteen dialogue centers, and eight dialogue groups that carry on this work; and it is spreading.

What benefits have accrued from all these activities? Nambiaparambil has summarized a few of them. Love, which builds bridges, has arisen between Hindus and Muslims, who hardly get along with each other in a city such as Aligarh. There is a shift from isolation to community. All too long the various religious communities have lived alongside each other without realizing that religious experience is something that can be shared; indeed the thought hardly seems to have entered their minds before. The "live-togethers" have gradually given rise to joint committees of a community sort. In the future they hope to work together, primarily in the spiritual area but in three instances in the area of social action, social projects, and work among the poor as well.

Of course there have been problems as well, and they still persist. Some are fearful of syncretism. Some are afraid that Jesus Christ will lose his uniqueness. Still others feel that missionary work will no longer be possible if people dialogue. A directory for dialogue in India is to appear soon. But Nambiaparambil knows how to take objections in stride. He maintains that the matter at hand involves a deeply religious experience of one's own faith-world and that of others; that there is no question of equating one religion with another. It is an experiment designed to help people get through a crisis and see light on the other side. Dialogue is a pilgrimage and has an eschato-logical perspective: people are looking for the oneness of all the faith-values in all religions, and those values reach their culmination in Jesus Christ. Only by way of analysis can we arrive at plenitude.

New forms of dialogue and contact arose around 1965 in Sri Lanka, which at that time was still called Ceylon. In that year a Congress of Religions was set up. The ten million inhabitants of that island are divided up religiously into Buddhists, Hindus, Muslims, and Christians; traditionally there was lit-tle communication between them. There was now a desire to achieve more harmony, understanding, and tolerance between the followers of these world religions. There was hope that this would lead to an integrated society that would serve the nation through its religious harmony. An inter-religious council was called into being, to which all difficult cases might be submitted. Leaving institutional competition aside, people sought to join together for social service to the population based on a religious background. For only in that way can the energies of the community as a whole be activated.

Thus four sections arose in the Congress of Religions. The first was the inter-religious council mentioned above. There tensions and disputes be-tween religions are brought out into the open so that some action can be taken: e.g., against conversions based on material motives, and for equal catechetical opportunities for every religion. The second section is the cultural unit. It organizes all sorts of activities to stress the fact that every world religion manifests itself in a distinctive culture. So far, for example, there have been discussions about the family, its social significance, and the responsibility of parents. On specific feast days of one religion there is no participation in the ritual of the other religion so as to avoid confusion; but a spokesman for the celebrating religion is permitted to express his view of the event and all the others come to listen. More searching dialogues are not public; they take place among small groups of experts. A third section is the social action unit. Two types of social services are already known in Sri Lanka. One type is promoted by denominational religions. They excel in expertise based on religious motives, but they also tend to confine themselves to promoting their own denomination. A second type is promoted by the State. In this case it is backed up by the community as a whole, but the quality grounded in religious motivation is lacking. Now people are seeking a third type of social service. It is to have an inter-religious character based on the perduring spiritual values common to all religions. This type of service must be capable of activating the whole community. Matters for action include good housing, fair wages, social responsibility, and so forth. The fourth sec-tion is an administrative unit. It looks after current activities and tries to get new initiatives off the ground.

My impression is that in Sri Lanka people have arrived at a good type of dialogue and contact. All the onesidedness noted earlier seems to be avoided. Perhaps the direct religious dialogue in small groups could probe more deeply than it has because it is all too easy for people to start with the assumption that all religions are alike. The question of a dialogue about salvation has not been resolved in this case, but the matter of turning towards the world has.[27]

A third initiative comes from Japan—again a country of Asia, the continent of the great world religions. In Japan we find a Conference for Peace and World Federation, which includes all the religions of Japan except the Soka Gakkai. In 1974 it held its sixth gathering in Nagasaki, and the organization of the meeting was entrusted to the Catholics. Undoubtedly influenced by the Holy Year, they chose as their theme: reconciliation between human beings. The import was clear. Reconciliation was viewed against the backdrop of the atom bomb, which exploded in Nagasaki, and of the persecution of Christians in Japan, which lasted for centuries and which is memorialized by a large monument at the harbor entrance. The desire was to forget the past, close a page of history, and start out towards a new community where respect for nature and friendship among all human beings would prevail.

Reconciliation was considered in three introductory papers, to which three discussion groups replied. The themes of these papers were: building the world on a foundation of friendship and trust; mutual understanding and real community among human beings in Asia; and the rediscovery of the Japanese human being. Two days were devoted to these topics. They were meaningful for those who were familiar with the role of Japan in the Asia of an earlier day and who are now looking for a new identity for the Japanese, both with respect to self and with respect to the new task that they must now carry out in a new Asia.

A solemn, Gregorian Eucharistic service was also concelebrated. It made a deep impression on the non-Christians, not only because it was held in a cathedral rebuilt since the war, but also because the atmosphere was so intensely religious. Afterwards one Buddhist monk said: "In this hour I tasted the joy of Amida's paradise." One evening there was a meeting of 250 young people from Nagasaki who belonged to various religions. Splitting into five groups, they spent four hours talking about the vocation of religious young people today. Msgr. Pietro Rossano, the representative of the Vatican at this meeting, gave several short talks in which he presented the Catholic and Christian view of reconciliation. He did so by citing and explaining passages from the documents of Vatican II, which maintain that the Church has the task of promoting unity and love among human beings and peoples. The conclusions of the conference, which were drawn up by representatives of all the religions present, were presented to the Japanese government.

Worthy of note in this Japanese initiative is the great role of the Japanese bishops. They were present and delivered speeches. They evinced great solidarity with the other Japanese religions and with the Church of Rome. A certain air of utopia reigned over the congress, and it goes back to the old Buddhism of Nichiren: so long as one submits to the Lotus Sutra, then the Japanese will achieve peace, salvation, and social progress, and their nation will become a holy platform that will enlighten all the peoples of the earth.

One could also detect a whiff of messianism, which is not alien to the new religions in Japan, almost all of which have arisen since World War II. They tend to be more pragmatic, while older Buddhism is more religious. In conclusion, then, I would say that here again we find a solid orientation towards dialogue with the world and hence one aspect of salvation for human beings; but in this case, too, there is no full or complete dialogue about salvation.[28]

Summarizing this chapter, I would say that I have tried to shed some light on the new forms of dialogue and contact from three different sides. First I considered the Catholic Church and its Secretariat for Non-Christians. Then I dealt with the outlook and activities of the World Council of Churches and its division for dialogue. Finally, I examined a variety of international and national organizations. My feeling is that this overview has been useful, though certainly not exhaustive.

Two things stand out clearly. First of all, dialogue is not just a matter for conciliar documents and theologians alone. It is now a practice in Churches and religious communities. Secondly, I must also point out that as yet there is no comprehensive, uniform view of dialogue. One may have a purely religious way of thinking about dialogue or one's dialogue may be more oriented to the problems of this world even though it is based on a religious standpoint. In many instances this religious standpoint is not clearly worked out. Our major problem, however, is the fact that a correct understanding of the concept of a dialogue about salvation is missing, except in the case of India. By this I mean a dialogue which recognizes that in all religions we find God's communication and a legitimate response to it by human beings. This poses a problem which is specifically theological: i.e., the relationship between religions and, above all, the view that Christians bring with them to any dialogue. For Christians believe that in Jesus of Nazareth something unique has taken place that has significance for all human beings, granting all the good responses and salvific values they all possess. These problems will now occupy us more closely.

3

Foundations for a Deeper Dialogue

We shall proceed slowly in developing this chapter because we must delve deeply into history in order to arrive at a correct modern formulation of the problem and its solution. First of all, there have been barriers to deeper dialogue on both the Protestant and the Catholic side. There have also been half-way solutions, such as relativism and syncretism, which in fact offer no solution at all. After we have done this preliminary work, we can probe more deeply and explore the biblical and patristic data for a positive theology of religions. Then we will examine later theological developments of a negative sort, also noting a few happy exceptions to the prevailing trend. Only then will the way be clear for us to make a positive approach to other religions through the work of various modern theologians.

This, in brief, is the setup of the present chapter. Of necessity the author must choose among the welter of data. I hope, however, to remain faithful to the real lines of development.

PROTESTANT INHIBITIONS
VIS-A-VIS A THEOLOGY OF RELIGIONS

In this section I do not mean to lump all Protestant missiologists together as if there were no differences among them. I know that there have been exceptions to the current standpoint. Such people as J. N. Farquhar and various Indian theologians took a positive stand vis-à-vis other religions.[29] And Paul Althaus vacillated between yes and no insofar as the presence of salvation in other religions was concerned.[30] But here I am considering a school of thought that has become current in Protestant circles and that still exerts great influence.

With all due respect I shall call it the exclusivist school, and one can encounter its thinking in publications to this very day. First we shall briefly consider its major spokesman and representative, Hendrik Kraemer, and then show that the spirit of his thinking has not yet been overcome. We have already seen that in considering the dialogue conference of the International

Missionary Council and the Division for Dialogue of the World Council of Churches. Here, however, we must explore the matter a bit more deeply.

Hendrik Kraemer wrote about this subject frequently throughout his life.[31] His major work falls between the publication of two books: *De ontmoeting van het Christendom en de Wereldgodsdiensten* (The Hague, 1938); and *Godsdiensten en culturen* (The Hague, 1963). Though Kraemer himself was Dutch, many of his books appeared in English before they were published in his native language. Viewing his works from a theological standpoint, we can say that we find no great developments in them. So here I shall rely on the 1963 book mentioned above to present his views, for it provides a culmination and a summary of his life's work.

Kraemer is familiar with the modern world and he knows that we are now living in the postcolonial age. He knows that in today's world there is a great deal of reaction against the invasion by the West. He also realizes the significance of this for the revival of other religions and for a new concept of mission. He is even prepared to use a new word in connection with the latter: i.e., dialogue. In any case he does use the latter word. The real question, however, is what he means by the term "dialogue," and that is discussed only at the end of his 1963 book. We can only answer the question after we see what Kraemer means by religions. He writes: "In the Bible religions are false or correct ways of showing loving obedience to God, who reveals his holy will."[32] This statement sounds more open than what we find in his earlier works. In one earlier work he discusses the realism of the Bible in the following terms:

> Jesus makes short shrift of all the means whereby human beings propose to become participants in God: e.g., holiness, enlightenment (Buddha), perfect insight and perfect discipline (saddha), and so forth. Jesus brushes all these aside with the remark: "Unless you change and become like little children, you will not enter the kingdom of God. Whoever makes himself lowly, becoming like this child, is of greatest importance in that heavenly reign" (Matt. 18:3–4). In the light of this remark, which articulates one of the major themes of the Bible with incomparable simplicity, all theological and philosophical discussion or debate as to whether human beings are in a position to know the true God is reduced to silence.[33]

Here, then, we see Kraemer rejecting universal revelation, natural revelation, and all religions (including Christianity) as efforts at self-deliverance and hence disastrous. The 1963 text cited earlier seems to be more open. But is it really? For one thing, it seems that the later book is not so solidly theological as his earlier ones. One gets the impression that Kraemer, because of his vast knowledge of religions and also the fact that these religions have become active again even in the West, now has some doubts as to whether his strong earlier judgment is still tenable today. His knowledge and the changed situation are compelling even him to reconsider dialogue, and he fully realizes that this new reflection will have an impact on one's whole missionary approach. At the same time, however, we find that even in his 1963 book Kraemer is still writing about the complete antithesis between other religions and Christianity.[34] And when he talks about this antithesis, he has the Eastern religions in mind primarily.[35]

Thus when we ask what dialogue really is, we find it difficult to get an answer in Kraemer's last works. In his later years he was still capable of noticing changes, but aside from occasional judgments about other religions he had become more circumspect. From this bulky tome one gets the impression that dialogue means primarily making contact with people of other religions who are involved in a process of development; and that in this contact Christians must first put their own house in order so that they can resolutely decide to be the Church of Jesus Christ both in the East and the West.

Hendrik Kraemer managed to exercise a major influence on Protestant thinking. Here I shall not delve further into the question of his dependence on Karl Barth, though it seems to me that it is enormous. My impression is that Kraemer himself has two kinds of followers. One group follows the youthful Kraemer while the other group follows the older Kraemer.

In the first group we must include Arend Th. van Leeuwen, who wrote *Christianity in World History.*[36] This book, too, is replete with a biblical realism, though that term itself is not used. One is struck by the fact that the religious history of Israel is set apart, and also by the parallel set up between this history and that of Christianity. In Israel there is a complete break between the religious life and thought of the pagan people and that of the Hebrews. Israel is led away from what the author calls the ontocratic pattern. It is removed from the domination of what is, from the feeling for the cosmic whole which keeps circling back in every area of human life, from cyclic thinking which is expressed primarily in symbols. Israel takes the big step from mythical to historical thinking, a transition that later takes place among the Greeks as well. The two come together later in the New Testament, and this transition comes to shape the restless dynamism underlying the history of Western Christianity. This is now in the process of affecting all religions, bringing them within the inescapable forward march of human history. Sacred traditions thus have been broken through from the early days of Israel to our own day. The task of Western culture is to carry this break through to its conclusion on every continent; and within Western culture itself the missionary movement is the dynamic force that faces this task pre-eminently. In other words, Western culture, and particularly Western Christianity within that culture, is the crowbar to be applied to any and every religion.

Here we meet the young Kraemer once again. Like Karl Barth, he sets up a radical opposition between other religions—including Christianity as a religion rather than as faith—and what we now call Christianity here, giving the latter the task of annihilating the others.[37] Thus there is no vision of God's one salvation history vis-à-vis human beings; no place for a cosmic revelation of God, which is written off as ontocratic, as an effort to effect self-deliverance and salvation; and hence no real vision of dialogue. And this line of thought is very much alive even today.

Others have felt more comfortable with the older Kraemer. Here I am thinking in particular of J. Verkuyl. He has often written on this matter, and has summarized his thinking in his latest book on recent missiology.[38] It is a book rich in ideas, and it also offers a good presentation of the various Catholic positions regarding dialogue. The author is well informed, but here we are interested in pinpointing his own standpoint amid the welter of Catholic and Protestant views that he presents.

It is pleasing to me to see that Verkuyl shares my view that the time is right for a new reflection on the theology of religions, and for new forms of dialogue. Like the older Kraemer, he is convinced that our greater knowledge of other religions in terms of the science of religion has rendered some of the older viewpoints impossible. Here he is in agreement with Kraemer's 1963 book, which was so sound in terms of the science of religion and so much in touch with what is actually going on in other religions. Hence Verkuyl also has real understanding for what Cantwell Smith is trying to do, however much justifiable criticism he may direct against the latter. Verkuyl is bold enough to ask such questions as the following: What did God do when the Vedas were handed down? What took place between God and Gautama Buddha when the latter received enlightenment (*bodhi*)? What occurred in the relationship between God and Mohammed when he contemplated in the cave in Mount Hira?[39]

Verkuyl assumes that God is not just operative in nature, the history of peoples, and religions, but that he also has a history with each and every human being. We cannot understand religiosity and religion if we pay no attention to the drama that unfolds between God and human beings. But the fact remains that Verkuyl views this religious reality in human beings with suspicion. The drama has three dimensions; but for all his stress on God's activity in nature (or creation), in history, and in human beings, his main emphasis is on the ambivalence in all this, on the human efforts at repression, projection, searching and groping, yearning and evasion. There is a struggle between good and evil, and the latter seems to win out again and again.

Verkuyl also does not go so far as Catholic theology, which still is willing to recognize other religions as ways to salvation so long as they have not been brought to knowledge of Christ. He calls that "theological apriorism." Verkuyl assumes that God is at work only when human beings detach themselves from their religious system and leave the latter behind them. Thus he has no real feeling for the reality of a cumulative tradition or for the fact that humans have joined together in social ties to give a response to God's invitation. Herein lies the big break with Catholic thinking. Verkuyl may indeed develop the trinitarian aspect of the theology of history. But when he talks about the activity of the Father, the Lord, and the Holy Spirit, one gets the impression that this activity does not take place in the religions themselves; that it only takes place when human beings become critical of their own religions and choose to abandon them. Here again he resembles the older Kraemer.

Thus we find serious inhibitions imbedded in much of the Protestant theology of religions, and hence their theology of dialogue as well. Basic discussion and solid ecumenical dialogue will be required to arrive at unanimity in this matter.

CATHOLIC INHIBITIONS
VIS-À-VIS A THEOLOGY OF RELIGIONS

One would have a mistaken image of the Catholic standpoint vis-à-vis the theology of religions if one imagined that all Catholic theologians share the very same viewpoints and are unanimous on this point. Here again I cannot recapitulate the whole recent history of this matter. What I can do here is elaborate a specific line of thought that has been very influential in the past and that is still influencing many missionaries. I am referring to the "theology of adaptation," which has deep roots in Catholic theology.

Our best line of approach to the theology of adaptation is through the work of Josef Mueller. He both offers us a history of this theology and also attempts to inject a more modern meaning into it. I shall follow him on the first point.[40] In practice adaptation was a reality much earlier, but as a theological system it has only been elaborated since the beginning of this century. One can distinguish a German, a French, and a Spanish school; and we also have a series of statements from the Church's magisterium. Connected with this theology are such names as Joseph Schmidlin, Johannes Thauren, Alphons Vaeth, Thomas Ohm, Joseph Masson, Edouard Loffeld, Ollegario Dominguez, and Angel Santos Hernandez. There are differences among these people, of course, but they also share a few features in common. First of all, all of them more or less view Christendom and the shape it has assumed in the West as the norm. Of course they make a distinction between the essence of Christianity and its external shape or garb, but almost everything is included under the essence that constitutes the oneness of the Church: e.g., the creed, cultic worship, the sacraments, and authority. In these matters no adaptation or accommodation to another culture or religion was possible, even if there was a clash between them. The shape of the Church was viewed in terms of such things as the Roman liturgy, scholastic theology, and canon law. All these things were viewed as so intrinsically bound up with the inner oneness of the Church that concessions could be made only in insignificant details. Indeed the term "concession" itself is highly significant in this context. Some theologians, Vaeth and Thauren for example, even went so far as to say that the shaping of Christianity in the form of Western culture was providential, and that this form is valid for all times and circumstances. The garb was the outer side of Christianity, such as feasts and devotions and art. That stood apart from the oneness of the Church, and in such peripheral areas one could indulge in adaptation.

This approach clearly offered no access to the authentic religious and cultural depths of other religions. There could be no talk of dialogue with them. The other religion was always viewed as nature, whereas Christianity was regarded as something supernatural. The supernatural must build on nature, of course; but it was taken for granted that nature (i.e., the other religions) was so buried under the weight of paganism, due to original sin, that this principle could hardly be implemented at all.

If boundary-limits were drawn by Christianity, there were also boundary-limits posed by the non-Christian religions. A distinction was made in the latter between customs and doctrines inextricably bound up with error, which must be eradicated, and those which could somehow be separated from error and then be adopted or adapted. One sentiment voiced frequently was this: certain customs have become civil customs and have lost their religious import, so they can be adopted. All this led to the game of adapting external, incidental elements. People never probed more deeply into the whole religious thought of the other culture or religion. With such an approach one could never arrive at one's own liturgy, one's own theology, one's own form of ecclesial life and official function. The theology of adaptation has been a major obstacle to any authentic dialogue with the core of another religion. By itself it simply led to the transplanting of a Western Church with all its concrete historical features.

In the Catholic Church today there are many other currents and practices, but that does not mean that the theology of adaptation has disappeared completely. Even in 1962 and 1963, L. Elders was writing that he could not go along with the process whereby Christianity divests itself of its typically Western ways of thought, worship, and life in order to adopt the forms in which other cultures express themselves. The long-standing bond between Christianity and Judaism and Hellenism in history is so intimate that it must be regarded as providential, as something that will last to the end of time. Moreover, the present-day world is on the way towards one civilization, and this is a condition favoring the introduction of Christianity.[41] Opposition to this view was assumed by H. Bruning in a witty article that poked some fun at those holding such a view.[42] In the meantime Henry van Straelen also got heavily involved in the debate, and this led to more reactions.[43] The debate has now quieted down a bit, but there are still many advocates of this theology and this approach to missionary practice.

Of course one can also try to give a deeper meaning to adaptation, as Mueller does. Indeed we shall see later that Vatican II also makes the same demand on us. But the term "adaptation" is so heavily weighted with historical connotations that at present people prefer to talk about the "incarnation" of Christianity.

RELATIVISM AND SYNCRETISM: NO SOLUTION

There have always been thinkers who have felt that the problem of the relationship between religions could be solved by simply adopting a relativistic standpoint. Here I would distinguish three types of relativism. *Cultural relativism* maintains that each religion is the appropriate expression of its own culture. Thus Christianity is the religion of the West, and Buddhism is the religion of Southeast Asia. *Epistemological relativism* maintains that we cannot know the absolute truth; that we can know truth only insofar as it is valid for us. We regard Christianity as true, but we may not assert that it is valid for all peoples. *Teleological relativism*, which might also be called *syncretism*, maintains that all religions are paths to the same goal. One can make a choice for oneself and mix elements of various religions together.[44]

Needless to say, these various types of relativism and syncretism are not always distinguished so clearly and neatly; they often are quite intermingled. Here I want to offer a few examples of this.

Teleological relativism or syncretism is still to be found in the East. A good example is the following poem by the secretary of Emperor Akbar, the Great Mogul, written in the latter half of the sixteenth century when India was still under Mogul rule:

> O God, in every temple I see people who are seeking you,
> And in every language I hear, people are praising you.
> Polytheism and Islam grope for you.
> Every religion says: You are one, without equal.
> In every mosque people murmur their holy prayer
> And in the Christian Church they ring the bell out of love for you.
> Sometimes I visit a Christian monastery,
> And sometimes I visit the mosque,
> But it is you I seek, from temple to temple.
> Your elect have nothing to do with heresy or orthodoxy
> For neither of the two stand behind the shelter of your truth.[45]

This attitude can still be found in Asia. In the eyes of Oriental human beings, all religious forms and systems are merely approximations when it comes to the question of truth. No human being stands in the shelter of God's truth.[46] There one finds that in Christianity everything is tied down already and that no forward progress is possible. The Absolute is formless for the Oriental; one can only surmise, leave it as a mystery, and surrender to it. This can be done through all sorts of forms and rites, philosophies and religions.

The same line of thought is evident in the West. It is proposed by people like Hocking and Bleeker, who plead for inter-religious contacts but who also maintain that each person must stick with his own religion. What we must do now is adopt certain elements from other religions in order to effect a rebirth or a reworking of our own religion.[47]

Cultural relativism is also still very much alive. A striking example here is Ernst Troeltsch's view of, and attitude towards, the task of Christianity vis-à-vis the world religions. He maintains that Christianity is not faced with any task of conversion. Instead it must see to it that other religions purify and realize their deepest and innermost intentions so that they truly express a religious awareness that corresponds to specific types of cultures. The case is a bit different with primitive religions, which are looking for cultural development and growth through some association with Christianity.[48] The same basic line of thought, but more generalized, can be found in Hubert Halbfas. He maintains that Christianity is entitled to influence the West, but not other cultures. In a Buddhist culture, for example, Christians must try to make Buddhists better Buddhists.[49]

Epistemological relativism can best be illustrated by citing Arnold Toynbee.[50] His publications are important because his original English text more frequently than not has been chosen as the textbook in various colleges throughout the non-Western world. One quotation may illustrate this point:

> I would not say that I expect to see a coalescence of the historic religions, but I think it may be expected, and also may be hoped, that all religions, while retaining their historic identities, will become more and more open-minded, and (what is more important) open-hearted, towards one another as the World's different cultural and spiritual heritages become, in increasing measure, the common possession of all Mankind. I should say that, in learning more and more to respect, reverence, admire, and love other faiths, we should be making progress in the true practice of Christianity. And the practice of the Christian virtue of charity need not prevent us from holding fast to what we believe to be the essential truths and ideals in our own Christian faith.[51]

Thus we Christians may view Christianity as truth for ourselves, but we may not transport it as truth to people whose basic convictions about life are different. Moreover, in our day we must be tolerant of other religions. All the monotheistic religions must therefore give up their claims to exclusivity, their conceptions of uniqueness, and their notion of a two-sided God. On the one hand the God of the monotheistic religions is a jealous God of some race or people (in Christianity, Judaism, and Islam); on the other hand he is also a loving God. We can only retain the latter concept now; then we will be in a position to deal tolerantly with others.

We have now reached the point where we must consider the above views critically so as to find some way out. We cannot accept or adopt the exclusivist outlook because in it the Christian faith is not open enough and because other religions really have not been taken seriously enough. In this age, when we have so many opportunities to become acquainted with other religions and peoples on both the practical and scholarly level, we simply cannot judge them in this way any more. Moreover, in this outlook the human element in religion is viewed too darkly on the basis of a specific doctrine of original sin. On the positive side, however, the exclusivist approach can teach us that dialogue is ultimately concerned with what God in Christ wants to do with us.

The Catholic theology of adaptation does not satisfy us either. I say that quite openly and emphatically. We can no longer maintain that our ideal is the transplantation of the Western Church with some incidental or minor accommodations. Here the theology of dialogue takes very different directions. The theology of adaptation also lacks any real grasp or understanding of the religious depths of other religions and of the totality of their religious life. It also seems to me that the distinction between natural and supernatural has an inhibitory effect here, that again Christianity is not yet open enough. Yet there is something positive to learn from this view also. In all our efforts at renewal insofar as the theology of religions and of dialogue is concerned, we must not neglect the element of conversion that is so strongly emphasized by the theology of adaptation. But then we must go back to the authentic biblical concept of conversion (*metanoia*): "Reform your lives! The reign of God is at hand" (Matt. 3:2).

Finally, there is the relativistic and syncretistic approach. Here both partners in the dialogue, both the Christian and the non-Christian, go to the dogs. One does not accept them as they see themselves even though that is a basic rule-of-thumb in any dialogue whether it be on a small scale (between Churches) or on a large scale (between religions). Both the absolute claims of Christianity—which we will certainly have to reflect on—and the essential reality of other religions disappear altogether. Everything is relative; everything is a mere approximation. Even before dialogue actually takes place, the assumption is that all are alike. One anticipates what the eventual conclusion must be, and that kills any real discussion. But there is something to be learned from this viewpoint also. Our insights are limited insofar as they are human ones, and this approach can stir up our longing for greater openness and genuine catholicity.[52]

So now we must probe a bit deeper to find a new approach to other religions, an approach that measures up to the demands imposed on us by the changed circumstances discussed in Chapter 1.

BIBLICAL AND PATRISTIC DATA

Whenever one searches out modern biblical studies on this topic, one ends up being disappointed. The two most recent books, those by Beyerhaus and Peters,[53] are so fundamentalist that they really do not carry us any further. They picture human beings as completely immersed in sin. The goal of mission is their spiritual salvation, which can only result from their total conversion. Furthermore, these authors have not the slightest inkling of the influence of mission on the social and political life of human beings. Here, then, we find no starting point for a theology of religions or of dialogue.

So like Verkuyl, I prefer to go back to a few earlier authors. In my opinion, they still have something worthwhile to say to us.[54] On the basis of these studies Verkuyl, who adopts a trinitarian approach, moves in two different directions. On the one hand he makes some surprising pronouncements and arrives at very positive insights; on the other hand he retreats from them to a great extent when he talks about the Father as Creator and to a lesser extent when he talks about Christ as *Kyrios* and the Holy Spirit. My reading of these studies leads me to a more balanced and consistently positive approach.

Noteworthy is the fact that in these studies the relationship between Israel or Christ and the nations is given central place.[55] Two facts have helped to bring our problem further along in this connection. First of all, people are now more open-minded in approaching the Bible. Writers do not begin by posing some theological question and then go looking in the Bible for instances that prove a point. Instead they look at the Bible as a whole and give due consideration to the reality of salvation history as the factor providing unity. As a result, a distinction is now made between "universal" and "missionary." The Old Testament is universal, i.e., geared towards the salvation of all nations and peoples. But it is not yet missionary, i.e., conscious of a duty to go out to all nations. In other words, in ancient Israel we find a centripetal tendency at work. Israel is the hub of the nations and the latter must come to Zion. Israel makes an appeal to the conscience of the nations, serving as God's instrument for the salvation of all. Only later in salvation history do we find a shift to a centrifugal tendency, so that God's people now go out to the nations.

Looking at salvation history as a whole, we can detect various layers or levels in it. One layer represents a broad, direct dialogue between God and the nations. I am thinking here of Genesis 1–10. Here we cannot think in merely temporal terms because this broad-based dialogue has never stopped; it still continues today. God as the Creator concludes a creation-covenant with Adam, and then later again with Noah. Let's call it the cosmic covenant. In spite of Adam's sin this covenant perdures, as is evident from its renewal in the person of Noah. It is also vulnerable, as we see time and again in the Bible. But the human being is the image of God, and God cares for his image: through the fruitfulness of nature, through the alternation of rainfall and sunshine, through the cycle of the seasons, and so forth. God guides human beings and wants their welfare. And they respond to him by joining together to create religious forms.

This direct dialogue has never ceased, and it crops up repeatedly in the Bible. We find it in the priest-king of Jerusalem, Melchizedek; in the Midianite, Jethro, the father-in-law of Moses; in Ruth; in the widow of Sarepta; in the Syrian, Daniel; and in the Edomite sheik, Job. All of these people are numbered among the holy ones or saints of the Old Testament.[56] He, who finds wisdom, finds life and approval from Yahweh. God made use of Wisdom in the creation of the world. Wisdom summons people to salvation, and hence is Word.[57]

However, there is also another level in salvation history. Abraham is specially chosen by God, and therefore so is the Israelite nation. Within the great dialogue there arises a special dialogue between God and Israel. We might also call this the beginning of the special salvation history. There is no clear picture right from the start as to the meaning of the relationship between the two. On this level emphasis is placed exclusively on the coming of the nations to Yahweh, to Israel, to Jerusalem, and to Zion. Their coming is Yahweh's work, which he will perform in the eschatological era. Thus Israel thinks in centripetal terms and does not feel any missionary sense. God will convert the nations insofar as he will appear at work in the midst of his people. The lordship of God becomes universal, and the Messiah is the focus of this expectation of salvation. But the servant of Yahweh receives the nations as a gift, not as a field for mission work.

A slight change in salvation history seems to take place when Israel finds itself in the diaspora, for then we find some minimum of centrifugal tendencies at work. Proselytizing goes on (until the fifth century after Christ). A Greek translation of the Bible is produced. It also serves as a tool for mission work insofar as certain texts are given a missionary import. Proverbs 1–9 and the sapiential literature fit into this context. Here we may see a preparation for the missionary consciousness of the early Church, which made use of this literature. But again we must not exaggerate. Proselytes represent individual conversions of people from among the nations. They find a spiritual home, and hence necessarily a material home as well, in Israel, so that Israel still remains the center, and a clearly centripetal tendency remains in force.

Another layer or stage in salvation history is the attitude of Jesus of Nazareth towards the nations. Many texts make clear that he has been sent to Israel, that his converts are not to go out to the nations, and that Jewish proselytes are not a good deal. There is no direct awareness of being sent to the nations. The only exception is in areas where Jews also live, and there Jesus works wonders from a distance (see Matt. 15:21–28; 8:5–13). Jesus follows the customary pattern: salvation will come for the nations at the end of time, when God's lordship will have fully revealed itself in Israel. To be sure, this situation is near at hand. Something is beginning to change. We recall his conversation with the Samaritan woman, the parable of the merciful Samaritan, the description of the last judgment, and his statements that in the end many pagans will find their way into the kingdom more easily than the Jews. We are told that Jesus is the Son of Man, the Messiah—a title that points towards universal lordship.

In fact the thinking here is centripetal, but there is a more universal perspective with the prospect of a new phase. The coming of the Messiah and of God's kingdom brings a provisional fulfillment of the promises given to Israel in the Old Testament. But it is provisional. The work of the Messiah is not over. He must first suffer, die, and rise (Luke 17:25).

A new stratum in the special or particular salvation history breaks through when the Lord has arisen. It is a phase of "no longer" and "not yet." On the one hand the period of waiting is over; on the other hand the time for the eschatological banquet of the nations in the perfected kingdom of God is not yet. In this interim period of tension and suspense the preaching of the gospel to the nations comes into its own.[58] Now the shift from centripetal to centrifugal also takes place. The midpoint is no longer Zion but the Christian community. The latter is the sign of a new order of salvation. The world must be brought to a new and positive relationship vis-à-vis Christ.

The carrying out of this hope-in-action is to be found in the activities and letters of Paul. Here everything is centrifugal. Paul wrestled with the eccentric aspect of God's salvation history because of Israel's attitude, to be sure, but he also accepted this mystery. Once again, as was the case in the first stage, there is a dialogue between God and all peoples. This fact is explored deeply by Paul and John in texts that are very difficult of access. In Christ they see a linking between the general and the special salvation history; in him the significance of the first stage becomes clear. The dialogue that began with creation proves to have its center in Christ from the very beginning. He is the first-born of all creation because all things were created through him (Col. 1:12–20).[59] John speaks in the same terms in the prologue of his Gospel. All came to be through Christ; he is the light and the life of human beings.

In this connection many speak and write about the cosmic Christ, who is at work in the whole history of the world and of religions. One can of course go too far in this vein, and then the warnings voiced by Verkuyl and Honig are in order. But at the very least one can say the following:

> The driving forces of history were revealed in the twofold happening of cross and resurrection. Christ is also the deepest secret of creation (John 1; Col. 1; Heb. 1). In all these passages the emphasis is on the historical work of the revelation of God's lordship (John), of reconciliation and re-creation (Colossians), and of the purification of sins (Hebrews). This historical work is regarded as the consequence and the fulfillment of his creative work in the carrying out of God's plan. The intimate relationship between what God aimed at in creation and what he fulfilled in Christ is expressed in these passages in the notion that the world was created in and through Jesus Christ. God's creation of the first Adam was carried out with an eye on the last Adam. The latter must bring creation to fulfillment and deliver the world from its incompleteness and alienation.[60]

Finally, we may state that there is a mutual relationship between the general and the special salvation history. This also means that the general salvation history has never ceased; through dialogue with the special salvation history it must be brought to completion and fulfillment. It is thus that its authentic and deepest import will be revealed. The special salvation history reveals God's real aim with respect to the general salvation history, and brings it to pass, despite all the opposition and sinfulness of human beings, Israel and ourselves. Thus Christ does not stand apart from the general salvation history, and the Christian community has deep roots in it as well.

This is of the utmost importance for our dialogic theology. All the religions of the world lie within the general salvation history, but inside and out they are already oriented towards Christ as the one who gives them their innermost meaning. Dialogue is to turn this into a reality and make it visible, and this is the task to be carried out by the Church until the final fulfillment. Mission, then, means carrying this dialogue forward in God's name because it was begun by him within salvation history and is gradually being unfolded by him. In their response to God's saving activity, religions must follow his progressive steps and arrive at some ultimate response to the fullness of his self-revelation in Christ. In this response they must include all the good that they already possess in their own response to God's invitation. Listening must take place on both sides, both from the standpoint of the general salvation history and from that of the particular salvation history.

God's salvation plan may thus be made clear, but the Bible was written by human beings living in specific social and cultural circumstances. Whether these authors were so positive in their judgments about concrete religions is a very different question and must be sharply distinguished from the former question. The answer is more difficult in this case because we are leaving aside the great overall vision of biblical theology and considering the concrete judgment of concrete religions. Of course there is no radical opposition between these two questions and their answers, but there is a real difference. The human response to God's offer of salvation is not viewed by the Bible with open and unreserved admiration. We find positive judgments in the Book of Proverbs and the sapiential literature, for example, but we also find criticism, condemnation, and exhortations to conversion (*metanoia*).

In the Psalms we find frequently reiterated condemnations of the worship of idols. There are many biblical condemnations of the cultic worship prevalent in Canaan, Egypt, Babylon, Assyria, Greece, and Rome. Even Paul, who did establish a link with the general salvation history, urged his listeners to turn away from the folly of worthless gods (Acts 14:15). In the Areopagus he makes it clear that God does not dwell in temples, that he is not a product of human learning or reason, and that the epoch of ignorance is now past (Acts 17:22–23). In Romans 1:18–32 he writes that the pagans are not to be excused. The human response to God seems to be ambivalent, therefore, and it seems to show up best in particular individuals rather than in religions as such.

However, we must not allow ourselves to be overly impressed by all this. In this concrete judgment certain factors and circumstances of a nontheological nature played a part. We must not forget that in those days there was no science of religion to bring out the inner depths of the religious life being practiced in other religions. Today we live in a period when our knowledge is much greater. Without going overboard, we must now re-examine our judgment and link up more closely with the positive overall vision of biblical theology. We must give more consideration to its view of layers or stages in salvation history, as I have briefly described it above: and then we must try to apply this view to concrete religions. Moreover, we must remember that the early Church found itself in a difficult position vis-à-vis other religions in its milieu, just as Israel did in an earlier day. This hardly fostered a positive evaluation of those other religions, or a more moderate mixture of praise and criticism.

Now I must say a few words about the development and elaboration of this

material in the patristic period. One could mention the most important literature on this subject, but I think it is more useful to follow the summary
overview that Drummond has provided.[61] The picture that emerges then is
quite varied. Since Constantine, the Christian theologians of the West have
never ceased to echo the old doctrine of divine creation and providence. But
up until a few years ago Western theologians, both Catholic and Protestant,
did not fully grasp the broader soteriological consequences of God's pater-
nity. Indeed the picture is not that clear and distinct to us right now.

The same holds true in the early Church. We find differences of opinion
and diversity. One school, of which Tatian and Tertullian were typical representatives, distanced itself from the religious and cultural milieu of its day;
but it was only one school among several, and during the first three centuries
it was by no means the characteristic embodiment of the contemporary theological attitude. Tertullian posed the question: What does Athens have in
common with Jerusalem, the Academy with the Church? This thought, however, was not the guiding thread in the thinking of the Church.

In the postapostolic era the question arose: If someone accepts Jesus Christ
as the definitive and normative revelation of the living God, must he or she
completely reject the wisdom of the world? Or were pagan culture and
science, including the religious insights of the philosophers, in partial agreement at least with God's wisdom and aim? Two different answers were given
to these questions, and both could appeal to an apostolic precedent.

In general, the early Church was very critical of the religious worship and
practices of Hellenistic paganism, of its popular forms in particular. In 313
Lactantius wrote that the first step towards Christianity was to see that the
various religions are false and to reject the gods fashioned by human hands.
Origen, who wrote to Celsus about 250 C.E., noted that the standard instruction of catechumens was designed to instill in them an aversion for idolatrous
images and all images.

A different trend of thought appeared among those who stayed closer to
the Johannine doctrine of the Logos. On the basis of this doctrine certain
elements of Hellenistic culture could be valued and preserved. The Fathers
among the early Christian writers who adopted this approach stressed God's
providence and grace from the very start of human history on. These two
elements played a pedagogical role in the divine economy of salvation before
Christ's coming. Here I am thinking of such people as Justin Martyr,
Theophilus of Antioch, Athenagoras, Clement of Alexandria, and Origen.
Clement said that the first-born Son, the co-adviser of God, was the real
teacher of the Egyptians, the Indians, the Babylonians, and the Persians. He
also said that God had made various covenants with human beings, and that
the Church had existed from the foundation of the world.

A classic formulation is that of Justin (c. 100–165 C.E.). He wanted to link
up the work and person of Jesus Christ with Mediterranean thought, and to
determine his place vis-à-vis other religious teachers. According to Justin, the
divine Logos appeared in all its fullness in Jesus Christ; but the "seed" of the

Logos was spread over all humankind long before it manifested itself in Jesus of Nazareth. In their understanding, every human being possesses a little seed of the Logos, and this is particularly true of the patriarchs, the prophets, and the pagan philosophers. Here again it is interesting to note that Justin had little respect for pagan religion as a whole because he found it corrupt. Like the biblical tradition, his interest is focused on individual people who lived in accordance with the Logos. Socrates, in particular, was such a person. The same thought was shared by Theophilus of Antioch (c. 180) and such early writers as Minutius Felix (early third century). The latter had great admiration for Plato.

In summary we can say that the biblical-theological vision of the whole of salvation history was positive, whereas the judgment of concrete religions was frequently critical. Only a few individuals were exceptions in the latter case. The patristic view presents us with a mixed picture. It was very critical of the prevailing religions, but it also has some appreciation of the work of the Logos in special individuals. As yet there was no positive view of other religions as an overall way of religious life.

This is understandable in view of the circumstances of the day. Before the victory of Constantine, Christianity was oppressed by non-Christian powers. After Constantine's victory it was intoxicated with success. Also lacking was any thoroughgoing study or real-life contact with the other religions. There was no awareness of the existence of such great religions as Hinduism and Buddhism, except in Alexandria perhaps. This heritage would leave its impact on succeeding generations.

LATER NEGATIVE THEOLOGICAL DEVELOPMENTS AND A FEW EXCEPTIONS

Here I cannot go into a detailed treatment of the whole relationship between Christianity and non-Christian religions throughout the course of history. That would require a book in itself.[62] What I can do here is suggest some of the general lines of development or offer an overall sketch, while at the same time stressing that there have always been people who did not see things in the traditional way.

On this matter the Catholic tradition is a longer one than the Protestant tradition, needless to say. The Catholic tradition takes a decided turn with St. Augustine, and we find strange and ambivalent notions taking shape in his thinking after the breakup of the Roman Empire in the West. He taught that souls could be saved only through the Christian religion, yet he maintained that God is the creator and ruler of the whole universe. According to him no one obtains definitive salvation outside the Church, yet he also wrote that the reality we now call the Christian religion was never absent from human history. Unbaptized children go to hell, but some philosophers had now and then chanced to say true things that are in agreement with our faith; we must claim them for our own use.

Fulgentius of Ruspe (467–533) was even stricter in what he had to say. He taught that not only unbaptized children but even babies who died in the womb were eternally damned. Eternal fire awaited all pagans, Jews, heretics, and schismatics who died outside the visible Catholic Church. Gradually this view became the prevailing one in the Church between the early and late Middle Ages.

The barrier created between East and West by Islam was a prime factor in preventing the doctrine of universal salvation from making further progress. Islam became a military, political, and religious rival. This impeded, if it did not practically preclude, an honest and objective view of its religious aspects. An attitude of aversion took root, and everywhere Islam came to be regarded as a Christian heresy. There was no salvation to be found in it. Lateran IV (1215) affirmed that there was no salvation outside the Church. This attitude, developed in connection with Islam, was applied in the fifteenth century and later ones when the Iberian nations found a sea route around the barrier of Islam and discovered more new regions and religions. Various Councils confirmed this teaching and turned the God and Father of Jesus Christ into the tutelary deity of the Western peoples. Later, of course, schemes were invented to preserve at least unbaptized children from the pains of hell by putting them in limbo. But there was no change in the plight of nonbelievers.

I must note here that in the sixteenth century other points of view were cropping up among some Catholic theologians.[63] A study of Suarez, Bellarmine, and Vasquez is well worth the effort. None of these three great theologians dealt explicitly with the problem of the relationship between Christianity and other religions. But it does underlie their teaching about the salvation of unbelievers. Three points recur repeatedly in their writings. Firstly, there is the opening of human beings to God. With varying degrees of emphasis all three assume that human beings can know God through their natural reason and through contemplation of creatures, in spite of all the difficulties involved. As far as the natural longing of human beings to see God is concerned, they differ. Bellarmine assumes it, the other two do not.

A second point brought up by these three theologians is God's universal salvific will. One may always ask whether the opening of human beings to God might not be a futile aspiration insofar as communion with God. The epitome of true happiness lies beyond the power of human beings. Human beings are wholly dependent on God when it comes to salvation. Our three theologians clearly assert that God wills the salvation of all human beings and hence provides for them. Thus God also makes provisions for all the means required to obtain salvation. God offers all humans the light of faith and grace, but this is always in relationship to Christ. How can that be in the case of unbelievers, who do not know Christ? Our three authors have no satisfactory answer to this question. They simply trust that in one way or another it is possible. Only Vasquez is quite negative on this issue, assuming that pagans frequently refuse the first grace and that God therefore does not send them any missionaries. The other two do not go that far. But they do stress the point that much sinning takes place in the epoch of natural law in which the pagans live.

A third point concerns religiosity and religions. The concrete situation of unbelievers is one of salvation or nonsalvation depending on whether they respond to God's summons or not. So the question is: To what extent do religions play a role in this situation? Our authors write that the religiosity of these human beings cannot remain a purely inner religious attitude. Human nature is social and finds expression in external rites. God has created human beings with a soul and a body. Thus human beings must create external rites when God does not do it for them; and these rites vary with peoples and regions. The concrete religions, then, are rooted in human nature, but they ultimately derive from an inner inspiration coming from God. Thus they possess a certain, if only provisional, legitimacy. It perdures until a meeting with the gospel message takes place.

Do these religions play a positive role in the attainment of salvation? We cannot really confront our three authors with this question because it is a modern one that has only come to the fore in our own day. The least we can say is that these cults or religions do represent a real value for unbelievers. But we must quickly add that not everything we find among unbelievers is authentic religiosity. Sinning increases steadily, morals grow slack, and knowledge of God fades. We get idols, wanton poets, haughty philosophers, and impious people. In particular, Mohammed and his followers come off badly. Our authors even go so far as to call religion itself into question. The task of the Church is to lead all human beings to the true faith.

Thus we find a lack of logical consistency in the views of our three authors. On the one hand there is salvation for all human beings; it is achieved in religions, and God does not stand wholly outside them. On the other hand their judgment of concrete religions is really a rejection and a condemnation of them. For centuries now, missionaries have headed out with this theology in their baggage. The reader can well imagine how they have conducted themselves vis-à-vis the religions of the world. This theology and its concomitant missionary practice did not undergo any basic change for centuries. We must wait for our own age, and for Vatican II in particular, to find other insights on the rise. Of course there were authors who talked about a baptism of desire, but that did not change much.[64]

At this point I must go into a bit more detail about some of the exceptions to the general trend in the course of history. There have always been people who, either because of a deeper acquaintance with other religions or because of deeper pondering of the matter, have arrived at a different view that is closer to our present attitude of dialogue. Here I can only mention a few figures who managed to get beyond the dilemma.

Shortly after the fall of Constantinople to the Turks, Cardinal Nicholas of Cusa wrote his celebrated work, *De pace fidei*.[65] He had been to that city shortly before, and he had brought home a copy of the Koran with him. He studied this work too and wrote a treatise on it entitled *Cribratio Alcorani*. But it is the first-mentioned work that is of prime significance for us here.

Nicholas is convinced that wars result from controversies between adherents of different religions. There must be religious discussion, and in *De pace fidei* he sketches such a discussion. It takes place in heaven. At the request of the Word (after the Incarnation), the Father seeks to arrive at an orthodox belief so that all the different religions may become one. But human beings are free, so this result can only come about through discussion and conversation. The participants in the discussion are: a Greek, an Italian (both philosophers), an Arab, an Indian, a Chaldean, a Jew, a Shiite, a Galilean, Peter, a Persian, a Syrian, a Spaniard, a Turk, a German, a Tatar, Paul, an Armenian, a Bohemian, an Englishman, and the Word. The spirit of dialogue pervades the discussion. It is assumed that all religions have had prophets and that they all know basically the same God, who is Wisdom and hence also Word. Here, then, Christianity is placed among the other religions and appears to have deep roots in the religious history of all humankind. There follows an attempt to ground typically Christian dogmas and the sacraments more deeply in the general religiosity of all human beings. Nicholas concludes that there is one religion amid all the variety of rites: *est una religio in rituum varietate.*[66]

The striking thing is that the backdrop for this dialogue is world peace and the establishment of tolerance. At the end of the dialogue the participants are given a mission as representatives of humanity. With the help of the Holy Spirit they are to go back to their respective peoples and lead them to the oneness of the true cult. Why? Because peace is founded on the oneness of faith! That is reminiscent of the modern organizations of religions that I discussed in the last chapter.

Another person who should not be overlooked here is John of Segovia.[67] He was a contemporary of Nicholas of Cusa, but he had thrown in his lot with an Anti-Pope who had then made him a cardinal. When the true pope took center stage, John withdrew to a cloister in the French Alps and devoted himself to the study of Islam and religious divisiveness. His approach can be characterized succinctly: not by the sword but by peace and study. Christ himself had never counseled war as the way to settle religious differences. Neither need we look for a miracle because God normally works through the activity of human beings. It is not yet time for the phase of mission work because two preliminary phases must precede it. First there must be political peace with the Muslims and also intense cultural contacts. When all fanaticism has been wiped out through such measures, then a real dialogue may take place. It would be a peaceable discussion over the fundamental points of difference, which would start off from the points of contact shared by both.

Here again, then, we find a dialogic approach. John calls it a *contraferentia*, which we would call a conference. He also zealously promoted his ideas through extensive correspondence with his contemporaries: with Nicholas of Cusa, who agreed with his peaceable plans; with Jean Germain, a French bishop, who preferred Crusades; and with Aeneas Silvius, later Pius II, who also agreed with him.[68] Indeed the latter also made a scholarly but eloquent appeal to the Turkish rulers to enter into discussions.

The aforementioned people went the furthest, but there were others who did not share the medieval attitude: e.g., Pico della Mirandola, Erasmus, Francisco de Vitoria, and other kindred spirits. They cast a very different glance at the ethics of the great Greek and Roman thinkers and found much in it that was in agreement with Christianity.[69] An interesting question, very much deserving further study, is to what extent the great missionaries who practiced a more dialogic approach were influenced by these thinkers when they were studying and going to school in the humanist centers of Europe. And here I am thinking of Matteo Ricci, S.J., and his later work in China; of Roberto de Nobili, S.J., and his later work in India; and of Bartolomé de las Casas, O.P., and his work in Central America.

We still come across similar personalities today, who arrived at a new relationship with other religions without a great deal of theological reasoning. Here again I shall confine myself to a few examples, though there are others whose work might be examined: e.g., Father Lebbe in China; Father Dournes in Vietnam; Nothomb in Rwanda; Bede Griffiths in India; Father Maurier among the Mossi in Africa; Gravrand among the Serer people in Senegal; Monchanin in India; and Father Aupiais in Africa. Here I shall choose three people to discuss: Father Placide Tempels, O.F.M., who worked in Zaire; Dr. Jacques A. Cuttat, who worked in India; and R. C. Zaehner, who taught in England.

Father Placide Tempels was one of the first to arrive at a new approach even before World War II. A Belgian Franciscan, he was sent as a regular missionary to what was then called the Belgian Congo. For ten years he operated in the traditional way, carrying his Bible and his catechism under his arm. He discovered that this did not work with the Bantu. They continued to regard him as the *bula matari*, the great teacher, but they themselves remained passive. At that point Tempels faced a crisis and changed his lifestyle. He went out and listened to the Bantu, sitting on the ground with them and asking them questions: What is life for you? What does living really mean? How do you see it?

Thus there arose a conversation between him and the Bantu peoples, and the latter began to express their deepest thoughts to him. Tempels began to understand them, and he was in a position to do what they could not do: i.e., to put their way of thinking and their religious life in words and give it formal expression in a book.[70] Tempels became a new person in the process and rediscovered his calling as a priest and missionary. Thanks to dialogue, he had gained insight into the deepest aspirations of the Bantu. Now he began to work this insight into his preaching and his catechetics.[71] The extraordinary result was that the Bantu in Katanga responded in their own way to this initiative by initiating a Christian movement designed to form an authentic Bantu Church: the *Jama'a* ("the assembly").[72] In this movement a major role is played by Bantu catechesis and a threefold initiation, which leads to a deeper living of the Christian faith in a Bantu manner. We know that this movement has encountered difficulties in the past and still does in Zaire, but it is basically sound and healthy.

The core of Bantu thinking seems to lie in a striving to strengthen and fortify life, to increase the life-force that is present in all beings. In human beings it exists in a hierarchical way, coming to the individual members of the tribe through God, the ancestors, and the clan chiefs. The Bantu cannot live without this vital link, which is both physical and spiritual. Here one is reminded of the words of Jesus of Nazareth: "I have come that men may have life, and have it in all its fullness" (John 10:10). The whole of Christian doctrine and praxis is conveyed in this spirit. What we have here is no longer merely adaptation or a question of tactics but a dialogue with the soul of the Bantu peoples. This new approach is being spread throughout Zaire by the Bantu, and even beyond the borders of that country.

We find a second modern example in Dr. Jacques Albert Cuttat, who was the Swiss ambassador in India and Sri Lanka at the time of his conversion. In his own life he has gone through the whole problem of religions, and he has arrived at the following view of the matter.[73] In India he has become the leader of a movement among Catholic, Protestant, and Hindu representatives to come together in dialogue. His views boil down to this. He rejects both exclusivism and relativism as solutions. In both instances one does not hear the other party at all, or only superficially, and hence one does not discover any differences.

When one goes out to meet all religions openly and lets them speak to one another, then there appear to be two spiritual hemispheres: that of the East and that of the Bible. There is a great difference between the two in their vision of God and humanity, the world, redemption, and salvation. The Eastern hemisphere leans towards the Absolute, the emanation of the world from the Absolute and its return to the Absolute for salvation, and interiorization in taking cognizance of one's self. The biblical hemisphere sees God as Person, human beings as created persons and free beings, and salvation as the encounter between this divine Person and human persons through grace; the human attitude towards the world is also a positive one.

The question is: Where does one go from there? What is the nature of a dialogue between these two different worlds, which are both authentic yet in contrast with one another? One cannot fuse the two completely because both are authentic. But neither can one leave them wholly alongside one another on parallel tracks because that will nullify the transcendent oneness of God and the immanent oneness of human nature. One can only proceed on the assumption that their relationship is a complementary one and begin by presuming that one is subordinate to the other. This raises the next question: Which of the two is in a position to incorporate the other without eliminating or mutilating it? Cuttat then proceeds to show that the Eastern perspective cannot incorporate the biblical one without nullifying essential elements of the latter, but that the opposite approach is possible. Thus mutual enrichment can take place.

The last figure I want to mention here is Robert C. Zaehner, who was a professor at Oxford and died recently. He wrote often on our present topic.

His thoughts are very original, though his style is often abstruse.[74] Zaehner, too, came to a solution of the problem of many religions through a personal crisis, and so his work strikes a very personal note. He distinguishes two chosen peoples: the Jews, who have influenced Christianity and Islam; and the Indians, who produced both Hinduism and Buddhism. The two view religion in wholly different ways.

Here we encounter two basic types, which also show up elsewhere: i.e., prophets and sages. This big difference calls for some clarification. According to Zaehner, there must be a dialogue between the two types and it must focus on mysticism. Zaehner starts off from the idea of fulfillment. The human being has been split by the fall. Body and soul are no longer in harmony with each other or with God. The Jews have no further vision of existence lasting beyond death; Zoroaster knows of the division and hopes for reunion; India stares fixedly on the spiritual; Buddha focuses exclusively on the aspect of suffering. It is Christ who fulfills all this and restores the original intention of them all. In him the two streams come together. The cross and resurrection repair original sin, the unity of soul and body, the oneness of human beings with each other, and their oneness with God. Thus Christ is the fulfillment of the prophets and the wise men. In him the two incomplete revelations come together to regain their pristine completeness. Through dialogue Christianity must prove this to be a reality throughout the world.

From personal experience the above-mentioned people arrived at their own views of the matter under consideration here and often expressed themselves in intuitive terms. These same views have now been brought to a larger public in Catholic circles, thanks to the results of Vatican II and to a handful of theologians and missiologists who have ventured to explore these new approaches. The latter will be discussed in the next section. Here I must say something about Vatican II.

I have already said what was necessary about the conciliar decree on the relationship of the Catholic Church to non-Christian religions. Here I shall simply cite the concluding section with its positive judgment of other religions:

> We cannot in truthfulness call upon that God who is the Father of all if we refuse to act in a brotherly way toward certain human beings, created though they be in God's image. A human being's relationship with God the Father and his or her relationship with fellow human beings are so linked together that Scripture says: "He who does not love does not know God" (1 John 4:8).
>
> The ground is therefore removed from every theory or practice which leads to a distinction between humans or peoples in the matter of human dignity and the rights which flow from it.
>
> As a consequence, the Church rejects, as foreign to the mind of Christ, any discrimination against human beings or harassment of them because of their race, color, condition of life, or religion.

Accordingly, following in the footsteps of the holy Apostles Peter and Paul, this sacred Synod ardently implores the Christian faithful to "maintain good fellowship among the nations" (1 Peter 2:12) and, if possible, as far as in them lies, to keep peace with all human beings (cf. Rom. 12:18), so that they may truly be children of the Father who is in heaven (cf. Mt. 5:45) [NA 5].

Earlier in this book I made the point that in this Declaration Vatican II urged dialogue and cooperative efforts. But we do fail to find any elaboration of a theology of non-Christian religions in this document. For that we must turn to other conciliar documents. The Constitution on the Church (*Lumen gentium*), for example, regards all that is good among those who have not received the gospel as a preparation for it (LG 16). It goes on to say: "Through her [the Church's] work, whatever good is in the minds and hearts of human beings, whatever good lies latent in the religious practices and cultures of diverse peoples, is not only saved from destruction but is also healed, ennobled, and perfected unto the glory of God (LG 17).

The same views find expression in the Decree on the Church's Missionary Activity (*Ad gentes*). It urges more thoroughgoing adaptation in every phase of Christian life and witness. To do this, Christians must be steeped in the wisdom and philosophy of the peoples in question. To this end study centers should be established in every region to foster this adaptation and make it a reality (AG 11-17).

I have already said enough on the doctrinal foundations of this new attitude. Here I might simply add that these principles are not just found in *Nostra aetate. Lumen gentium*, too, asserts that those who have not received the gospel are somehow related to the people of God, and that he is present among those who seek him with a sincere heart (LG 16). Missionaries must seek out the riches cultivated by other peoples and detect the secret presence of God and his Word in them (AG 9). Here Vatican II picks up a patristic line of thought. But it continually stresses the need for conversion as the main thing, because the good in other religions is not yet fully Christian and other elements in them must be rejected (LG 17; AG passim).

The elaboration of all this in Catholic theological and missiological reflection will be the subject of the next section. Here I want to give a brief overview of the general situation within the Protestant tradition.

In general one can say that the great Protestant reformers had just about the same view of the pagans as did Francis Xavier. It was impossible in their eyes for heathens to be saved, but at first they did not draw any conclusions about the necessity of mission work from this premise. Zwingli was of the opinion that the Spirit of God was also at work outside the formal boundaries of the Christian Church. Certain Anabaptists and spiritual writers also seemed to have shared this thinking. But a mission movement first arose when the Pietists appeared on the world stage. They took very literally the doctrine of heathen damnation and headed out to save them. The Moravians,

who were also very active in mission work, were more flexible in their thinking. They maintained that God had for a long time been present and active
throughout the world in order to win disciples for his Church.[75]

I have already discussed more recent theological developments within the
Protestant Churches in section 1 of this chapter. But here again we must
realize that there have been exceptions to the general trend, which we shall
have to consider later. Here I am not thinking so much of the Anglo-Saxon
theologians who have adhered a bit more closely to the patristic line and who
have been more positive in their views. I am thinking rather of the Indian
theologians who rejected the rigid view of the young Kraemer and formed a
group: Rethinking Christianity in India Today.[76] I am referring to A. J. Appasamy, P. Chenchiah, V. Chakkarai, and the younger theologian, P. Devana-
dan,[77] who died at an all too early age. They all did ground-breaking work to
arrive at a positive relationship between Christianity and Indian religiosity.
Starting out from Indian thought-categories, they arrived at an authentically
Indian theology, and in particular a Christology which made it clear that
Christ can be preached in a way that is comprehensible and accessible to
Indians. While one may have criticisms about these first initiatives, they were
definitely worthwhile. They are now being implemented and further elaborated by Catholic theologians.[78] Whole new perspectives for theology and
missiology are opening up in this area.

OVERCOMING THE DILEMMA WITH THE HELP
OF OTHER SCHOLARLY DISCIPLINES

Here we come face to face with a multitude of modern theological and
missiological ways of thinking. We must make a selection, and that will necessarily be subjective to some extent. So here I shall try to give consideration to
the major trends at work.

One of the first authors we must consider here is Karl Rahner.[79] I shall
follow his most well known and current line of reasoning, though I am aware
of the fact that at the 1975 international missiological conference in Rome he
chose not to use the term "anonymous Christians." He did this for practical
reasons because the term had aroused much debate and misunderstanding.
Insofar as its content is concerned, however, his thought has remained un-
changed over the course of years.

Rahner poses the problem against a specific backdrop. On the one hand we
have the fact that two thousand years after Christ there are still so many
different world-views around. On the other hand all these together are confronted with an explicit a-religiosity. This raises the question as to the meaningfulness of remaining a Christian today. Rahner chooses to speak as a
dogmatic theologian, not as an expert in the science of religion. Thus his first
thesis is that Christianity is the absolute religion intended for all human beings; it cannot accord any other religion equality with itself. God created his
new relationship to human beings in Christ. It represents a free self-
revelation on God's part, and Christianity is the interpretation of it. But that

leads us to a wholly different question: Can the absoluteness of Christianity, which has a historical beginning, be existentially imposed on all human beings as a demand at the same time. The answer to that question is: no. It can only be demanded of them when Christianity has become a visible reality within another culture, an historical factor in that culture. This introduces into the picture an historico-sociological factor that will help us to surmount the dilemma. Christianity must first have assumed a social form within the other culture and religion, and that form must be part and parcel of the culture or religion in question.

In his second thesis Rahner poses a further question: How does a given religion look at the moment when the gospel message actually enters the situation of a given human being? Every religion possesses elements of a natural knowledge of God. For example, human beings are familiar with transient beings and thus come to the idea of absolute being; human beings are anonymous theists. These elements having to do with natural knowledge of God are intermingled with human depravity, which is the result of original sin and its further consequences. But every religion also has supernatural elements of grace, given to human beings through Christ, which ensure the presence of a supernatural existential. Among these supernatural elements of grace one must include God's earnest and universal will to save all even after the fall; and this salvation must necessarily come through Christ. Thus God in Christ is the horizon of every human being before any acceptance or rejection takes place, and one can talk of an anonymous Christian if one chooses to retain that term.

What, then, is a legitimate religion? It is an institutional religion whose "use" by human beings at a given time can be regarded as a positive means to enter into a proper relationship with God and thus attain bliss. Such a religion gains a positive place in God's salvific plan. In the concrete manifestations of such a religion we may find many errors, as was the case in the religion of the Old Testament. In the Church, however, we have an institutional body which can make the necessary distinction in an authoritative way. The Church is eschatologically definitive and hence infallible. Thus the other religions are not wholly and completely from God, but neither are they merely human constructs.

Rahner's third thesis is that the non-Christian is already an anonymous Christian in certain respects. He or she is touched by grace and already possesses revelation, but these two things are not yet recognized in the concrete. Christian preaching makes them concrete and explicit. This is the very spirit of dialogue, for the task of dialogue is to make things explicit. Thus human beings are granted a greater possibility of salvation.

A fourth and final thesis concerns the Church. It is the historically visible vanguard, the social expression in history, of the reality which Christians hope is present outside the Church as a hidden reality. It is thus meaningful to remain a Christian amid the present religious pluralism and the nascent epoch of a-religiosity.

Glancing back at this perhaps too simplistic summary of Rahner's abstruse line of thought, we see that he has taken a step forward. There is no open admiration of other religions, but they are given a place as a totality in God's salvific plan. In a given historical and social context they are responses to God's grace and revelation. To me it seems that here we have the beginning of an answer at least. On the other hand, in Rahner's thought it would seem that too much stress is placed on the individual human being; that he has not chosen to go all the way and overcome the dilemma posed to us by religions as social totalities or responses. For that we must consider another author.

Before I move on to him, however, I want to point out that I do not go along with some of Rahner's pupils, who draw conclusions which he certainly did not have in mind. H. R. Schlette, for example, regards other religions as the ordinary way of salvation and Christianity as the extraordinary way. He then asks whether it is really intended that the two should converge in history. I cannot find a place for this view in the biblical vision of salvation history that I outlined earlier in this chapter.[80] I have less difficulty with the book by Josef Heislbetz, which puts the matter in stronger terms than Rahner does but which basically agrees with him.[81] The beginning made by Rahner is worked out even more trenchantly by Raymond Panikkar. He concludes that within the Church there is room not only for a theological pluralism but also for a religious pluralism. Christ is present in the other religions and therefore they must be elevated to the sphere of Christianity. A Christian Hinduism or a Hindu Christianity must be possible.[82] It seems to me that the time is not yet ripe for such a concrete effort to go back and find Christ in certain Hindu texts and rites. That strikes me as much too mysterious and artificial. I also have difficulties with authors who pursue and develop one part of Rahner's theory: i.e., the substitution of Christianity as the vanguard for other world-views and for a-religious humanity. They elaborate and present this element exclusively so that it does not really fit in well with Rahner's synthesis. It can easily lead people to the notion that the task of mission is now outdated and superfluous.[83]

The author who, in my opinion, has probed our subject most deeply is Piet Schoonenberg.[84] I shall present his views in detail with only a few criticisms of them. My own line of thought has been heavily influenced by his. Schoonenberg has continued to elaborate his theology of religions over the years. Among Dutch authors he was the first to see the urgency of this issue and to seek out a solution for it. It seems to me that Schoonenberg's contribution to the solution of our problem stems primarily from his great knowledge of the history of Hinduism and Buddhism as religions and, in general, from the development of cultural history as he sees it. One can indeed criticize particular points of his view, and I shall do just that; but his view basically stands up. He has overcome the dilemma in such a way that his theology has benefited from the reality of other religions. Here, then, is a brief summary of his views.

Schoonenberg makes a distinction between the self-interpretation of a given religion, which involves both critical and further creative thought, and outside interpretation of that religion by some other religion. The latter is the case in our present subject, for example, where we are considering the theology of religions. Schoonenberg explicitly acknowledges that the possibility of such interpretation today is due to the scholarly science of religion. The latter is a precondition for any theology of religions. Outside interpretation is now a right to which both sides are entitled because of the openness in our modern world. It is also a human duty because no encounter or community is possible otherwise. In this process of outside interpretation the standards of fairness and love must be maintained, and stress must be placed on a willingness to learn from the other party.

Here I shall not go into the self-interpretation of Hinduism as Schoonenberg elaborates it. He follows the works of Cuttat and Ratzinger, adding some nuances of his own. My concern here is the question of outside interpretation of all other religions by Christianity. Schoonenberg uses some of Daniélou's terms,[85] but he uses them in a far more positive sense and elaborates them much further. For example, he accepts the notion of cosmic revelation which Daniélou introduced, although the latter elaborated it in a Barthian sense. Schoonenberg writes that this revelation is not a natural one but rather a general (or universal) supernatural one. It is universal because God reveals himself to all human beings through creation, and this is accessible to all. It is supernatural because in it God is revealed as a God who seeks out human beings, who wills to have community with them, and who wants to conclude a covenant with them. In and through cosmic revelation God unites with human beings, giving them salvation and redemption. Already here, then, God is implicitly a Father in Christ. Human beings can respond to this divine invitation, to his offer of a covenant. Every human being receives the grace to do this. However, human beings are free. They can refuse to respond to God, and then we have the fact of sin.

Now the human being never responds in isolation, because he or she is social by nature. Thus the response has a social character. It is that of a group or tribe or people. It takes the form of a religion, which consequently is also a social fact. Human refusal to respond to God also has a social aspect. The person who refuses to give a response brings the whole community into danger, and sin affects the whole community. In human response to God or refusal of him we find the origin of every religion.

But God did not stop with cosmic revelation in his saving activity. After it comes his historical revelation in the history of Israel. There God manifests himself as a guiding God, and then comes his personal revelation in the person of Jesus Christ. These two latter revelations, to which humans again have given a communal response (Judaism and Christianity), are explications and consummations of the first revelation. The relationship between them is one of progressive advance, not of opposition. So what we have is a progressive revelation in the course of human history. Since the three revelations do not contradict one another, neither do the three responses of humanity in the form of religion: Hinduism, Buddhism, and primitive religions; Judaism;

and Christianity. Human religions find themselves in one of the three stages of religious history. Elsewhere Schoonenberg speaks of five stages, but that view of his seems less fortunate to me; it is based on a rather antiquated and arbitrary classification of the history of human cultures and religions. It is always risky for a theologian to venture on this terrain because the views in these disciplines are continually subject to change. So I shall stick with the three stages mentioned above because they seem to provide a more correct theological interpretation of the history of cultures and religions.

Now these three stages coexist in the religious history of humanity even after the coming of Jesus. Only a real, thoroughgoing encounter or dialogue with Christ and Christianity can change the situation and bring about the transition of a religion to a higher level: Christianity. Even then the earlier revelation and the response to it remain important; for it is a piece of God's work, and as such must be integrated into Christianity so that the latter may assume a pluriform character in accordance with the culture and the religion where it takes root.

God works progressively in his revelation and he wants the response of human beings to him (i.e., religions) to follow this progressiveness. The Father and Christ, who are implicitly present in other religions, choose to make themselves explicit in the incarnate, manifest Christ. The task of mission work is to work this out in cooperation with God. The mission of the Church is an invitation to respond to this appeal of God, which is more perfectly present in Christ. Mission work is an invitation, a modest dialogue in Christ's name. The missionary must be consciously looking to find the salvific work of God as Creator already present and operative in every religion. He may then escort it to its fullness in the Church, in the name of Christ the Redeemer. This demands a real conversion on the part of the missionary: no imposition of self, humble invitation, positive listening, and acceptance of all that is good in the other party. It also requires conversion on the part of non-Christians. Sin has affected them too, and they may all too quickly be convinced that they have already given a complete and perfect answer to God's revelation.

Here, then, we have a clear vision of dialogue. It is theological and at the same time it was fashioned in a dialogue with other scholarly disciplines that helped to get beyond the dilemma: i.e., the science of religion, culture history, and sociology. I am of the opinion that it offers us a consistent vision that will serve as a good starting point for a more fully developed theology of the concrete religions. It should also be clear that the dialogue proposed by Schoonenberg is a dialogue about salvation and is in no way opposed to mission work.

In addition, in his study of Hinduism and Christianity Schoonenberg brings the world into his reflections. Let me cite a few examples of that fact here. He points out that in the Eastern hemisphere there is a different conception of the person than there is in Christianity; this has repercussions on the whole issue of activity in the world. The notion of "world" is also different in the two realms. Christianity is positive about activity in the world and, on the basis of the Judeo-Christian tradition, it seeks to initiate the kingdom of God here in peace, love, unity, and justice. Eastern tradition, on the other hand, is more focused on rejection of the world and ascent to the Absolute. The notion of "history" is also different in the two hemispheres. In the East history is viewed cyclically while in the Christian hemisphere it is viewed linearly. In the latter, it is viewed as coming from the past, through the present, towards the future prospect of a new heaven and a new earth.[86] Thus this theology of religions has important implications for cooperative development work, for the humanization of all human lives, and for liberation.

Now I should like to deal with a few additional points of view on the theology of religions that could be useful for our exposition. To begin with, I am pleased to be able to report that in their prolegomena a few dogmatic theologians are now grounding their treatment solidly on the phenomenon of religion rather than on one or another modern philosophical system. In his latest work on dogmatics Hendrik Berkhof adopts this approach, though I cannot agree with him on every point.[87]

Berkhof describes the phenomenon of religion as the relationship to the Absolute. I agree with him when he says that this phenomenon points up the realization of human beings that they stand in a wholly different relationship to something that is not part of their phenomenal world, but that is even less knowable outside and apart from that world. The phenomenal world would include such relationships as our profession, social structures, culture, technology, and nature. The wholly different relationship is a relationship to a reality that serves as our supporting ground. Human beings have need of some ground that in turn does not require a supporting ground.

The fascination of religion lies in the fact that it arises out of an interaction between need or question on the one hand and certainty or answer on the other. First of all, we have need: human beings are not satisfied with the life-fulfillment offered them by the answers of the world. In one way or another they experience the certainty that they do or can possess the ultimate answer. In religion they feel that they have found a revelation of the divine and some sort of revelation of the way to human salvation. Thus religion is a relationship above and beyond phenomenal relationships, but it is also bound up with the latter in an intimate and complementary way. Hence we get the multiplicity of religions, the wide variety of questions and answers.

Structurally speaking, we find a great deal of uniformity, of course. Almost all religions have three elements: that of myth, teaching or preaching; that of rite or cult; and that of moral rules of conduct. There is also an immanent set of problems confronting all religions: they are different from one another because they are interwoven with different fields of experience, because the Absolute can never be known apart from such fields. Isn't it a contradiction to go looking for the Absolute in the relative?

Here atheism proposes an answer, or at least an alleged answer. For atheism shares the religious questions, although it does not share the answers. It offers no answer to the universal, ineradicable questions of human beings. Atheism does not unmask the religious question. The question of our relationship to the Absolute remains, and human beings cannot get away from the religious problematic. (Note that Berkhof does not say that they cannot get away from "religion.") Human beings keep reaching out towards their ultimate limits; only then are they fully human. Berkhof thus places more stress on the question than on the answer (religions). The variety of the latter prevents him from reaching a solution to the problem of the truth of religion. It would seem that in their religions human beings keep trying to rise above themselves and their world but fall back into the latter time and again.

Over against religions Berkhof sets the Christian faith. Of course the latter is part of the broad field of religions. But when viewed against the bewildering variety of religions, Christian faith has a specific character of its own. It does so for an historical reason. Around 1700 B.C. something happened in the area of the central Euphrates: a migration of tribes, the forefathers of Israel, to Palestine and Egypt. Abraham could no longer count on the old gods that he had left behind, and he had no support from the gods of the unknown land to which he was going. He dared to take the leap into the unknown on the basis of a new kind of trust: i.e., that he would be guided by a higher, nameless God who had called him. This God had dominion over his old land, his new land, and the dangerous region lying between the two; and he was not confined to a specific natural locale. Because of this God's transcendence, he was mobile and could safely move on to new worlds. Abraham's trust was not disappointed. So we find a deepening and enrichment of his faith from one generation to the next.

This brings us to the difference between this reality and religions. In the latter human beings can give expression to the Absolute only through the immanent and the relative. In Jewish tradition the situation is otherwise. God is transcendent and, when he chooses to do so, he steps into history. This implies a de-divinization of the world. Thus with Abraham humanity begins to experience a break between the godhead and the secular world. Religion loses its self-evident nature, which had been taken for granted. However, one cannot say that the immanent problematic of religion is overcome here, for it is bound up with the very fact that we are human beings. What one can say is that it has now acquired a wholly different structure. Faith in a God who crops up now and then was difficult by comparison with the omnipresence of the earlier deities. It involves a groping journey from promise to fulfillment, a life lived on the edge of unbelief. The prohibition against idols fits in here, as does the centrality of the word. The latter becomes a reality insofar as the omnipotent God freely chooses to let that happen, and not otherwise.

Thus it is no longer satisfactory to talk about "religion" here. Berkhof calls it "faith." This faith-religion necessarily came into conflict with the prevailing religions around it. The latter could not make any promises, or actually render assistance to helpless human beings. The new faith was indeed a difficult one, and aberrations cropped up time and again. Great figures had to arise to set things right again in God's name. Thus it is all the more amazing that this faith-religion has had such an important impact on world history as the structure or infrastructure of later religious forms. Indeed it has served as the womb for three world religions: Judaism, Christianity, and Islam.

The transition from religion to the faith-religion of Abraham might also properly be called a leap: on the one hand it is in continuity with the past; on the other hand it represents a break with the past. Faith is not just a variant or a higher level of the broad phenomenon known as religion, because it adopts an uncompromising attitude or stance vis-à-vis any and all forms of religion. But faith and religion are not really opposites (Karl Barth and Hendrik Kraemer) because they lie within one and the same field, offering contrasting answers to the religious problematic they share. Thus a dialectical relationship exists between faith-religion and other forms of religion, and it is in this context that we may pose the question of truth. It can arise only through a choice. Thus it is subjective and, at the same time, it reveals itself to us in such a way that we are overwhelmed by it. Truth, then, involves both choosing and being chosen. And the choice has consequences for the relationship between the deity, humanity, and the world.

I can agree to a large extent with this view of Berkhof, and readers will discover many thoughts in his view that are dear to me. One must ask, however, whether it is really true that only the other religions are obliged to seek out the Absolute in the relative. On the basis of Schoonenberg's view one is forced to arrive at a different conclusion, and this seems to be related to a different view of revelation. In any case we again find an ecumenical openness that makes mutual dialogue possible. And the notion of a monotheistic revolution seems to me to be an important contribution to dialogue, primarily because it brings Islam into the picture.

I must also consider the theology of Paul Tillich in this connection.[88] He, too, elaborates a theology against the backdrop of the other religions, basing his work primarily on the philosophy of religion. He himself said that he would have to go much further along those lines if he ever wrote another dogmatics. Tillich, too, had some personal experience in this area through his participation in non-Christian religions during his stay in Japan. Tillich, too, works with the schema of question and answer, or natural and supernatural theology. In natural theology the question of God is posed and the human situation is analyzed; in supernatural theology an answer is given to the questions raised. Between the two lies his method of correlation, which takes away the opposition between them.

A phenomenological approach is required in posing the question of God. Concrete experiences are analyzed so that we may arrive at clearer concepts. What "ultimately concerns" a human being is the thing that becomes God for him or her. On the one hand this ultimate concern is concrete, because only in that way can it affect and touch human beings; on the other hand it also transcends the finite and the concrete. Herein lies a conflict, and that is the key to understanding the history of religion.

In his *Systematic Theology* Tillich proceeds to elaborate a typology of religions. Christianity is included in it insofar as it is a religion. Insofar as the ultimate concern ever remains concrete in the idea of God, there is a tendency towards polytheistic structures. On the other hand, the impact of the absolute element tends towards monotheistic structures. We find three subtypes under the polytheistic category: the universal, the mythological, and the dualistic. The first subtype is pantheism, the second concentrates divine power in individual gods, and the third stresses the ambiguity and conflict between creation and annihilation, life and death, good and evil. We also find three subtypes under the category of monotheism: monarchism, mysticism, and exclusivism. The first is very close to polytheism: the ruling God reigns over the lower deities. The mystic subtype evaporates all concreteness in favor of the ultimate. Only the third subtype, exclusivist monotheism, can radically withstand polytheism: one concrete God is elevated to the Ultimate and the Universal without either losing concreteness or turning into a daimonic force.

However, such a possibility is not deducible from the history of religion. It has arisen from the prophetic strain in the religion of Israel. But Israel itself, the concrete medium of revelation, is not raised up to the Ultimate. Its relationship to God is based on a covenant which demands justice and humaneness from Israel. This process continues through the New Testament and repeatedly triggers reform movements when it falters. Thus the world relevance of this monotheism is quite clear.

According to Tillich, there is progress in the history of religion but it is confined to the human answer: i.e., to religion. In the revelation as such there is no progress, but there can be progress and retreat in the cultural aspect of religions. Tillich's angle of vision, then, is horizontal. No religion is revealed. Religion is based on revelation, to which it is a reaction; but it may also entail the distortion and demonization of revelation. To be sure, there is a uniqueness in the revelation to be found in Jesus as the Christ. In this context Tillich talks about the ultimate revelation; but he also stresses that it is not unconnected with the past and the future, with history.

The self-same God who reveals himself everywhere manifests himself in some crucial and ultimate way in Christ. Christ is the center of history. God's manifestations before and after Christ must be consonant with him. So we have a period of preparation and a period of acceptance. Life before Christ must not be viewed in temporal terms. It must be viewed as a life lived prior to any existential encounter with Jesus insofar as he is the Christ. Many human beings still live in this stage.

So there is a universal revelation: humanity has never been left alone by God. Tillich therefore distinguishes between a latent Church and a manifest Church. The first would include socialism, Christian humanism, and the various religions. God is present in them, but only partially or fragmentarily. Only in Christ is the Spirit fully and completely present. This distinction is important for missionary work. Non-Christians must be regarded as potential members of the latent Church rather than as aliens outside who are to be invited into the Church. The function of mission work is prophetic purification of human religious awareness. For the Spirit or the New Being is fully a reality only in Jesus as the Christ.

On the basis of this viewpoint in his *Systematic Theology,* Tillich moves on to describe what dialogue must be in the concrete in another work entitled *Christianity and the Encounter of World Religions.* We must first recognize the value of other people's convictions as religious convictions, which is to say, as convictions based ultimately on revelation. Secondly, both religions must know how to convey or transmit their religious core with conviction. Thirdly, some common basis must be presumed as the setting for both dialogue and conflicts. Fourthly, people on both sides must accept criticism of their own religious foundations. Rather than conversion, then, Tillich wants a dialogue in which both sides expose themselves to criticism.

Again I can recognize my own thinking in this view. My only reservation is to Tillich's notion that there is no progress in revelation. Here again I would appeal to Schoonenberg's analysis, which talks about a progressive divine revelation in the course of salvation history, to which human beings must respond with ongoing answers in and through their religions. I would also retain the notion of conversion, but in a biblical rather than a negative sense. In that sense conversion would be a repeated opening-up to God's initiatives and a refusal to close off the process. I also have christological reservations, but I do not think they need be brought up here.

The important point here is that Tillich turns the religions of the world into a source for theology. We could also delve further into the consequences of Tillich's "Protestant principle" for the theology of religions. The principle basically calls for continuous, ongoing criticism and nay-saying. Insofar as it has repercussions on his restricted view of God's saving work and regards God as imprisoned in the ineffability of his own transcendence, I cannot go along with Tillich. But taken as a whole, his thought represents a big step forward in Protestant theology. We can readily admit that he has made possible an intra-Christian dialogue about the theology of religions.

Before drawing a few conclusions, I should like to at least mention the fact that there are a few publications which provide a more complete overview of the present-day theology of religions.[89] The most solid and compelling work is that of Georg Evers. But although I find his view very attractive, I do not agree with him on all counts. Let us first consider what his conclusions are, since he is the latest to venture an overview of the matter.[90]

Evers regards a variety of points as real gains and profitable points for development. He praises the acceptance of God's universal salvific will, and of the positive relationship between the order of redemption and the order of salvation. He endorses the conviction that in principle salvation history and profane history take place in the very same locale. Here and now we may not be able to make a neat division between the two, but that does not mean that they are identical either. Evers also favors recent developments in our understanding of revelation—from word revelation to the transcendental orientation of the human spirit to God's grace-filled revelation of self. He also approves recent developments in the notion of faith insofar as the latter is viewed from an existential rather than an intellectual standpoint and thus considers the stance of human beings vis-à-vis their total situation. Evers also mentions the close connection between love of God and love for human beings; in the present order of salvation the latter is what gives us access to the former. Another valuable gain, in view of the social nature of human beings, is the realization that salvation is not isolated in the interior life of the person, that it is to be found in a socio-historical milieu.

One is pleased to see Evers enumerating these points. But one cannot help but wonder why the author, after devoting a section to the theology of the non-Christian religions, presents a separate section on the secular world. The gains cited above lead directly to a theology of religions or dialogue that is directly connected with the world. For the salvation sought by human beings is directly connected as well with the world and the concrete situation of human beings and their society. Thus one gets the impression that the book is a loosely connected compilation of a number of authors rather than a real synthesis.

Here I want to focus on his conclusions, which are more directly connected to the non-Christian religions. In principle those religions have been annulled by the absolute bearer of salvation, Jesus Christ. But so long as no existential encounter with Jesus Christ has taken place, they remain legitimate paths of salvation and religions. It must be added, of course, that false forms and depravities have found their way into the historical religions, thus severely curtailing and, in some cases, eviscerating their function as means to salvation.

One could indeed say that this new vision has created some disquiet with regard to missionary work and missiology. Is mission work still meaningful? The insight that has been gained now is the realization that it is not a matter of saving souls but of gathering together the people of God and bringing closer the existential meeting between Christianity and other religions and cultures. Mission and Church, therefore, fulfill a vicarious role for the whole human race. Rules for adaptation must therefore be laid down in connection with mission methods.

I am not wholly in agreement with this summary. As we have already seen, dialogue does indeed have significance for the world. This is spelled out clearly by such people as Schoonenberg and Tillich. But insofar as its significance for mission work is concerned, I should like stress to be placed on the fact that dialogue here means a dialogue about salvation. This indeed is what is brought out by other authors we have considered here. In the last analysis it is a matter of bringing more salvation, and ultimately the fullness of salvation in Jesus Christ. This point is not stressed enough by Evers. We shall see that this salvation may not be regarded as merely spiritual; it relates to the total human condition.

Evers then goes on to mention a few points which he regards as open questions. He points to a faulty scriptural basis for the theology of religions. Perhaps our considerations here have brought it a bit further, though admittedly modern authors must pay more attention to this subject. Evers also points out that the socio-historical aspect of religions and its influence on the life-attitudes of non-Christians must be spelled out more clearly, so that the social conditioning of salvation may be made clear. Here again I feel that Evers lacks knowledge, particularly of the non-European literature on this matter; otherwise he could not make such a statement. Evers also maintains that there must be a clearer and more explicit treatment of the relationship between the theology of religions and theological reflection on secularization. I grant this necessity, but again I am afraid that he is talking too much from a strictly Western perspective. The amazing thing, in fact, is that the non-Christian religions and cultures are engaged in a process of renewal and reform, and that this opposition to secularization does not exist for them. Japan has indeed modernized; but at the same time it has managed to satisfy existing religious questions, of which Vatican II speaks, with a host of new religions. The same is true in Africa, where one can find a striving for authenticity, African humanism, and African socialism. We must not simply try to transpose the Western problem of secularization to other areas of the world. A pluriform approach is necessary here, and Westerners may well be able to learn something from other continents in this respect.

With this I hope I have laid down the groundwork for a deeper dialogue in the area of the theology of religions. As I see it, it is a dialogue about salvation; and here salvation is taken in its fullest sense to include both the immanent and the transcendent aspects. In the next chapter we shall return to the realm of practice to see whether or not these theoretical expositions have found any echo in reality.

4

Examples of a New Evaluation of Other Religions in Theory and Practice

In this chapter I simply want to offer a few case studies related to the topic under discussion. I hope they will prove that the reflections presented in the previous chapters have already been fleshed out in theory and practice when it is a matter of concrete encounter between Christianity and other specific religions. Drawing on a large number of potential examples, I have chosen those which give some indication of the geographic spread and the theoretical approach involved.

I will begin with a new approach to Buddhism as it has been worked out by Richard H. Drummond.[91] This is the realm of the special theology of religions, the point where the theses presented in earlier chapters are applied to a concrete, specific religion. In this area Buddhism itself represents a particularly difficult challenge, and the prejudiced judgments of Christianity have been numerous and varied. It has been claimed that Buddhism is really atheism, that it lacks any notion of "person," and that it has no relationship with the world. Some have even wondered whether Buddhism should be called a religion at all.[92]

Drummond starts with a thorough-going analysis of original Buddhism, basing it on the work of modern Japanese experts in Buddhism. In my opinion, that is an important and useful starting point for a special theology concerned with the encounter between Christianity and Buddhism. Drummond is not led astray or confused by later developments or accretions in the history of Buddhism. He describes for us the pristine, original inspiration of the Buddha, thus opening up ways for it to make contact with the pristine, original inspiration of Jesus of Nazareth. His basis is a very positive theology of religions whose spirit is that which I have indicated in the preceding chapter. Both original Buddhism and original Christianity are total views of life wherein God is present and at work. And it must also be noted that we need not diminish the greatness of the Buddha in order to salvage the unsurpassed treasure that we have received in Jesus of Nazareth.

Drummond derives his criteria from the totality of salvation history as it is presented to us by the Bible: God is the God of all. He is the creator of the universe. His providence and paternal concern go out to his whole creation, and through the persons of the Trinity God is active at all times. God reveals himself and redeems. We have now discovered that truth again, but it is time to apply these basic criteria to human beings who are living in different spiritual traditions. What about other human beings and movements? To what extent do they possess spiritual and moral qualities which clearly reflect the presence and activity of the Father who has been revealed to us in Jesus of Nazareth? Drummond attempts to apply these questions to Buddhism in particular.

At one point Drummond starts off from the following text: "Whoever receives a holy man because he is a holy man will have a holy man's reward" (Matt. 10:41).[93] Thus in Jesus' view a holy man is not just one who is a Christian. Consider his remark about the Roman centurion: "I tell you solemnly, nowhere in Israel have I found faith like this" (Matt. 8:10). Thus he bade his followers to recognize and accept a morally good human being as such. Now everything indicates that Gautama the Buddha was such a good man. This is evident from the earliest Buddhist texts, which tell us that in his day men and women of every rank and station regarded him as a person who was lofty in his attitude and conduct towards others. Not everyone agreed with him, but we never hear of anyone accusing him of a moral flaw.

We may also think of Peter's remark: "Anybody of any nationality who fears God and does what is right is acceptable to him" (Acts 10:35). Now the Buddha may not have "feared" or revered God as a personal being, which is the way God was seen in Israel; but he did respect karma (the law governing retribution for good and evil deeds), which is righteous. He also respected dharma and its beauty, dharma being the real truth in the cosmic and interior senses. Finally, he also sought to reach nirvana, the full and perfect realization of reality (his version of the kingdom of God). Thus there is no doubt that Gautama the Buddha acted uprightly. One cannot imagine such a human being apart from God's presence and activity in the world.

We note the same thing in the teaching of the Buddha. It consists in an analysis of the empirical situation of human beings, which he found unsatisfying, and in a description of the way to get free of this situation and arrive at a fully satisfying life. For the Buddha, living is suffering; and suffering arises from desire and an incorrect feeling for values. Human beings attach themselves to the fleeting and the transient, which is necessarily unreal for that very reason. He had a keen and poignant feeling for the fact that we tend to express as follows: All created reality is contingent, not strictly necessary, and hence unsatisfying in the last analysis. To that extent the Buddha is fully in agreement with the teaching of the Bible: one cannot find any ultimate reality in the phenomenal world.

Now this feeling may lead to various reactions, either positive or negative. We find both types in both religions. The real Buddha never went so far as to despise empirical life or negate it through great asceticism. He simply said that the ultimate is not to be found here, that we must go further than that. We must overcome karma (our dependence on the empirical) and follow dharma (an inner dynamism of goodness and beauty which leads us to the goal of nirvana). Thus there is a gracious Presence in the world. And once we attain nirvana, the imperfections of this world and the wickedness of our past fall away. Nirvana, which is hard to describe in words, is not an extinction of our existence; indeed it can even be attained in this life. This idea should be familiar to good Christians, who know that moral and spiritual conversion is part and parcel of their ultimate vocation.

So we find that Christianity and Buddhism are not so far apart as we might have imagined. It is no longer necessary for them to stand in opposition to each other and see nothing but differences between them, once we realize what is implied in the differing words they may use. Differences remain, of course. There is, for example, the issue of personalism, which has always been viewed differently in the West. The East is not so mindful of an interpersonal relationship with the Other, be it the divine Other or human others. Hence it tends to lack any notion of the reality of divine revelation and self-communication.

At the same time we must be cautious here. We should note that the Buddha does ascribe quasi-personal aspects to nirvana. He invited people to come and see, he experienced love for "the beautiful," and he lived in intimacy with it much as Francis of Assisi did. It was an ongoing and intimate relationship, even though one may not be able to call it "interpersonal." We must be sensitive to these points. On the basis of all this, Drummond is led to conclude that the Buddha was indeed in contact with aspects of the reality that Jesus called "the kingdom of God." At the same time he feels bound to say that the teaching and person of Jesus Christ revealed the aspects of this kingdom in a unique and fuller way. The point, then, is that to some extent the teaching and the life of the Buddha may be viewed as revealing the presence and activity of the same God to which the history of Israel bears such wondrous testimony.[94]

In my opinion this book by Drummond, so rich in its concrete experience of Buddhism, has laid a new foundation for a dialogue about salvation with Buddhism. And I am particularly pleased to see such an effort coming from the Protestant camp. Such an approach is also evident in the Catholic camp, but in the latter we find more reservations and inhibitions.[95]

Since I can only present a few views in this part of my book, I must try to make a responsible selection. Here, then, I should like to move to North Africa and let a Muslim voice be heard. It will show that the desire for a new relationship between religions is also evident among other religions. As an example, then, I will discuss the views of Professor Mohammed Talbi, the chairman of the history department at the University of Tunis.[96]

Like us, he starts out from the fact that in our day all monolithic ideologies are disintegrating and giving way to cultural pluralism. Islam cannot evade these facts, especially because it is still weighed down by the unfortunate consequences of its darker ages. These consequences have not been overcome as yet, despite the fact that a certain measure of renaissance is evident. If Islam is to get a hold of itself once again, then dialogue is of vital importance. Contact with the world must also be restored. No religion has lost contact with the world as much as Islam has. In this respect Christianity finds itself in a particularly privileged position.

When one probes deeply into the Koran, one encounters the necessity for such dialogue. Revelation invites the prophet and Muslims to engage in discussion and to enter into dialogue with other human beings. They must dialogue with human beings in general and, in particular, with believers who belong to the biblical religions. However, this does not eliminate the task of the apostolate. Dialogue and apostolate can and must go hand in hand. So here again we find a view advocating a dialogue about salvation.

Now the fact is that people are often led to wonder about Islam in this respect. They wonder how Islam can envision dialogue when it has made so much use of the sword. Two points must be made in this connection. First of all, it is certainly true that Islam has made use of the sword, but not always and at all times. Countless other methods have been used to spread Islam as well. It is also true that some verses in the Koran do urge a holy war in the name of Allah. But we must also remember that they were written in certain historical circumstances, at a time when other world powers were also trying to extend their sphere of influence. Moreover, the holy war is a second line of approach. We can now say that all of that belongs to the past. It is not the deepest core of the message, which really represents a hand outstretched to one's fellows with an attitude of courtesy and respect.

Thus the task for our day is clear. We must try to clear away all the misunderstandings of the past and the present. The latter aspect must not be neglected. The fact is that an enormous gap does separate the two potential partners in dialogue. For the most part Muslims live in underdeveloped lands; both in terms of attitude and study they are not yet prepared for dialogue. Christians enjoy a great advantage in this respect, and so far it is they who have taken the initiative. (Talbi wrote this before the 1976 dialogue in Tripoli, Libya.)

Associated with this fact is an uneven pace of theological development. Christianity has had to engage in discussion and explanation with all sorts of thought systems. Islam must now proceed to do this. Christianity possesses a whole series of experts in the field of Islam, and thus it is "ready and equipped" for dialogue. Islam must make a start in the same direction. Right now they are hardly partners. There is no Muslim christology, and its theology came to a halt in the twelfth century. How can we talk about real dialogue when one party has a superiority complex and the other has an inferiority complex? Islam must proceed to overcome these difficulties.

Human beings cannot deny real developments, not for long at least. The modern world rules out isolation. Schooling, development, and other such factors are eliminating the social shelter that once surrounded the Muslim way of life. Adherents are now being forced to make a personal choice. But that is possible only if Islam enters into dialogue with today's world, and hence into dialogue with Christianity. Starting out from the reality of its own witness, Islam must dialogue with all other thought systems without exception if it is to revitalize the spirituality of its followers and assimilate all worthwhile values. Otherwise a process of de-islamization will take place. Indeed the first indications of such a process are already evident in the universities, among young people in general, and among the more educated classes. They retain only a vague emotional attachment to Islam, and it is more cultural than religious in nature. It makes no sense to maintain a rigid attitude or to defend barriers that have already been breached.

Thus it is necessary to consider the preconditions for dialogue. Two things must be avoided: the spirit of contentious argument and the spirit of compromise. By the first, Talbi means that we must avoid the urge to proselytize, though that does not rule out any and every sort of apostolate. The right attitude is to be found in the witness of one's way of life, in which one strives for moral perfection. Here the various religions can indeed compete with one another in the service of the world. Such an attitude also rules out compromise, while allowing us to accept the fact that there is a plurality of paths to salvation. The time is past when any religion could say: no salvation outside the Church. In short, he advocates a plurality of paths to salvation, but he does not advocate relativism. The game is honest only when each religion is truly convinced of its own set of values. There is only one truth, but our conceptual capacities are not always the same. When we explore this matter in real depth, our faith will cease to be merely a matter of sociological adherence and will become a real inner conviction.

This brings us to a question: Does dialogue have any real object? Is it meaningful? Yes it does, says Talbi, because at bottom it is a disinterested and unrestricted effort at collaboration in the service of God—which is to say, in the service of goodness and truth. Dialogue must be fruitful for everybody; otherwise it will never take place or lead to anything. The object of dialogue is to remove barriers and to increase the stock of goodness in the world through a free exchange of thoughts. Together with human beings who profess other religions or ideologies, we confront the same awesome tasks of our day; and we must make our contribution to the solution of these tasks precisely as members of various religions. Together we also face the great questions of life that touch every human heart, as Vatican II pointed out in *Nostra aetate*. So there must be encounters between people of all religions, whether they possess sacred scriptures or not.

Prudence is in order, of course. It might be wise for the monotheistic religions to initiate this process of encounter. One feasible topic, for example, might be how to reconcile human freedom with divine omnipotence. Finally, the question of the aim of dialogue must be considered. Talbi formulates it in clear and forceful terms. The aim of dialogue is to arouse human beings, to get them moving, and to keep them from clinging rigidly to their own convictions.

Every faith must face up to this challenge. This is particularly true in the case of Islam, which has refused to do this for centuries. God's word is eternal, yet audible everywhere. Why, then, should people not be willing to learn from others? Today Muslims must listen to the word of God even though it may be voiced outside the Muslim faith. In this way they will gain a better understanding of it. We really do not know if one faith will arise in the future out of all this dialogue. Believers may hope for this eventuality, but right now we must face up to the task of endlessly patient dialogue.

Happily, in the case of Islam these fine sentiments have not remained a matter of mere words. Talbi expressed the above views in 1972, and they came to the attention of the West in 1975. Since then three dialogues have taken place, and I should like to report them here.

In September 1974 a dialogue took place between Muslim and Christian scholars in Cordova (Spain).[97] A variety of topics were discussed. An attempt was made to present Islam in such a way that the Muslims present could recognize themselves in it. A similar attempt was made to offer a presentation of the Christian religion. The mutual implications of political developments and the spread of religions were also discussed. Attention was also devoted to the crisis of faith and to real-life experiences in Muslim and Christian religious education.

An unforgettable experience was the Friday prayer-service in a Cordova mosque and the Eucharistic service that took place in a portion of the mosque later converted into a cathedral. The conference clearly had political dimensions, thanks to the makeup of the delegations and the messages that were sent. The congress produced what is known as the Declaration of Cordova.

I can only summarize parts of that long declaration here. It acknowledged the monotheism of the two religions, their defense of the same moral values, and the need for both religions to deepen their shared faith in God. All this was to be done for the sake of benefiting the world, and misunderstanding had to be eliminated. Another point mentioned in the document was the discovery of areas for joint activity, where Muslims and Christians could work together. Stress was placed on the need for joint study. The manuals used in schools had to be examined so that false conceptions of the two religions might be eliminated and real dialogue might be fostered. Within two years the participants were to meet again in Cordova and other places. The two sides had to respect each other's religious convictions, protect minorities, and avoid proselytism. They must work for peace and justice, support the human and national rights of the Palestinians, and form a committee to work all these matters out. Here again we find traces of the same thrust evident in other national and international congresses. But here the religious element obviously plays a major role. It is to serve as the driving force behind cooperative efforts on behalf of the world's welfare. I think that a very important point was discovered and adopted at this conference.

Another dialogue took place in Tunisia the very same year (November 1974).[98] In this case the initiative came from a group of Tunisian scholars. It was the first time that a dialogue was sponsored by Islam itself. Here the Christians were the guests. The Muslim composition of the delegation was varied; the composition of the Christian delegation was less solid because some of those invited were not in attendance. But Protestant Christians were present. The theme of the conference was: the Christian conscience and the Muslim conscience in relation to the challenges of development. The delegates discussed uneven development, the current population explosion, the plurality of existing cultures, development, and ties to the past, and finally, violence. In the final two sessions the participants were to exchange information on the current status of biblical and Koranic studies.

Such was the plan, at least. In fact, the second day saw the start of a confrontation over exegesis of the sacred scriptures. It was both courteous and heated. It began with the remarks of Professor Mohammed Arkoun of Paris, who stated that the point was not to talk as a Muslim or a Christian but rather as an involved and inquiring person. Later he also maintained that reflection in the two religions should not start off from the "God" hypothesis or assumptions about a supernatural revelation, but rather from an analysis of individual and collective experiences. In the latter case such humanistic disciplines as linguistics, anthropology, and history are now in a position to offer their contribution. At the end of this analysis people would be in a position to find the word of God.

No one had any difficulty with adapting human disciplines to the exposition of God's word; in Islam that in itself represents a major step forward. The difficulty lay in the fact that some, both Muslims and Christians, maintained that faith is basically grounded on a divine intervention in history, that it is the latter which constitutes their faith. A rigorous, ongoing examination as to how the holy books were received, understood, and handed down to later generations would be a very different question.

Thus the colloquium strayed into side-issues more than once. These had not been foreseen at the start, but at the same time they were far from uninteresting. People also realized that it was not possible to talk simply about development and progress without interjecting the religious factor as a closely related element. Both aspects are intimately connected because religion, alongside other factors of course, either does or does not give impetus to the process of development. Discussion of the other topics mentioned above led to forthright statements on both sides and a fair amount of agreement—e.g., on the use of violence.

The dialogue became truly religious in nature when the congress moved to Kairouan, the holy city of Tunisia. Reservations and timidity were left aside; people got to know each other and devoted themselves to the study of the Bible and the Koran. The basic theme had to do with showing respect for the word of God and at the same time measuring up to the legitimate demands of human scholarship. Mutual discussion and questioning took place, and then the participants would pray together for a few moments before listening to a few verses from the Koran or the Bible.

It cannot be said that everyone agreed with everyone else. But it was clear that a profoundly religious atmosphere and respect for each other's religious convictions prevailed. I would say that it contained all the elements we would expect in a real dialogue. It focused on salvation and avoided compromises. It was a dialogue focusing on the whole and integral salvation of today's human beings and seeking to help resolve all the specific problems involved from a religious standpoint. For besides the work of economists, politicians, sociologists, and other specialists, the various religions and their adherents have their own distinctive contribution to make.

A final meeting in this series was the seminar on Muslim-Christian dialogue held in Tripoli, Libya (February 1–5, 1976). The papers and discussions of this conference have not yet been published. But since I myself participated in this seminar as a Vatican representative, I can say something about it. I shall not go into the political aspects that occupied the meeting at times and that found expression in a few of the final resolutions. It seems to me that such things are unavoidable right now, considering the present situation of Islam in the Middle East. The press paid too much attention to this whole aspect, rarely reporting on the deeper issues that came up for discussion.

In Tripoli, the public was very different from what it had been at the earlier meetings. Besides scholars, there were faithful representing both religions from the Philippines to Argentina. There must have been a total of about five hundred people at the meetings. The number of official representatives from Islam and Christianity was quite limited, coming to a total of about twenty-five. The dialogue went back and forth between them. Thanks to a hastily organized secretariat, questions in writing could be presented to one delegation or the other. The latter could decide whether to deal with a particular question or not.

The topics included religion as an ideology for living one's life, the common bases of Islam and Christianity and their points of convergence with respect to life, and social justice as the fruit of faith in God. The participants also considered how they might break the negative judgments about each other's religions and the lack of trust that has kept us divided. Every morning one Muslim and one Christian speaker took the floor. The rest of the day was devoted to discussion and dialogue.

It cannot be said that the discussions always reached the level of genuine dialogue. There were moments of tension and fierce outbursts from the Muslim side. But the patient attitude of the Christians present and the understanding approach of the Lybian delegation helped to move the participants towards more conciliatory statements. On the Christian side Father Lanfry gave a moving talk. He acknowledged our guilt and asked for forgiveness. The response was a big round of applause and an embrace from two Muslim leaders.

Much discussion centered on whether a religion must tie down every aspect of life or allow more freedom for further developments. It is fair to say that the Muslims leaned strongly towards the first alternative while the Christians leaned towards the second. The latter stressed that the Bible provides us with certain truths which we must continually adapt in each succeeding period of history. I should like to dwell on this point a bit longer by summarizing my own talk, which dealt with social justice as the fruit of belief in God.

I adopted an empirical approach for the most part, and this was new to many of the participants. I did not cite extensively from the sacred books of the two religions to show what a good job we are doing with everything. Instead I offered a comparative study of the monotheistic religions—Judaism, Christianity, and Islam—vis-à-vis the other religions. My basic thesis was that the former represent a monotheistic revolution, and I sought to show that this imposed on us a common task in the face of today's world and its pressing needs. At the end I underlined this vision with a few citations from the Bible and the Koran.

It is my conviction that great injustices exist in the world, and everyone who has done some travelling is well aware of them. We find famine, inadequate housing, unemployment, resignation to one's sad plight, a lack of interest in improving oneself, and so forth. Upon investigation it would seem that this is not the result of conscious injustice practiced by some human beings against others but rather the result of a way of life based on specific religious and cultural convictions.

Thus we may admire Hinduism in many respects, but it also puzzles us on many points. There is the caste system, the large number of untouchables, and the fact that so many poor people live out on the street without adequate housing. We fully realize that reform movements are under way in Hinduism to do something about all this, but the fact remains that they have not been able to solve these major problems. The big question remains: Wherein lies the cause of this attitude of human beings towards one another? In the core of Hindu religious life, it seems. For it does not accord any real value to one's own person, the person of another, or the world. Instead the Hindu seeks to return to the source from which one has come and of which one is a part: the Absolute. Liberation and redemption does not mean working in this world with others to turn it into some small portion of the kingdom of God while we wait for the definitive kingdom; instead it means returning to the Source from which humanity has come. This can be accomplished through yoga and meditation. In this case, then, one can say that a religious view of the world serves as a brake on development. This raises the question: Do we people who are the beneficiaries of a monotheistic revolution have the responsibility to help India, through dialogue, to change its Hindu view of life as a preliminary step towards development?

In ancient Buddhism, which is still very much alive in some lands today, we find much the same difficulty. As we have noted earlier, Buddhists have a keen feel for the transient character of earthly things. Nothing is perduring. It is better to give up all striving and seek nirvana. Here again we find obstacles to a social life based on justice and the elimination of hunger and poverty.

One can proceed to do this with other religions as well, examining them under a microscope as it were. One will discover many good and beautiful things, and one can learn a great deal. But the fact remains that the developing course of religious history, in which we see God's salvific plan unfolding, eventually led to what we call the monotheistic revolution. Thus it is important for us to consider what sort of values are part and parcel of this revolution, and also what role they might be able to play in solving the world's problems. That is a task for the upcoming decades.

First of all, the monotheistic religions share the belief that God is a person, and that we human beings are also persons in God's image. During the course of history these persons are working together to fashion a better world. Connected with this is a conviction shared by the monotheistic religions: that the world and all human beings have been created by God and that the latter had a goal in mind. They are meant to be happy, and all created things ultimately are designed to help human beings to reach that goal. The monotheistic religions also look positively on the world of created things. These two developmental values can help people to attain a greater degree of social justice and to progress towards world peace.

Thirdly, there is the conception of history shared by the monotheistic religions. Human beings are not to retreat towards the past from which they have come; instead they are to move ahead into the future. The monotheistic religions share a linear notion of time, as opposed to the cyclic conception of some other religions. Christian tradition refers to the kingdom of God, and Muslim tradition views human beings as the viceroys of God on earth who have the task of establishing his kingdom.

Finally, there is the distinctive view of community that is shared by the monotheistic religions. The fashioning of a new world is not something that we do alone by ourselves. We do it in joint activity with God and with each other, in cooperation with human beings both inside and outside our religions. We must step beyond the barriers, go out to others, and assemble them all into a people of God on its way to complete fulfillment. So we can say that the monotheistic religions have their own distinctive place and task, both in the world and in God's saving dispensation. They must enter into dialogue with other religions for the sake of all humanity and move forward towards the fulfillment of salvation history. Thus the intimate connection between the values deriving from the monotheistic revolution and the progressive development of the human world should be clear.

This view caused a sensation at first at the Tripoli meeting because the participants were not used to this type of thinking. Some would have preferred that I stick to the Koran and the Bible and point out the similarity in the thought of each on a given matter. The subsequent discussions made it clear that people were slowly coming to see the reality and nature of the communal task placed before us. In later personal conversations this came out clearly.

The final conclusions of the meeting are also of importance.[99] There it was stated clearly that the participants had come together to help remove mutual misunderstandings that had existed for centuries. But self-criticism with respect to the past (at which Christianity is stronger than Islam) was not the only aim. The participants also were interested in the future. They wished to examine and express the values of the two religions in order to overcome the material and moral crises of our day. The dignity of human beings and their liberation from any and all sorts of oppressive factors had to be examined from the standpoint of religion. The findings were presented in twenty-four paragraphs. Two of these paragraphs were not accepted by the Vatican, which served as the host dialogue-partner jointly with Libya. One example may show that not all the problems and prejudices of the past have been overcome. One section states that Islam offers human beings a complete system of tasks and duties in life (hence a kind of ideology, though this is denied) whereas Christianity stresses spiritual and inspirational values. My feeling is that this is not a full and accurate reflection of what Christianity is.

On the other hand the concluding statement did make clear that both religions are monotheistic, something that was denied more than once in the past. It also stated that there was agreement on a common goal: promoting spiritual and moral values for the benefit of human beings. And it asserted that the two religions recognize each other's prophets and messengers. The document then dwelt in some detail on joint efforts to eliminate hunger, war, and inhuman living conditions because these things are in conflict with God's aim and purpose. Great emphasis was placed on the education of young people, who are to be given objective catechetical instruction about the two religions. The point was made that Christians expect Muslims to examine their holy books in a truly scholarly way even as Christians do theirs. Thus there is a need for a mutual interchange of university professors. Finally, a resolution was passed to set up a permanent mixed commission, which would have the task of seeing to it that these resolutions were implemented.

Looking back at that week in Tripoli, I can see that it measured up a great deal to what we have envisioned here as a proper theology of religions and real dialogue. On the whole, its outlook was very much oriented towards the world and not alien to real life. Dialogue about salvation also played a role at the meetings, however modestly. A plea was made for religious freedom and a free exchange of religious experiences, the only stipulation being that the latter take place in a scholarly way and in the spirit of mutual understanding.

Now let us consider the situation with regard to African religions. Here I am not going to deal directly with the burgeoning African theology that is evident today. Instead I want to relate my view of dialogue and the theology of religions to the rapidly changing valuation of the many independent Churches that are arising in Africa. Some of them are offshoots of the Catholic Church; most of them are offshoots of Protestantism. Once upon a time people talked about schismatic Churches, or separatist Churches, or even about post-Christian movements in Africa.[100] A few years ago there were about 600 such offshoots. Today there are many more. But now people talk about African initiatives in the area of religion[101] or about independent Churches. Some of these Churches are already members of the World Council of Churches. Leading the way is the Church of Simon Kimbangu in Zaire, which has a million members.

What is the reason for the change in our judgments about these Churches? Well, we have probed more deeply into the genesis of these Churches and thus entered into dialogue with the authentic desires of the men and women who have founded or joined them. We have learned how to get a better feel for Africa and this has led to a changed evaluation of the impressive phenomenon. This has been the concrete result of a deeper dialogue with Africa.

Here I shall consider only one example: the Southern Shona Independent Churches in Rhodesia.[102] Daneel has given a detailed examination of these Churches in a three-volume work, of which two volumes have already been published. The two published volumes deal specifically with the subject I am interested in here. Daneel chose four Churches for his study: the African Apostolic Church of Johane Maranke, a Zionist Church with many subdivisions, the African Congregational Church of President Zvekare Sengwayo, and the First Ethiopian Church of Bishop Nheya Gavure.

Thorough investigation and active participation over a course of years brought the following facts to light. There is a profound difference in approach between the Catholic Church and the Protestant Churches with respect to both traditional customs and their convictions of faith. This is bound up with the teaching of the two Churches. People in the Protestant tradition started off from the assumption that human beings are wholly depraved, even though they might voice views that sounded quite different: e.g., that human beings are the image of God and that there is some *sensus divinitatis.* All such latter notions had no real effect on the total corruption of human beings. Catholic tradition acknowledged original sin, but it also maintained that the rational soul escaped total corruption and could know God (natural theology). This knowledge of God was incomplete, of course; but thanks to the analogy of being between God and humans, the latter could attain rational knowledge of the First Cause apart from supernatural revelation.

This difference in view led to a big difference in missionary approach. While the theological differences between Catholics and Protestants may have been small, their consequences for practice were great. Both Churches wanted to see the rise of native churches. In the Protestant tradition, however, this did not imply any assimilation or absorption of indigenous customs or religious practices. A complete break with the pagan past was emphasized. Only after conversion to Christ could one proceed to ask: What elements from the old way of life can be renewed in Christ? By then it was frequently too late, however. Rome acted otherwise. It acknowledged seeds of the Word and accepted indigenization. Customs and habits that were good in themselves were accepted and taken over by the Church. It talked about building bridges between paganism and the Church. There was accommodation and assimilation. Catholic missionaries adapted themselves to the other culture and native elements were assumed by the Catholic Church. To be sure, some in the Church held more rigid views, as we noted earlier in the case of Vaeth, Thauren, and Ohm. But the fact remains that Catholic missionary practice was often better than its missiological principles.

Now the interesting thing is that this theological difference did not find expression in the early phase of missionary work. Missionaries regarded Shona culture as an alien thing. The dominant position of the ancestors and the influence of spirit-mediums was regarded as a serious matter. Polygamy and successive marriages had to be wiped out, and dances had to stop. It was only at a later stage that the different approach of the two Christian traditions of the West came to the fore: specifically, when the community began to grow and take fuller shape and when people had to make a more clear-cut choice. According to Daneel, this is one of the most direct causes of the splintering of the African church membership and one of the most important reasons why the Protestant Churches have lost more members than the Catholic Church.[103] Even on the difficult matter of polygamy the Catholic Church was more indulgent and more flexible, particularly in the case of the wives of polygamists.

But the difference in approach can be seen most clearly in the case of ancestor worship, which is a vital part of the life of Africans. In the Protestant Churches all forms of ancestor worship and divination were regarded as violations of the first commandment. Fundamentalist missionaries were the most rigid in this area, of course. Precisely here a complete break with the past was demanded. At first the Catholic Church also rejected these practices, but it soon came back to its old approach in practice. Catholic missionaries began to attend rituals and to bless sacrificial offerings and beer with holy water. Now there are efforts to incorporate Shona rituals into the Catholic liturgy. In particular, the modern Catholic theology of religions opens up vast new perspectives in this area, which go far beyond the mere adaptation of external rites. They are ultimately concerned with the ways of thinking that lie behind such rites. Once again it should be clear how important an open theology of religions is for a total renewal of missiology, particularly in this modern era when other peoples, cultures, and religions are demanding their rights.

This chapter could be extended indefinitely. I could discuss Indian christology, which arose almost two centuries ago. It began with Hindus, and it has remained Hindu.[104] However, I must bring this chapter to a close, so I will confine my remarks to a question that is now under serious discussion: May non-Christian holy books be used in the liturgy? There is much debate about this subject in many Asian lands, but it is particularly heated in India.[105] So I shall consider the question in terms of India, focusing on the line of thought expounded by Mariasusai Dhavamony in *Concilium*.[106]

Dhavamony bases his remarks primarily on the findings of a research seminar which dealt with this question in Bangalore (India). The seminar met to resolve difficulties that had arisen among Catholics in the process of studying ways to use Hindu texts in the liturgy. The book work comes to more than seven hundred pages. First of all, one must have a good acquaintance with the Hindu holy scriptures. There are primary texts that were written down by seers long before our era and that are regarded as containing the eternal word. The secondary texts came later, comprising things remembered by people of subsequent generations; thus they contain a mixture of divine truths and human truths. Both the primary and the secondary texts are part of the holy books for all those who are reared in the Hindu tradition. They receive their authoritative status through recognized religious authority in the Hindu community: i.e., from the Brahmans, saints, and other religious leaders.

A large process of development is to be found in Hindu rituals and the Hindu holy books. The outlook can range from some specific form of polytheism to worship of a personalized God with pantheistic traits. In the holy books, which also include the ritual material, we again find much variation. But basically they teach people how to come to a realization of the divine in human beings through the spiritual pathways of action (including ritual acts), knowledge, and love of God. The degree of divine realization varies with the different ways, as also does the object of the experience. Sometimes the object is the one, supreme God; sometimes it is various deities; sometimes it is the Absolute (Brahman); and sometimes it is something divine or holy, such as the power of the rite itself. The pathway of rite does not stand opposed to that of knowledge or love, but rather in the service of the latter.

In considering this whole problem one must also take due account of what the modern Hindu actually performs in the way of holy rites and the extent to which he or she uses the holy books. While much has been dropped, much has also remained: e.g., domestic rites and a few "sacraments." Exquisite hymns can be heard on everyone's lips, both at home and in the temple. Ceremonies with fire-offerings, interspersed with scriptural readings, are widespread; and so forth. Hinduism is a living religion.

The opinion of Dhavamony is that the Hindu scriptures were not "revealed" in the real sense of that word. That is to say, they are not a divine self-communication in both words and salvation history. He regards them as human attempts to solve the whole question of the divine. They are human verbal revelation and efforts at self-fulfillment. Thus there is also a great difference between inspiration in the biblical sense and inspiration in the Hindu sense. The salvation preached by the Hindu holy scriptures is also different from Christian salvation. For the Hindu the Absolute, with which one unites, is the goal of salvation; it puts an end to the transmigration of the soul. There is no hint of the biblical God, who is intensely personal and who is at work in history in and through his people. So can we really use the Hindu scriptures in Christian worship?

Here I will not offer my own judgment of the views advanced by the author above, except to say that my judgment might be a bit milder. Here, however, we want to see how an Indian resolves the difficulty. At the research seminar in Bangalore and in their practice of a renewed liturgy, others have gone much further. They have also been subjected to the same criticism from the highest sources. Again I want to emphasize that a sound theology of religions should be able to lead us further along in this area. But let us get back to our author.

Dhavamony maintains that many texts speak beautifully about the One, the unique one that truly exists, the really real. He cites many moving passages, regarding them as fleeting glimpses of a higher divine personality and the experiencing of it. He also underlines their pantheistic or monotheistic context. In this connection he talks about theologically objectionable dogmas. These must be stripped away while the religious experiences, which are valuable and authentic, should be assimilated into Christian prayer and the Christian liturgy. When the Hindu texts are incorporated into the Christian liturgy, they lose their Hindu connotations of monism or pantheism. This means that we do not generally adopt them as they are to be found in the Hindu scriptures: "In their Christian, assimilated form they retain their authentic Hindu religious value, but without the Hindu dogmatic content that is objectionabie to a Christian."[107]

Thus Dhavamony is not in favor of the adoption of Hindu texts, but he would like to integrate the underlying religious experience into prayers of intercession and Eucharistic prayers. He would like to see the same thing done in the liturgy of the word. It seems doubtful to me that the authentic Hindu religious values are retained when this is done. It seems to me that he has been led astray by the pastoral problems involved in the liturgical use of Hindu texts by people who have been Christians for centuries and no longer live in the Hindu milieu.

Perhaps one could make greater progress by probing more deeply into the notion and reality of revelation in Hinduism, exploring the place of Hinduism in God's salvation plan and continuing the experiments that are taking place in the new Christian communities and ashrams (where small groups of Christians try to live together and follow a Hindu life-style in order to break down opposition to Hinduism). One need not be afraid of syncretism or relativism in doing this, for the Christian texts used in the liturgy provide a counter-balance and should make clear what completes and perfects all the rest.

This set of examples should suffice to show that there are new evaluations of other religions in both theory and practice. My aim here was simply to point up a trend, to give the reader some idea of the new forms of ecclesial life that can result from a dialogue based on a sound theology of religions. Much of this is applicable in the West as well, for today many people professing Eastern religions are living there. In Europe and America we should be able to relate to them and enter into dialogue with them, thus looking for the best solution to their religious problems. Those problems result from the fact that they are far away from the homeland of their culture or religion. But right now we stand at the very beginning of such an effort.

5

A New Vision of World Christianity

On the basis of their studies concerning dialogue with other religions or the theology of religions, many authors have arrived at a vision of a renewed and revitalized world Christianity. In this final chapter I should like to consider the vision of a few authors, and then conclude with a brief statement of my own position.

I will begin with a few observations made by van de Pol.[108] He maintains the exclusivity of the Christian proclamation, but he also stresses that empirical Christianity may in no way be identified with the biblical or Christian proclamation. Even that proclamation itself is bound by time and place. So the absoluteness and exclusivity of the saving message goes hand in hand with the relativity and specificity of Christianity as a world religion. However, this does not rule out the possibility or the factual reality that God has willed to prepare all humankind for his saving message through the activity of his Spirit; and that the non-Christian religions in general, and the religion of Israel in particular, are the fruit of the activity of God's Spirit.

In our age conventional Christianity, with its negative judgments of other religions, has become an impossibility. We are living in an age of encounter and dialogue. In this context van de Pol poses the issue of the common basis for dialogue. The question cannot be answered in any general terms because it depends on the concrete religions in question. Of course it is true that all world religions possess holy books and are familiar with prayer, sacrifice, meditation, adoration, and worship. Besides these shared elements is the shared fact that all religions face a common problem: their credibility in the modern world. Thus there are reasons enough for encounter and dialogue, which must go together.

Van de Pol shares Tillich's view of the crisis being faced by all religions. Whether their adherents are aware of it or not, it is a period of ongoing and serious crisis for all religions. The question that faces them now is: How are they to withstand present-day secularism and the quasi-religions (or ideologies) based upon it? But it is a period for purification rather than one of decline. Something new is born out of every crisis. Human beings are inescapably religious, whether they will it or not. Thus van de Pol sketches thoughts which offer much hope for the future of Christianity. The latter, however, must go back to its pristine proclamation that is grounded in the Bible and the message of Christ. Only then will it be able to make the new start that it must now make. But van de Pol does not tell us how Christianity will actually look in its new garb.

The topic is worked out more clearly and explicitly by Kenneth Cragg.[109] His book was the result of a shock, of a sudden realization of the contrast between the nineteenth-century view of mission in this world and the apostolic precedents in the first century. Geographically speaking, we can say that Christianity had just about become universal, but it had done so with a thoroughgoing partiality for Western culture. This is not to say that Christianity is not to strive for universality. That point is made clear in the Bible. In Christ there is no longer Jew nor Greek, slave nor free man; all are children of God through faith in Jesus Christ. But gradually stipulations and specifications arose in the course of history. Mission work went hand in hand with colonialism. The cross and the flag were intertwined, and we got the three *m*'s: the merchant, the missionary, and the military. Whatever may have been their mutual influence on each other, the fact is that evangelization went hand in hand with pacification, and that this gave rise to a relationship of domination on the part of the Western powers and Western missionaries.

We cannot go back and change the facts of history, but neither can we maintain the old relationship at this point in the twentieth century. Western domination is a thing of the past and even the Churches are adapting to the new political circumstances. It is no easy matter, needless to say. With great difficulty the Churches had always erected and maintained hospitals, schools, social centers, and similar institutions for the native population— but often without the involvement of the latter. Now all these establishments must be turned over to people not fully motivated by our "doer" mentality. At the same time it is also true that the Churches have contributed a great deal to nationalism in various parts of the world. Many native politicians have gone through their studies in mission schools, and there they acquired a deep love for their land.

In this era of independence and nationalism the old faiths are recovering their strength. Buddhism, Islam, and Hinduism are underpinning national yearnings and giving new cohesiveness and confidence to people in Burma, Thailand, India, Pakistan, Indonesia, the Arab lands, and so forth. We are moving into a new situation that can lead either to greater secularization or to a pluriformity of faiths with minorities and majorities. Among the Christian minorities we also see a change; there is a gnawing fear that they, as minorities, will be forced to retreat on the political front. Even in areas where primitive religions prevail, with their seemingly slim chances for survival, we see efforts being made to maintain their identity. Such is the case, for example, with the concept of negritude and with the revitalized African theology.

On the other side we note that the interdependence of cultures is coming to the fore as a counter-weight to extreme emphasis on one's own distinctive identity. So there is a struggle between individual identity and universality. Like me, Cragg does not believe that the result will be one world in which faith is irrelevant and cultic worship will disappear. In this one but divided world Christians look to Christ and his mediation, laying aside prejudice in favor of the fascinating fact of human diversity and all that it can contribute. The New Testament itself arose out of such a situation! One must continually strive to overstep and overcome the limits of the world, while trusting in the Lord's message. The early Church sought the Logos everywhere.

Today we face much the same problem, for it is through religions that cultures are defined and spiritually inspired in history. Hence Christianity cannot harangue people and ignore their gods. If we wish to have world relevance, then we must accept a multi-religious world. So we need a theology of religious pluralism. We must acknowledge the historical fact that there are many religions and go out to meet them; and we must meet them, not in the old way, but in terms of their current spirit of self-affirmation. Exclusivism is gone once and for all, and we can no longer regard the wide world as a spreading circle of inanity. Despite the indirect influence of Christianity on human beings such as Gandhi, and also despite the good that it has accomplished, the fact remains that the various faiths of the world still continue to exist. They have not succumbed to capitulation or disintegration.

In a spirit of prudent realism and of deep loyalty to Jesus Christ we must take this pluralistic religious situation seriously. We can do so by patiently working towards a Christian theology of religions, taking due account of their continuity and their present-day responsibilities. Our Christianity must be an open faith that faces up to two questions: What does the diversity of human faiths signify for the inner form and state of the Christian spirit? And what does it signify for the external relationship of the Christian faith with these other faiths? In this process we must give up using the term "non-Christian." It makes no more sense than using the term "non-Buddhist" to describe a Christian. We must find positive words to fill with positive content. We must give up self-preservation and intolerance, and cease to regard our former privileges as a perduring status. This does not mean that we have to give up the exclusivity of Christianity, as Toynbee would urge; but we must find other words and ideas to express what we mean by that. Starting out from the gospel message, we must develop an openness towards other faiths through attentiveness and communication, using the latter as the focus of our shared relationships. We can no longer maintain the attitude or the theological line of reasoning of Hendrik Kraemer vis-à-vis other religions. Though Cragg is critical of the notion of "anonymous Christians," he finds Rahner's view more closely akin to his own. Be that as it may, the aforementioned steps will open Christianity up from the inside so that it can tackle the problems of our day.

Now how will all this work out in Christianity's external relations with other beliefs? First of all, Christianity must take the latter seriously. It must acquire a deep inner feeling for those religions and try to comprehend them. It must serve them in their own society, inviting them to express their own understanding of reality in a full and positive way and to practice a radical and critical form of self-consciousness. If we do this, we will discover some wonderful things: an understanding of grace in Hinduism; a feeling for compassion and self-transcendence in Buddhism; a notion of mutual dependence and human solidarity in the philosophy of negritude; a conception of saving indignation in communism; a sense of orientation to God in Islam; and the notion of a people's dedication in Judaism. Cragg develops these ideas further in specific chapters dedicated to Judaism, Islam, and the African spirit.

There follows a chapter dealing with Christianity in an increasingly secularized world. Finally, he comes to his overall vision of Christianity in this new world. His conclusion is that Christianity in the world must be ready to give up its Western forms in order to live an authentic life within the full panorama of human cultures.[110] The Christian Church must have a diversified identity along with a loyal universality. It must retain its identity vis-à-vis its past and vis-à-vis the new world. It must become a real *ecumene,* spread out over the whole inhabited earth. The Christ of the West must become the Christ of the World.

This problem is also tackled by Robert Lawson Slater.[111] He, too, poses the issue of religious pluralism and the quest for a world community. Most of his study is an attempt to evoke the distinctive visions of Hinduism, Buddhism, Islam, Judaism, and Christian yearnings in the West. The problem is thus posed in sharply etched terms.

In Chapter 8 Slater comes to three possible solutions. Many people of different religions agree that one world also means one religion. That result, however, can be achieved in any one of three ways. The first approach comes down to replacement. One of today's major religions will become the world religion; the others will cede their places to it. That presumably is the only way to effectively insure world peace. This is how the major religions usually view the matter. Many Christians and Muslims share this view, thinking along strictly confessional lines; this explains their energetic missionary activity. Most Buddhists and Hindus would presumably reject this view. But when one probes a bit deeper into the thinking of a few of their modern authors, one finds exactly the same mentality. This solution cannot be adopted, however, because in fact a great revival is now under way among the major religions. They have no intention of being replaced by some other religion. Representatives of all the major religions, and of Christianity too, have been advocating some sort of religious pluralism for years. So this solution has little chance of being implemented.

The second possible approach is synthesis. All religions are to remain on the scene. They will compare their doctrinal teachings and rules of conduct, choose what is best among them, and thus produce a new religion embodying the finest insights and aspects of all. This is not syncretism because real syncretism would imply overlooking differences. Others in the past and present have tried to reduce all religions to about five basic points or aspects, but such attempts have never found favor with religious leaders. They have consistently been regarded as offshoots or stepchildren of relativism. Moreover, they seem to be the work of a handful of scholars sitting around a table, and one wonders what the common people think of such ideas.

At the same time, however, there is some measure of truth in this view because all religions have incorporated elements from other religions over the course of history. The process is usually called "adaptation." Hocking calls it "reconception," and Slater has discussed his view. This is the third possible solution, and some would use it to arrive at one world religion. It lies somewhere between the view that one religion is to replace all the others and the view that all present religions are to be replaced by some synthetic religion. There is to be no surrender of traditional affirmations, but neither will they perdure in their present-day form. Instead a "reconception" is to take place in each of the major living religions on the basis of a new inducement and a new challenge. The inducement is the rise of a world community, a new civilization; we stand on the threshold of that community now. The challenge is the influence of other faiths. Reconception must take place in each religion, with Christianity leading the way. It is not to be a reworking of isolated elements but a revision of one's faith as a whole. People will first explore what is essential in their own religion and try to realize the full implications of their faith. Rather than discarding their own convictions or simply allowing them to be replaced by others, believers will be challenged to explore their own beliefs more deeply and to see what is vitally essential and what is not. In this way their religion will become more truly itself.

Hocking writes so much about Christianity that people of other faiths may get the impression that the coming world religion is to be Christianity; that it will be so organized and widespread that others will be inclined to accept it. The difficulty, however, lies in determining what exactly is essential in each religion. Hocking believes that this approach will be one way in all religions, a summit of all religions. Slater, however, feels that no single religion will replace the others in the near future; and also that synthesis and syncretism offer no solution to the problem. He thinks there is something to the notion of reconception. It is true that all religions have borrowed from each other in the course of history; and the setting of reconception in the modern age is correct and appropriate. The weakness of Hocking's theory lies in the fact that one cannot easily assume that the quest for what is essential in each religion will automatically bring them all closer to one world religion. Does this underlying unity or oneness actually exist?

I agree with Slater that it is more realistic to stress what is particular, special, and different in each religion. The various religions proceed from sources of inspiration that are deeply different. Even looking at religion from a phenomenological point of view, we can say flatly that Hocking's theory is very weak. The major religions will perdure, and one may justifiably wonder whether a united world community must necessarily have one world religion.

The feeling for some sort of natural law does provide one basis for religious unity, but it is hardly an underlying unity in itself. It merely offers a coincidentally common ground or basis amid many other bases for difference.

Some may call this pretty vague. Others will advocate a well-ordered community and all sorts of institutional measures to exclude schism and heresy. But such an approach will never lead to any deep conviction, and it can do no more than tolerate religious pluralism.

On the basis of these two very different starting points one would say that the ideal of one world–one religion seems to remain a very remote prospect. But the prospect of one world is real enough and one can hope for cooperative efforts despite religious divisions.

M. M. Thomas has also wrestled with the issues raised in this chapter, dealing with them in the context of India.[112] He, too, realizes that changes are taking place in various religions because they are being confronted with the social and spiritual problems of the modern world. He attempts to explore the significance of all this for encounter between religions.

According to Thomas, we are now living in an inter-religious world that cannot be compared to that of a past age. Many factors have contributed to this new situation, and Thomas goes into them just as I did in the first chapter of this book. Thomas stresses that there is no real opposition between studying the interaction of religious traditions with modern history and the modern spirit (which seeks to solve humanity's problems in the modern world) on the one hand, and seeking out the deepest reality on the other. There is an integral relationship between anthropological and theological yearnings. The relationship between self, world, and God can never be interpreted by isolating these realities from one another. While the connection is viewed differently in different religions and ideologies, it is also true that in the modern world dialogue between them can best take place at the point where they come to grips with the spiritual self-understanding of modern human beings and their efforts to achieve authentic self-realization and fulfillment within the modern situation.

Against the backdrop of the modern human situation Thomas attempts to spell out the meaning and significance of dialogue within different religions and between them; and he focuses especially on dialogue with Christianity. Thomas spells out clearly the revolutions of our age, the struggle against poverty and oppression, the process of secularization, and the self-understanding of modern human beings. The latter seek to fashion their own history and to attain freedom, self-determination, and their own identity. They want to achieve this freedom in and through universal love. In other words, they want to achieve it in open dialogue and community with other persons and communities, with whom they share a belief in the unity of humanity and the universality of man's dignity as a human being.

It is here that the notion of world community comes to the fore. Once again Thomas stresses that the feeling for God goes hand in hand with the feeling for one's own self. Human beings realize that they transcend their own selves and also the world. This brings them to an awareness of the Ultimate Reality, the source and ground and goal of the human self. Thus religion or faith has to do with the way that a person comprehends and expresses the significance of selfhood in relation to nature, society, and self; but it also has to do with the symbolic expression of humanity's life in the realm of the holy, where the faith-adherence of a person can be renewed and revitalized continually.

Now there are two types of religions. One is the Jewish-Christian-Muslim tradition, in which history is the basic sphere of God's self-revelation and saving activity. The other is composed of the religious traditions of Africa, India, and China, in which release is viewed as a perduring vision of the undifferentiated spiritual oneness or harmony of nature, human beings, spirits, and deities. Thomas describes the first as the messianic approach to reality, and the second as the unitive approach to reality. In the messianic approach we find two different conceptions: that of the Conquering King and that of the Suffering Servant. The latter conception was difficult for the Jews to affirm because they were wedded to the conception of the Conquering King. But this latter conception of messianism (in terms of the Suffering Servant) lies at the root of the modern spirit of freedom and self-determination, of the revolutionary forces of our age. The other conception of messianism (in terms of the Conquering King) merely leads to new forms of slavery and inhuman totalitarianism. It still perdures today, fostering the destructive capabilities of modern humanity. We must go back to the messianism of the Suffering Servant, grounding our faith on the cruciform humanity of Christ as the ultimate goal of humanity.

In our day we also find the followers of the other type of religiosity (the unitive approach) expressing criticism of messianic religion. They say that the latter leads to aggressiveness, self-destruction, and unrest, while their type of religion offers spiritual contentment to the restless human beings of the West. Messianism is also being criticized by the Western counterculture. On the other hand it is also true that the peoples who adhere to the unitive approach are coming under the influence and reach of the anthropology and theology of messianism—either in its secular, theocratic, or prophetic form. They are being affected by the influence of Western education, the struggle for national independence and nation-building, technology, and the demands of social justice and secularization. We see them turning to a religious messianism such as Christianity or to some secular messianism such as nationalism, radical humanism, or communism. Thinkers in these lands are now busy trying to lay the new spiritual foundations for the new society that is taking shape, and the result is always some form of messianism.

Thus dialogue is already a reality in Africa and Asia. It is a dialogue between the basic native tradition of "primal" mystical faith or a natural humanistic one and the messianic core of Western secular and religious faiths. The ideal is a synthesis of the unitive vision and the concept of the crucified Messiah in order to harness the unbridled dynamism of the conquering Messiah. I find these latter ideas to be the most important ones in Thomas's book, and we shall have to explore them more deeply here.

The second half of Thomas's book is very concrete. It is a detailed application of his basic ideas, as he examines the "primal" vision and modern human beings. We can already note the effects of dialogue in the above-mentioned sense. There is the African humanism of Senghor, the Ujaama ("togetherness") movement of Nyerere in Tanzania, the African humanism of Kaunda in Zambia, the whole distinctive socialism of Nkrumah, and the whole movement in favor of "negritude." Here we also find the modern religious movements that have broken away from the ancient notion of time as something without a future and that I referred to as the "independent Churches" earlier. Thus Africa is in dialogue with Christ. Already there are African theologians—e.g., Mbiti, Sawyerr, and Idowu—who are working up an African theology so that African Christianity may be truly at home in a modern Africa which is oriented towards the future.

Then there is India, where we find the Hindu renaissance with its new concern for spiritual deliverance and the goal of history. It all began with such great Hindu reformers of the nineteenth century as Rajah Ram Mohan Roy, and it is still in progress today. We find wholly new interpretations of the ancient writings. In the *Bhagavad Gita,* for example, some now are discovering a stress on activity devoid of personal desires and on the well-being of the world as the aim of all action. The Vedanta, too, is now viewed as a sort of social gospel: Because human beings are divine, they can be strong, provide for their own needs, and have boundless self-confidence. How different that all sounds for the age-old emphasis on humanity's ascent to the Absolute! Radhakrishna, India's great philosopher and statesman, has also given new interpretations to old notions that once imprisoned human beings. He maintains that the quest for possessions and happiness and the performance of social obligations are means to attain redemption. The old alienation from the world is now past. Sri Aurobindo, one of India's greatest thinkers, views humanity in the process of cosmic evolution and regards humanity as the goal of that process. One can go further and say that there are now Indian socialists and communists.

Investigation shows that this revival in India owes much to the influence of Christianity, but that it also has led to an indigenous form of Christianity in return. In Buddhism there is now talk of some sort of messianism. Some thinkers view the world as a process of continual change or as some type of creative evolution. Even in Hinayana Buddhism some consideration is being given to the situation of human beings and the practice of those who are filled with universal love and seek to improve the lot of human beings on earth. Sometimes one even hears the notion that Buddhism is a revolt against religion in the name of human dignity in religion and society, and that it therefore is an authentic humanism. Sometimes Marxism is also viewed as a tool in this connection. There are also many studies about Buddha and Christ. I have already analyzed one such study, that of Drummond, in some detail. All these things are indications of a dialogue in process, and a messianic consciousness is also evident in Buddhism. It still has the aspect of a theocratic messianism because it is designed to counter Western domination. Thus, in their dialogue with Buddhism, Christians will have to say more about the messianism of the Suffering Servant.

Islam is also on the move. There are thinkers and reformers who are advocating the principle of change and movement in a religion that had been static for centuries: e.g., Iqbal in Pakistan. There is also a turning towards the world after centuries of withdrawal, and even some radical criticism of religion. A closer Christian approach to Islam is still difficult; but as we noted above, there is at least a Muslim elite seeking to make this possible. One is reminded of the encounters in Cordova, Tunis, and Tripoli.

Marxism must also be mentioned in this connection. Thomas thoroughly explores the deeper dimensions of human alienation, from which Marxism seeks to liberate human beings. Discovering and spelling out the deeper dimensions of alienation will provide the opportunity for a dialogue about freedom and humanism that can counteract the alienation which keeps occurring—even in the Marxist way of life. We also find new Marxist ideas about the relationship of Marxism to religion. Some Marxist authors are even saying that a future open to the Infinite is the only transcendence known to them as atheists. So a dialogue between Marxism and Christianity is now under way, and such major theologians as Rahner and Metz are involved in it.

Thomas concludes with his own vision: the modern human being and the new humanity in Jesus Christ. The early Church identified the crucified Jesus with the awaited Messiah, the Christ. The saving goal of history is viewed in terms of the new cruciform humanness of Jesus Christ. Jesus is the new human being, through whom a new humanity is created in the image of God. He is the authentic Adam, through whom all of humanity has been reconciled with God and all creation has been brought to completion and perfection. Jesus introduces a movement of the Spirit that leads to the ultimate future of God's revelation in humanity and nature, to the completion of the kingdom where God will be all in all.

That is the traditional theology. The challenge facing us is to discover how we are to link up this new human being in Jesus Christ with the problems of today. A few examples may suffice here. Christianity has done a complete reinterpretation of the vision of creation, the fall, and redemption. We no longer cling to myths. The whole point now is to look at creation in terms of the final goal: the redemption of creation in Jesus Christ. Creation is a foreshadowing of, and a yearning towards, a new creation: God's creative future in the resurrection of Jesus. Creation is the world moving towards its fulfillment in the coming *eschaton*. The *eschaton* is the creative force, the inner dynamism, of a world in the process of becoming, of a human history moving towards its full integration in the lordship of Christ. To be sure, opposing forces are at work as well. Thus Thomas also talks about the new cruciform humanity in Jesus Christ, while noting that the Spirit gives us the power to overcome these opposing forces.

More important, however, is the fact that the Christian theology of messianism is being forced to rethink its definition of the people of Christ (the Messiah) and their divine election. And this rethinking must take place in the context of Jesus Christ's universality and the oneness of humanity. On the one hand we have the particularism of the Church, the people of God; on the other hand we have the universalism of the final goal. The question has always been around, and it has always been resolved in terms of mission. That is the answer even now, but we must now reconsider the nature of mission in the light of the self-understanding of modern humanity and its quest for a pluralistic world community.

Here Vatican II offers one answer in *Lumen gentium*. It asserts that the Catholic Church is the central stream in the process of salvation in this world, but it also acknowledges its intimate ties with all Christians. Moving out from there, the circle takes in the Jews, then others who recognize God as the Creator (e.g., Muslims), then those who seek the unknown God in shadows and images, and finally all those who truly seek God and try to live an upright life according to their conscience. *Gaudium et spes* divides the latter into two groups: those who acknowledge God and those who cultivate the beautiful qualities of the human spirit without yet knowing the source of those qualities. The mission of the Church applies to all of them. The Church must preach its message, serve all humankind, and try to bring about the conversion of human beings to Christ in his Church.

In this document, then, we see no more attempts to set up rigid boundaries for the people of God that is in community with Christ. At the same time it is debatable whether the conciliar document is clear enough in expressing the fact that the community of faith is wider than the Church. Elsewhere the document says that since Christ died for all human beings and since the ultimate vocation of human beings is one and divine, we believe that the Holy Spirit, in some way known to God, offers everyone the possibility of being associated with the paschal mystery. Here we have a community of faith that is wider than the church.

This notion can be elaborated further in a number of ways. One may talk about anonymous Christians, or the hidden Church, or the unknown Christ. Readers will recognize the views of various authors treated here in our discussion of the theology of religions. In any case the way is opened up for Christians to stress their unity in Christ by entering into full fellowship with people of different races, classes, ages, religions, and political convictions. It will be fellowship in a pluralistic community that goes beyond the boundaries of the Church, thus offering the testimony of the Church to the goal of humanity's renewal in Christ. Right now a secular fellowship in Christ is at the forefront of Christian thinking. Both political theology and the theology of religions is occupied with that topic, and so we need a theology of religious pluralism. We now view Jesus Christ as the humanism of God, and that is a good step forward from the exclusivism of Karl Barth, Hendrik Kraemer, and Emil Brunner.

Others are moving in different directions. John Hick writes about differing religions as the historicization of God's agape in the history of different peoples.[113] More recent Catholic thinkers view other religions as legitimate means of divine salvation in what can be regarded theologically as a pre-Christian situation. The novelty of Karl Barth's thought is that it embodies a christocentric relativism which radically relativizes any and all expressions of religiosity.

Thomas finds the latter to be the most fruitful starting point for interpreting other religions and quasi-religions. At this point Thomas follows the teaching of Karl Barth and his followers concerning the human being. The latter is created by God but also alienated from him. The human being defies God but cannot escape him. Humans move away from God to find their own self-justification, but they only end up in endless self-frustration. The various religions will be abolished at the end of time. Until then we must involve ourselves in religions but be prepared at all times for their abolition by Christ. This implies a theological relativizing of all religions in the name of God's grace in Jesus Christ. Thus human beings are already liberated from religions and quasi-religions and actively occupied with their new humanity in Christ through implicit or explicit faith. For this reason they can enter into dialogue with other religions, doing so in the spirit of concern for human fellowship. In fact, the two processes—secularization and relativization—go together.

There is much to admire in the initial phase of Thomas's exposition. He places the theology of religions in its proper context: the context of a world that is changing, becoming one, and seeking to be more humane. There is also a gain in the fact that he, like other authors discussed here, views Christianity as a force for humanization and feels that this fact is inextricably bound up with the religious inspiration of Christianity. (Indeed in all religions the images of God, human beings, and the world are inextricably bound up with each other.)[114] What I cannot understand, however, is his lapse into a long outmoded position of Karl Barth. Someone like Thomas, who has solid knowledge of both religious and profane realities in our present-day world, should be a bit more critical-minded in discussing this particular topic. Indeed it does not really jibe with his previous remarks, which suggest a very different solution to the problem. They point towards a Christianity stripped of its historically determined traits and engaged in dialogue with the views of humanity, the world, and God held by other religions. Such a dialogue would maintain an even balance between social and political involvement on the one hand and religious inspiration on the other.

Having come to the end of Part One, I should like to offer my own summary vision of world Christianity. I agree with those authors treated extensively above who plead for a religious pluralism within Christianity. Christianity must be properly understood, however, as a group of human beings living the ideals of Jesus Christ. In a previous chapter we saw that these ideals of Jesus Christ are rooted in the general salvation history. Thus they are imbedded in the interplay between God's invitation and humanity's response to his self-communication through the course of history. This pageant has gone through different phases, and it still is doing that. Every social response or religion has its own input into the dialogue. It contributes its own color and shape and content to the group effort to live up to the ideals and essential values brought by Jesus. In the Christianity of the future, therefore, a great deal of pluriformity will prevail in theology, catechesis, official functions, service to the community, ecclesial structures, and so forth.

In this theology of religions lies the basis for a missiology that is still to be worked out, and for the self-realization of the Christian essentials in specific Churches and groups.[115] Yet there will be a recognizable identity too. For all the forms of Christian identity elaborated by different cultures and religions will go back to the essential thing that Jesus brought us: i.e., his vision of the human being, the world, and the Father. Thus we are striving for a world Christianity and we retain the hope that it can come to be once again. But we fully realize that a long history lies before us and that the major work remains to be done. The time is now ripe to get started.

PART TWO

The Way, the Paths, and the Ways: Christian Theology and Concrete Religions

In Part One I dealt with a general theology of religions. I spoke about the responsibility facing Christianity to make a new, positive approach to other religions in the spirit of dialogue. And I suggested that other religions have their own specific contributions to make towards salvation.

Here in Part Two I wish to propose a more concrete theology of religions. Again and again I will be trying to answer such questions as the following: What precisely is the conception of salvation—in the broad sense of the term—that this particular religion holds? What contribution does it make to ongoing dialogue, even for us Christians? What, therefore, is the task and obligation of Christians in this dialogue with other religions?

I fully realize that this is no easy subject and that my thoughts hardly represent the last word on it. Too much remains to be said and done in this area. In the brief compass of these pages I must limit my remarks to certain observations. I cannot go into any lengthy discussion of particular issues. For example, I cannot even explore in detail the full conception of salvation held by this or that particular religion. No single religion is a static datum. It is constantly undergoing change and development, revision and adaptation. It is also being influenced from the outside, perhaps even by Christianity. But I do hope to treat other religions fairly here, so that my remarks may encourage further dialogue of an authentic sort. Such dialogue assumes that both participants are open to each other, that together they are working for the total salvation of the whole human race which is announced to us in the coming and already burgeoning kingdom of God.

As was true in Part One, readers may find that there is more in the Notes than in the text itself. The wealth of material indicated in the Notes should not dismay my readers. I want the text itself to be as simple and readable as possible, and the Notes will provide reading material for those who wish to explore the subject further.

In the chapters of this part I will attempt to dialogue with a variety of religions: Islam, Hinduism, Buddhism, the new religions of Japan, the Bantu religious outlook, the religious practice of the common people in Latin America, and the ideal of the new human being in China. There is a plethora of material involved, but that is the result of fifteen years of study and teaching. In a concluding chapter I will try to sum up the results and to stress the possibilities for renewed dialogue and rapprochement. I will suggest that dialogue must go hand in hand with a maieutic approach. We must, in other words, combine dialogue with thorough questioning of other religions and Christianity in order to find out how they represent Ways and the Way towards greater progress in the overall salvific situation of the human race. We must dig deep and find a new standpoint for examining the whole issue.

I had my reasons for the title of this part: "The Way, the Paths, and the Ways." Religions are not first and foremost institutionalized systems but Ways. Aren't the Old Testament and the New Testament full of talk about the Way of the Lord? Weren't the first Christians called followers of the Way (Acts 9:2)? Doesn't the first sura of the Koran talk about the straight Way? Doesn't Hinduism know three Ways to salvation? Doesn't Buddhism talk about the Eightfold Path? Here, it seems to me, we have a good starting point for dialogue.

6

The Supreme, Almighty God: Islam

Islam is the youngest of the great world religions. It is the only one that arose after Christianity, so from the very start it had to adopt some position vis-à-vis Christ and Christianity. Here I shall try to reproduce some of the essential elements of Islam that have perdured despite historical changes. They go back to the Koran, which contains the divine revelations proclaimed by Mohammed between A.D. 610 and A.D. 632. The setting was the South Arabian peninsula around Mecca and Medina.

THE CORE OF ISLAM

Mohammed was a religious personality, who withdrew into solitude one month each year. He would spend that month in a cave on Mount Hira, which was located near Mecca. Mohammed was seeking the true religion, and he was not satisfied with the polytheism of his clansmen. He became convinced that Abraham, the ancestral forefather of the Jews, Christians, and Arabs, had known only one God, just as the Holy Scriptures of the Jews and Christians said. The Arabs, like others before them, had strayed away from this fact. So God constantly sent prophets to bring them back to the one true God and the straight path. Moses, David, and Jesus were three of them; but the Arabs had their prophets also. In the course of time, however, all the followers of these prophets turned away from the straight path and began to worship several deities. Mohammed wanted to dispel this ignorance, first among the Arabs but also among Jews and Christians.[1]

Mohammed is the last of the prophets to echo the divine message. He is the seal of the prophets. This essential message is summed up in the following passage of the Koran: "Say: 'We believe in Allah and what was sent down to us, and what was sent down to Abraham, Ismail, Isaac, Jacob, and the tribes, what was brought to the Prophets by their Lord. We make no distinction between one and another of them, and we have surrendered ourselves to Him.' "[2] We must now analyze the main points of this revelation.

First of all, we must note that the message has been "sent down." In other words, all the prophets are transmitters of one single heavenly book, and so no distinction is made between them. They are all in one line and they all speak out of the same book, even though they may use different languages. So there is no progressive revelation and the content of this revelation is simple. Allah is the creator of heaven and earth. He is almighty and sublime. In his inscrutable wisdom he has foreordained whom he will lead to the right way and whom he will allow to go astray. After this life comes the next life. On the day of resurrection God will demand an account of everyone. Eternal grief and punishment or eternal blessedness will be their lot.

This simple message is delivered by all the prophets: by Jewish prophets such as Moses, Christian prophets such as Jesus, and also by Mohammed. The message remains the same always, but human beings are constantly straying from it. When they do stray, God must send another prophet to impress the age-old message on them once again. Humanity must constantly be brought back to monotheism. The last to do that was Mohammed, who imitated his Arab predecessors.

Three points stand out here: (1) The message proclaims a simple, straight-forward monotheism; there is one supreme, almighty God. (2) The prophets play no part in the making of the holy book. There is no human author of the holy book, which has been sent down. (3) There is no development in revelation, and hence no salvation history in the Christian sense.

Next we must note the last phrase in the passage cited above: "We have surrendered ourselves to Him." It means that they are Muslims and profess Islam: i.e., total surrender to the one God (Allah). That is why it is so typical for Muslims to say: "As God wills it." This has an impact on Islam's view of the role of the human person in history. The human being may well be termed God's vice-regent on earth, but that should not be readily equated with the Christian notion that the human being works together with God in building up the kingdom of God. For Islam the keynote is submission, resignation, and even fatalism at times.

And so Islam comes to its core pronouncement: "There is no God but God, and Mohammed is his Prophet." Islam sees itself as the one true guardian of the one true religion. It must even protect Jesus from what Christians have falsely made him: one of three gods.[3]

Islam's specific conception of salvation should now be somewhat clearer. Salvation consists in total submission to the almighty, sublime God who rules all. Human beings must be constantly brought back to this outlook, and the call of Islam is precisely this. Here I need not go into the fact that Islam has fashioned a whole system around this core, a scheme of precepts and tenets which may differ somewhat for differing sects and factions. The point is that the core remains the same. The straight path is right up front!

DOES ISLAM HAVE A MESSAGE FOR US CHRISTIANS?

We might ask what this first post-Christian world religion has to say to us Christians. The question is usually answered in generalities. With the help of a recent publication,[4] I will try to offer a more nuanced answer.

To Muslims we are "people of a book": the gospel message. So we, like the Jews and the Muslims themselves, are not pagans. That in itself is a positive judgment. But a Christian feels more here. He or she has personal relations with the living Word of God in Jesus of Nazareth. Still, it is good that Islam challenges us to test our actions against the gospel message and expects us to quote the Gospels when we dialogue. Muslims may ask us, for example, why we eat the flesh of pork when that is forbidden in the Old Testament. They expect us to answer with a quote from the New Testament. That is of fundamental importance in dialoguing with Muslims, even though we may not always find that very satisfactory. We can benefit greatly from measuring our practices by biblical standards!

Another point deserving mention is the fact that Islam accepts a religious pluralism. It is not simply a matter of converting all Christians. Muslims will vie with us in good works and leave the rest to God: "To each of you have we proposed a way of acting and a well cleared path. If Allah had so willed, He would have made you a single people. But His plan is to test you in what He has given you, so strive to be first in good deeds. All of you will return to Allah. Then He will inform you about the things over which you differed."[5] This opens up a whole road to joint efforts in countless fields for the benefit of our fellow human beings. As yet we find few joint efforts by Muslims and Christians on behalf of the many migrant or foreign laborers in the West. This passage offers a solid support for such efforts, as well as for international efforts on behalf of justice and peace. Here again the Christian will not be wholly satisfied and will want to enter into deeper dialogue. But we certainly must face up to this challenge to compete in good works.

The Koran goes further and shows respect for monks and priests in particular. Let me cite this passage first: "Strongest among people in enmity to the believers will you find the Jews and [Pagans]. . . . Nearest among them in affection for the believers you will find those who say, 'We are Christians.' Because among them are priests and monks who do not indulge in arrogant pride. And when they hear what was sent down to the Messenger, you will see their eyes overflow with tears for what they learn of the essential. And they say, 'Our Lord, we believe, write us down among the witnesses.' "[6]

This passage tells us that Muslims expect love and humility from Christians, and from priests and monks in particular. Our dialogue will have to be characterized by the same traits. More striking is the fact that Muslims expect us to shed tears when we become acquainted with the essential point of the message to Mohammed: i.e., that there is one supreme and almighty God. They expect recognition of this essential point. This obliges us to profess our monotheism clearly and to be wary of all sorts of conceptions of the Trinity, even though it may be true that Islam has a different picture of the Trinity than we do. (The Trinity is pictured as composed of the Father, Wife or Mary, and Son Jesus.) In our dealings with Muslims we must bring out much more clearly the fact that we, too, are monotheists in the literal sense of the word. We must attempt anew to make plausible to Muslims the being-Father, being-

Word, and being-Spirit aspects of God; and we must not give the impression that we are backing away from one God in favor of three.

Here is one of the great tasks facing dialogue. The text cited above expresses a very positive attitude towards Christians. Very different texts can be cited, of course, but they arose in different historical circumstances when strife had already arisen between Muslims and Christians.

I might sum up the matter this way. If we Christians truly act as people of the Book, as people who listen to the word of God, the Bible, and have a strong sense of God's majesty, then God will surely use this attitude to remind our Muslim brothers and sisters of those texts in the Koran that speak well of Christians. We can meet each other as believers, mindful of the fact that our lives are subject to the word of God. We can meet, not as rivals and opponents, but as people who have renounced fruitless controversies.[7]

TOPICS FOR DIALOGUE

The goal of dialogue is to bring both partners within closer reach of complete salvation. What can Christians contribute to this conversation with Muslims? Here we must consider the specific difficulties facing Muslims in their quest for complete salvation. We must first track down these difficulties. Then we must ask ourselves what help we can offer them in patient dialogue without negating the essentials of Islam.

What, then, are the difficulties facing Muslims? Dr. Smail Balic, a Muslim from Yugoslavia, is a librarian in Vienna who has been a participant in many dialogues. He makes the following observation.[8] Islam lies buried under a shackling system of legislation, theology, and science which had not changed since the Middle Ages, and which cannot address human beings in the twentieth century. Contacts with Christians make this all the more obvious because Christians, despite many difficulties, have been able to adapt successfully to the present century.

Many Muslims, including Khaddafi of Libya, plead for a return to the source, to the Koran. I don't think all problems can be solved that way because a return to the Koran itself confronts people with fundamental problems. I shall summarize them briefly here on the basis of my own experience in dialogue situations. First of all, we find a completely different concept of revelation in Islam than we find in Christianity. According to Islam, revelation took place only once: i.e., to Adam. It comprises the oneness of God, his role as creator, human responsibility vis-à-vis God, and reward or punishment in the next life. In the course of history this revelation was perverted again and again. God had to keep sending new prophets to get the message across again. Mohammed is the last of the prophets, but he does not bring anything more than was given to Adam.

The Judeo-Christian view, by contrast, sees a progressive revelation. God reveals himself not only in nature, the history of Israel, and the person of Jesus of Nazareth but also in the events of this age. The latter take place under the ever-active Spirit of Jesus. So there is development, progress, and constant adaptation to new situations in every area of life. This dynamism, which is characteristic of the Judeo-Christian view of life, makes Christianity a religion that is open to the modern age. The means to liberation and justice are there to be discovered, despite opposing forces.[9]

This theological conception of revelation and time is of basic importance for the total salvation of humanity. It must be brought up in our dialogue with Islam because we can get to the real problem only when we get down to that depth. In my opinion it is possible to arrive at such a development within Islamic thought itself. If one studies the Koran with modern scholarly methods, one becomes convinced that the same sort of historical progress in revelation is present in the Koran. Countless statements cannot be understood without knowing the historical circumstances of Mohammed's life. We find important developments taking place throughout the life of Mohammed as he grew from a purely religious leader into a statesman. And we can legitimately ask whether it is not possible to extend this process of development to later times. Are all the prescriptions and statements of the Koran meant for all ages and all circumstances surrounding Islam? Or can we say that many of them had merely temporary value, that they dealt with the typical situation of tribes who in past ages had lived amid deserts and oases? How should Islam look when there is no desert: e.g., in Indonesia?

This introduces a significant relativization, which also constitutes a big problem for Islam. Is it permissible for people to deal that way with a sacred book that lies open and ready in heaven and that is merely sent down to the prophet? Evidently a completely different concept of inspiration lies at the core of Islam. Exegesis, textual criticism, and historical considerations are the works of human beings; they cannot really affect the divine book. Here we have another important point for consideration, and fortunately that is now being realized by some Muslims. One simply cannot proceed further with the old, rigid concepts of revelation and inspiration. That does not mean that Islam is finished. After all, Christianity has managed to survive all that. It should be a valuable point for rapprochement between the two religions. It should help open the way to finding a new relationship or connection between Jesus of Nazareth and Mohammed, and that is what must ultimately take place, it seems to me. Christianity does not seek to cancel out Mohammed. Rather, it seeks to give him fresh validity within Muslim culture so that people can gather as disciples of Jesus around him in their own distinctive way.[10]

Now we come to one final but important point in our dialogue with Muslims. Religions cannot be imagined or conceived apart from some relationship to the world. Every religion has its own view of humanity and the world. When we examined Islam's conception of revelation and inspiration in the preceding paragraphs, we noted that Islam faced problems in trying to arrive at a dynamic attitude vis-à-vis the world. Indeed there is a further question that might be raised at this point: Is Islam actually fatalistic or not?

Must Muslims resign themselves to whatever overtakes them, or can they take their fate in their own hands to some extent at least?

In this case, too, one must explore the whole tradition of Islam. But right now Islamic scholars find it more important to direct the question back to the source, to the Koran, in order to get away from the tangle of various opinions and to put an end to the fatalism that is actually widespread among Muslims. The point worth noting is that in prophetic religions the world and history are regarded as the locale where God's word is actually realized. Hence the world must be approached in positive terms. The case is different with mystical religions, as we shall see. In them the world is associated with the pervasive reality of pain and suffering that embraces all existing things. If one wants to attain salvation, one does better to flee from the world. So the world is judged in negative terms.[11]

Now Islam is certainly a prophetic religion, so we must ask ourselves whether the observations just made above apply to Islam as well. I simply am not convinced that Islam can, without further ado and comment, be ranked among the prophetic religions and all the consequences which flow from them. The whole matter is a bit more complicated, it seems to me. I have the further impression that Islam deviates from the normal paradigm for prophetic religions. In this respect I disagree with R. Friedli.[12] I am convinced that Islam must still go through a whole process of development in order to arrive at the view of humanity and the world that is typical of prophetic religions. Here we have another valuable point of contact for dialogue with the prophetic religions specifically. Is it really true for Islam that the world and history are to be viewed as locales where the word of God is actually realized? One gets a different picture every time one picks up the Koran and reads it.

On the one hand it is certainly clear that the earth and everything on it is a wondrous sign of Allah. It invites human beings to contemplate and praise God's omnipotence, and it leads them to the realization that there can be only one God: "And the earth We have spread out, and thereon set pillars, and produced on it all sorts of things in due measure."[13] Human beings are to travel around the earth, gaze in wonder at Allah's works, and then await resurrection: "Say: 'Travel the earth and see how He made creation the first time; thus will Allah accomplish the later rising. For Allah has power over all things.' "[14] It is in this spirit that the human being serves as Allah's "vice-regent."[15]

On the other hand we must not inject Christian notions into this picture. We must not imagine that the Koran pictures human beings working together with God to complete and perfect creation. That notion is not evident in the Koran. By the same token, however, Muslims will not go so far as to embrace a harshly ascetic life or spurn the world, as happens in mystical religions. They will relish and take delight in the world in many respects. Thus the outlook of the Koran cannot be classified straightforwardly under the basic typology mentioned above. Neither do we find in Islam the asceticism that has been linked with Calvinism and that has supposedly led to social and economic progress.[16] The correct human posture vis-à-vis Allah is servitude and subjection, humility and lowliness. Secularization and humanity's taking the future into its own hands are not data to be found in the Koran. Hence it is very difficult for Islam to raise these issues.

Here I am not writing about modern apologetes for Islam who attempt to give a new twist to the Koranic texts in rather unscholarly ways. It seems to me that here we have a wide field for dialogue between Islam and Christianity, and that such dialogue is needed if Islam is to preserve all the good things it has to offer. The approach must be maieutic, and the starting point must be the Koran. We may well be able to move further along by applying modern scholarly and historical methods of interpretation to specific texts. It will not be so much a matter of literal interpretation and exegesis, in my opinion. Instead it will be a matter of viewing them in their historical specificity and then prying them open for the possibility of further development. It will also be worth exploring why Islam experienced a period of flourishing art, science, and world mastery centuries ago, and why all that has gone by the boards.

7

The Absorbing Absolute: Hinduism

It is practically impossible to envision the task of dealing with Hinduism in this brief chapter. Hinduism is already thousands of years old in India. It is a complex whole made up of different currents, schools, and tendencies. Here again I cannot hope to go into all the reform movements that have appeared in the course of history. Sticking to the basic thrust of Part Two of this work, I shall instead try to offer a typology of Indian religiosity, a glimpse of the constant amid all the variety. In doing this, I shall rely on the classic work of Hajime Nakamura.[17] Some of his observations also apply to Buddhism, which likewise arose in India.

THE CONSTANTS IN HINDU THINKING

A first characteristic is the fact that the Indian stresses the universal. The people of India like abstract speculation, and so the individual recedes into the background. Abstract concepts are preferred to concrete realities when it comes to contemplation. The Indian spirit may be described or typed as one that grows inward in the most abstract manner.

As a result there is a preference for the negative. The people of India like to describe things in negative terms. Even the Absolute can only be comprehended in negative ways. It is the Not-Finite (the Infinite), the Negative. The Supreme must be free of any and all qualification. This view is expressed very clearly in an old school that is still very much alive: the Vedanta.

The Absolute, therefore, is also not a personal principle. That leads to monism. Only the Absolute, Brahman, is real. All else is illusory: maya. While this view is not held by all Indians, it was present in India from a very early date and it has undergone constant elaboration and development. It has influenced the whole range of Indian thought and its view of God, the world, and humanity. Even today we must reckon seriously with it.

From this view we also get a different conception of time. When that which lies behind the phenomenal realm is more important, then the notion of time is squashed and human beings live unhistorically. Human existence is a mere succession of lives which are marked by timelessness and which are therefore meaningless. It is an eternal rebirth. Another consequence is that political and social conditions receive no attention. In the economic realm this means that stress is laid on sharing rather than on production or output. In the spiritual realm one is led to contemplation, to the acquisition of knowledge, or to pious devotion. One must come to realize that the human being is not really a person, that the human being belongs to the world of illusion, that it is meant to fade away and dissolve in the Absolute. That is salvation.

Salvation, then, has nothing to do with the earthly condition of the human being. This earthly condition is illusory and unsalvific: maya. Human beings must go back to what they were: a part of the Absolute. To do that, they may travel along one or more of the three ways just mentioned: contemplation, acquisition of knowledge, or devotion. Our little selves must enter into the Great Self (Atman).

WHAT DOES HINDUISM HAVE TO TELL US?

This brief typology of Hinduism and its essential core brings us to the question: What does this outlook have to say to Christians? Here we must proceed cautiously to avoid taking over things that do not fit in with our religion.[18] It is all too easy for Westerners to adopt this Eastern outlook without calling due attention to the underlying background elements and the fundamental differences involved. At the same time it should be noted that the Indian spiritual outlook can offer us something. At present numerous critical studies of the subject are being published.[19]

The first thing to be noticed here is the fact that studies of the Indian mentality, particularly in India itself, have led Christian circles to pay more attention to St. John's Gospel. This is evident in the work of many modern Indian theologians.[20] John has much to say about the oneness between the Father and the Son (his Word) and about our ascent into that oneness. Liturgy, preaching, and catechesis in India cannot overlook that fact. Perhaps only in India is John's Gospel being truly grasped and lived. Aside from a few great mystics, we in the West have neglected one side of Christianity: i.e., the contemplative side and becoming one with God. Of course there still remains the problem of combining this aspect with a genuine interest in the earthly condition of the human being and the human race. I shall go into that a bit further on.

Hinduism can help us Western Christians, and Westernized Christians elsewhere in the world, to regain our feel for certain truths and attitudes that are very worthwhile in human terms but that have been shoved into the background by us. It can help us to comprehend our little self more clearly in the light of the Great Self. It can also teach us ways and techniques to do this: e.g., yoga and contemplation. It can draw out the deeper level in us and point us towards the ultimate why and wherefore of our lives. In this way we can become more harmonious human beings and overcome the splintered character of Western human beings. Hinduism can help us in trying to ponder and answer such questions as the following: "Wherein lie the limits of our technology? Where must we stop with concern for mere progress in order to avoid becoming inhuman monsters? Have we properly understood our mission of creation, and have we always properly distinguished between domination and stewardship? Are we not so absorbed in the concrete and the individual that we no longer can make contact with the All-Surpassing and Ineffable? Don't we all too often reduce God to history, assuming the latter will lead to a perfectly happy and blessed life for human beings and calling that the kingdom of God? Isn't that a one-sided approach to the mystery of God, who embraces and fulfills history on the one hand but surpasses anything and everything on the other?

Hinduism confronts us with questions that cut deeply: questions about interiority, spirituality, the supra-personal character of God, and our attitude towards the world and creation. These questions can be broadened, but they can be fully explored only in real encounter. Fortunately, this sort of encounter is taking place frequently in India at the present time, and on all levels.[21] Already there are ecumenical and mixed religious communities which are seeking an answer to the questions raised above. Dialogue is already a reality in India, and it is leading to astonishing experiments.

CHRISTIANS IN DIALOGUE WITH HINDUISM

What contribution does Christianity offer Hinduism in the process of dialogue, particularly in India? The question can be answered in various ways. On the one hand there is the historical influence. It is a plain fact that Hinduism has been influenced by Christianity. The influence was particularly strong in the nineteenth century, but it has also been felt in this century. It is particularly noticeable in various reform movements of the last two centuries: e.g., the Brahma Samaj, the Church of the New Dispensation, the movement centered around Mahatma Gandhi, and the secularism of Pandit Nehru.[22] In these movements one detects greater sensitivity to the historical situation of human beings, to their social condition and political independence. This sometimes leads to monotheism. One surprising result is the exemplary role attributed to Jesus of Nazareth. He is seen as the ideal human being whom Indians are to imitate. This has even led to missionary movements aimed at the West, whereas in an earlier day Hinduism was pretty well confined geographically to the Asian subcontinent.

Another answer to the question raised at the beginning of this section can be found by studying the Indian theology that has been in the making since the nineteenth century.[23] Today, as in the past, contributions are being made both by Hindus who have remained loyal to the Hindu religion and by Hindus who have converted to some Christian denomination. In this theology we again detect greater sensitivity to the earthly situation of human beings, of the pariah and the socially sheltered on the subcontinent. The social teaching of the gospel message plays an important role here, as does the person and influence of Jesus of Nazareth. Jesus is viewed in a wholly Indian way. He was the selfless one, who could therefore open up to others and especially to God. As a result God and others could abide in him. Here we have the basis of a whole Indian christology that is quite distinctive.

There is also a third approach to the question raised above, and I should like to pursue it here. It takes off from the brief typology of Hinduism which I offered in the first part of this chapter. It seeks to determine the role of Christianity vis-à-vis Hinduism on that basis. I prefer to adopt this approach because it lets us probe deeply while freeing us from historical initiatives that are always incomplete to a greater or lesser degree. It seems to me that readers will find it easy enough to make connections with the other two approaches just mentioned, which will be treated again in Part Three of this book.

The first thing that must be taken up in any dialogue is the notion of God. According to Eastern spirituality only an unconditioned, unlimited, and infinite Indefinite deserves to be called the Absolute. It is regarded as super-personal, as devoid of name, form, and quality. From this standpoint the God of the Bible is a relative and anthropomorphic form of existence for the Supreme Being. This would appear to create a wide gulf between the two viewpoints. But I have the impression that the biblical perspective can be incorporated into the Eastern perspective without mutilation. What we must do here is appeal to the theology of John the Evangelist. Just as the Hindu seeks dialogue with the Absolute, so the Christian seeks it in contemplation with the Father. Christians find their inspiration for this effort in the dialogue that takes place between the Word and the Father within the divinity. God is in dialogue with his Word. In other words, God is in dialogue with that other "I" that is the expression of himself. The only difference between them is that it is God the Father who utters the Word, and it is the Word that is uttered. The expressed and begotten Word gives full and perfect expression to the Father: "To have seen me, is to have seen the Father "(John 14:9).

That is what our dialogue with God should be as well. We have received from him everything that we are. For we have been made by him in his image and share in his nature. We can enter into the dialogue between the Father and his Word. Dialogue is no mere human affair, for then it would have little value. Dialogue is contemplation of the dialogue between the Father and the Son and participation in it. Thus God can be supremely personal and yet absolute. Our union with this Person is really what the Indian seeks to attain.

Of course we should always stress the fact that we do not become God. We are not some small fragment of the godhead that has been flung into space and that now strives to return to it. The wondrous thing is that we have been placed in the divine milieu, that we are from him and through him; but we are not God. Our identification cannot go that far. There is participation in his life and a communication of the gift of his being in a most intimate way; but it takes place by way of creation. The latter is a reality unknown to Hinduism, and it is the second matter which we shall have to inject into any dialogue.[24]

Hindus do not think or talk about creation. For them there is no way that leads to the divine. The world and all that relates to it in social, economic, and political terms is unreal and illusory: maya. There is no sense trying to find salvation there. That will only lead us away from salvation, which consists in our total disappearance and absorption into the Absolute. We must return to our Origin, from which we have strayed. It is against this backdrop that we can understand many conditions in India which seem to be shocking at first glance: the millions of untouchables; the countless poor people who have no homes, who live and die on the streets, and who are the object of Mother Teresa's concern; the failure to pursue economic development for the whole population; the political misconduct; and so forth. All such things can be traced back to the Hindu religious view of salvation.[25]

Working in the world is unsalvific, so Hinduism does not encourage it. India has factories and an economy, of course, but all this only leads to a conflict of conscience or a falling away from Hinduism. One feels one is doing something that is unsalvific and that will lead only to another rebirth; or else one drops Hinduism and tends towards religious indifference. Herein lies one of India's greatest problems and one of the main tasks facing the Judeo-Christian tradition. Patient dialogue may try to bring about a change here, a change that will redound to the welfare of countless suffering people.

For Christians creation is a gift and a task. Inspired by Jesus of Nazareth and the prophets, they will continually try to push back injustice, discord, inequality, poverty, illness, and so forth. They hope to let people glimpse what the kingdom of God will be like when God finally establishes it to crown our efforts.

Once again we must ask the maieutic question: Can this Judeo-Christian vision be incorporated into the Indian one without nullifying the latter? I think it can. Even in Christianity it is normal to remain conscious of the fact that created reality is not the ultimate reality. Christians believe that here they will not obtain what has been ultimately promised them. Salvation lies far in the distance: "These all died in faith, not having received what was promised, but having seen it and greeted it from afar, and having acknowledged that they were strangers and exiles on the earth. For people who speak thus make it clear that they are seeking a homeland. If they had been thinking of that land from which they had gone out, they would have had opportunity to return. But as it is, they desire a better country, that is, a heavenly one. Therefore God is not ashamed to be called their God, for he has prepared for them a city (Heb. 11:13-16). Christians conduct themselves like people waiting for the return of their master from the wedding feast. They are dressed for action and their lamps are lit (cf. Luke 12:35-36). They must provide themselves with purses that don't grow old and store up treasure for themselves in heaven (cf. Luke: 12:32).

Hindus will have much inner feeling for these aspects of Christianity. Starting off from the common experience that underlies both, it should be possible for both sides to draw closer to each other. But Christians will be able to bring in the dimension of hope, of future expectation, which also has to do with the material welfare of human beings. Hinduism, which has always had an inclination to negative theology and renunciation of the world, can thus be led to new ideas about the welfare of human beings within Hindu culture.[26]

To conclude this brief treatment, I should like to offer a few observations made by Swami Abhishiktananda. His original name was Henri Le Saux, and he is a Benedictine. After living in India for a long time, he adopted an Indian name. He has probed deeply into the nature of Hinduism, and this has led him to a better understanding of Christianity. Like Monchanin and Bede Griffiths, who took the same road, he is one of the most valuable thinkers for furthering dialogue and one of the best at turning it into practice. His conclusion is that the Advaita doctrine of Hinduism—the doctrine of nonduality or monism—makes Christians more consciously attentive to the interior dimension of their own spiritual tradition. Christians are made to realize that all too often they remain fixed on the level of law, morality, commandments, and so forth. Christianity thus remains functional. It fashions a functional theology which strongly marks the preaching and training of priests and religious. Hinduism helps us to move on to the ontological and existential order, thanks to its mystical side. Thus we recover authentically biblical insights and thoughts. Intellectualism can take a back seat to authentically spiritual experiences once again. The reading of the great Christian mystics should have a powerful impact on the people of India, and it is high time that good translations of the Christian mystics were available in India. This holds true for both Christians and Hindus in India because both need such reading material, though perhaps for different reasons. Indian Christians need to unlearn their Westernized Christianity, which confines them to a spiritual ghetto. Indian Hindus need to find out how rich Christianity is, and how it can bring fulfillment to the deepest Hindu aspirations.

Thoroughgoing rapprochement is involved here, not superficial adaptation or accommodation. It begins with study of the holy scriptures of both Hindus and Christians. It continues with an interchange of deep, religious experiences. Contemplation and ascesis come in here. One thinks, for example, of yoga and other disciplines for calming the senses and the spirit. The process continues with Hindus and Christians living together in ashrams or small cloisters. There all theory fades into the background. The reality of spiritual experience plays the main role. Thus within Hinduism we can get new forms of being a Christian and forming community around Jesus of Nazareth. Already there have been many good experiments started in India, some of an ecumenical nature. I shall discuss them in Part Three of this book.[27]

8

Experiencing the Transiency of All Things: Buddhism

If it is hard to write about Hinduism and offer a typology of it, that holds even more true for Buddhism. We shall consider it a religion here, but even that point is still debated. Buddhism arose in India. Its founder was Gautama, who was born about 560 B.C. For a long time Buddhism exercised a dominant influence in India itself. Then its influence there dwindled, but it spread to many other Asian lands: e.g., Sri Lanka, Burma, Thailand, Laos, Cambodia, Vietnam, China, and Japan. In recent times Buddhism has again revived in India itself. I need hardly mention that it is also active in other areas of the world right now, and that Buddhist missionaries are actively at work.

One might surmise that a religion with such a long history, which has spread to many lands, would produce numerous currents and schools of thought. That is indeed the case. Yet, unlike the case with Hinduism, it is relatively easier to arrive at a typology of Buddhism. For one thing, Buddhism did have a founder! We can still go back and find out what some of the fundamental insights of its founder were, and we can see how these insights were elaborated over the course of time and in various lands. Moreover, every Buddhist typically tries to get back to the original roots of Buddhism and to give them new life today.

GAUTAMA'S EXPERIENCE OF LIFE

The founder of Buddhism came from a noble family whose name was Gautama. His first name was Siddharta. He was born in Nepal, and he lived amid the sheltered luxury enjoyed by his family until a turning point in his life occurred. He encountered the experience of death when confronted with the sight of a corpse. Experiencing human transiency in this way around the age of thirty, Gautama left his wife, his children, and his relatives and started a homeless quest for inner peace and security. He became a monk, a disciple of other teachers, in his desire to find the answer to his questions. First he looked to the ancient teachings of the Vedas for guidance; but neither severe asceticism nor rigorous meditation brought him liberating, saving insight. After many years of rigorous searching, a second turning point in his life occurred. It was this experience that transformed Siddharta Gautama into the Buddha—i.e., the "enlightened one." While sitting under a tree in quiet meditation, he was suddenly given *bodhi* (enlightenment). He suddenly perceived the root problem affecting human and cosmic existence: i.e., suffering. And he also perceived the answer to the problem, the way in which human beings could escape the vicious circle of rebirth and find freedom. This perception or insight made a missionary out of him. He went out to offer the way to deliverance to all, preaching compassion or love for all human beings and things. One of his first great sermons was preached in Benares, the holy city of the ancient Brahman religion of India. Until his death as an old man of eighty years and more, Gautama was a tireless preacher. He was especially active in northern India. He founded monastic orders for both women and men, but his teaching is aimed at everyone; it is universal. He was a down-to-earth preacher and teacher, not a prophet or a priest. Just before his death, before he passed over to nirvana, he exhorted his monks to work out their salvation with care and caution.

There are four essential insights in the Buddha's teaching. In the course of history they have given rise to a wealth of commentaries. They are insights, not dogmas, and they can be achieved only by people with experiential knowledge of life. The first of these insights, of these four noble truths, is that human existence in the world means suffering. Human beings necessarily experience the fact that everything is ultimately transitory rather than lasting or definitively satisfying. They must ponder grief, pain, sickness, old age, and death. Buddha never tarried over metaphysical questions concerning the world, humanity, or God. His attention was focused on the practical, concrete question of how to attain liberation from suffering.

The second noble truth has to do with the origin of suffering. It is born of desire, of longing in all its forms. This includes even the longing for well-being and eternal life in a new reincarnation. Human beings are not free; they are in bondage to what they desire. Even concern for one's own soul (as in Hinduism) must be exorcised.

The third noble truth has to do with the extinction of suffering. That can happen only through the extinction of the ego, the self, the soul, and desire itself. Only when complete egolessness is attained, only when desire for anything and everything is rooted out, only then is one wholly loosed from this earthly existence and empty. And once suffering comes to an end completely, one enters nirvana, a state of absolute and ineffable deliverance.

What is nirvana exactly? This is still a debated question among scholars of religion and various currents of Buddhism. It is better not to pose the question since, according to the Buddha, it is more important to become acquainted with the way to nirvana. One might justifiably ask whether there is something transcendent for a Buddhist, something such as God, and whether Buddhism is therefore a religion. But even though these are valid questions, they take us beyond the actual teaching of Buddha himself. To him it was more important to know the way to nirvana: the four noble truths and the eightfold path. His is a middle way which avoids extremes. The eight features of his pathway are hard to describe exactly, but they may be summarized as follows: right belief or insight into every earthly situation, right resolve, right speech, right conduct, right occupation, right effort, right contemplation, and right meditation. This is not a merely individual ethics; it also includes a social ethics. But the latter is guided by the aim of making it possible for all human beings to seek and attain nirvana.

EXPLORATORY QUESTIONS

Now we come back to the question raised earlier: In the teaching and practice of the Buddha is there a God or something divine that stands over against humanity? If so, what does that signify for human beings? Christian tradition, the thought of Western Europe, and all humanity are interested in this question, as the history of religions teaches us. The Buddha himself is silent on this question, yet it is not proper to call him an atheist. Certainly he is not an atheist in the sense of modern materialism, which actively opposes God. The Buddha never did that; he simply kept silent.

We can talk about the Buddha's a-theism, in the sense that we find no conception of God in his teaching. There is certainly no notion of a personal God who addresses and summons human beings, who chooses to appear as their partner. Neither is there negation or denial on this score. The Buddha's attitude is that right now the issue is of no importance because human beings must free themselves from suffering and enter nirvana. What comes later is something we shall see later.

To be sure, nirvana is presented in negative terms. But this wholly Other in which human beings are to lose themselves is merely the negative expression of an infinite fulfillment. Thus it also signifies hope and happiness, even though there are no proper words for it in human language. So clearly the Buddha's silence has nothing to do with modern atheism, and his nirvana is not the nothingness of a nihilistic materialism devoid of hope. As one might imagine, various schools and currents of Buddhism have sought to explore these issues more deeply over the course of time.[28]

I should point out that the Buddhist does indeed live an experience of transcendence. The reality of infinite fulfillment, which signifies hope and happiness, has served as the inspiration for many thoughts. Whereas the monastic Buddhism which took shape in Hinayana Buddhism has concentrated on one's personal experiencing of this transition, the emphasis is different in Mahayana Buddhism. Widespread in the Far East, the latter reveres those who postpone their entrance into nirvana in order to bring as many other people as possible into nirvana with them. They are known as bodhisattvas. One could say that in the nothing the Buddhist seeks something.

Sometimes a universal Buddha is placed above the historical Buddha. Sometimes there is talk about an Absolute Buddha. Male and female bodhisattvas help people to get to nirvana, to the Absolute Buddha. In Japan we find many deities entering the picture, of which I will mention two here. Amida is the Buddha of Boundless Light. Jizo is a bodhisattva who delivers the souls of the dead from suffering in hell. Thus one could say that the closer Buddhism has drawn to the average person, the more it has felt a need to answer the ultimate question. In Japan we find Pure Land Buddhism, for example. That state is to be attained by calling upon the name of Amida. One is then reborn into the Pure Land of Amida. Deliverance and salvation are not the result of personal effort. They are due to the power of another, Amida in this particular instance; but Amida is not to be dissociated from the Buddha.

So the result has been pietism and reform movements, which in turn have been challenged by such later movements. It simply means that the problem has not been solved, that questions remain on people's minds. We find many such developments in Chinese and Japanese Buddhism, not only in the past but even today. People are studying whether there is something transcendent in Buddhism and what it is exactly, and various efforts are being made to discuss and write about the matter.[29]

I shall cite only one such discussion here, that of a noted Japanese philosopher of religion. Professor Keiji Nishitani of Kyoto writes about the "great doubt" which arises in human beings as they experience the negative realities of life: e.g., human worthlessness and death. This raises the question of the meaning of existence, of one's own life and that of others, and one succumbs to all the distress associated with the issue. The process goes so deep that one loses the distinction between the doubter and what is being doubted, between the subject and object of doubt. That distinction is transcended, and the human being itself becomes the "great doubt." The person thus enters into the "great death," where the big change or turnabout takes place. Once the great death takes place, the whole universe is made new. Under the great death lies the great enlightening, and Professor Nishitani talks about transcendence in this connection. It is an enlightening of the self, but in such a way that the ego is no longer the operative force. Joy and rejoicing enter the picture. Standing before the abyss, one lets go with both hands, falls into the deep, and thus the self is annihilated. One thereby escapes slavish bondage and finds liberation. From this basic standpoint Professor Nishitani offers his critique of the philosophy of being and of interpersonal relationships. In the last analysis it is a matter of carrying through a radical negation to the end in order to arrive at the ultimate reality. This ultimate reality lies beyond and outside all such oppositions as beginning and end, existence and nonexistence, something and nothing. Otherwise it would entail limitation of some sort. It is hard to say much about it, but it is something like an absolute nothing in which a wondrous state of being or existence is revealed. But this state of being should not be viewed in dualistic terms as something possessing ontological priority over against nonbeing.[30]

From such remarks it is clear that we cannot maintain that those who came after Buddha have not gone any further in trying to reflect upon nirvana. It is we who will have to re-examine and revise our notions about the Nothingness of Buddhism. Certainly it contains an experience of transcendence. The real question is whether we, with our Western notions, can really grasp and comprehend it aright.

IS CHRISTIANITY IN A POSITION TO ENTER A DIALOGUE WITH BUDDHISM?

Following the plan of Part Two, we find ourselves at the next basic question: What contribution does Buddhism have to offer in any open dialogue with Christianity? Buddhism can make us Christians receptive once again to the notion that all existing things possess no ultimate worth. Even our own being and personhood, viewed in themselves, are not irreducible or underived values. Buddhism can stimulate us to give deeper consideration to the words of Jesus: "Anyone who loses his life for my sake will find it" (Matt. 10:29). It can help us to see what a truly kenotic way of life means, what it means to live wholly for others, and particularly for the Father.

We are not supposed to live by greedy desire either, as Paul tells us: "Now that is hardly the way you have learnt from Christ, unless you failed to hear him properly when you were taught what the truth is in Jesus. You must give up your old way of life; you must put aside your old self which gets corrupted by following illusory desires. Your mind must be renewed" (Eph. 4:20–23). Buddhism may help us to see more clearly what it means to be truly light, an image that is often mentioned by John the Evangelist and Paul: "You were darkness once, but now you are light in the Lord" (Eph. 5:8). It seems to me that a Buddhist will have little difficulty in understanding the kenotic attitude of our Lord Jesus Christ, as Paul describes it: "His state was divine, yet he did not cling to his equality with God but emptied himself to assume the conditions of a slave, and became as men are; he was humbler yet, even to accepting death, death on a cross. But God raised him high and gave him the name which is above all other names" (Phil. 2:6–9).

In dialogue with Buddhism, therefore, we can recover a lost aspect of Christianity. We can recover a healthy ascesis bathed in the light of kenosis or self-emptying. This will lead to a deeper self-knowledge. Such self-knowledge was evident in St. Francis of Assisi, who is greatly admired by Buddhists.[31] Empty of all craving and desire, Francis opened up to his Lord and discovered him in all his creation in some mysterious and ineffable way.

There is a second point with which Buddhism can help us to get on the right track again. Our Western mentality and our Western philosophy and theology are riddled with affirmative pronouncements about God. We know how to define God so well, and we can fill whole treatises on the subject. Buddhism teaches us to be cautious and circumspect. The mystery of the Ultimate is really incomprehensible and ineffable. It can only be alluded to in a negative way. When we think or talk or meditate about God, we can usually be found guilty of an excessively anthropomorphic approach. There is much for us to learn from a dialogue with a worldview that describes the Ultimate as Nothingness or Emptiness. For all too long we have shuddered over such an approach, or merely shrugged our shoulders at it. Only now, after much experience and study, is it becoming possible for us to glimpse what Buddhism is really driving at. Real dialogue can now begin, and it promises to offer us unexpected fruits.

Christianity must also ponder the image and example of the bodhisattvas. They postpone their own attainment of salvation as long as possible, in order to bring as many other human beings as possible along with themselves. One cannot avoid the impression that modern Christians are so preoccupied with fashioning their own identity and developing themselves in courses and training sessions that they never really reach out or touch others. But Jesus' words remain true: "Anyone who loses his life . . . will find it."

THE BENEFITS OF DIALOGUE FOR BUDDHISM

Our final question is: What contribution do Christians have to offer in their dialogue with Buddhism? For the Way has a message to bring to the Ways, transforming them into new forms of this Way. The literature on this subject is growing. Here I should like to bring out some of the outstanding points being made.[32]

We might ask ourselves whether Buddhism really does full justice to human beings in terms of their concrete, existential needs. As I suggested above, there is a danger that the social ethics of Buddhism will focus merely on making it possible for others to attain nirvana. Indeed today there is a growing realization that too little has been done to change social, economic, and political structures; to eliminate poverty; to cure sickness; to promote human freedom; and so forth. It is not without reason that in eastern and southeastern Asia we have seen the rise of political regimes that dissociate themselves from Buddhism and are making efforts to do something in those areas. As I shall discuss more fully in Chapter 12, some are calling for the appearance of a new human being even though it may entail great sacrifices.

Jesus said: "Insofar as you did this to one of the least of these brothers of mine, you did it to me" (Matt. 25:40). This point still needs to be realized and implemented in the Buddhist world. Total disregard for one's own ego as the chief concern should never lead to disregard for the dire needs of others. Here we do find points of contact, of course, in such Buddhist schools of thought as that of Amida Buddhism. They talk about moving away from human beings and the world and also about drawing closer to them. Using a maieutic approach within the inner context of Buddhism, one can turn Buddhism in this direction. Judeo-Christian ideas can find points of contact with Buddhist notions, so that the two together may work towards a new synthesis.

There must be a dialogue between the Buddhist and the Judeo-Christian vision of humanity and the world if we are to realize salvation in all its fullness; for salvation has an earthly dimension as well. In the last analysis, our dialogue will have to dig down deep because that Buddhist vision is closely bound up with the whole spirituality of Buddhism. Escape from suffering, liberation, plays a major role in that spirituality, but suffering is not subjected to complete examination and interpretation in Buddhism. Buddhism focuses on the realization that nothing is perduring in this world. Now it must also take in the realization that much suffering is due to injustice, discord, poverty, sickness, and so forth.

This means that the notion of nirvana will also have to be interpreted in broader terms. It is not enough to restrict it to a feeling of spiritual uneasiness and a subsequent attempt to overcome this by a purely spiritual process of awakening. No one in the Judeo-Christian tradition would ever dispute the value of that insight and that spiritual process of enlightenment. But he or she will not rest content with that. Other realities must be brought in here: e.g., the kingdom of God, the elimination of estrangement between human beings and God, joint responsibility for one's fellow human beings and for the world. Dialogue must explore what salvation really entails in all its depth. Is it merely something confined to the spiritual plane? Or is it something more complete that takes in the whole human condition, both on this earth and beyond? What is real, total liberation? And how does one type of liberation affect the other?

We must pose these deeper questions to Buddhists. In so doing, however, we must start out from their thought-world and from the experience of transcendence that is present among Buddhists. Paul Tillich sensed this very well during his stay in Japan, and he had this to say:

> This dialogue leads to the general question of whether the controlling symbols, Kingdom of God and Nirvana, are mutually exclusive. According to our derivation of all religious types from elements in the experience of the holy, this is unthinkable, and there are indications in the history of both symbols that converging tendencies exist. If in Paul the Kingdom of God is identified with the expectation of God being all *in* all (or *for* all), if it is replaced by the symbol of Eternal Life, or described as the eternal intuition and fruition of God, this has a strong affinity to the praise of Nirvana as the state of transtemporal blessedness, for blessedness presupposes—at least in symbolic language—a subject which experiences blessedness. But here also a warning against mixture or reduction of the concrete character of both religions must be given.
>
> The dialogue can now turn to some ethical consequences in which the differences are more conspicuous. In discussing them it becomes obvious that two different ontological principles lie behind the conflicting symbols, Kingdom of God and Nirvana, namely, "participation" and "identity." One participates, as an individual being, in the Kingdom of

God. One is identical with everything that is in Nirvana. This leads immediately to a different relation of man to nature. The principle of participation can be reduced in its application to such a degree that it leads to the attitude of technical control of nature which dominates the Western world. Nature, in all its forms, is a tool for human purposes. Under the principle of identity the development of this possibility is largely prevented. The sympathetic identification with nature is powerfully expressed in the Buddhist-inspired art in China and Korea and Japan. An analogous attitude in Hinduism, dependent also on the principle of identity, is the treatment of the higher animals, the prohibition against killing them, and the belief, connected with the Karma doctrine, that human souls in the process of migration can be embodied in animals. This is far removed from the Old Testament story in which Adam is assigned the task of ruling over all other creatures.[33]

Insofar as the relationship between participation and identity is concerned, Christianity and its traditions can offer some help. The history of Christianity makes it clear that the two do not exclude one another. We find a long tradition of nature mysticism in Christianity in which the principle of participation can scarcely be distinguished from the principle of identity. One thinks of a figure like Francis of Assisi, or of the Protestant mysticism which derived from Luther's nature mysticism. One also thinks of the great Flemish and German mystics of the Middle Ages and their negative theology.[34] Translations of such authors and works should benefit dialogue enormously. They could greatly aid mutual understanding and recognition.

9

Seeking the Meaningfulness of a New World: The New Japanese Religions

A whole book could be devoted to the new religions and new religious movements that have arisen in our own day. They are now beginning to receive attention from authors, particularly from theologians and other scholars of religion.[35] Here I think it would be advisable to restrict our attention to one of the most striking examples of the whole phenomenon: i.e., the new religions of Japan. The literature on them is more extensive, and some of the titles go back to an earlier date. Moreover, the relevance of these religions for a dialogue with Christianity has become increasingly clear over the years, due in no small measure to personal experience with these religions. Perhaps the outlines sketched here may be of some use and importance for dialogue with other new religions, whether they be found in North America, Europe, or elsewhere.

THE IDENTITY OF THE NEW JAPANESE RELIGIONS

If we wish to comprehend the new Japanese religions, we must go deep into the Japanese way of thinking and its basic religious dimension. This holds true for all the religions in Japan, which have had to adapt to this underlying religious dimension: e.g., Shintoism, Buddhism, Confucianism, and the newer religions of today.

This basic religious dimension in Japan consists of four features. First of all, it could be said that the Japanese are cosmically oriented. For them the absolute or the divine is anchored and made manifest within this phenomenal world. Their feeling and sensitivity is drawn towards an all-pervasive numinous reality that reveals itself in the world. This leads to an intense effort to live in accordance with the rhythms of nature, to share life with nature in a harmonious symbiosis. The world and nature are viewed in positive, optimistic terms. As a result, there is strong interest in this world and no distinction is made between nature and supernature. The hereafter remains obscure, the natural dispositions of human beings are considered good, and the notion of sin is shallow and undeveloped. Along with all this goes a spirit of tolerance and forbearance, and the Japanese readily assimilate foreign elements.

The second feature is the habit of the Japanese to group around a specific and restricted social nucleus. The group transcends the individual, and the rules of the group also define the conduct of the individual member. The group has a head, who is entitled to respect and deference. So Japan is erected on the basis of households, families, kinship groups, and the like, and the nation as a whole found its identity embodied in the emperor at the top. That can lead to sectarianism and narrow nationalism, of course; but it also offers such advantages as mutual help and a feeling of security about one's place in society. Another consequence has been that the notion of the person has never been able to assert itself over the long course of Japanese history. Even today one can talk about a certain impersonalism in Japan.

A third feature is the distaste and the difficulty which the Japanese experience when it comes to thinking in abstract and purely rational terms. The sacral realm is concrete: this tree, this beautiful mountain, this blossoming branch. Also sacred is the concrete community, be it small or large. The Japanese capacity for expression, then, does not tend towards the universal, the abstract, or the logical. It is inclined to be intuitive and emotional. The Japanese find difficulty in using words to indicate the Absolute and the transcendent; they much prefer to use expressions that are concrete, graphic, experiential, and emotionally toned. To them the heart is more important than logical reasoning.

The fourth feature of the Japanese mentality is their tendency to tolerate and combine different elements in the area of religion. In this connection we have often failed to understand the Japanese, and we have too readily tended to accuse them of superficial syncretism. As the Japanese see it, the sacred shows up in countless different forms. They react to it as complete human beings, using their intuitive sense and their attachment to concrete situations and realities. That is why Japanese religious life shows so many shifts and turns, and why it does not tend to be static, exclusivist, or uncompromising. Many different feelings can be at home in one and the same heart, whether they derive from Shinto, Buddhism in its various forms, Confucianism, Christianity, or modern currents of thought and life. More than one religion may have taken root in a given Japanese individual. The Japanese say: whatever road a person may take, they all lead to the top of one and the same mountain (Fuji) where the same moon shines down on all.

It is out of this basic dimension and its various features that all the concrete Japanese religions have grown. It has structured them all in one way or another. All those religions transcend any merely human horizon. They are a response to what God has to say in this world. But I do not mean to suggest that this response might not suffer mutilation on the human side.[36]

Before I try to relate the basic Japanese features to the new religions of Japan, I must say something about the latter. Some of them were around even before World War II, but most of them arose after it. It was at the end of the war that their big opportunity came, for Japan had turned into a spiritual vacuum. The old Shintoist and Buddhist values had failed. Confucian morality, with a divine emperor at the apex of the pyramid, had collapsed. The new religions might be called crisis-religions, but they have now acquired enduring value. This does not mean that all Japanese have solved their religious crises in this form, however. Many of them are still seeking a solution to their problems.

Perhaps it is a bit misleading to refer to these religions as "new." First of all, some of them date back to pre-World War II days. Secondly, they all tend to hark back to age-old values. So some authors prefer to refer to them as "modern" religions. In many cases we are dealing with popularized forms of Shinto or Buddhism. Their novel aspects are to be found in such things as the following: the way in which human beings are concretely addressed in their daily lives; the critical attitude of the founder or founders of the new religious group; and the adoption of certain Christian ideas by these groups. Thus they fit into the multireligious character of Japan, as a few examples will show.

My first example is the *Seicho no Ie* (House of Growth), whose founder was born in 1893. He views his religion as one which reduces all religions to one. As he sees it, he really teaches only one truth which is common to all religions and ideologies. This religion has a large and splendid center in Tokyo, and Christian influence is noticeable. The founder is familiar not only with the teaching of Buddha and Japanese Buddhist masters but also with that of Jesus, Paul, and John.

Like many of the other founders of the new Japanese religions, he heard a voice. It said: "Only spiritual reality exists. You are reality. You are Buddha. You are Christ. You are infinite and inexhaustible." The so-called bible of this religion begins with John's vision of the Son of Man in the middle of the seven lampstands, as we find it in the Book of Revelation (1:12–13). There follows a revelation about the lighting of the seven lampstands, a summons in biblical style to seek reconciliation, bring oneself in harmony with the universe, and express gratitude to all human beings. This leads to a promise, offered with many biblical allusions and as if Jesus himself were speaking. The promise is that this reconciliation and gratitude will result in the solution of all human problems and the manifestation of Christ.

The founder also wrote a commentary on the Gospel of John, which brings the figure of Nicodemus to the foreground. Jesus' crucifixion is also given an interpretation. It proves that the body does not exist, that matter is nothing, and that the spirit rises. When one stands in front of the large building with round towers where the religion is headquartered, one can see a huge white figure placed in one huge niche. One gets the impression that one is looking at a Christian church. When you ask who the figure represents, you are told that it is the one who is still to come. Perhaps more than any of the other new religions of Japan, this one seems to be on the look-out for Christianity.

My second example is the *Tenri-kyo* (the Religion of Divine Reason). It is the one that has made the greatest impression on me. Occupying a valley lying between Kyoto and Nara, the great cultural and religious centers of Japan, its members have transformed the area into an earthly paradise. It is a large, sumptuous garden with all sorts of buildings: a hall of worship, dormitories, infirmaries, hospitals, schools, a university, a library with old and new books about Christianity in Japan, and so forth. This particular religion was founded in the previous century, but only now has it begun to systematize its teaching in order to become a worldwide religion.

The ultimate reality is the Divine Reason. Those who live according to it will be blessed, all others will perish. Egotism and self-seeking cause misfortune and sickness. All wickedness must be rejected. Evil is viewed as soiling matter. It includes such things as gluttony, avarice, improper love, hate, selfishness, resentment, and anger. Believing in God and trusting in his goodness, human beings must remove this matter, become happy, and unite with God. Then sickness will be cured and suffering will be turned into joy. The soul will then be prepared and ready.

Believers cling to the notion of reincarnation. Virtue and vice from the past still play a role now. The aim of reincarnation is to turn all human beings into virtuous tools. It is not enough to try to remove all the filthy matter within oneself; one must also try to get rid of all the evil elements in society. People must serve their fellow human beings. It is in this way that the ideal kingdom of God will be established.

These beliefs have led the Tenri-kyo to tireless work in many different fields: pedagogy, education, priestly training, library science, caring for pilgrims and the sick, etc. One notes that many Christian expressions can be found in their teaching: "As you sow, so shall you reap"; "How incomprehensible are God's ways." And they use such terms as ascension, sacrament, and mediatrix. There is a strong missionary movement under way from the Tenri-kyo.

My third example is the *Odoru-shukyo* (the Dancing Religion). By comparison with some of the other new religions, this one has a smaller membership: 120,000. But it is one of the most striking and surprising. Its founder was a peasant woman, born in 1900. Thanks to divine revelation, she became securely convinced that she had inside herself a female and a male deity; thus she formed a trinity. She received the mission to save the world, and she considers herself to be divine. The absolute God of the Universe is the same as that of Christians and as the eternal Buddha. Sometimes she refers to herself as Christ or the Mediator of God. Buddha preached the message 3,000 years ago. Christ preached it 2,000 years ago. Today she is the Christ. She supposedly gives oracles, is a prophetess, heals the sick, and works miracles. She also talks about a heavenly kingdom and is familiar with a prayer like the Our Father.

One important means of reaching the kingdom of God is the "Non-Ego

Dance," from which this religion has gotten its popular name. It is an ecstatic dance which leads to liberation from one's self and from evil spirits. (The latter play a great role in her view.) Thus the kingdom of God can become a reality here and now in this world and among human beings. There will be neither sickness nor war. When human beings are prepared to preserve peace in their own hearts and to relay it to their families, their countries, and the whole world, then the kingdom of God becomes a reality in this life.

It can be said that the Christian influence is increasing in this religion. The foundress has begun to equate herself more and more with the Christ of the New Testament. She will have to work three and a half years for the salvation of the world (hence she is more important than Christ). She says that it will be difficult for people of the upper classes to enter the gate of heaven. Like Christ, she was tempted by evil spirits who wanted to make her queen of the angels. She also says that people should focus more on their own sins than on the sins of others.

My fourth example is one of the largest new religions, which certainly should be mentioned here. It is the *Rissho Kosei-kai* (Association for the Establishment of Uprightness and the Promotion of Friendship), also head-quartered in Tokyo. Its founder, Niwano, was born in 1906. He is a well-known figure in the World Conference of Religions and Peace, which I mentioned in Part One.[37] Originally there were two founders, but only Niwano is left.

Worship is directed to Buddha Sakyamuni, who achieved buddhahood from all eternity. The rites have Buddhist and Shintoist elements. Reverence is paid to all the Buddhas and bodhisattvas, and also to various Shinto deities. The aim is to ensure the full development of all human capabilities. That is buddhahood. To attain this, a contrite and dutiful way of life is necessary. This enables people to overcome want, suffering, and ignorance; to build a happy family life; and to establish friendship with other human beings. Membership in this religion is now approximately three million.

Some of the appealing features of this religion are the promise of healing and earthly well-being, the organizational talent of Niwano, and the stress upon the family. One very modern feature is the use of group sessions for talking out issues and counselling people. The sessions are small, and directed by a leader. In the main headquarters two to four thousand people are given instruction by this method every day. The same system is operative in local areas where the religion is represented. Since 1959 this religion has also worked indirectly on the political front in connection with local and national elections.

Of all the new religions in Japan, this one is the most interested in the ecumenical movement among Christian denominations. In 1965 Niwano was present at the opening of the fourth session of Vatican II, and he also had a meeting with Pope Paul VI. Afterwards Niwano stated that the Christian God and Buddha were in fact the same, and that he would welcome the entry of Christians into his movement. In his talks he makes frequent reference to

Christianity. He is very ready to work with Christians in trying to find a common spirituality that will promote peace, as is evident from his work in the World Conference of Religions and Peace.[38]

Careful readers can see that the four basic features of the Japanese outlook are mirrored in the new religions I have just discussed. There is a strong interest in this world here and now, where the numinous reveals itself. There is also the formation of new groups since World War II. In them people can gather around a small nucleus and actively live their lives as part of a group. Abstract, speculative teachings are pretty much absent; the emphasis is on practical issues. And if anything is obvious, it is the tendency to tolerate and combine different religious elements. One striking note is that Japan seems to be approaching Christianity on its own two feet, and this should make us stop and ponder quite a bit.

WHAT DO THE NEW JAPANESE RELIGIONS HAVE TO OFFER US?

This is our usual second question in Part Two. What do the new Japanese religions have to contribute to us in any dialogue with Christians? This question is new, of course, since they represent a new phenomenon. It is difficult to answer such questions because there has not yet been enough dialogue with these religions, but I would like to make a few points.

First of all, these new religions of Japan teach us not to overstress the difference between nature and supernature. When religion swings too much towards the supernatural, it gives an unearthly impression. It then fails to address either the Japanese or Western Christians. The new Japanese religions are teaching Christianity in Japan not to be overly suspicious of the basic religious dimension there and its four features. Such suspicion has been in evidence all too long. As a result, Christianity has been regarded as an alien plant and it has not been able to strike deep roots in the country. In our dialogue we must adopt a maieutic approach, explore the basic features and dimensions of Japanese life, and move from there towards the Christian message.

In particular, we must not be too frightened by the fourth feature discussed above: i.e., the Japanese tendency to tolerate and combine various religious elements. We are too quick to regard such an approach as syncretism or an arbitrary mixing of religions. But that certainly is not the aim of the Japanese, nor of Easterners in general. Underlying their approach is the intuition that there is some connection between the experience of the divine in any and every religion. To put it in Christian terms, it is an expression of the fact that God has never left himself without some witness in human history.

The new Japanese religions can also make it clear to us that it is impossible to approach Japan in purely pietistic, spiritual, or fundamentalist terms. In dialoguing with these religions Christianity must join them in building a better world on both the national and international level. In the process both sides must start out from moral insights that call for mutual clarification. The new Japanese religions are sharply oriented towards the world and they have started to move beyond the boundaries of Japan. They are missionary. We shall have to work with them elsewhere in the world as well, seeking to come to deeper understanding and agreement. Thus a whole new set of challenges faces Christianity. The new Japanese religions compel us to explore more deeply the issue of total salvation for all humanity.

THE CHRISTIAN CONTRIBUTION TO DIALOGUE

Finally, we come to our third basic question: What does the Judeo-Christian tradition have to contribute to a dialogue with the new Japanese religions?

A starting point, it seems to me, is the whole concept of sin. One cannot escape the impression that these new religions are overly optimistic about the ability of human beings to change themselves and the world. Christianity will not deny that beauty and harmony in the cosmos are worthwhile values, and that the lack of these features is sinful. But it will explore the issue more fully, trying to make clear why these ideals fail to succeed, why there is so much disharmony and physical ugliness in the world. It is certainly a relevant question in any industrialized society such as that of Japan. The deeper reason for human failure must be brought up for discussion.

This should not be viewed as a negative observation. We are simply trying to find a way towards a world that resembles the kingdom of God to some extent. That would include, among other things, a respect for asceticism and an attempt to master our drive to exercise domination over nature. Here, too, Christians must avoid excessive optimism while retaining their spirit of dedication and perseverance. Again and again we must fight for the kingdom of God in new circumstances, until it finally arrives in all its fullness through God's grace and power. Christianity can also help the Japanese to avoid a conception of the kingdom of God that is too material and exclusively this-worldly. We will have to dialogue about soteriology, the doctrine of redemption, which means that we will have to consider the matter of eschatology. Christianity itself has undergone a whole line of development regarding this point, learning much in the process.[39] And here I am talking about the whole of soteriology, which includes the human question of meaning as well as sociopolitical and economic issues.

More could be added here. In his fine book Ernest Pirijns listed a large number of topics that deserve close theological examination. He arrived at them by a careful analysis of Japan's past and present religious situation. I shall merely touch upon a few of his points here.

The concept of God is barely outlined in Japan. Yet it is an attractive notion for the Japanese, even as it is for other people of East Asia. Moreover, the Japanese view the divine as intramundane, as something to be found within this world. There is no higher plane over against some lower level.

Pirijns urges us to talk about a way of life rather than about concrete religions or conceptions of God. The individual Japanese person is seeking a way of life and is approachable in religious terms, whether that person adheres to one single religion or more than one. We will have to make it clear that the God of Jesus of Nazareth gives strength, peace, and equanimity to human beings who believe in him.

Although the Japanese have a keen sense of the fact that everything is transitory and contingent, even the deities, they also have access to the transcendent. Here again the dictum holds true: the heart is more important than logical reasoning. Using intuition and emotion over the years, the Japanese unconsciously try to break through the limits of the relative and the contingent in order to reach the ineffable and unnameable. Through dialogue a new Japanese theology must be worked out in this area. In it negative theology will play an important role, as will the doctrine of kenosis. For the reality of emptying and self-emptying penetrates to God insofar as God suffers affliction for the suffering of his Son.[40]

We shall have to get across the uniqueness of Christ more clearly to the Japanese. It is our belief that Christ is truly present in other religions and working for people's salvation there. So those religions possess much that is good and beautiful. But it is also a fact that human failings can put obstacles in the way of the salvation willed by God. Two approaches are necessary, therefore. Christianity must bring whatever is good and beautiful to fulfillment; and it must also reject or purify all negative elements. Jesus of Nazareth must be presented as an historical person rather than lined up as just another mythical figure. This concrete person is a unique reference to God. This point must be made clear to the Japanese, who see the Absolute as something realized in this world here and now.

In doing this, we must avoid an excessively rational approach along Western lines. That will not suit the Japanese at all, as I have indicated more than once. We do not need treatises filled with hard and fast dogmas of the Western type. They must be rethought and reformulated along the lines of Eastern thought. There must be a place for subjectivity as well as objectivity, for intuition as well as reason, for the negative approach of non-knowing as well as positive assertions.[41]

Here we face a whole new task. Through much dialogue and experiment we must work our way towards the right approach. It is my conviction that the best chance of doing this is through cooperative efforts with the new Japanese religions. In a certain sense Christianity is spreading there beyond the confines of Christianity and Christendom. It is an instructive lesson. Clearly it is time for the Christian mission to adopt a qualitative approach. The Judeo-Christian vision of God, humanity, and the world must be gotten across to those religions in a deeper way. Then it will be able to take more solid shape in a truly Japanese way.

10

Seeking Vital Force and Fulfillment in Life: Bantu Religious Life

Now I am going to speak about Africa, and specifically about the Bantus in Sub-Saharan Africa. Though they occupy much of that region, they are not the only native inhabitants. My remarks are necessarily limited, even when it comes to the Bantus themselves. There are now many case-studies of Sub-Saharan Africa, and indeed much has been written on the Bantus. I choose them as my example because such information is available, and because my own personal acquaintance with Africa is limited almost exclusively to them.

A TYPOLOGY OF BANTU RELIGIOUS LIFE

The Bantus are scattered over much of Sub-Saharan Africa, and they are divided into many different tribes. Nevertheless it is possible to offer a typology of Bantu religiosity. I am well aware of the fact that much change has been going on in that part of Africa, due to urbanization, industrialization, education, and nationalism. The social change has been great, and yet a Bantu remains a Bantu. The Bantus have their own character and inner convictions, and that is what I would like to describe here.

Our tendency is to overlook the African religions almost completely. In the document of Vatican II dealing with the attitude of the Church towards non-Christian religions, reference was made for the most part to the great world-wide religions. One reason for this is the fact that it is difficult to tackle African religions. They do not possess written sources or holy books. Neither do they form a unity. So there are many detailed monographs and many different methods for approaching the subject. Indeed it is only in recent times that people have begun to offer us texts and prayers of oral tradition that have survived.[42]

For us the main problem is the question of methodology, because otherwise there is no possibility of arriving at a dialogue. According to Shorter, it is a matter of being confronted with the essential values and meanings of African traditional religions. One will then discover that they are quite capable of the loftiest religious goals and intuitions.[43] There are various methods of approach, however. Some use the particularistic approach, focusing their study on one particular group and avoiding any comparisons with other groups. Some follow the enumerative approach, merely listing different beliefs and practices because they feel that no real comparison is possible. Another approach presupposes that comparison is possible and arrives at a basic worldview (as does John V. Taylor,[44] for example). The historical approach is based on oral tradition. A more restricted comparative approach emphasizes differences rather than similarities, though an underlying similarity precedes the differentiation. The categorical approach goes a bit further than the above. Rather than focusing on historical proximity, it takes note of structural, cultural, and ecological similarity despite geographical distance. Then there is the thematic approach, which examines a given theme (e.g., the concept of God) in different contexts.

Shorter's judgment is that the best thing to do is to use a multidimensional approach, one which combines the historical approach, the restricted comparative approach, the categorical approach, and the thematic approach. Here I shall briefly report the conclusions which he derives from the application of this multidimensional approach, since it brings us closest to a typology.[45]

The religion of any African people is the product of countless interacting factors. These factors derive from the surrounding environment, the economy, sociological relationships, historical realities, and psychological conditions. But none of these factors, taken separately or all together, can account for everything that goes to define the ultimate form of an African religion. Religious experience is both the inner experience of the individual and the mutual affirmation of shared insights by a community. So religion is also a further dimension of ordinary life, which is defined by all those factors. Religion is a transcendent quality of the life process, and the believer is privileged to recognize this. Religion is the living community of human beings with a spiritual world. The latter is not sharply separated from the world or set up over against it; it is discovered and lived in this world.

In Africa religion is more a matter of relationships than of practices. What forms do these relationships take? What do they look like? With whom are these relationships established? All this finds expression mainly in prayers, which bear witness primarily to a deep faith. In them we meet supreme beings, deities, ancestors, mediators, and so forth. Thus we cannot be satisfied with such simplistic categories as theism and deism.

In most traditional African religions the notion of a Supreme Being is more or less distinctly present. Associated with the Supreme Being are three other levels of spiritual beings: forms of existence of the Supreme Being (whose uniqueness and oneness is only vaguely grasped at times), mediators, and deities. Mediators are created beings who are nevertheless associated with the activity of the Supreme Being. Deities are subordinate beings whose activity is more or less independent of the Supreme Being.

All this can be lived out by Africans in terms of different models. There can be a pure and strict theism. There can be one supreme spiritual power which is pictured in a variety of spirits, the latter mirroring the manifold variety of human experiences. Another model pictures go-betweens who play an important role in certain situations of life. In marriage, for example, both partners use the go-between as a channel for communication with each other and with the Supreme Being. The tribal chief, the ancestors, and the spirits are go-betweens of this sort. It can also happen that they are not the exclusive go-betweens with the Supreme Being; sometimes one may turn directly to the Supreme Being. There can also be a relative deism. Then the deities play a prominent role, sometimes operating in intimate relationship with their king but usually in some degree of tension with him. It is the deities that are venerated in local cults and sanctuaries. Finally, there could be a model of pure and strict deism, but it is debated whether this category actually exists in African religion.

Now one cannot simply apply all the above remarks to the Bantus. However, they do fit into these categories somehow. This is particularly true with regard to the ancestors being mediators or go-betweens with the Supreme Being. The tribal chief also plays a major role. He takes care of communication between the tribal members on the one hand, and between them and the Supreme Being on the other hand. The Supreme Being is also referred to as the Creator frequently.

That brings us to the thematic approach. Themes express values, and they are the most enduring and important elements of traditional African religions. Long after the visible aspects of African religion have disappeared, long after cults and practices have ceased to exist, these values and themes continue to live on in the hearts and minds of human beings who have adopted some imported religion or given up religion altogether. For a real dialogue, a "dialogue of meanings," we must focus specifically on these values and themes. What are they precisely? A few examples may help to make it clear to my readers.

It is often said that in Africa being a parent is a more important aspect of marriage than being a partner. This is an African value. In an African community consumption is preferred over the accumulation of wealth—another African value. These values are expressed in a variety of images and symbols, which produce a regular pattern of thinking among a tribe or a culture. That is what we are calling themes here. They may be confined to one culture, or they may have to do with universal human experiences of life: birth, puberty, marriage, sickness and health, old age, death, friendship and estrangement, happiness and sorrow, work and leisure, etc. Now these values or themes can lead to explicitly religious experiences: human inadequacy and sinfulness, the experience of God, creation and creatureliness, judgment and salvation, etc.

One can readily come across all this in African prayers. One must listen closely and pay heed to it before one starts chattering about the role of Christianity. That is the first step in dialogue.

One of the most outstanding themes is that of "remembering" or "commemorating." The more people discovered that Africa has a history, the more this theme came under study. One could say that the African lives in continuity with the past. This provides an understanding of the present and a basis for hope in the future, although the notion of a future culmination is absent. One can find this theme in historical recollections of great leaders in the past, but it stands out even more clearly in the need to live in harmony with one's ancestors. One of the main ways of doing this is to carry on the religious traditions which they established. One must honor the Supreme Being as they did. One must carry out the rites and sacrifices at the holy places established by them. In all the details of one's life one must follow in the footsteps of one's ancestors, the friends of the Supreme Being. That will guarantee divine favor in the future.

Prayers must be in harmony with those of the ancestors, for then the Supreme Being will hear them. The stronger the influence of the ancestors as go-betweens is, the more likely Africans are to pray *to* them rather than *with* them. Africans are particularly pleased to direct their prayers to the immediately preceding generation or generations: "You, our ancestors, enjoyed life, let us enjoy it also. We have been faithful in making our offerings to you; look after us in your turn. You were good parents, caring for your children; continue to care for us now."[46]

A second major theme is that of co-creator. Modern Christianity has rediscovered this notion and thereby resolved many problems connected with the relationship between faith and science. Pre-literate communities are often accused of having a magical outlook and of viewing created things in wholly sacral terms. The question is whether the accusation is in fact true. Certain African communities may well possess a poorly developed technology. Yet these very communities sometimes possess a human being-orientated cosmology wherein human beings, using relatively few religious activities, believe that they can control their environment by magic and other means. This suggests a tendency towards secularization. Even more frequent, however, is the existence and elaboration of the notion of co-creator. That does not mean that Africans have thought deeply about creation *ex nihilo*. For them creation means God's lordship over human beings and the world. Nor should one assume right off that Africans view creation as an ongoing reality. They do not have any clear notion about history culminating at some acme, or about the steady accumulation of human knowledge and technical expertise. To the African the most important thing is that God is the master, the guiding providence, and that human beings play a role in the whole process.

This finds its clearest expression in the process of transmitting life. There human beings participate in God's creative work in an eminent way. God is first and foremost a giver of life, and here the ancestors play an important role. Children are often regarded as the reincarnation of some ancestor. Thus such themes as fertility and fulfillment in life through fertility play a major role among the Bantus. They seek fulfillment in life, and God is involved through the ancestors. Perhaps this is the most noteworthy of all their themes, though it is not treated so fully by Shorter.[47]

As I said, the African has no real feeling for the culmination of history in some high point. Thus we do not find any real eschatology in our sense of the word.[48] It would be surprising, then, if we were to find the theme of a last judgment for human beings in Africa. And yet caution is in order here. In the gospel message of John, Paul, and the Synoptics we find the notion that the last judgment has already begun, that we are being judged here and now. In times of oppression, persecution, and enslavement, it is easy for people to push back or postpone this judgment to a later time. In communities where there is little interest in this life, people's thoughts turn to the hereafter and the last things. I am not suggesting that there is no hereafter. The question is when it begins. Africans see themselves as living in present-day reality. They are attached and dedicated to living in this world, but they also hope for a deliverance. As they see it, they are undergoing a time of testing in this life, and it reaches a climax at death. Then the Supreme Being is the judge, and his judgment is immediate. The situation is a bit different among tribes where the mediators play a major role. There judgment is in the hands of one's descendants rather than in the hands of God. One's descendants will reward good deeds by remembering them, and will punish evil deeds by consigning them to oblivion.

A final theme I want to mention here is the African's sense of community. He or she readily uses the words "we" and "us." An African cannot live or operate outside a community, and this is evident everywhere in everyday life. They are members of a big family and a village. If they live in an urban environment, they belong to newly created communities, which frequently are church communities. What gives a religious dimension to this sense of community loyalty? In a few exceptional cases it is the conviction that one's own group enjoys God's favor while other groups do not. Usually, however, the underlying feeling is much more positive and conciliatory. The ideal of the community is to maintain harmonious relationships by following solidly established patterns, structures, and role divisions. Each individual has his or her place. The structure of the community is a God-given gift, and maintenance of the expected social relationships is a religious duty.

Does this divinely ordained community consist solely and exclusively of the living? No, the primary members of the community are the deceased. They are seen as the guardians of the community, who are actively involved in its life and growth. They are the creators of the community, even as God is the creator of the cosmos. So in Africa it is a community composed of the living and the dead.

The dead are honored at their graves and called upon in difficult circumstances. They receive offerings. Their graves are near the houses of the community, and they are maintained properly. In short, the dead are a channel between the living and the Supreme Being. Theirs is a vital community with the living, and they guarantee the stability and progress of the whole community. The dead possess more than human knowledge. They know hidden thoughts, hidden causes, and things that will happen in the future. They can take possession of human beings and communicate secrets to them. They can impose sanctions, causing illness and misfortune. They can also heal illness and wipe away misfortune. There is of course a precondition for being an ancestor of this sort. During one's earthly life one must have upheld and lived the ideals of the community. Social success, then, is a very decisive factor.

Following a somewhat meandering course, I have tried to trace out a typology of the African person that applies to the Bantu as well. In many external features it is not too different from that presented by such people as Tempels and Mulago, but I do think that my description is more justified in scientific or scholarly terms. According to my typology, Bantus are concerned with fulfillment in life and life-force. All this resides in the Supreme Being. It can be conveyed to the individual who is living in community with the ancestors and the tribal leaders. The orientation is clearly towards this world here and now. But it is also religious in nature, revealing some slight openness to the future and the transcendent.

WHAT LESSONS HAVE THE BANTUS FOR US?

So we come to our usual second question: What can Bantu Africans offer us in a dialogue? If we truly listen to them, what can we discover that would enrich us religiously? A whole book could be written in answer to this question, so my remarks are obviously limited.

First of all, I would like to stress the fact that we should not think that the African outlook described above will disappear with modernization, urbanization, and so forth. It now seems quite clear to me that we are dealing here with categories and themes that go very deep. At times they may change their outer forms or even become shapeless, but they will never disappear from the African heart. In the past we have spoken all too negatively about them, and we have acted thoughtlessly in our efforts to uproot them. One clear consequence has been the rise of independent Churches, since Africans did not feel that they were understood by Western Christianity.[49] These splinter movements of varying size and importance now number well over six thousand, and the figure is still growing. We might well try to ponder the reason for the appearance of such movements. I shall deal with the matter to some extent here, and pick it up again in the next section when I consider the potential contribution of Christianity to Africa.

We must begin to pay more attention to the all-embracing nature of Bantu religiosity. All too often we have viewed particular practices and convictions in isolation, trying to dissociate them from the whole complex of which they are a part. In Africa religion is an all-embracing category, harmoniously linked up with the sociocultural, economic, and political life of human beings. We in the West need a similar philosophy of life. That does not mean we must try to resacralize everything once again—something which the African doesn't do either. But our lives are now so compartmentalized that we find it very easy to view ethical considerations in isolation from micro- and macro-economic realities and their impact on societal structures. The result is a bad situation for the downtrodden and oppressed all around the world. Our God has in many instances become a Sunday-God who has little influence on our weekday lives. Religion may be on its way back,[50] but we see precious little evidence of concrete consequences. We might well find much inspiration in the African view of life and its consequences, as they were sketched above.

I noted earlier that African religion meant a living community of human beings with a spiritual realm that is not dissociated from this life. It is to be discovered and lived in this world here and now.[51] Religion is a transcendent quality of life, a further dimension, but not a dimension viewed as disso-ciated from existence in this world. How modern the African is in this re-spect! Consider how long we have labored under an excessively sharp distinc-tion between the natural and the supernatural, and suffered from the consequences of it! And have we really outgrown it completely? The har-monious vision of the African can give us a final push in the direction that the message of Jesus of Nazareth and its implementation is urging us. We are still trying to answer the question: What exactly is the role of religion in the whole of human life? The African's vision of life has much good to offer us in this connection.

There is also much for us to ponder in the African theme of "remem-brance." Our Western culture has taught us to forget the notion, even though Christianity is full of it. The memory of the life, passion, death, and resurrec-tion of Jesus lives on in Christianity. What is the Eucharist if not a memorial, a remembrance? Yet how difficult it is for us to express that in an updated way so that it becomes a living reality for Christians! We have beautiful doc-trines and learned books on the subject, but practice follows far behind. Jesus is our great ancestor, and what is there that we do not have to thank him for? Here we have a rich field for thought. Aren't we now so future-oriented that we are almost incapable of remembering? And how are we to find the right balance once again? I hope you can see all the questions that surface once one begins to think about the matter.

Then there is the whole matter of being a co-creator. Modern Christianity has recaptured this truth, but voices are being raised to warn that we are now going too far. Once again we are forced to ask ourselves whether we have fully distinguished between maintenance and domination, or whether our domina-tion of the earth and its resources is not in danger of going too far so that exhaustion and pollution stare us in the face. In dialogue with Africans we may be able to recover respect for creation and a real feel for its beauty.

As I shall point out in the next section of this chapter, I think that the Christian vision of creation has much to offer to Africans in any dialogue. So I would simply note here that on this point both partners in the dialogue must find the way to arrive at the golden mean; for the issue is of cardinal importance insofar as the world's future is concerned. It might be very good, for example, if we were to view the transmission of life much more as an eminent way of participating in God's creative activity. For how many Westerners today is that a truly living conviction?

African eschatology has a very interesting side for us. Focusing on this present life, the African tends to move the notion of judgment closer in time; it is not pushed back to later centuries or eons. The same tendency is evident in contemporary Christianity. Distinctions between a particular judgment and a general judgment have become more problematic, especially in the light of thoroughgoing biblical studies. We may be able to learn from the African view and thus give more concrete form and content to our own thinking. But I would insist again that such a process would involve give-and-take on both sides. African conceptions of these matters are often vague. Insofar as the African view of punishment and reward has to do simply with being forgotten or being remembered by one's descendants, I don't think it does full justice to the Christian vision of the matter.

The community existing between the living and the dead has much that is attractive for us. It can help to bring home to us the Christian doctrine of the communion of saints. In our modern Christianity it is a fairly forgotten notion. Only in various forms of popular or folk Catholicism do we find real vestiges of the doctrine. On this issue, too, certain aspects will have to be purged. We shall have to determine whether we can hold on to all the concrete details regarding ancestor worship and its concomitants. But that is normal in any dialogue where the participants are prepared to seek mutual understanding and agreement.

I would like to offer one final remark about one of the chief traits of the Bantus: i.e., their quest for ever-increasing fulfillment and strength in life. The quest has to do with life here and now and with life hereafter. Life-force has many different dimensions. It includes health, happiness, fruitfulness, spiritual fulfillment, and good relationships with the tribal chieftain, ancestors, and the Supreme Being. The chief focus is on this earthly life here and now. Indeed we might well ask whether death must not somehow be experienced as a break in the quest, even though one becomes an ancestor thereby.

Here again there are two sides to the story. We can learn something about living from the Bantus. We can learn to find life in ordinary things that we all go through but enjoy all too seldom. We, in turn, may be able to offer the Bantus an answer to the mystery of death. But we shall have to do it in such a way that it is meaningful within the context of their African conception of life.

CHRISTIANITY AND BANTU RELIGIOUS LIFE

What task faces Christianity in its dialogue with the Bantu way of life? Here one could explore Black theology and African theology and come up with any number of points. It is already obvious that Christianity is taking on its own particular shape in Africa. Native theologies are clearly on the rise, and only now are we beginning to get general overviews. Moreover, non-Western theologians are beginning to organize and meet, and Africans are playing a significant role in this process.[52] However, I shall postpone discussion of these theologies for Part Three, since the topic fits in better there.

Another possible approach is to study the independent Churches in Africa, for in countless different ways they are embodying what we seek to achieve in dialogue.[53] This topic, too, will be postponed until Part Three, where I shall consider the implications of a dialogic approach for the Church's missionary task. Right now I should like to focus on certain topics or subjects which will come up in any dialogue, and which can to a greater or lesser extent fulfill the deepest aspirations of the Bantus.

I do not mean to suggest that there will be no difficulties in achieving even a partial fulfillment of Bantu aspirations. The clear fact is that human beings in Sub-Saharan Africa are now striving for self-affirmation, and that there is real danger of a conflict between the cultural heritage of Africa and the Church. Consider, for example, the difficulties that still linger from the past in Zaire. There people are striving for authenticity, a return to the heritage of tradition in the use of names, more veneration of their ancestors, etc. In less explosive forms the same thrust is evident in other African countries, where people are working towards an African socialism, an African humanism, and so forth.

Problems are to be expected. It would be wise for the Churches to look ahead and to take seriously the topics for dialogue that are posed by modern Africa. Preliminary work along these lines is being carried out by various African theologies and Black theologies, and it is also embodied in the practices of the independent Churches. Here, however, I would like to plunge below the surface and explore some of the problems at a deeper level.

As the starting point for dialogue, I would bring up the notion of God. In my treatment I noted that there is no unanimity on this matter in the part of Africa under discussion. The notion of a Supreme Being is more or less distinctly present in most cases. Sometimes there is no complete grasp of the oneness of the Supreme Being. It takes on different forms of existence, and these various embodiments are given more attention. There may also be other deities and mediators. Christianity may help Africans to think this whole matter through and to arrive at a clearer conception of God. They may thus come to revere the one God who created everything and who is accessible to human beings in their times of need. God is a God of human beings, and the Father is present to us as a father in his Word and Spirit. And it is an ongoing, perduring presence.

That raises the question: How are we to encounter and accommodate Africa with respect to its great need for mediators, whether they be spirits, deities, or ancestors? My impression is that a revitalized angelology would be a valuable contribution to Africa, and I would expect to see African theologies delve into the matter. The only proviso is that angels would have to be seen as extensions of God's presence in this world. Insofar as ancestors and chieftains being mediators is concerned, I don't think the matter is so problematic. Deeper study is necessary, to be sure, but it is already in progress in some countries.

My impression is that God is being viewed as the Great Ancestor, who is sometimes called Father. This Great Ancestor is very closely associated with human existence. God made human beings and shared his life with the archetypes. The newly born child comes into the world gifted with a divine principle; this places it in the line of descent from God. How does all this take place? This is a matter for perduring reflection among Africans. We shall have to explore whether the ancestors and tribal chieftains, who are or were earthly beings, play a role somewhere in this scheme. Do they mediate divine life? A new theology of the ancestors is becoming very necessary, since no African can live without them. Here again I must say that African theologies fall short of the mark. They frequently stick to ethnological considerations, failing to proceed to the solution of the problem that confronts a Christian African.[54] Here the Christian doctrine of the communion of saints and their relationship to God and us could well be of service.

I noted earlier that in any dialogue with Africans we must pay heed to typical African themes which have to do with such universal human experiences as birth, marriage, death, and so forth. In this connection the theme of "remembrance" came sharply to the fore. This raises another issue that must be resolved. Africans do not tend to view history as a process arising out of the past, moving on in the present, and culminating in some future. It is the last phase that presents the problem. Here African and Christian eschatology must be brought in contact with each other.

I would not go as far as some authors, who assert that the notion of "future" is entirely missing in Africa.[55] But I am convinced that Jesus' message about the coming kingdom of God can be a liberating one for Africans. According to Jesus, this coming kingdom has already begun to make its appearance here and now. Such a message can open up the outlook of Africans, giving them more courage to go out and work in this world. Needless to say, the point must be presented in a way that dovetails with the typical African outlook, which tends to focus on the ancestral past and the present. It should be possible to make clear that the future stands in continuity with the past and the present. This is another task to be undertaken by African theology.

That brings us to a closely related point: i.e., the view of creation as an ongoing reality. For Africans creation tends to mean God's lordship over human beings and their world. It does not so clearly include the notion that human beings are co-creators with God, that they must develop the world through improved techniques and methods. The absence of the latter notion poses obstacles to progress in agriculture and industrialization. The African notion of creation does not inspire Africans to play an active role in these areas as it might, particularly when the busy Westerner finishes the initial work and heads home. If Africa really wants to get involved in building a better, more humane world, then it will have to dialogue about the notion of creation. It can be a maieutic process, however, since most Africans do possess a concept of creation.

The point is that they must push on from this starting point. Dialogue should lead Africans to a deeper appreciation for human know-how and technology. At the same time, however, we must remember that all these things are supposed to contribute to the desired culmination: the establishment of the kingdom of God. Otherwise scientific knowledge and technology may turn into independent realities posing a threat to human beings and their future. We Westerners can learn something about moderation from Africans. In this connection we should also realize that Africans do possess a very clear notion of co-creation, particularly when it comes to human procreation. There God, human beings, and the ancestors work together. This may serve as a starting point for extending the notion of co-creativity to other areas of life.

I have already had something to say about eschatology. We have no objections to a more proximate eschatology, such as that found among Africans. But they must be opened up more to the notion of a future culmination in the coming kingdom of God, and to the notion of the ongoing life of the human person after death. Right now the notion of continued survival is too closely bound up with remembrance of the dead by the living. In some cases that is not verified: e.g., among widows, orphans, and unmarried people. Even when remembrance is a fact, it often lasts no more than a generation or two. Here the biblical view of life and the Life could offer more joy and hopeful anticipation of the future. It is at least a point of contact, but it would have to be explored and elaborated in dialogue.

The typically African notion that the community is composed of the living and the dead is a rich one which can only be admired by Christians. Here we have countless points that could be tied together and elaborated further on the basis of biblical thought and the Christian heritage. Christianity is a community centered around the risen Lord. This is reflected in concrete earthly communities centered around him, including the basic ecclesial communities and smaller groups that are found throughout Africa. We must make sure that these new communities dovetail with the extended-family system in Africa so that they will be genuine, living communities. We do not want to give the impression that they are being imposed on the Africans from outside. Here we touch upon the whole matter of new forms of ecclesial life, which will be discussed in Part Three.

On one point real critical thinking must take place: i.e., on the role of the deceased in this community composed of the living and the dead. So far this role has been almost completely confined to preserving the existing setup and sanctioning punishment when people try to undertake change. Here Christianity can play a liberating role. It can help Africans to see that their ancestors, too, were active in their own day. But that whole matter would properly be a part of any new theology of the ancestors.[56]

11

The Residue of Religious Oppression: Folk Religion in Latin America

We now move to a different continent and a different culture world: Latin America. My concern in this chapter is not with official Catholicism or mainline Protestant movements; it is with various folk forms of Catholicism which reveal the scars of earlier conquest, enslavement, and oppression. More recent trends will be discussed in Part Three. Nor is my view restricted solely to folk Catholicism, though it receives much attention, because then I could not introduce such movements as spiritualism, Umbanda, and the like. I would like to suggest how we can and must dialogue with the religious life of peoples who have been deeply affected by historical oppression.

THE SLOW RISE OF RELIGIOUS PLURALISM

Ever since the days of the Iberian conquest, Latin America has been Roman Catholic, except for pockets of unconverted Indians here and there. Religious pluralism was a rather late arrival on the scene. For a long time Latin America managed to keep out the ideas of the Reformation and the Enlightenment, at least during the colonial period. Successful movements towards political independence in the early nineteenth century led to the founding of various nations. The ideas of liberalism and the Enlightenment crept in, though only among a small group. Even the rise of this liberal oligarchy did not prevent Roman Catholicism from being recognized as the state religion. Real change came only with the social alterations that began to take place in the middle of the nineteenth century.

The ruling oligarchy consciously chose to encourage immigration for the sake of economic growth. Most of these immigrants from central and eastern Europe were Protestant. Their ideal was not mission but rather social and economic progress. They lived in their own little national enclaves with their own hospitals, schools, newspapers, and churches. Mission efforts from the United States failed to call Roman Catholicism into question. It was only in the twentieth century that they became a significant factor.

Here again a distinction is in order, however. One must clearly distinguish between the historical mainline Churches and the sects. The Pentecostal movement, in particular, was very much present among the lower classes. It played a political role insofar as it called things into question and offered alternatives. It raised questions about such traditional values as wealth, profit, possessions, family connections, educational degrees, and professional work. Its open access to the Spirit created a force that tended towards liberation from exploitation and oppression. Yet even that did not lead to real emancipation. In most instances earlier forms of power were simply replaced by some form of church power.

So gradually religious pluralism appeared on the scene. I should like to begin with a discussion of *spiritualism*. It entered Latin America around the same time that Protestantism did, but one cannot make a sharp distinction between it and folk Catholicism. There is a loose and somewhat slippery relationship between the two. We find brands of spiritualism in Cuba, Haiti, Puerto Rico, the Dominican Republic, Mexico, Argentina and, above all, Brazil. A distinction is usually made between a stricter type of spiritualism, known as Kardecism, and Umbanda. Kardecism derives from a man named Alan Kardec. Umbanda is a syncretistic movement incorporating Kardecist, Indian, African, and Roman Catholic elements.

Let us consider spiritualism first, as we find it in Brazil. It was introduced there in 1865. There is now a spiritualist federation in Brazil, but it does not include all currents of spiritualism. A brief typology of this spiritualism might include the following points. Spiritualism is a communication with the dead, with disembodied spirits. There is an unconditional connection between cause and effect, so that good deeds are rewarded while bad deeds are punished. Thus spiritualists tend to talk about merit rather than about grace. History is an ongoing process of purification. Repeated reincarnations enable people to be cleansed of their earlier misdeeds. The earth is only one of the inhabited planets. Indeed it is seen as the low planet on the totem pole, the planet for penance. The fundamental virtue is love for all human beings, including the spirits. God is so far removed from human beings that God's essence or nature cannot be known. Spiritual leaders function as intermediaries for revelation addressed to living human beings. The revelation of Jesus, viewed as a completion of Moses' revelation, is now being supplemented by the ongoing communication of spirits in and through mediums.[57]

Umbanda requires a bit more detailed treatment. During the colonial period, and particularly in Brazil, the introduction of Roman Catholicism to the native Indians and imported Black slaves was often done in a very superficial way. Old images of African deities were simply replaced by those of Christian saints in order to provide Blacks with easier access to Catholicism. But the old deities lived on, and many of the old religions survived under a Christian guise. Ancestor worship and spirit cults remained alive. At important moments the spirits of the ancestors were consulted through the mediation of priests and priestesses. In the nineteenth century this tendency surfaced and flourished, thanks to contact with the more scholarly type of spiritualism then in vogue. It was now possible to regard the native version as another brand of spiritualism. Umbanda, then, is a form of spiritualism which has African and Indian roots, and which has been strongly influenced by modern forms of spiritualism.

Umbanda is still undergoing steady development, thanks to its contact with scholarly spiritualism. Proponents do not dwell on its African origins. Instead they maintain that Umbanda really goes back to ancient forms of religion in Egypt and India, from which the African forms derive. The African forms are viewed as imperfect derivatives, which degenerated further under the impact of the slavery to which African Blacks were subjected in Brazil. The task now is to clear away the polluted elements and restore the pristine stream of Umbanda. The first Umbanda Congress agreed on its divine origin. Umbanda was placed on the side of the world religions and found a summons to mission. Its members now want to hold their own vis-à-vis scholarly spiritualism on the one hand and Macumba on the other. Macumba retains sharply African features, which Umbanda is trying to play down. So such features are disappearing from Umbanda: e.g., drums, alcohol, intricate dress, magic elements, and the cult of the demon, Exú. However, these elements continue to survive elsewhere in Quimbanda, to which people turn in dire need.

The teachings of Umbanda can be briefly summarized as follows. There are different currents in Umbanda, so again I am offering a general typology. There is a tendency in African religion to rationalize. This dovetails with the new social situation of Blacks in the big cities, where social progress and integration are now becoming possible. The racially rooted aspects of Umbanda are waning, therefore, and membership is being swelled by mulattoes and whites. The assumption is that the spirits of the dead, particularly the ancestors, have been divided into groups, depending on their degree of perfection and other affinities. The mediums, who absorb these spirits, are likewise divided into groups or legions. They are basically divided into seven series, which are primarily based on ethnic origin. Each series is guided by an *Orixá* or its Catholic counterpart. Through a trance experience, which involves contact with a medium and hence with a disembodied spirit, African cults are reconciled with, and in a sense sublimated by, this form of spiritualism. There is now an enormous literature about Umbanda in Brazil. There are recipe books for all the various problems of life. People can find out whom to turn to and how to do it exactly.

Spiritualism, and specifically Umbanda, is viewed as fulfilling a variety of functions. It serves a therapeutic function insofar as it carries on the physical and psychic healing of the age-old religions. Sickness once was due to magical forces that attacked a victim malevolently. This is now done by the spirits, who must be exorcised or overcome by an even stronger spirit. Sick people may also be the cause of their own illnesses: e.g., by neglecting to honor the spirits. Another function of spiritualism is to provide for the social integration of marginal groups in urban society by ensuring assimilation and compensation. By assimilating modern scientific, political, and ethical viewpoints, members choose to participate in the evolutionary spiral on both the mental and material level. They can promote racial equality, equal opportunity for social advancement, and enthusiasm for Brazil as a land of unlimited opportunity and a great future. All this finds expression in love of neighbor, sociopolitical action, and a contented worldview based on the certain knowledge of evolutionary progress and Indian ideas about karma.

Social integration is also fostered through compensation. While Umbanda and Brazilian spiritualism do foster adaptation to a progress-oriented society, they have not lost their spiritual orientation in the process. Many people remain only partially incorporated into the existing social system. The potential for upward mobility remains slim among many marginal groups, and traditional obstacles of class remain. Given this fact, the various forms of folk devotion continue to serve a strongly compensatory function. Through his or her contact with a higher realm, a medium enjoys high esteem in the cultic community. This relativizes the social function of others. Moreover, anyone can acquire this function as a medium; if it so happens, then the man or woman involved must try to develop this capability.

Another compensatory function can be seen in the fact that the redeemed spirits of former slaves stand over against the spirits of their masters who are still doing penance. The latter are the object of pity and compassion. Thus there is such a thing as a "right order," and existing social relations are viewed as bad by comparison.

The most important form of compensation is embodied in the law of karma, taken over from Hinduism. Earlier good deeds and bad deeds accumulate in the process of reincarnation. Thus one's present life on earth is seen as merely one brief moment in the incarnational series, which may entail progress or backsliding. One's lower social status at present can be interpreted as a penance, and those somewhat higher on the social scale can find some way to explain the suffering and misfortune of the lower classes.

Another factor fostering integration is social assistance. Umbanda appeals to authentic Christianity, preaching the practical exercise of goodness towards everyone. It is also convinced that human beings can be improved by benevolence and education.[58]

So there is real religious pluralism in Brazil, as the above treatment of spiritualism and Umbanda suggests. Now I would like to focus on *folk Catholicism*, which cannot be explained without looking at the mission methods of the colonial period. The spiritual conquest of Latin America was simultaneously a mission of state. Church and state went hand in hand. Every conquistador was at the same time a mission pioneer, and every missionary was at the same time a land occupier. There were exceptions, and sometimes marked exceptions to be sure, but that was the general picture. In the eyes of native converts the priest was a government official in league with the hated oppressors. In Brazil, for example, there was close cooperation between the large landowners and the clergy. There the priest, as house chaplain and educator, was an ally of the feudal plantation-system. As a result there was no authentic development of an indigenous Latin American religiosity within Catholicism for centuries. It is only in our own day, and particularly since the Medellín Conference in 1968, that such native developments have come to the fore in a remarkable way.

Except for those missionaries who were members of religious orders, colonial clergymen hastened to establish such formal church structures as episcopates, deaneries, and parishes. The process of missionizing was often minimal and superficial. The assumption was that Christianity could be established among the Blacks and Indians only if paganism was crushed and eradicated. Of course the old pagan beliefs lived on, insofar as people were baptized *en masse* without proper preparation. The Jesuit Reductions represented one major exception to this picture. There large groups of Indians were brought together to live in relatively independent surroundings, and much better care was taken of them.

For the most part missionaries latched on to old customs and habits. This often meant that old pagan beliefs were continued under Christian names. The old deities were replaced by Christian saints and Mary, the mother of God. There was no longer a god for every natural phenomenon; instead the one God was differentiated into a plural God. Ceremonies, processions, and rites from Iberian Catholicism fitted in surprisingly well with the customs of the converted natives; unfortunately people disregarded the deeper, underlying differences. And so the feasts of various patron saints took on great importance, and they were accompanied by lavish festivities, merrymaking, and fireworks.

What Christ did the missionaries bring to Latin America? It was not the historical human being, Jesus of Nazareth, but the dead Christ on the cross. It was the latter Christ who was revered as the Lord of the living and the dead in the hereafter. Christ had nothing to do with life here on earth. The saints and Mary took care of that. Everything would be set right in the next life, and thus religion came to function as a source of consolation and comfort. It was also a means whereby people could forget their suffering and oppression. The result was unlimited trust in the Church, combined with a sense of fatalism. History was seen as the locale of God's activity, and human beings were not to interfere at all.

I can recall a procession that I witnessed deep in the interior of Colombia. A high Mass was celebrated in the large, open village. Then a very old picture of the just-scourged Jesus was placed on boards and raised high on sticks by a group of *campesinos*. The barefoot peasants carried it around the churchyard, accompanied by girls dressed in white, choirboys, a priest holding incense, and almost the whole population in their bare feet. As they moved along in procession, they sang mournful songs. It was at that moment that I realized for the first time what folk Catholicism meant there. The people identified with the suffering, scourged Jesus. They interpreted their own plight in the same terms. Human beings, too, must suffer in this earthly life; no change can be expected on that account. Only after humiliation and death will one find release, happiness, and redemption in the after-life. Obviously when the masses of people shared that outlook, one could not expect to see them promoting social, economic, and political improvements; they simply were not motivated to move in that direction.[59]

However much religious change is taking place in Latin America today, it should be obvious that we must keep in mind the long backdrop of colonial oppression, which was both material and spiritual. It should also be obvious that folk religion has assumed many forms in Latin America, and that I have discussed only a few examples. Macumba, for example, would merit detailed consideration of its own. But I think we have enough material already for our present purpose, which is to initiate a dialogue by asking a few questions.

IS THERE SOMETHING WORTHWHILE TO LEARN FROM FOLK RELIGION?

Here we have our usual second question: What do these various forms of folk religion have to tell us? They are certainly an indictment of the way in which we have exported and preached the Christian message. Such religious forms are the fruit of a Christianity transmitted in bondage. We must first delve deep into past history in order to be able to grasp the present situation and begin meaningful attempts at reform and renewal. In this connection it is good to hear that an ecumenical church history of Latin America is now being prepared there.

The centuries-old situation in Latin America teaches us to show understanding for peoples suffering from oppression. But it also indicates that such peoples have their own defense mechanisms, with which they try to adapt to existing circumstances and solve the problems of life in a way that is meaningful for them. In Latin America this led to worship of ancestors and spirits, who lived on under the guise of Christian saints. It led to an image of Jesus which fitted in with their own suffering and oppression. And it led to native forms of neighborly love and social integration.

In approaching those religious forms, we must be extremely cautious and prudent, it seems to me. We may not wish to view their approach to life as a be-all and end-all, and we may well want to encourage efforts on behalf of progress, change, and liberation. But we must remember that it is very perilous to undermine the certainties achieved in that integration process without at the same time joining the people involved and working out meaningful, livable alternatives for them. The native religious forms can fill us with respect insofar as they arose in a very unequal contest and enabled the people to hold their own in life. Respect is the first thing that we must learn from them in our encounter and dialogue.

That sets us thinking about our own local situation as well. How did our forms of religious expression arise here in Europe and the Netherlands, for example? Were factors associated with oppression at work here too, and did they produce more or less similar phenomena? Are there no forms associated with folk religion to be found in European Catholicism? What about processions, penitential practices, worship of the saints, fatalistic acceptance of what God wills, and an image of Jesus that is theologically incomplete? Indeed aren't these phenomena sharply on the rise? If so, why? Isn't our official faith, be it Catholic or Protestant, a bit too intellectual so that it goes over the heads of the faithful? These are the sorts of questions that will surface in dialogue. They will make us a bit more cautious here, forcing us to consider what the average believer really lives by. Moving on from there, we will be able to consider new approaches and developments that deserve to be integrated into the picture.

We must also pay heed to what Latin Americans themselves are doing in connection with these problems. We must consider their new pastoral approaches and their new theology of liberation and captivity. I shall not delve into that issue here, since I intend to discuss it in Part Three of my book.[60] But again I would say that we must be critical-minded listeners. We cannot rashly adopt things deriving from another continent. Instead we must do our own exploring and arrive at our own solutions. This is not to suggest that all folk forms of religion are way off base, however. The question is whether they promote or impede a correct relationship to the Father in Jesus and through the Spirit.

POTENTIAL LINES OF DIALOGUE

We must consider seriously what the role of Christians might be in any dialogue with folk forms of religion in Latin America. Again I shall not discuss liberation theology or basic ecclesial communities here, since they will be brought up in Part Three.[61] Instead I shall proceed from the typology outlined in the early part of this chapter.

In connection with the more scientific or scholarly types of spiritualism, Christians will have to bring up the Judeo-Christian vision of history. They will assert that history is indeed progressive, but that Christianity sees no need for an ongoing process of reincarnation based upon some sort of automatic requital for evil deeds in a previous lifetime. The history of a human being is a one-time process, and it is qualified by the forgiveness and reconciliation offered by a good Father. In dialogue with spiritualism it might be best to start with its lively concern for love for all human beings. Here automatism is completely absent; human freedom begins to assert itself against the pressure of spirits, fate, and constraint. This love must be seen as an imitation of a good Father, who gifted us with his Son and Spirit because he loved us. The Holy Spirit is more important than any influence exerted by the spirits of spiritualism.

Umbanda is more complicated. In any dialogue we must first get back to reality, letting fantasies about ancient Egyptian and Indian origins fall by the wayside. The need for ancestor worship must be brought out clearly as a venerable cultural and religious element in Africa and India. The Churches must recognize that element in Latin America, even as they must in Africa, as I noted in the previous chapter. In Latin America, too, there is real need for a new theology of the ancestors. Unfortunately one can find little evidence of this in Latin American publications, which are almost exclusively concerned with political liberation. Here we have another major area for cooperative efforts among theologians and catechists of Latin America and Africa.

It is not up to European theologians to work out such a theology. Those involved will have to consider to what extent the evocation of spirits, the use of mediums, and trance experiences can be integrated into an acceptably Christian notion of ancestor worship. Here again I see no concrete proposals being offered by the theologians, and I am simply throwing out the question. It will have to be resolved in dialogue with the followers of Umbanda; and in the process one will have to pay heed to the deeper aspirations underlying such actions and procedures. I would guess that points of contact and the ultimate solution will come from there.

As I noted earlier, Umbanda offers a certain degree of integration to marginal groups through assimilation and compensation. Here again we must proceed cautiously, being careful not to upset the balance when we have no alternative to offer. That would create a psychologically intolerable situation. Our ideal, too, is that these marginal groups play their proper role in society even as other groups do; that they have their proper measure of social, economic, and political influence. To be sure, there must be structural changes in Brazilian society. Some Brazilian Christians are just as responsible for the current oppression as outside forces are. But there must also be a change in the image of God, humanity, and the world which the marginal groups themselves hold.

The three are closely bound up with each other. Insofar as God is not regarded as a Father in the biblical sense, people do not trust in his concern and provident care. He is seen as an almighty Father rather than as a provident Father who loves his children. Insofar as Jesus is seen only as the suffering Messiah with whom people can identify fatalistically, little thought is given to the risen Lord who is active in our midst today and who is seeking to lead the world to freedom, justice, peace, and unity. In dialogue this incomplete image of Jesus will have to be filled out. People will have to be brought to the realization that Jesus did not retreat or withdraw from human history after his sufferings were over, that he still lives in our midst.

Particularly noteworthy is the fact that the Holy Spirit is not much in evidence in Umbanda. Here again the link between the Father and human realities seems to be broken.[62] So for centuries the images of God, humanity, and the world have remained partial and incomplete in the folk religions of Latin America. They must now be made complete in the process of dialogue. This is a task for a revitalized catechetics among basic ecclesial communities and in the schools.

Many of the above remarks apply just as much to any dialogue with folk Catholicism, where we find many of the same traits: fatalism; religion as a source of comfort amid the misery of human existence on earth; the quest for happiness after death; and the same basic image of God, with the same resultant attitude towards human existence and this world. Here again reflection must go hand in hand with action on a wide variety of fronts. Folk Catholicism must be changed from within in the proper way so that people are not left with nothing, or confronted with impossible political situations.

I am thinking at the moment of the integrative function of folk Catholicism. It is not without reason that during the decade of the seventies the theology of liberation developed into a theology of liberation and of captivity.[63] Latin Americans know that they are imprisoned in defective sociopolitical, economic, and religious structures. They know that those structures cannot be changed by doing theology alone, even when that theologizing derives from praxis. In dialogue we may learn how to stretch out our hands once again. Perhaps our own history can provide models of truly successful liberation, which can serve to stimulate and inspire unfree human beings in Latin America.

12

Mao's China and the New Human Being

Readers might well wonder whether this particular topic belongs in my treatment at all. What does continental China have to do with the subject of dialogue between religions? Does China want any religion? In the course of my discussion I hope to show that there are real questions of this sort to be asked. We must probe beneath the surface and remain open to what China wants if we are to comprehend it at all.

I fully realize that I am going to broach things which some will find hard to appreciate. First of all, there are the missionaries who were driven out of China after 1949. I have no doubts about their immense dedication, and I would not blame all of them for deliberate colonial misdeeds and mistakes. I know that if I myself had lived and worked during that period, I probably would have had difficulty with the ideas developed in this chapter.

But time has not stood still since Mao's takeover in 1949. He himself ruled for about thirty years before he died. We would do well to look at those thirty years, to study Mao's work and a bit of his poetic writings, to get a close-up view of the various revolutions in China, and to explore the slow elaboration of a distinctive way of thinking. I know that Mao and his followers began to rule with an iron hand and a tough approach, and I have no intention of merely lavishing praise on his actions. But are we to do nothing but keep harping on our complaints forever? If that is the case, then other peoples could keep harping on our own misdeeds in history for all eternity.

Missionaries are not the only people who may have trouble with my exposition, however. During the decade of the seventies various groups voiced growing opposition to suggestions that Christian Churches might show more openness and willingness to dialogue vis-à-vis Communist China. This opposition movement was directed primarily against the World Council of Churches, and it found much support among fundamentalist Christians. In Germany there was the Berlin Declaration of 1974, which discussed China in two of its many theses. Questions were posed in terms of sharply contradictory alternatives: Christ or Anti-Christ? World Community or the Kingdom of God? In this spirit a large group gathered around Professor Peter

Beyerhaus of Tübingen, who was very active. We must hear what these people have to say also, and then try to dialogue with them—not an easy task. A similar movement was also evident in the United States. And a Love China Congress in the Philippines some years ago, which was sponsored by several Churches, was also critical of any new rapprochement with Communist China.

The whole problem of discussing Mao's thought is further complicated by developments in China since his death. On the one hand some difficulties seem to have been removed. China has established relations with the United States and is now opening up to Western business and technology. Excesses of Mao's regime have been condemned, and Mao himself is no longer deified. On the other hand this may render any discussion of Mao's thinking and the new human being in China somewhat belated and academic. But in my opinion such a discussion, as an example of the dialogic approach, has value for many reasons.

I do not propose to offer the final word about Mao's thought or Mao's regime. No such definitive judgment seems possible to me. Here I am simply pleading for the value of a dialogue with the new China, using the notion of the new human being as a focal point. We must keep our ears open to what is coming out of China and try to comprehend it. It is all too easy for Westerners to interpret the voice of China in a one-sided way, to forget that China is an oriental country with a very different mentality and a very different form of symbolic expression.

Many people viewed Mao's China simply as a Marxist state, with all that implied. In my opinion the matter is not that simple. We must set aside our *a priori* view of Marxism and try to hear the authentic voices of the Chinese people themselves. Perhaps then something new will get through to us, paving the way for real dialogue after the long years of silence and loss of contact. Such an attitude is the starting point for dialogue, or the precondition for it, and we may hope that China will see it in that light also.

LACK OF FREEDOM AMONG THE CHINESE
BEFORE MAO'S REGIME

Before I proceed to offer a typology of Mao's vision of the human being, I want to fill in some details in the historical background. Without some knowledge of the historical backdrop, we cannot possibly comprehend Mao's view. To understand the new human being of Mao's China, we must first have a good idea of the past oppression of the Chinese. This oppression was multifaceted. It stemmed partially from the old regime in China itself, and partially from the impact of the Western powers on China in the nineteenth and early twentieth centuries.

China was familiar with all sorts of unprivileged human beings. There were hereditary, caste-like groups of slaves and servants; by Confucian standards these people were morally inferior. The majority of people were good and decent, but there also existed a minority of people who were regarded as lowly and base. Later on, others were added to this minority: e.g., beggars, actors, prostitutes, and lowly workers such as hairdressers and domestic servants. Some civil servants also belonged to this group: e.g., messengers, jailkeepers, and local police officials. Others belonged to the lower social strata because of their regional origin: e.g., the boat people in Kwantung and Fukien. Sometimes these people were of obscure origin. But to them were added others: e.g., unassimilated ethnic minorities, defeated groups, rebels, families of criminals, and people who were sold in times of famine.

All these groups suffered discrimination from the law and society. They could not marry decent people. They could not climb the bureaucratic ladder based upon the Confucian system. And when they broke the law, they were punished more severely. Moreover, their status was hereditary. When the Confucian state was toppled in the early part of the twentieth century with the downfall of the emperor, those laws and norms were abolished in theory; in practice, however, they continued to prevail. This situation ended only when new values and a new legal system were introduced after 1949.[64]

The Confucian class-system also operated in an oppressive way. Here I am not going to discuss the philosophic aspects or religious implications of Confucianism. I am concerned with Confucianism as a sociopolitical phenomenon. As such, Confucianism was a bureaucratic system of civil servants. Social mobility was tied to examinations. Successful completion of the exams could raise the candidate to a higher level of civil service and social status. These Confucianists formed the class of the literati, beneath which stood three other classes of people: peasants, craftsmen, and merchants. The Confucianists formed a world of their own, which stood apart from the rest of the population. Thus an almost unbridgeable chasm opened up between the culture of the elite and the culture of the common people.

In the early part of this century the Confucian system was slowly but surely undermined by Sun Yat-Sen's revolutionary movement. The real assault on the rigidified system, however, came with the May Fourth Movement, which held the Confucian system responsible for the stagnation of traditional Chinese society. Modern Western ideas began to compete with Confucianist ideas. The contest was decided finally during Mao's regime. After fierce debate Confucianism was condemned.[65]

Oppression also came from outside China. Here I must say something about extraterritoriality,[66] the complex system of interrelated privileges and interests which the Western powers had extorted from the Chinese government. For almost one hundred years they had eaten away at China's sovereignty by forcing China to sign various treaties with them. Prior to Western inroads, China had been a land apart, the Middle Kingdom. Its contacts with the outside world were confined to trading posts in Macao and Canton. Then the increasingly industrialized West of the nineteenth century began to seek new markets. The Western nations began to dream of opening up China, where one-fourth of the world's population lived. The military might of the

West had grown greatly, so it was now possible to force China to open her borders. Gradually Western countries proceeded to demand certain favors and privileges, and thus extraterritoriality became a reality.

It took all sorts of forms. Western citizens, for example, no longer were subject to Chinese laws. They had their own national courts on Chinese soil. They might take the form of consular courts for Western nationals, a larger court of the same type in Shanghai, or a mixed court composed of Chinese judges and Western consular officials. Westerners had their own customs houses, postal services, telegraph lines, tax offices, and military barracks. They were free to travel the inland waterways without having to pay Chinese tolls. Their missionaries could operate freely and acquire land without restriction. There were also Western enclaves and concessions.

All these things were affirmed and reaffirmed in various treaties: e.g., the Nanking Treaty of 1842 between Britain and China, the Wang-hsia Treaty of 1844 between America and China, the Whampoa Treaty of 1844 between France and China, the Tientsin Treaty of 1880 between the United States and China, and so forth. In the twentieth century efforts were under way to get these treaties rescinded, but the increasing incursion of Japan into China after 1931 aborted such efforts. It was only around 1943 that signs of change appeared and Chinese national awareness began to assert itself.

I must say something about the concessions. These were treaty ports where Western citizens could freely engage in trade. In this century there were more than one hundred such ports at one point. There were also exclusive residential enclaves for Westerners. In theory the Chinese emperor remained sovereign, but in practice he did not exercise his legal right. Western enclaves had their own boundaries and government, headed by the consul. The concessions were under greater Western control than simple trading posts, where Chinese officials continued to exercise authority. In both areas, however, land was leased to the foreigners, usually for ninety-nine years. (Such is the case with the newer sections in Hong Kong, for example.) The leased areas were right by the treaty port, of course. Concessions and trading posts were held by Britishers, Americans, Frenchmen, Germans, Austrians, Belgians, Italians, and Russians. Japan joined the party by its conquest of northern China. One such international settlement was in Shanghai. In 1935 it covered 22 square kilometers and contained a population of 28,000 foreigners and 1,000,000 Chinese. The French part of this settlement had 19,000 foreigners and 500,000 Chinese. However, no Chinese were allowed to live in the concessions. Japanese influence grew during the decade of the thirties in the Shanghai settlement. And embassy row in Peking was a marked exception, especially after the failure of the Boxer Rebellion in 1900. The embassies could have their own military personnel, a diplomatic commission ruled the district, and no Chinese could live within it.

The significance of all this was primarily political and economic. China had traditionally been an agrarian land where small farmers worked the fields of large landowners and enjoyed little freedom. In the concessions and trading settlements, however, industry and trade of the Western type developed. It was designed to serve the imperialist powers, of course, but it also had an impact on the rest of China. The old economic and social order was being undermined, and the imperialist enclaves offered crucial protection to Chinese capital. Capitalism grew in China.

It is against this backdrop that we can understand the later dispute within the Communist party. Where should one begin with the revolutionary process: among the oppressed majority of poor peasants or in the industrialized cities? Mao opted for the first alternative as his way. Political tensions with China resulted in the flow of Chinese capital to foreign countries. The social and psychological consequences were even worse, since China felt humiliated. One good result was that China came in contact with a new line of thought. This line of thought gave rise to an elite which was in a position to rise above its own tradition and tackle the modernization of China.[67] Since Mao's death, the leaders of China seem to be re-examining the whole issue of how to proceed with the Chinese revolution vis-à-vis the West and capitalism. And the change in attitude towards the Soviet Union further complicates the whole matter.[68]

It is against this background that we must view the missionary activity of the Churches. I do not intend to retrace the church history of China, which goes back to the heyday of Nestorianism. I shall restrict my remarks to the modern phase, which began in the nineteenth century. On the Protestant front we see then the first efforts to associate with secular forces. The first Protestant missionary accompanied the British East India Company as an interpreter in a journey from Canton to Peking. This soon led to ties between missionary and commercial interests. The aims were well intentioned, but they would prove to be doomed to failure in the long run. Another missionary also acted as an interpreter for British opium dealers in order to make contact with the Chinese people. The foreigners were convinced of their cultural superiority, and their missionary zeal was shot through with such feelings. Matters became worse after the Opium War, when five port cities were opened up and more followed. Missionaries took advantage of the privileges now guaranteed to Westerners by treaties.

Express provisions were now made for religious matters. At first pressure was exerted primarily by Catholic missionaries. Protestants were less organized at first, and it was some time before they took full advantage of the system. France demanded the exclusive right to protect Catholic missionaries, and this led to later problems with other Western nations: Germany, for example. From the protectorate territories, then, much varied missionary work went on. Catholics put more stress on the building of communities, care of souls, and charitable works. Protestants stressed the spoken and printed word (Bible translations), publishing activities, medical studies, education, and so forth. Thus Western scholarship and science also spread to China, which was now opened up to the modern world.

There were harmful side-effects also. Due to missionary reports, Europe began to form a distorted and erroneous picture of China. Westerners heard mainly about such things as military revolts, child-abandonment, poverty, famine, and banditry. Little was said about the great culture of East Asia and its higher ideals. Similar side-effects resulted from missionary methods in China itself. Not every missionary was guilty, of course, and missionary intentions were not consciously malevolent. But one can readily understand why a reaction against Christian missionary work set in when Mao took over in 1949. A few examples will make this clear.

Both the missionaries and their Christian converts were under the protection of the Western powers, and they took advantage of it. The very creation of the German lend-lease area in Kiaochow (Shantung Province) was due to the killing of two German missionaries by bandits. Although the Chinese police went to work immediately, Germany stepped in with strong demands. For some time Germany had been trying to gain a territorial foothold on the coast, and this seemed to be the perfect opportunity. Within two weeks the German fleet had blockaded the port of Tsingtao, and Germany began to make its demands. China was to pay the costs of the German military action. Germany was to be given the right to lay railways and exploit coal mines. It was merely the start of a long process which went much further. The same thing happened in other Western protectorates. Either the Western government jumped into action when Christians were molested, without any objections from missionaries, or else the missions themselves explicitly asked for protection. One vicar apostolic in Peking allegedly expressed his ideal to be this: a Catholic Church everywhere, with a Vatican and French flag on either side.[69] This church-state coziness proved disastrous later on. It again helps to explain what happened after 1949.

Other strange procedures and events entered the picture to alienate the Chinese, particularly after 1860. I can only mention a few items. There was the matter of Christian trials. With the help of their respective governments, Christian missionaries intervened in court proceedings where the Chinese defendant was a Christian parishioner. One cannot avoid the impression that this fact must have led to conversions for something less than the right motive. That there was already a lively hatred of Christians and Westerners seems evident from the infamous Tientsin massacre of 1870. The French consul, his aide, ten sisters from an orphanage, two priests, nine other foreigners, and thirty to forty Chinese Christians were tortured to death by a raging mob. The reprisal by the West took the form of gunboat diplomacy.

The hatred nurtured by the Chinese was very evident in the Boxer Rebellion of 1900. It claimed thirty thousand victims, including two hundred foreign missionaries and their subordinates. It was clearly an anti-Western demonstration, and the court in Peking was not out of sympathy. Western reprisals were shocking. Until 1949 China had to pay a high annual indemnity to the missions for the killing and destruction.

I must also note another fact, pertaining to Catholics primarily. In difficult times they made it awfully easy for Chinese parents to abandon their children. At the front of a Catholic cloister was a big cylinder which opened out on to the street. Desperate parents could tuck their baby into the cylinder, turn it around, and thus deposit their child anonymously with the good sisters. The latter would baptize the child and raise it as a Christian.

Another widespread fact was particularly true in northern China. Missionaries bought up large tracts of land. Converts and catechumens were allowed to work these lands and were established in fortified villages against bandits. Thus the missionaries became sole overlords. I shall not go into the merits or demerits of another practice: i.e., the work of making "rice Christians" in times of famine, which recurred periodically.

Another point should be noted about Christian missionary activity in China. Many schools and universities were built in China, and Protestants led the way in this area; Catholics followed later. Yet the process of transferring authority to Chinese natives moved slowly and painfully. It was only in 1922 that a majority of the Protestant Churches decided to form a national Christian council, and it was not until 1926 that the pope in Rome consecrated the first Chinese bishops. There was much opposition to such moves, but gradually voices in favor of them grew among participants in the Chinese national movement and even among some foreign missionaries. People began to demand revisions in the unfair treaties, native Chinese leadership in schools and universities, and the abolition of compulsory religious instruction. Little progress was made, however, because China was so dependent on financial aid from abroad. Few changes were feasible during the difficult decades stretching from the Japanese invasion to the civil war. When the Communist Party took over the government in 1949, there remained many things that could only be regarded as abuses.[70]

It is not surprising, therefore, that the Chinese People's Republic almost immediately sought to break the ties between Chinese Christians (about 3,000,000 Roman Catholics and 800,000 Protestants) and the outside world. Even the Christian Churches themselves sometimes viewed the move as one of liberation. There was a campaign to foster the threefold independence of the Churches, which was known as the Three-Self-Movement. The Chinese Churches were to be self-shaping, self-governing, and self-sufficient. About 400,000 Christians signed the 1951 manifesto which officially established the movement. The Korean War and the attendant threat of invasion strengthened the movement in the eyes of Christians and the government.

Of course the government had its own aims in mind. It clashed sharply with fundamentalist groups, which were not very flexible. The Catholic Church had difficulties, too, because of its allegiance to Rome (a foreign power). In the early fifties members of the Legion of Mary, mostly young intellectuals, were very active in discussions with Communists. In 1954 a few Chinese Catholic priests organized a Catholic independence movement, and in 1957 the first bishops were consecrated without permission from Rome.

Service to the people as advocated by communism attracted many activist Catholics at the start, and they joined in the reconstruction effort. During the

Great Leap Forward (1957–1959), Catholic collaboration was evident in many parts of China. Liturgical activity in communities and parishes disappeared almost completely, due to lack of time and lack of clerical leadership. Christianity in China went further and further into seclusion after that. During the period of the Great Proletarian Cultural Revolution (1965–1969), however, religious services did take place in various areas because freedom of religion was theoretically provided for in the Chinese constitution. Whether the decline of Christianity in China will terminate in extermination remains an open question. We lacked information for many years, and only now are relations with China beginning to normalize.[71]

A TYPOLOGY OF MAO'S NEW HUMAN BEING

It is high time I came to our real subject. What exactly was the new human being that Mao wanted to fashion in China? Needless to say, I am not going to explore all the phases of Communist rule in China, nor even all the revolutionary processes.[72] I simply want to bring up a few lines of thought that will help towards a sketchy typology. In the last decade or so, various visitors returning from China have reported several things. There apparently has been great material progress: i.e., no famine, decent housing for all, adequate clothing and work for all, and a slow but steady buildup of industry. But witnesses have also reported the rise of a new human being in China. These human beings possess self-respect and dignity, displaying admirable camaraderie, goodness, and self-sacrifice. They seem to be able to give concrete expression to whatever good qualities are buried in the human heart. They work well together, showing mutual understanding and mutual consideration. There is also a large measure of self-discipline and community feeling.

One American visitor in 1973, a Christian, was deeply struck by the Christian resonances of what he saw and heard. He sensed a Christian brand of ethics in the life of Chinese society and in the teachings of Chairman Mao. Without really knowing anything about Christ or his work, the Chinese people seemed to be adapting Christ's teachings to their society and their lives. School children were being taught to develop their talents as much as possible, not to further their own selfish interests but to place their abilities in the service of the society around them. The Chinese were horrified by the moral suffering associated with sociopolitical conditions in the West. They saw no hope for redemption in its seemingly impotent social and religious institutions. Hope for a new future in China and elsewhere arose out of the revolutionary experience through which the Chinese were passing. This is the sort of positive testimony that more than one visitor to China brought back in the last decade.

Questions remain, however. Are these reports of converted hearts and spirits empirically verifiable? If so, will the conversion into new men and women be lasting, or will human nature come back to nullify it all? What were the new values of revolutionary China in Mao's lifetime, and are they somehow related to accepted, traditional values in the West? By what methods were those values introduced and maintained? Can those values be transmitted to nations in the developed West and the Third World? What exactly is the relevance of these Chinese experiences for the rest of the world? Finally, what theological truths are brought out by the Chinese experiment?

There are questions we must ask ourselves, too. Are we perhaps so wedded to Christian loyalties, sociopolitical relationships, and individual rights and freedoms that we are no longer in a position to look at China objectively? It is also possible that some of us may have given up on our own traditions and institutions, that we therefore tend to admire the Chinese model uncritically. As Christians, we must also ask whether such a fundamental change can take place without the witness and leadership of an authentically religious community. Is it perhaps that China has indeed fashioned a new secular religion? There are many religious analogies in Marxism and Maoism, but they remain merely suggestive unless they are explored more deeply. We must get down to the basic issue and related matters. What is God's objective with humanity? How is God at work today trying to consummate creation? What exactly is the relationship between social justice and salvation in a secular context?

We must now acknowledge the fact that when human beings strive for social justice, human fulfillment, freedom, and communal peace, they are striving for things in history which are viewed by Christianity as good. But we also cherish the conviction that the job cannot be done without a transcendent perspective, without taking into account God's broader hope and goal for humanity within the completed Kingdom of God. The prophetic relationship intertwined therein sustains our hope, despite adversity and opposition. The same holds true for China. Within its secular society does China possess a holy community that keeps alive the ideal of utopia? It is certainly not Chinese Buddhism or any other old-time Chinese religion or philosophy. And it is certainly not Christianity, from what we have already recounted above. And yet the religious dimension is present in China.

This was clearly evident during the Cultural Revolution (1965-1969), when two contending currents of thought clashed. On one side stood Chairman Mao, who seemed to stress the priority of the person as an individual embodiment of his new ideas. On the other side stood the revisionists, who stood for bureaucratic routine and the careful rationalization of political and economic life. It was a long and murderous struggle, but Mao seemed to win at the time. With the new leadership in China now, it is the other side that seems to have won out. Here I simply want to point up some of the underlying ideals in Mao's position, while acknowledging that the implementation of ideals by force and political power raises many questions and doubts.

One could say that for Mao the voluntaristic principle was central. Unless the mind and heart of individuals is changed, society cannot be changed. The people, and only the people, are the driving force of history. The Cultural Revolution was meant to effect this change in individuals. Mao stressed personal conversion rather than technocratic processes as the proper way to institutionalize revolutionary change. The spiritual aspect of society as a whole was to be transformed by the proletariat through their embodiment of new ideas, habits, customs, and cultural patterns. There was, it seemed, a cosmic struggle between the forces of good and the forces of evil, both vying for the hearts and souls of the Chinese people. It was a spiritual struggle.

This represented a complete deviation from orthodox Leninism and Marxism. It reversed the whole picture. There were no pre-established economic criteria rooted in class-structures, nor was social change to be viewed as an historically defined degree of development. The achievement of communism and socialism first presupposed a change in the hearts of human beings and in their communal values. It was new men and new women who would make the revolution, not vice-versa. Underlying this view was the belief that the basic nature of human beings can be changed, that the process of change is not determined a priori or immutably fixed. It could be speeded up, and the new human beings involved were active subjects of the revolution rather than mere objects of it. Through his revolution Mao kept trying to stress to the people that they had been freed. They were now leaders, not slavish followers. It was they, not the party, who were to lead the nation. The Cultural Revolution was a summons to permanent revival: "Serve the people! Combat selfishness! Away with revisionism!"

All this raises some interesting questions. What was implied in references to soul, spirit, personal transformation, spirits and demons, human nature, liberation, happiness, and the darker aspects of the people? It all resembles a religious terminology. Mao was a realist. He knew that the Chinese would have to carry on an ongoing struggle, a continuing revolution, in order to convert and transform themselves as persons. That is why he never ceased to fight against Confucianism and the cultural corruption of the West. Liberation was a historical process which began in 1949, but which was to make deeper inroads among the people as time went on. Liberation from imperialism and feudalism was to lead to the resurrection of the Chinese people on every front. It would free women, peasants, party cadres of a too dogmatic and authoritarian cast, bourgeois intellectuals, earlier capitalists and landlords. It would entail liberation from internal as well as external factors: the unfree political system of an earlier day, the clan system and ancestors revered by Confucianism, the religious system which ranged from worship of the ruler of the heavens to worship of various deities and spirits, and various brands of popular Buddhism.

A few points must now be elaborated in a bit more detail. First of all, it should be noted that Mao's values were both spiritual and material. In the last analysis his concern was with collective values. Private, individualistic goals were to be sacrificed so that people could work together for the greater objectives of the community. Individuals were to be selfless, to devote themselves wholly to the public good. Wholehearted dedication to the welfare of others was demanded. At the same time, however, people were to strive for adequate clothing, food, and fuel. There was to be a decent burial for all the deceased, and decent education for everyone's children. The aforementioned spiritual values are implicit in all this because such material values can only be realized if the collective spiritual values are also given concrete embodiment.

Mao, then, reversed the orthodox Marxist order. Mao's values did not grow out of the socialist revolution. Instead the revolution had to flow from personal conversion to such community-oriented values as dedication, self-sacrifice, sobriety, selfless moderation, uprightness, and service to others.

Now if we assume that to be true, we must ask where and how those communitarian values arise. Readers must first realize that in Mao's thinking there was no such thing as *the* human nature, human nature in the abstract. Human nature existed only in the concrete. In a class-based society this concrete human nature bore the marks of class. A human nature above and beyond social classes did not exist. All that existed in reality was a pre-given, concrete human person who was always undergoing development. The nature of a human person was always changeable, according to Mao. There is always the possibility of some change from the inside taking place; and such a change was more a response to mental stimuli than a mere reaction to natural or socio-economic forces. Mao believed that one could speed up the process of conversion to new values, that such changes in values were not tied to rigidly historical forms of determinism. That is why he promoted a separate school system, one which stressed such value-changes besides teaching other subjects. That is why he promoted political discussion, political study, and political criticism; that is why he also emphasized social practice. University students were to experience manual labor, and the old feudal and capitalist classes were to go to training camps. Instruction and education were to play a major role in Mao's China.

But we still face real questions. For a long time we had little empirical data about China's new men and new women. We don't know to what extent and material incentives played a role. We don't know how transferable this Chinese approach is to industrialized and underdeveloped countries. Indeed we don't know to what extent Mao's model had fully crystallized in China itself before his death, and how well it will survive the change in leadership.

Clearly China does tell underdeveloped peoples that liberation is possible, that it can be done. The personal discipline evident in China also has significance for the world at large. The Chinese do seem to cherish an underlying vision that is eschatological in nature, for they feel that their experiment has important implications for the world of the future.

Another question we might raise, however, is: Where is the transcendent, prophetic perspective so needed to keep such a hope alive? How does such a thing fit into a secularized society? China has ditched all superstition and rejected the social relevance of religions. Are human beings the only source of their own salvation and welfare? Isn't it taking the easy way out to maintain that Christ is working incognito in China? The Chinese would regard such a view as a vestige of imperialism.

Another task which remains to be done is to make clear that the freedom achieved in a secularized society does have something to do with freedom in Christ. It will only be accomplished when a Christian community arises in China once again. Living within Chinese society as it exists today, it will have to be a Christian community bearing witness to the transcendent God and God's promise of fulfillment. While this promise will be completely fulfilled only in the coming kingdom of God, we cannot fail to recognize that it has been partially fulfilled already in China and this world.[73]

There is an opening to transcendence in Mao's own thought, as I hope to show from some of his own poetry. I am interested here in his thoughts and allusions, not in his poetic style or ability. Consider these lines:

> I stand by myself
> Here in the cold autumn
> By the Xiang River,
> As it streams northward. . .
> On the wide stream,
> Jade-green and clear,
> A hundred small boats
> Struggle with the waves.
> Eagles soaring through the air,
> Fishes gliding over the shallow bottom—
> All things living in this chill air
> Are feeling sorry for their freedom.
> And I, dissatisfied with infinity,
> Ask of the green and azure earth,
> Who is the master of the waves,
> Of the human adventure?[74]

What exactly is the struggle of the boats? Why are all things feeling sorry for their freedom? What is this dissatisfaction with infinity? Why does Mao ask about the master of the waves and the human adventure? Mao's poem is suffused with the cosmic thinking of the Chinese, which suggests an answer to us. There is something higher that the Oriental approaches only by way of allusion and suggestive imagery. Mao's "system" is not a closed worldview, and certain motifs recur often. We live on hazardous waves. We are travellers who find only brief rest-stops here. As human beings we are forced to ask ourselves where all this is leading to.[75] Elsewhere Mao wrote:

> Once born, the human being
> Quickly its youth has lost,
> The sky not so fast . . .[76]

In another poem addressed to the Kunlun mountain range, he bids the mountains not to rise so high amid so much snow. He threatens to take his sword and cut it into three:

> I'll put one part in Europe,
> Offer one to America,
> And give one part back to the Orient.
> The whole world would live in Great Peace,
> Sharing your cold and your warmth.[77]

Here a transcendent ideal comes to the forefront: Great Peace for the whole world, and in particular for the three areas mentioned. Notice that one part is to be given back to the Orient. In another poem he has this to say about it: "The chill sigh of the autumn wind is still there today, but humanity has changed."[78] Despite all his criticism of Confucianism, Mao wrote the following in 1956: "Even as the Master stood by the river and said: we float through life as did he."[79]

After thirty-two years had gone by, Mao returned to his home town of Shaoshan in 1959. The visit evoked poetic thoughts. He cursed the water streaming by so fast, but he felt that much had been accomplished through the sacrifices of many people: Tyranny had been overthrown, and a new heaven and earth had been opened up:

> Thanks to the willingness and sacrifice of many,
> I may bid the sun and moon
> To stand in a new heaven.
> Now rice and vegetables are seen to wave . . .
> And heroes from everywhere return
> To quiet, domestic adventures.[80]

Mao's feel for the cosmos is evident in many of his poems. Here I will merely cite a few lines from two poems:

> The human being grows old all too quickly, but not Nature.
> Year after year the Double Nine returns . . .
> The yellow blossoms on the battlefield
> Acquire a sweeter scent. . . .[81]

> Even sitting still, I travel with the earth ten
> Thousand miles a day.
> Far off in the sky I glimpse myriad Milky Ways.[82]

Was it perhaps the cosmos and its message that gave Mao the strength to carry on the struggle for his people's liberation over many decades? Can we here glimpse an answer to our question about the presence or absence of a transcendent dimension in Mao's thought? Is that the element of transcendence which could keep the hopes of his people alive? To answer such questions, we will have to probe deeply into the Chinese and Oriental modes of feeling and expression. We cannot judge them a priori in terms of our own

Western categories. Even Mao Tse-Tung, for example, spoke about a new heaven! But he did so in very concrete terms, which were very much in line with the thought, culture, and religion of his own people.

POSSIBLE LESSONS FOR US

After this lengthy but necessary introduction, I come to our basic questions. What did Mao's ideal of the new human being have to tell us? Is there some message in it for us? There has been much consultation and discussion about this subject, and the literature is growing. It has been under study by Pro Mundi Vita, the research institute of the Roman Catholic Church located in Brussels, by the Lutheran World Federation in Geneva, and by a department of the National Council of Churches in the United States. European Christians concerned about China are also studying the matter on both the national and international levels.[83] We can no longer disregard the questions posed to us by China, and we certainly cannot fall back into older, outworn attitudes. However, much study and research will be needed if we are to develop a new and better attitude. With one-fourth of the world's population, China cannot be overlooked by us Christians, even though some people within the various Christian Churches oppose any rapprochement.

Of particular interest to us in Mao's vision of the new man and the new woman is the fact that personal spiritual renewal must precede sociopolitical and economic changes. There is an ongoing dialectics between the two poles, a dialectics which is sustained by the revolutionary process itself. This represents a great change from orthodox Marxism of the classic brand, and also from the static outlook which prevailed in the China of old. Mao was fully aware that the Chinese were not free human beings because of various internal and external factors. He wanted liberation and the establishment of a new nation. Every individual was to serve this cause of the Chinese people as a whole. In the last analysis he was concerned with collective values, but those values were to be achieved through the total dedication of individuals. He wanted people to be selfless, to throw off the shackles of enslavement and become leaders. They were to discard the old Confucian political system, their old religions, and the dominating influence of their ancestors. The public welfare was to take first place, and it was to be served with total dedication. Mao also spoke about sobriety, moderation, self-control, and uprightness. People displaying such qualities would be working towards the establishment of a real community. They would be promoting tranquillity, justice, equality (even in material things), happiness, and world peace. All of this could come about if people underwent a conversion of mind, heart, and spirit.

Mao also talked about a cosmic struggle between the forces of good and the forces of evil. He was fully aware of the weakness of the human person. We must be constantly on our guard against opposing forces both within the human person and in surrounding societal structures. Hence the revolution would have to be an ongoing one.

Now it seems to me that we in the West can learn much from these two points: i.e., the ongoing dialectics between spiritual and material values, and the perduring struggle between good and evil in human beings and in societal structures. Must we not seem awfully materialistic to the Chinese? Must we not also seem awfully utopian, insofar as we assume that economic and sociopolitical measures alone will give us the new society we seek? We Christians should be able to detect an attitude of *kenosis* in Mao's vision of human life. For, as he saw it, individuals had to empty themselves and open up to others. Or, as Jesus put it: "Anyone who finds his life will lose it; anyone who loses his life for my sake will find it" (Matt. 10:39).

I suppose that some people will accuse me of excessive enthusiasm for Mao. They will say, as did the 1974 Berlin Ecumenical Declaration, that some Christians want to discard Jesus Christ and replace him with an Anti-Christ.[84] Opponents of any openness to China claim that no good came out of the events of the past thirty years in China; and they have no memory of what went on there over the past century and more. They talk about the cruelties of the Communist regime, but they never say anything about the cruelties connected with the religious wars in the West!

One can detect a feeling of deep anxiety in all such remarks which hint at Communist infiltration. These people suggest that we are trying to get rid of the historical Jesus as a description or model of the new human being for today. Quite the opposite is true! We maintain that Christology must still remain the critical norm in trying to interpret any modern conception of the new human being. Indeed we can go further and suggest that anxiety-ridden Christians lack the courage to criticize their own past history in China and to offer positive praise for China's sound achievements in the past thirty years. Evil and sinfulness remain, but even Mao himself spoke about the continuing struggle between good and evil.

POSSIBLE CHRISTIAN CONTRIBUTIONS TO CHINA

I do not advocate uncritical veneration of Mao, which may well have had its day even in China itself. I am not going to suggest that Mao was one small step away from Christianity because he used words that are familiar to Christians. I know that it is nature mysticism and Confucian ideals, not Christianity, that underlie his worldview. But some of the resemblances are striking nevertheless. Let me offer a few comments here, while insisting once again that much remains for further and deeper study and contact.

A healthy starting point for any dialogue with China might well be common human values. They must be viewed as such, not labelled Christian right from the start. In trying to establish those values, we will see where the similarities and differences lie. Human freedom, for example, might come up in our dialogue. Were people free to criticize Chairman Mao during his lifetime? Are they free to criticize the present Chinese leadership? Can the Chinese freely debate such issues as the proper model of the human being and the societal order? The Chinese certainly have freed themselves from older forms of societal and foreign oppression. But is it possible that social pressure prevents the Chinese, as individuals, from exercising their new freedom in their personal lives? We Christians might also ask ourselves what freedom really means in Christianity. We might ponder how Christianity could lead China to an even greater measure of freedom than it has already attained.

We must also be careful about equating Mao's "new heaven" with the Christian "kingdom of God," the latter being the great consummation for Christian people of faith. Any such easy way out would prove ineffective and abrasive in the end. There have been achievements in China which point towards greater justice, equality, peace, and happiness. But it seems that the grounding of those achievements on a transcendent perspective is vague and weak at best, and there is still some question as to how enduring they can be on such a basis. That does not prevent us from seeing God at work in all the good that has taken place in China. But any future Christian community in China will have to bear witness in dialogue to God's ultimate and definitive work: his kingdom.

We must also not be too quick to equate Mao's Long March with the Hebrew Exodus from Egypt, much less to equate Mao with Moses. That is going too far. It will put off both the Chinese and Christians. But that does not mean that there aren't similarities of some sort. In dialogue with the Chinese we will be able to exchange experiences and get a clearer picture of the whole matter. We cannot simply baptize or christen Maoism. In dialogue we would do much better to try to appreciate the underlying basis of Maoism and the Chinese Communist approach. I think we will find much that is authentically Chinese: e.g., a basic optimism about human nature as opposed to the more reserved attitude of Christianity. The latter believes in the possibility of human fulfillment too, but it is perhaps more mindful of the obstacles involved. Conscious of human frailty, it puts the stress on God's grace and help.

Another topic for dialogue is the Christian image of the Church: i.e., ecclesiology. In the past China dealt with many different Churches. Despite all the good they may have done, there was much to find fault with in their way of living. When and if such Christian communities come to life in China again, they will have to avoid an excessively institutional cast. They will have to identify with the work of God's Spirit without equating that Spirit exclusively with the Christian Church. They will then be free to encounter the activity of God's Spirit elsewhere as well, and that could lead to fruitful dialogue. In short, we must foster communication at every level and pay particular attention to horizontal communication.

God's word and the propagation of his message take place amid the circumstances of history. We will have to discover what those circumstances are in China here and now. We cannot go in for polarization. Our outlook must be open and humble. We must realize that certain elements in a communist or socialist view of the world, humanity, and history are not totally opposed to Christian convictions. We must be prepared to learn from the Chinese and their experiments. We must be able to detect a note of religious dedication in their efforts. It may not be fully worked out or crystallized, but it is there and it is worthwhile. What is going on in China certainly does not stand outside the bounds of salvation history. Great progress has been made away from the old China of the past.

There are questions, of course. Is human welfare so subordinated to the prevailing ideology that further progress is impeded? Are revolution and re-construction the only program for liberation in the sociopolitical order? I sympathize with the theology of hope and the theology of liberation, in which traces of Marxist inspiration can be found. They have taught us once again to take seriously our Christian responsibility for the sociopolitical order. But the question of violence in revolutionary activity remains unresolved, and there is no doubt that Christian living cannot be reduced one-sidedly to mere political activism.[85]

13

The Renewing Force of a Dialogic Approach

In the preceding chapters of Part Two I have consistently used the same approach. To be fair to members of other religions, I first did the best I could to sketch a typology of their conception of human salvation. I made no attempt to play off one conception within a given religion or worldview against others. I have tried to go way beneath the surface, and that was only possible at all after much study of history and the science of religions. I tried to get to the core of other people's views of God, humanity, and the world, insofar as those views are perduringly present.

My second step was to enter into dialogue with those various religions and worldviews. It entailed two basic steps. First I asked: What is the significance and relevance of this particular typology for us Christians? Then I modestly tried to point out ways in which Christians might enter into a comprehensive dialogue about salvation with this other religion, starting out from the salvific data and values which they possess in Christ. It strikes me that this is a fair approach, one which does justice to other religions and to Christianity.

To conclude Part Two, I would like to focus on several points. First of all, it should be clear by now that I am advocating a comprehensive dialogue about salvation. I am not talking about a merely religious encounter that focuses on pertinent religious exchanges. Nor am I talking about a merely sociopolitical or economic approach to human welfare and salvation. From what has been said in the previous chapters, it should be clear that both approaches to salvation are closely interconnected and mutually related in every religion and worldview that I have discussed. Again and again we have seen that religion is a motivating force, prompting people to be salvifically present and active on various fronts in the world of human beings.

Perhaps this fact finds clearest expression in Maoism. The socialist revolution must come, but it does not come by imposing a new sociopolitical and economic system on people; it comes through a thoroughgoing series of spiritual changes in human individuals themselves. The new human being comes first. As we have seen again and again in Part Two, salvation is a totality embracing both material and spiritual factors.

As I see it, there is a lesson here for modern Christianity. It should become conscious once again of the real task that it has. If it confines itself merely to religion, it will quickly become irrelevant for the world. If, on the other hand, Christianity is reduced to sociopolitical or economic activism, it will soon lose its inner force and its perseverance. Thus dialogue will undergird modern Christianity in its efforts to integrate all areas of life and to find its own proper mission. Salvation once again has been brought into relationship with the reality of human existence, as it was in the Old Testament and in the preaching of Jesus and his first disciples. Secularization has contributed much to this process. It has planted our feet firmly on the ground and enabled us to comprehend and live pristine Christianity once again. Salvation means striving for a promised land of happiness and peace. It means moving towards a kingdom of God marked by justice in personal and societal relations, peace between human beings and nations, and unity among all human beings. That is not merely a glimpse of some far distant future. It is also an ongoing, constantly renewed effort to realize those goals here and now in the face of opposing tendencies and forces.

Thus the historical dimension of total and comprehensive salvation comes to the fore once again. History has become salvation history. As Christians, we are constantly trying to overcome our experience of impotence by living in the hope and expectation of God's own power. It is God's strength that will bring all things to a good conclusion in the completed kingdom of God, but without our persevering efforts the latter will never be established. Our sense of human and Christian responsibility for the world has grown, and it now takes on many forms. What we manage to achieve in the way of salvation now is a sign of the great salvation to come. Here is the task facing Christian mission efforts, therefore. Through a process of dialogue with the practices and conceptions of salvation to be found in other religions and worldviews, we must try to inject Christian hope and renewed strength into them as they now stand. Mission work, in the form of a dialogue concerning total, comprehensive salvation, has a future.

In this task Christians make use of three intermediaries. The first is christology. Christians know that they are associated with other human beings in a common human history. They express this in Christian terms by thinking and working in terms of the Body of Christ. Through incorporation into this Body, the community and solidarity of single individuals become comprehensible—so much so that any collective absorption of the individual must be ruled out. Here the person of the risen Lord plays an important role. As the resurrected Lord, he not only continues his life on earth but also remains in an immediate relationship with the present day. He lives! The salvific activity of the Lord is not restricted to the past; it continues in our salvific work within his Body.

The second intermediary, ecclesiology, builds upon christology. The universal significance of the Christ-happening precedes all ecclesial mediations. But the Church and its service to redemption is necessary. For, without concrete human witnesses to salvation, people would merely have a supernatural alibi for shunning responsibility. The whole people of God has the mission of salvation, which has a totally human content. The various services within that salvific mission must not be distinguished in terms of temporal-earthly on the one hand and spiritual-eternal on the other. Human beings know that they experience themselves as corporeal, worldly beings in their personal existence, and hence also in their eternal existence. So we must begin with the mission of total salvation, and only then start to differentiate strands within it. That is why Vatican II referred to the Church as the sacrament of the world as well. The Church's mission is to introduce everywhere unity, peace, justice, and love; to "infect" the world with its ideals. The Church is the sacrament "of intimate union with God and of the unity of the whole human race" (LG 1 and 48). One could also say that the Church is the sacrament of peace. This all indicates that the Church must work together with other religions and philosophies of life. The Church is not alone in this work, but it is the promoter and advocate of unity and peace among human beings. This is of great importance in terms of mission.

The third intermediary is the Holy Spirit. The Spirit is not a parallel force, but one that suffuses the other intermediaries and is related to them. The Spirit renders present the origin, person, and history of Jesus, his words and his actions; but he prevents all forms of historical petrification and tries to ensure that the presence of Christ will ever remain new and inspiring. The Spirit points towards the future, keeping alive the eschatological reality that began with the Lord's resurrection.

Thus, in and through the risen Lord, his Church, his Spirit, and the mutual interrelationship of all three, the dialogue about total and comprehensive salvation penetrates the whole world. Service on behalf of salvation, of Christian salvation, consists in proclamation, ministry (*diakonia*), and committed involvement in society. And whether one focuses on human capabilities or human failings, Christian witness to salvation soon arrives at the same borderline-limits. Indeed long before it arrives at those limits, Christian consciousness of salvation and Christian witness experiences itself being sustained by the life and mandate of the risen Lord and his Spirit, who resurrects the world and human beings from death.[86]

Thus this comprehensive dialogue about salvation reveals to us Christian developmental values that are both spiritual and material. They are implicit in all that has been said above, but here I should like to explicate a few of them once again. First of all, Judeo-Christian revelation has given us a particular concept of the person. This notion stresses the immeasurable worth of the person, its freedom and uniqueness, while at the same time underlining the fact that the person is part of a larger whole: i.e., the people of God, the Body of Christ. It is in the latter that Christians find their strength. They know that in their struggle they are united with Jesus, the risen Lord, who lives in their community. This is a Judeo-Christian datum about salvation that must be shared, in dialogue with other religions and philosophies of life about their different views of salvation. In this way the impulses and expectations of others can be synthesized and fulfilled.

Another developmental value in the Judeo-Christian tradition is our conception of history and time, of the future. Coming from the past and living in the present, Christians continue to keep their eyes on, and to work towards, a future that surpasses all human possibilities. The kingdom of God waits for them. That remains their hope, and they work on its behalf unceasingly. In dialogue Christians approach other religions, reinforcing small impulses in the same direction or encouraging greater efforts. Salvation is worked out in and within history. This point is not seen by some religions, such as Hinduism and Buddhism. It can also add something to any religious outlook, such as that to be found in Africa, which focuses merely on the ancestral past and its impact today. The latter view, with its very restricted view of the future, does not really do justice to the all-embracing nature of salvation and of the human task in this world.

A third developmental value offered by Judeo-Christian revelation is its view of the world. The world is not some place to withdraw from. It is not condemned in negative terms as a place of punishment and reincarnation. The world is not unsalvific because it keeps us from rising to the Absolute and nirvana. The world is, in fact, the place where we are able to work out our salvation by an ongoing willingness to serve each other. We find the grace and strength to do this in the resurrected Lord. With us he lives for a future in which all our human hopes will be fulfilled, in which we will find justice, peace, love, unity, and so forth.

A fourth Judeo-Christian value is the notion of community and its reality. The Christian community gathered around the living, resurrected Lord is a Church, from which comes a force for unity and peace among all human beings. The Church is the sacrament of unity and peace for all human beings. It does not stand off by itself. Moving out in an ever-widening circle, it seeks to bring all these values into dialogue with other religions and worldviews. It "infects" the world, hoping thereby to arrive at a quantitative approximation as well, but in a very different way than once upon a time. This time it will work together with all those who are involved in the same task, including secular and religious institutions on the national and international levels. It does not claim any exclusive right here, only a motivating force deriving from the Spirit of Jesus.[87]

Before I close, I want to say a few words about the renewing or revitalizing force of real dialogue. My preceding treatment may have indicated already how I view the matter. Dialogue is revitalizing for the Church or the Christian community insofar as it brings to the fore the ever new yet age-old tasks. Through dialogue about total, comprehensive salvation, the Church again comes into relationship with the world, human beings, religions, and worldviews. The Church can again be the pioneer on the road to a better world, spearheading the drive and inspiring others. Christians, too, emerge from dialogue as better, provided they are willing to be vulnerable and not to withdraw into some ivory tower.

Such a dialogue is revitalizing for other religions and worldviews as well. On the one hand they will see that they have much to offer the world, and Christians too. On the other hand they will see their own desires, initiatives, and efforts fulfilled in the living Jesus and his community. Like Christians, non-Christians willing to be vulnerable will come to see their need for humility and correction. They will experience their own frailty and sinfulness.

One of the benchmarks of the revitalizing force of such a comprehensive dialogue is what I have repeatedly called the maieutic approach. It is now time for me to go into this a bit more deeply. The word "maieutic" comes from Greek, and it originally meant "to serve as a midwife." Well, the new world and the new human being must be born out of two profound encounters. One is with the risen Lord. This encounter will give them strength, courage, and hope. Paying heed to him and his message of salvation, they will be able to attain a full, new life. The second encounter is with the deepest inspiration which lies buried in those religions and worldviews, but which has sometimes been obscured by centuries-long developments. People will have to go down deep inside themselves and let their good impulses come to new life.

Christianity must help non-Christian religions in this process. Sometimes, as we saw in the case of Islam, it is very difficult to detach oneself from traditional insights that pose obstacles to a more comprehensive view of salvation. That is why my approach to other religions in Part Two was typological, why I did not go into historical developments and reform movements that may have obscured the authentic underlying desire and thrust of a given religion. They must be reborn out of themselves, finding new life through a dialogue with Judeo-Christian values.[88]

Let me briefly summarize what I have tried to get across so far. Every religion is a response to God's self-communication in nature, history, or the person of our Lord. God issues a universal invitation to all. It goes so far that God asks all to meet him ultimately in Jesus, who is the Way. Religions are Ways to salvation, but as yet not always to total, comprehensive salvation. Thus Christians are continually on the road, moving towards the other side, towards the new Jerusalem. Going along this Way, they encounter other human beings who are also on the way. They include all those we have met in this book, from Muslims to Maoists. The Way and the Ways meet in an encounter to further the well-being of all humanity. But each has its own contribution to make. Thus the Church, or the Churches, is no complete fulfillment; neither is present-day Christianity. We still look forward to a time of unity and fulfillment. The same process is also taking place within our own boundaries, where so many non-Christians live and where so many no longer know the Way.

By way of conclusion here, I would urge the Churches in the world to view their mission in this new context of the world. Let them try to detach the Judeo-Christian vision of God, humanity, and the world from the Western context and go back to the authentic Way. Only then will they manage to comprehend the other Ways from inside. Only then will they be in a position to link up the message of Jesus with those other Ways. Let the Churches work together on this task and offer each other help, since it is so enriching for both sides.

This may also help to detach us from older historical categories that have become petrified, that have made us incomprehensible to many human beings in our own environs and beyond. The core of the message must be pinpointed in and through dialogue. It must again become flesh and blood, even in our own small world. It seems to me that mission, in the form of a dialogue about full and complete salvation for all humanity, is a good, modern term for the worldwide task that faces us on every continent, including our home continent.[89]

PART THREE

No Dead-End Way:
Local Churches in Dialogue
with Their Surroundings

We have been talking about a dialogue that would deal with the total salvation of human beings. Such a dialogue would entail committed action by Christians and the other participants. The dialogue would have to produce results, and those results should be tangible.

As I have already suggested, it is in local Churches that those results should take visible shape and form. Those Churches draw on the rich resources that God has given each and every people, and that have found their fulfillment in the richness offered to us in Jesus Christ. Then they repeatedly exhibit new and original ways of living as a Church. Their individual form of ecclesial life is integrated into the context of their religious, cultural, social, and political milieu. A new birth will take place out of the dialogue between native, God-given resources and the richness offered to us in Christ. Thus I am pleading for a grass-roots Church, a Church of the people built from the bottom up, a Church that is at home in its milieu, a Church that offers its own particular embodiment of God's catholic (i.e., universal) salvific work.

Here in Part Three I propose to explore to what extent traces of all this can already be detected. The local Church in the context of its milieu is the Church in which I believe. It is the Church of the future. But that does not mean that we cannot see initiatives in that direction already. By bringing the data together here, I hope to encourage further work along those lines.

Perhaps I can give some direction to a development which I regard as salutary and providential in our time. And of course this vision and this reality compel us once again to reflect upon the oneness of the Church.

From the above remarks it should be clear that we must begin with some basic considerations about what is called "ecclesiogenesis" in Latin America. The big question is: Where and how does Church enter the picture? How and where does it really arise? That will be the subject of Chapter 14. I hope that Europeans and North Americans will not be upset by the fact that I mainly draw my data from Churches on other continents. It may do us good to become acquainted with the thinking and activity of other Churches, for that will show us how relevant our own views and activities are. There are Churches outside the Western hemisphere, too, and they are very active and dynamic; but their voices rarely get through to us. The thoughts and models furnished by the Third World might prompt us to reflect anew on these matters. Mutual assistance by the Churches is one aspect of the new relationship that is developing between them.

I shall then proceed to discuss particular aspects of the local Church. We see the rise of native theologies, liturgical forms, and prayers. Distinctive, indigenous views of church offices are being discussed and implemented. There is a desire to serve the national and international community in distinctive ways, which sometimes diverge sharply from our Western way of doing things.

I could go on to mention many things, but obviously I must restrict my treatment here. I cannot cover all possible examples, nor delve into all the related literature. What I can do here, however, is point out the basic line of development whereby the Church develops into Churches that are at home in their milieu. This is not to suggest that such is already the case everywhere. I am realistic enough to know that there are obstacles, thanks to my own personal experience with Third World Churches and my contacts with students from the Third World.

My treatment, then, is meant to offer a sign of hope. It suggests that things can be different, and that changes are indeed taking place. It is meant to encourage two types of people. First of all, it offers an account of what is actually being done by those who have struck out on a new pathway. We can hope that this will encourage them to further effort. Secondly, it is meant for those who are suspicious of the new trends and find it hard to handle the stresses involved. We can hope that it will encourage them to look for the positive side in the new developments, to trust them a bit, and to experiment with them on their own. We learn by doing. By experimenting, we can often get rid of the inhibitions we feel inside.

Here again a major factor will be a willingness to dialogue with the living experience of many young Churches. And in the final Chapter I shall make a point of showing how we still believe in the oneness of the Church of Jesus Christ, and how we propose that this oneness is to be realized in the actual practice of ecclesial life.

14

Where and How Does Church Enter the Picture?

Later in this section of the book I will return to the matter of the unity of the Church. Of course the issue cannot be sidestepped completely in our attempt to describe where and how Churches come into being. One cannot talk about particular or local Churches without keeping in mind *the* Church, because the relationship between the two cannot be overlooked.

It is perhaps Leonardo Boff, the Brazilian theologian, who has expressed the point most clearly and explicitly. He writes: "The particular Church is wholly Church, but it is not the whole Church."[1] That may sound a bit mysterious on first reading, but his words embody a profound truth and point to a profound reality. He explains it in the following terms. The particular, or local, Church is wholly Church because the mystery of salvation is fully present in each particular Church. But it is not the whole Church because no single particular Church mirrors all the richness of the mystery of salvation. The latter can and must find expression in other particular Churches in all their varying and distinctive forms. In the early Christian centuries this was very much so, and the Catholic Churches of the Eastern rites show this variety. The identification of the universal Church with *one* local Church (the Church of Rome) is *one* moment and *one* historical concretization of the universal Church in the West. Historically speaking, we know that meant the dominion of sameness: one language, one liturgy, one code of canon law, and one way of doing theology. The result was the universalization of the particular Church, i.e., of the local Church of Rome. In the course of history, then, the particular Church of Rome tended to impose itself on all the particular Churches. But in fact it still continued to be a particular Church! Universality does not mean uniform homogenization. It means openness to all sides, and particularly to the salvation mystery which reveals itself in each local Church. Without that sort of openness and community a particular Church ceases to be Church, because it ceases to be universal.

My use of the word "particular" may strike readers as odd. It stands in contrast here to the term "universal." My use here is based on the conciliar documents of Vatican II. There the same term "particular" is used to refer to several different realities. Most of the time it refers to larger entities or areas possessing cultural unity: e.g., a diocese or an episcopal conference (*Ad Gentes* 22). The stress is on diversity in unity, and the conciliar documents talk about sociocultural areas and "young" particular Churches. But the conciliar documents also use the term "particular" in connection with the missionary duty of smaller Christian communities. They talk about the duties of the People of God who are living in dioceses and parishes (*Ad Gentes* 37).

My impression is that Vatican II did not pursue this line of thought down to the level of basic ecclesial communities. As far as I can see, the latter are a postconciliar development, a further elaboration of the whole notion of diversity-in-unity. In Part Three of this book, I shall use the notion of "particular" Church in all those varied senses. I shall have to talk about basic ecclesial communities, in which case the meaning of the term will be clear. But I shall also be talking about African theology and Indian Christology. In that case I will be using the notion of a particular Church in a broader sense. I will be talking about a larger sociocultural unit, which may embrace one diocese, several dioceses, an episcopal conference, or even several episcopal conferences on one continent.

In the present chapter the distinction is not of any great importance, though it lurks in the background. Here we want to consider where and how Churches arise, and all the aforementioned gradations are Churches.[2] Even basic ecclesial communities are Churches, as they themselves make plain. It is their ecclesial nature that sets them apart from other groups formed to promote sports, music, folklore, and so forth. They are church realities because they are a community response, based on Christian faith, to the gospel summons to conversion and salvation. Religious and Christian inspiration is the thing that binds the people together and gives the group its various goals and its evangelizing characteristics. The basic ecclesial community sees itself as the presence of the Church, as a communal living out of the gospel, as an organism and an organization promoting salvation and liberation in the world. The Church is formed when human beings pay heed to Jesus Christ's summons to salvation, unite in community, profess the same faith, celebrate the same eschatological liberation, and try to live their lives in the following of Jesus Christ.[3]

In exploring the where and how of the true origins of the Church, we have good reason to focus our attention specifically on basic ecclesial communities. It is not simply a matter of practical necessity, of some need to tackle the issue differently. We are dealing here with a new vision of what it means to be a Church, of ecclesiality; and this new vision may be of the greatest importance for the universal Church and the future of the Christian faith. It is important that we join in taking this turn, and that we do so with all our heart. The following remarks are meant to point up the legitimacy of this turn to the grass-roots Church, the Church built from the bottom up.

History can teach us a great deal, though of course we cannot simply reconstruct past history. We must be a Church in our own time and situation. Bishop G. Matagrin, Vice-President of the French episcopal conference, put it this way in 1976:

> We are talking about a revolution in the Copernican sense of the word, a turnabout that ties in with the theology of the Church understood as the People of God. We are talking about a shift from a Church based on the top of a pyramid, a Church of bishops and priests, to a Church based on the ground level, on the community of the baptized. This must be linked up with what we said about the need to restore community ties by creating more groups, cooperative ventures, and communities. The image of a Church which puts too much stress on the vertical relationship between the individual believer and the priest—the latter being regarded as the only one who exercises responsibility—must be replaced with the image of a Church built on Christians who embody solidarity in groups and nuclear communities. These Christians and their groupings must be seen as the basis of the Church, arising out of their communal faith and impelled by their common will to accept responsibility for the life and mission of the Church.[4]

We are sharply reminded of the Churches that came into being in the early days of Christian history: the Church of Jerusalem, the Church of Antioch, and a host of others. We are reminded of Paul's *modus operandi*. His aim was to set up self-reliant Churches as quickly as possible and then move on. Paul got things going, came back to visit perhaps, or maybe sent a letter. In little more than a decade he started Churches in four provinces of the Roman Empire: Galatia, Macedonia, Achaia, and Asia. He let those Churches make their own history. What is noteworthy is the fact that they were financially independent, practicing charity through the use of their own resources. Their charitable generosity to the Church of Jerusalem is a case in point. Moreover, despite the distances they maintained fraternal relations. Greetings were passed (1 Cor. 16:19) and letters were exchanged (Col. 4:16). They saw themselves as the one Church of the holy and elect (Rom. 1:7; 1 Cor. 1:2). Distinctive individuality and character were fully developed. Each had to listen to the Spirit even when a reprimand was involved, as was the case in the seven letters to the Churches (Rev. 2–3). Each Church displayed something of God's richness and fullness.[5]

In the first centuries of Christian history there were many Churches which resulted from an enculturation or incarnation in the surrounding culture: e.g., the Syrian, the Greek, the Latin, the Coptic, the Armenian, the Ethiopian, and the Indian. They were individual forms of ecclesiality with their own liturgy, theology, and church structure. The Irish Church, for example, had its own distinctive ecclesial model for many years, and it spread to

Europe through the work of missionaries. This basic model was operative up to the twelfth century:

> There was continuity between the small domestic communities of the first few centuries, where 20 to 60 Christians came together, and the development of parish-dioceses in small towns or the rural parishes which were "founded" by rulers, feudal lords, abbeys or chapters, and which rarely had more than 300 members.[6]

From the twelfth century on, however, towns became increasingly important centers of trade and commerce. The clergy tended to become a distinct and separate estate, enjoying power through its monopoly of education, its sacred qualifications, its civil functions, and its concentration of financial resources. The change took place slowly, gradually taking on a universal character. Then the medieval parochial structure itself ran into problems, as reform and reformation movements went hand in hand with rapid changes in social and ecclesial life. Existing relations were disrupted by increasing urbanization, a growing scientific attitude towards nature, and estrangement between the laity and the clergy. The great social upheaval of the French Revolution brought divisions between church and state, and between parish and community.

The medieval parochial structure faced its biggest confrontation in the changes that began to take place in the nineteenth century and continued into the twentieth. Large numbers of people moved to the cities, and the megalopolis began to make its appearance. A few comparative figures will make this clear:

> In the fourteenth century . . . Paris had 70,000 to 90,000 (?) inhabitants, Ghent about 50,000, Bruges about 35,000, and London between 35,000 and 40,000 (?). In 1500 no single city in what is now the Netherlands had more than 20,000 inhabitants; indeed only five cities had around 10,000. In the fourteenth century Italy was the most urbanized part of Europe. But even Italy had only four cities with more than 50,000 inhabitants: Milan, Naples, Venice, and Florence. Cologne, with 15,000 inhabitants in the thirteenth century and 30–40,000 in the fifteenth century, was by far the largest city in Germany.[7]

Everyone knows how large Western cities are now, and the same problem applies to other continents as well. In 1980 the urban population of the world was around 693.4 million. The old nineteenth-century model of the rural mission has been completely undermined. And we all know how difficult it is to get the "urban apostolate" on its feet![8]

The old ideal of a people's church based on small groups of human beings who know each other is going by the boards. Now we have huge administrative units. The supply of priests is meager, and even they are moving away from village centers to the big cities. That is why people are again looking for communities tailored to a more human dimension. This brief historical overview indicates where and how Churches are arising today, and why they are taking the form of basic ecclesial communities. The Church is springing up from the grass-roots level because the larger units—parishes and dioceses—have become too big and are no longer viable.

This does not mean, however, that we are going back to the past. It is not a matter of trying to resurrect the small rural communities or town groups of the past. We are living in a new era with its own demands. We may well grant that a basic reorientation of parish life was attempted by Catholic Action, the movement for liturgical renewal, the worker-priest movement, and the theology of secular realities. We may also grant that great efforts were made by some theologians, even before Vatican II: e.g., by De Lubac, Congar, and Karl Rahner. There was the prophetic cry of the book entitled *France: A Mission Land* (1943), and the pastoral emphasis of Michonneau in describing the parish as a missionary community in 1945.[9] All these things created a climate for making change possible, but they do not explain the rise of basic ecclesial communities in our own era.

The basic ecclesial communities under discussion here stand in a dialectical relationship with the larger church institution embodied in parish and diocese. They are bringing the institution back to life from the bottom up, and they cannot do without the support of the larger institution. In later chapters we shall see in detail how this is being achieved in different lands and continents. The point is that community and institution always go hand in hand, and the question is exactly how that takes place. It is the combined interplay of the two that is the distinctive feature of our era, and this interplay can assume different forms. I shall come back to this matter in the last chapter, when I consider what the unity or oneness of the Church might mean today.

The brief historical sketch given above sheds some light on the rise of basic ecclesial communities. Now we must explore history a bit more deeply. It is not just historical insight that has led to the rise of such ecclesial communities. At least equally important is a new vision of ecclesiality, of what it means to be a Church. From a theological standpoint basic ecclesial communities signify a new ecclesiological experiment, a revived feeling of what a Church really is. In short, they represent the action of the Holy Spirit against the backdrop and horizon of our own time and its needs. So we must critically examine our earlier theological and pastoral conceptions and open up to the new thing which the Holy Spirit is effecting in our midst. At the same time we must keep our critical sense alert so that we may be able to distinguish true and authentic approaches from false ones. What we are seeing today is a new type of church institutionalization. As Clark puts it:

> The holistic approach gives us the vantage point from which to ask what are the most important tasks facing the Church today. It is not enough to deal with the problems (clerical celibacy, papal authority, birth con-

trol). Nor is it enough to develop new activities (parish councils, ecumenical dialogue, parent-educator programs). These may be important, but they can be handled only in the context of an overall strategy
or blueprint for building the Church. What is needed is a clear grasp of
the goal (what it is that we are trying to do in the Church today, what
ideal the Church should be heading for) and a way of bringing the
Church as a whole (the whole Church) to it. What is needed is a plan of
development that will deal with the needs of the Church in the
twentieth-century world.[10]

What ideal ought the Church be heading for? Boff has written some penetrating remarks on this very question. He raises such questions as the following. Is it possible for us to recover and recognize the Church once again?
Wasn't the Church founded by Jesus Christ and provided with the necessary
structures? May we enjoy a taste of the essence of the Church? Must we hold
fast to the *de facto* way in which the episcopate functions, with priests as
administrators of the sacraments? Hasn't this led to the immaturity of the
People of God, to dependence on one class? Or must the people rediscover
the sacramental (symbolic) significance of life, eliminate clericalism (not the
priesthood), and aim at taking control over their own care? Can we move in
that direction without doing harm to the Church willed by Jesus? Or are we
too quick to assume that something was fixed and established once and for all
by Jesus? Is there room for facing up to new needs in new times, for meeting
the obligations of the Church in today's world?
When we say that the Church is a structured community, where should we
place our emphasis: on the aspect of structure or the aspect of community? If
we stress structure, then we get a Church running from the top down: pope,
bishop, priest, deacon, religious, and lay person. This view has prevailed as
the official one in the West for centuries. But if the stress properly should be
on the aspect of community, then the Church is a community of brotherhood,
mutual relations, and participation. The hierarchy is realized within the community and it is meant to benefit the community. Jesus' chief aim was to
establish brotherhood, mutual participation, and community between human beings. No believer doubts that the Church was founded by Jesus Christ.
The real question is whether he established it once and for all on certain
specific structures. Did the historical Jesus do that?
More recent theological and exegetical studies show us the way here. Jesus
felt that he himself had been sent solely to the people of Israel. Could he have
been contemplating the establishment of a community that would be one
among the many already existing in Israel? It seems quite certain that Jesus
saw the end-time as near (imminent eschatology). How, then, could he establish a Church that was institutionally organized and clearly defined in historical terms? Jesus' preaching focused on the idea of the Kingdom of God,
which was meant to be universal and cosmic. How, then, did the Church
come into being as a reduced and ambiguous actualization of God's

Kingdom? According to the New Testament, isn't it the Kingdom of God, not the Church, that is the ultimate aim of God's plan and the perfected image of salvation for the whole world? Viewed in terms of Jesus' preaching, is the Church a direct consequence of that preaching on the Kingdom, or is it a tiresome replacement which he did not will? Is the Church the fruit of disenchantment or a realized implementation?

Modern exegesis does not simply pose such suggestive questions. It also offers certain matters as established. Catholic exegetes are agreed that in the New Testament talk about the Church comes only after the Lord's resurrection and through the coming of the Holy Spirit. The Church is a post-paschal datum. To be sure, through his preaching and activity Jesus laid the foundations for the appearance of that Church. Through his death and resurrection there arose a community which wished to bear witness to Jesus as the Living One. The cause and person of Jesus did not come to an end with his crucifixion. They show up later as the causes and constituents of the ecclesial community. There is a discontinuity between the preaching of the Kingdom and the Church: the death of Jesus on the cross. But there is also a continuity: the resurrection, through which Jesus Christ continues to be present.

Both moments must be stressed. The Twelve symbolize the effort to turn all Israel to the Kingdom of God. Only after the resurrection do they become apostles; only then do we get a post-paschal missionary conception. Simon becomes Peter because he is the first to proclaim the resurrection. The Church is grounded on that belief, on professed faith in the resurrection. Peter makes the Church a Church of Jews and Gentiles. He goes to Antioch. He becomes the doctrinal authority because he is entrusted with the interpretation of Jesus' teaching. But the same power of binding and loosing is also entrusted to the whole community (Matt. 16:19; 18:18). Peter is the guarantee and representative of Jesus' teaching rather than the head of the community. Here we already have a view of a grass-roots Church, a Church from the bottom up. But when people isolate the texts in question from the whole New Testament, then they end up with, not an ecclesiology, but a hierarchology: i.e., a Church viewed from the top down.

Let me bring these remarks to a conclusion. The Church is clearly a substitute for the Kingdom of God. On the one hand it is the Kingdom of God because the Risen One is present in it, testifying to the fact that death, the ultimate enemy of the Kingdom, has been defeated. On the other hand the Church is not the Kingdom because the latter is to become a reality in the (eschatological) future. There are still sick people, human beings still die, and we still have sinners and unliberated people. The Church is in the service of the Kingdom. It is the sacrament of the Kingdom, a sign and instrument of the Kingdom's appearance and realization in this world. After Israel's refusal, both the Kingdom and its instrument are in fact addressed to the world of the pagans. Like Jesus himself, his disciples must be bearers of a revolutionary idea of the Kingdom of God; and they must view its existence as a being for others, even as Jesus lived for others.

Israel's refusal has profound significance. Thanks to it, the Church was stripped of its Semitic language and outlook. The message of Jesus was translated into a Greco-Roman outlook and culture. This was completely legitimate since it concretized the fact that the Church had now become a Church of the Gentiles. Christ's return is not imminent. The Church must repeatedly preach and actualize its message about the Kingdom in a historical situation, taking into account the variations that may surface over the ages and the future that lies open. The mission of the apostles, therefore, continues in this way right up until today.

Inspired by the Holy Spirit, the apostles went out to the Gentiles. The Eucharist is the nourishment of the community, the place where the People of God partakes of Christ's body and is turned into the body of Christ. The Church arose from a decision of the apostles after Pentecost, a decision prompted by the Holy Spirit. The turn to the Gentiles was a logical conclusion after the rejection of Jesus by the Jewish people. From that time on the Church has viewed itself as a sign of salvation addressed to the whole world; its aim is to bring about the coming of the complete Kingdom of God. But that is to be done in ever new situations: first in the Greco-Roman world, later in the West of the Middle Ages, and now in the distinctive situation characterized by many different peoples and cultures.

These are the views offered by Leonardo Boff. What conclusions follow for ecclesiogenesis, for the birth of a Church? From Boff's investigation it seems that the Church arises from the context of the Christ-happening. Here Christ's death and resurrection, and the activity of the Holy Spirit, play a preponderant role. For they led the apostles to the decision to establish Christian communities, Churches, as a preparation for the full coming of God's Kingdom. It is in that sense that faith tells us that Christ founded the Church. It is a complex profession, but a correct one.

What sort of institutional form did Jesus want his Church to have? We can see that from the way the apostolic community operated under the guidance of the Holy Spirit and in response to the needs of a given situation. The episcopate, priesthood, and other functions would perdure. But it is evident that those structures are in the service of the ever-present needs of the communities: i.e., the need for unity, universality, and a link with the great witnesses of the apostolic past. More important is the lifestyle of those leaders in the ecclesial communities. They can lord it over the communities by monopolizing all the services and forms of power. They can also live within the communities, integrating their tasks and showing respect for the various charisms that are to serve the oneness of the whole body. The latter style translates the gospel lifestyle and the praxis that Jesus willed for the messianic community. The latter is supposed to maintain the presence of the risen Jesus and his Spirit; to make audible his liberating message of grace, forgiveness, and unlimited love; and to make it easy for human beings to respond to it. And it is to do this in ever changing situations. It is a process of tradition and ongoing adaptation in the course of history. Today, when we are trying to rediscover the Church, these reflections can be extraordinarily liberating. They can give rise to a new presence of the Church amid human beings, with new services, tasks, and lifestyles replacing the old, traditional ones.[11]

My concern in this chapter was to consider where and how Church enters the picture. Thanks to help from competent dogmatic theologians and exegetes, I think we have the basis for an answer to our question. The Church arises over and over again in historical situations, in imitation of what the apostles did after the Lord's resurrection and the coming of his Spirit. That points us towards tradition and inventiveness. In the coming chapters I hope to show what is happening today in the area of ecclesiogenesis.

15

Indigenous Forms of Ecclesial Life Today

Here I am restricting myself to basic ecclesial communities. There are larger associations taking shape, and I shall allude to them in passing, but they are not yet too sharply defined. I shall offer a few examples from different continents to give my readers some insight into the general phenomenon. And I shall begin with Latin America because it is there that basic ecclesial communities surfaced first and most visibly.

LATIN AMERICA

It is now common in Latin America to talk and write about basic ecclesial communities and a new Church.[12] At the time of the 1974 Synod of Bishops in Rome, almost all the Latin American representatives characterized the basic ecclesial communities as a hopeful sign.[13] One of them described a basic ecclesial community as follows: "The primary cell of the whole ecclesial structure, the center of evangelization and most important factor for human development, the formation of which demands the presence of ministers of the Word and the Eucharist . . . coming from their own ranks for their service."[14] It is a pleasure to note that this form of ecclesial existence has the basic approval of the hierarchy—which is not always the case everywhere.

The studies which I was able to consult on this topic explore the circumstances which allowed for the rise of these ecclesial communities. All sorts of revolutions have been taking place, ranging from technology to education. Changes have taken place in human beings, and the Church itself is on the move. Psychosocial relations are transforming communities.[15] After Vatican II people began to stress the social task of the Church, envisioning a more accelerated and just form of development. Among many there was a growing desire to make the Church a sort of pressure group, and this desire found inspiration in liberation theology. People came to the conviction that the Church ought to detach itself from its old ties with the economic and political forces which made real liberation for the people impossible. Naturally this led to repression and persecution by political groups.

A grass-roots constituency which lacked motivation and was often fatalistic had to be aroused to undertake a process of liberation and move towards genuine community. For this a new pastoral approach was needed. What was needed was a process of consciousness-raising that linked up with the deep-rooted religious feelings of the people, a creative synthesis of popular religion and liberation theology. This was to be effected in basic communities. Instead of planning things out for the people, the planning was to come from and through the common people themselves. They were to have their own leaders and their own tempo of growth. Respect was to be shown for their own cultural values.[16]

If it is obvious anywhere in the world that basic ecclesial communities are the outcome and fruit of an open dialogue concerned with human salvation and welfare, then it is certainly obvious in Latin America. I will not go into the theoretical justification for such communities here. Instead I think it is better to offer a few concrete examples, fully realizing that the phenomenon takes many different forms and that I can hardly cover everything. In 1976 it was estimated that the number of basic communities in Brazil was approximately 40,000, in Honduras 6,000, and in one diocese of Guatemala more than 700. They can be found all over the Latin American continent, and a special department of the Latin American Episcopal Conference (CELAM) is dedicated to the training of these groups.[17]

Dominique Barbé describes how one such basic ecclesial community arose in Brazil.[18] It happened in Osasco, in the State of Rio de Janeiro. There a group of priests began operating as worker-priests in July 1964. The first year was seen as a period of silent friendship. Only then did more deliberate evangelization begin. Fifty people took part at first, of which twenty-five remain. Attention was first focused on those who were practicing the faith, just as Paul addressed himself first to Jews. Every Sunday people met in a little chapel, seeking to reshape their faith and traditions. They wanted to move away from devotions, veneration of the saints, a passive and superstitious faith, and ignorance of Jesus Christ; to get back to the gospel message. Audio-visual techniques were used in catechesis. By 1967 it was reported that twenty-five to thirty people were participating regularly, not in the small chapel any longer but in the home of the priests. The content of the catechesis was strongly missionary in its thrust. Jesus called his apostles. Right away the question is raised: Who is this Jesus? He is a human being, God and Lord. He shares his treasures with us: first and foremost his word, his offer of life, and his bread of life. He also shares with us his most intimate things: the goodness and forgiveness of his Father, the life of the risen one that comes to revitalize our lives, his Spirit, his family and community (the Church of Jesus Christ and his witnesses).

One notices that it is precisely those elements which are missing in folk religion, and to which I called attention in Part Two, that are emphasized here.[19] Here is where a missionary attitude begins; before people turn their attention to others, they try to form themselves and get to know Jesus better.

Towards the close of 1967, a further step was taken. People were sought among those who came faithfully every Sunday who would join and take responsibility for a small group. The members of such a group would not meet in the church or rectory but in their own homes. This was a big step, since people had the idea that nothing could be done without a priest. The first two groups formed: the first basic ecclesial communities. Four or five people were to be responsible for them, and some twenty people joined them. There was a priest to assist each group, of course, but the starting point for missionary activity was to be the home, not the priest. Why? Because the family is the cell of the Church. The assumption of responsibility by lay people was a new birth, and it entailed labor pains as every birth does; but it was a healthy thing.

What were involved in the meetings of a basic ecclesial community? At first the members met every week or every two weeks. People reported what had been happening since the last meeting, then a gospel text was studied. Meetings were led by the father of the family in whose house they came together, but sometimes the lay person responsible for the whole group might have to assist him. The members dealt very concretely with the problems of that family, and then with a gospel text. This gave rise to a family spirit. People got to know each other very well because everyone can join in a conversation about the simple things of everyday life. It also gave rise to a missionary spirit insofar as each person reported what he or she had done since the last meeting. Jesus' disciples lived with him and reported to him the results of their mission. Gradually people came to experience everyday life as a part of salvation history. They began to understand that salvation is precisely for human beings here on earth, in these specific conditions of poverty. Hearts, eyes, and ears were opened up to the activity of the Spirit of Jesus. To this was added the reading of the gospel message. Sometimes it was read three times, so that it might soak in. It was amazing to see how well the people involved, often uneducated, were able to grasp the gospel message and put it into practice. The meeting then ended with a prayer, just as it had begun with a prayer. The closing prayer was a communal prayer before a picture of the risen Christ. This was designed to counteract the excessive concentration on the suffering and crucified Jesus which had characterized much folk religiosity. The Lord lives and works among us! So there is no sound reason for fatalism. The picture of the risen Lord is left with the family. It remains a center of prayer and activity until it is carried to the next family's home. So we see coming back the home-churches of the first Christian centuries.

As the movement spread, other structures arose. A core group of leaders and advisers was formed. Two or three people were chosen to represent each group. They would meet and then report their findings to their basic communities. The core group has a president, a vice-president, two secretaries, and two treasurers. In this way people learn to work together—something that is not exactly the strong point of such communities. The core group works for the spiritual and material well-being of all. The core group decides what gospel texts are to be read in the communities, and it makes an effort to find solutions to the problems raised there. Communal activity is fostered, human progress is promoted, and mature adulthood is thereby encouraged in the laity. Every three months or so there is a general meeting in order to reach wives and mothers too, since the latter would find it difficult to come otherwise. Four or five Sundays during the year, the whole community takes a trip to engage in missionary reflection, relax, and solidify its sense of fellowship. The aim is to arrive at a living community, one united by the proper balance of spiritual and material cohesion.

This does not mean that large parishes, which cannot possibly be served by one priest, are given up. Instead new life is injected into them. The role of the priest is to be the animator, who is to turn over more and more duties to the lay leaders. Obviously this raises questions about new ministries (or services) and offices in the Church, but I shall come back to that point later. The following priorities have been laid down for Latin America:

> The construction of a living Church rather than a growth in material structures. Living and authentic participation by the people, and a decrease in merely passive Christian masses. The training of leaders and an increase in the number of well-chosen ministries and ministers. Increased involvement in the lives of human beings and the realities of this world rather than holding on to a faith in Christ which is exclusively individualistic, alienating, and alienated. All must hear and heed the missionary summons to help one another, so that all may come to recognize the fatherhood of God and the mutual solidarity and brotherhood of all human beings. In this way they may come to realize the task of liberating the whole human being and all human beings. The liturgy must come out of living experience and be celebrated by all. In Jesus and through the Spirit it must be geared towards God and the life of all; it must center on the essentials of the faith. It must be a celebration of the universal Church rather than a complex of devotions geared only to certain persons or groups.[20]

The basic ecclesial communities in the diocese of Divinópolis are complying with those priorities. They will serve as our last example here. The diocese has 300,000 inhabitants, of which 35 percent live in rural areas. There are few priests for the 32 parishes, and in the past they were able to visit the faithful only a few times a year. The Eucharist was celebrated in a chapel, there was almost no religious instruction, and illiteracy was high. By 1974 there were already 275 basic ecclesial communities, each having an average of three leaders. There are Sunday services throughout the rural areas. The community comes together for a liturgy of the Word. There is a reading of the bishop's or priest's message and a reading from the Gospel. Then there is a homily and the recitation of prayers. As soon as the community is functioning well, the bishop permits one or two responsible married people to give out

Communion. Once a month the priest in charge comes to celebrate the Eucharist. There are now sixty people responsible for distributing Communion, conducting funeral services, giving catechetical instruction before baptism, and administering baptism. They also are in charge of education, social action, and health care.

Similar basic communities can be found in town areas, but they are more liturgically oriented. Thus there are leaders and other responsible parties, and a variety of functions are beginning to emerge. Twice a year three or four officials from each community take part in a five-day training session. So far 862 people have received formal, appropriate training in scripture, theology, catechetics—and also in first aid and leadership techniques. Emphasis is shifting from the parish as the administrative center to small basic units that are truly alive.

AFRICA

One of the most impressive pastoral letters was written by Bishop Patrick A. Kalilombe, pastor of the Church in Lilongwe (Malawi).[21] He has thought through the shift inaugurated by Vatican II and drawn the full conclusions:

The Church is composed concretely of local communities, which bring together the members of the Body of Christ as they live and work in their natural, geographical, cultural, and human milieu. Just as Christ, through the incarnation, was present in the world in a distinctive people, culture, place and time, so the Church is present insofar as it is made incarnate in specific human situations. The universal Church exists in and through these local Churches. As Vatican II put it: "This Church of Christ is truly present in all legitimate local congregations of the faithful which, united with their pastors, are themselves called Churches in the New Testament" (*Lumen Gentium* 26). The local Church is not simply a fragment—as if we had to put all the fragments together to get *the* Church. The local Church is *the* Church in and for this particular place, be it Camden Town or Harlem. This is the Church that lies within our reach, our experience, and our comprehension. It is here that Christ is present in the gospel message which is read and explained, in the Eucharist which is shared, and in the love which issues from both.[22]

Kalilombe goes so far as to say that his remarks about the local nature of the Church are more applicable to way-stations and sub-parishes than to large parishes and the diocese as a whole. In other words, he makes a strong plea for authentic basic ecclesial communities.[23] He wants to build the Church of Lilongwe on such small communities. This means that there will have to be new offices and new institutions, as well as really creative thinking.

In Africa much emphasis is placed on the fact that these communities must be self-ministering, self-propagating, and self-supporting. Africa seems to have severely felt its total dependence on the Western Church, and so the issue of basic ecclesial communities arises out of a totally different backdrop than that to be found in Latin America. People want a Church in which the offices and services are performed by people themselves in a wide variety of ways; they do not want consecrated ministers. Here we might recall the active lay people in the *Jama'a* movement in Zaire, which I mentioned in Part One.[24] The charism of the religious life is also given recognition.

These basic communities must also be missionary by their very nature. Missionary work is not something which has to do with foreign missionaries primarily, so new methods and initiatives are required.

Third, the Church must also take care of its own needs, both in its witnessing and in its service to the world. Again inventiveness is called for. Instead of dependence on wealthy Western institutions of all sorts, they must use their own resources. They must shape their own development model, one which is suited to their own needs and culture. There are to be no new projects which do not entail the direct involvement of the native population. There is to be no more reliance on some infinitely powerful and wealthy Church outside the country. To achieve these goals, new leaders must be trained.

Much is already under way in Africa, and I can only mention a few examples. A fairly old but still good study is the one on Tanzania by Marie-France Perrin Jassy.[25] Here I will simply focus on the view of Christopher Mwoleka, Bishop of the diocese of Rulenge in Tanzania. It is he, perhaps, who has done the best to form basic ecclesial communities in East Africa. Mwoleka pleads for small Christian communities with a human face, as opposed to large parishes where people can hardly be touched by priests or their bishop. What is needed is a group in which a network of interpersonal relations is feasible. A feeling of belonging is also needed. But those things come only when we have services that promote solidarity. It is within such a community that ongoing religious formation can take place. That is why a decided option for such small communities was recently made by the episcopal conferences of Ethiopia, Kenya, Malawi, the Sudan, Tanzania, Uganda, and Zambia. It is in such communities that people can truly live as a Church. Then one can proceed to seek out larger structures.

What functions can be discerned in such small groups? There is a prayer leader, who teaches the group to pray. Every week the leader meets with the group to study the Bible. The prayer leader also conducts a Sunday service without a priest. There is someone responsible for religious education; this person helps parents with their responsibilities towards their children and also handles adult catechesis. A marriage counsellor assists young couples before, during, and after marriage. Another person is responsible for the sense of community among the members of a given group; this person fosters fellowship and solidarity, and he or she also instigates projects designed to abet the welfare of all. Another leader seeks to bolster the sacramental life in every way possible. Another person has charge of economic matters, making the financial needs of the Church clear to all and trying to collect the necessary funds. There is also a coordinator who tries to make sure that everything runs smoothly.

All these people with responsibility attend special training sessions. It is encouraging to note that pastoral institutes are taking over this training work in many parts of Africa. Priests, religious, and catechists are given the special task of training and guiding these lay officials. Only with such training will lay people be able to assume real responsibility for the growth of local Churches. Only then will they be able to ensure that their local Churches do full justice to the indigenous culture and to the authentic values of the gospel message.[26]

ASIA

Here again I must be selective. In another paper I dealt to some extent with movements in Asia,[27] so here I shall confine my attention to India. In India there has been a growing realization that for centuries that country has been slipping into a Latin captivity.[28] Even the large Churches, including the Catholic Church, are dependent Churches. While that may no longer be true in terms of personnel, it remains true financially; the stream of money flows from the West to India. Culturally it is difficult to arrive at an Indian Church, and many Indian faithful regard that as a return to a forbidden past. So we see laborious efforts in the realms of liturgy and theology. The same holds true for other large Churches, and indeed it may apply most to smaller sects of a conservative or fundamentalist nature.

Despite all that, we do find breakthroughs in India at various points. Here I shall concentrate on the effort to form new groups with the Church, noting two basic orientations. The first type of group is very active, and wholly in service to the poor. Its best-known representative is Mother Teresa of Calcutta, who made a total commitment to the poor in 1946. By 1975 there were 870 sisters in her group and 180 novices. She had 41 communities in India and 16 in Sri Lanka, Tanzania, Venezuela, Italy, Israel, Jordan, Peru, England, Australia, and Mauritius, and now at least one in the United States. She has also founded a congregation of brothers that includes 140 brothers and 6 priests. These communities look after the starving poor on the streets, lepers, orphans, and abandoned children. All the members take a special vow: to serve the poor gratis. Mother Teresa's movement continues to spread both in India and around the world. Her communities are basic communities of authentic evangelical poverty, and they also exert missionary influence on the surrounding milieu. They are changing the outlook of Hindus, whose spirituality does not focus their attention very much on the plight of their fellow human beings. Some monks from the Ramakrishna Mission in Calcutta are reported to have said: "In these sisters we see the Lord Jesus returning in the midst of human beings and going around to do nothing but good." Wealthy Hindus have become more action-oriented, and some are now adopting abandoned children. Some people no longer pass by dying people on the streets; instead they contact the police, call an ambulance, or carry the afflicted to the sisters. Thus a Christ-inspired community is growing and spreading around Mother Teresa and her sisters.[29]

A similar movement was started by a German nun in North Kerala in 1969. Sister Petra Moenningmann established a congregation dedicated to the poor exclusively. Its Indian name is Ninasēvanasabha: i.e., the Congregation of the Servants of the Poor. The members live in poor houses, spend no more than $1.50 a day on themselves, and wear Indian saris. There is no special requirement for admission, except a total commitment to the poor. The members do social work for at least four-and-a-half hours a day. Three years after its founding, the congregation already had 143 members, 30 postulants, and 13 houses in Kerala. The sisters now do medical work, but they seek to tackle the causes of society's ills and to raise the standards of education and hygiene. They are active in farming and cattle-raising, in developing trades, and in creating job opportunities. Through these services to the poor they create communities without any direct focus on evangelization.[30]

Alongside such activist communities there are others of a more contemplative bent. The members live in ashrams, small cloistered communities modelled along Hindu lines. More and more ashrams are appearing in India. Sometimes they are ecumenical Christian communities and now we even find ashrams where Hindus participate with Christians. Hindu ashrams were settlements in a forest or along a river where people retired to ponder their holy books during their third stage of life. In modern times ashrams have also taken on social and educational tasks.

Christians have begun to glimpse the value of this institution. First, however, they must get a clear picture of the most important current in Hindu thought, the Advaita doctrine. This is the doctrine of non-duality. It asserts that there is only one absolute reality, Brahman; everything else is Maya, non-reality. The goal of life in an ashram is to pass over completely into the Absolute. Many Christian theologians have devoted their attention to this view of the world, trying to reconcile it with Christianity. Christianity, of course, cannot go so far as to say that there is no difference between "I" and "Thou," and we must make this point clear in our dialogue with Hindus. We can, however, learn much from this mystical Hindu experience. We can learn to go deeper into ourselves and find God there. We can realize that through our union with Christ, as described in John's Gospel, we can actively participate in his oneness with the Father in some sense. In our dialogue with Hindus, both sides must be open to the treasures which the other side has to offer. People in a Christian ashram can also listen and learn.[31]

In any case many Christian ashrams have arisen in India, most of them exclusively Christian. One example is the monastic Kurisumala Ashram in South India. It arose in March 1958 through the initiative of a Belgian and an English monk. The cloister has a hall where people gather in the evening, and there are also three guest rooms. Off to the left is the main building containing the chapel, the library, the refectory, the dormitory for younger monks, and the cells of the older monks. Behind it lie stables and workshops. The ashram supports itself with farming and stock-breeding. The native population also benefits from learning new methods. There are three meals a day; people sit on the ground and eat with their hands. The liturgy is that of the local population and its rite (Syro-Malankar). There are alternating periods of prayer, study, and work. Hospitality is lavishly displayed. The cloister is open to seers, Hindu brahmacharis and sannyasis, and all who are dedicated to the quest for truth and the Supreme Lord of the Universe.

That is merely one of the hundreds of ashrams in India today. They are small communities where a new form of Indian ecclesial life is being cultivated. People are still groping, and there are problems. But there is also high hope that these experiments will eventually leave their mark on the Indian Church. It clearly indicates a shift to a grass-roots Church, out of which will grow an indigenous spirituality, theology, liturgy, and service to the people.[32]

The question which we posed to ourselves in Chapter 14 is now being filled in with more concrete data. We could go on to discuss basic communities and the Jama'a movement in Zaire, the Barangay Sa Virgen in the Philippines, the Tonarigumi in Japan, and many others.[33] Clearly we are on the way towards a fresh discovery. Perhaps it was expressed most beautifully by the inhabitants of Enarotoli in the Indonesian province of Irian Jaya. They attended a sort of pastoral council in the capital and brought a huge package with them. It was placed in the middle of the gathering. The packing material was made up of leaves, which is what they use to preserve foodstuffs. Then they began to unpack the bundle. They unpeeled the outer layer of leaves: "This is the pope. Is this the Church? It is a skin-layer of the Church." They peeled off another layer of leaves: "Here are the bishops. Are they the Church? They are a skin-layer of the Church." On they went until they came to the vegetables inside: "These vegetables are the people. That's us. We are the Church." They began to eat up the vegetables. "But we are not the kernel." A little speck of bacon remained. "That is the kernel, the bit of bacon that gives flavor to the vegetables. That is Jesus, the kernel of our community."

Has anyone ever put it more beautifully?

16

New Forms of Service

In the course of the last chapter it should have become apparent that new forms of ecclesial life entail new forms of service as well. Now I must consider the latter a bit more in detail. Again I must restrict myself to a few examples of a rapidly developing phenomenon. Again I see no need to elaborate any theological justification for the rise of these new forms of service.

ASIA

This whole matter has been thoroughly explored in Asia. Asians have a penchant for congresses and thorough studies, preferring to lay down the guidelines before they proceed to action. I will discuss two Asian congresses here.

The first was a Research Seminar held in Bangalore (India) from June 2 to June 7, 1976. It examined our present topic from a more thoroughly theological viewpoint. The seminar included forty-three bishops, scholars, and a few participants with pastoral experience. The follow-up was a Pastoral Consultation attended by 120 bishops, priests, sisters, and lay people. At their gathering they sought to offer clearcut recommendations. It is the latter that are of particular interest to us here.[34]

It seemed that the laity were more ready for change than the clergy were. The latter often voiced the old saw: "Don't change that because the people are not yet ready for it!" The lay people were also frightened off by the word "ministries." Viewing it as a term which suggested further clericalization, they preferred the as yet unspoiled term "services." The clergy, on the other hand, did not care to see further institutionalization in the Church. Thus the beginning of the consultation was not too auspicious, since the participants had to get acquainted with each other in many senses.

There was a gradual shift from a pyramidal view of the Church to a concentric view; the Church is a community of service; in it all persons are equal, co-responsible, and mutually dependent, although they exercise a variety of functions. Even as this reality was fleshed out in the early Church, so it must now be fleshed out again in the concrete cultural situation of India. The Church is local by nature; it must be incarnate. It is also missionary by nature, carrying on the mystery of the Incarnation. Since the whole Church is missionary, it is also service-oriented. Charisms, services, and functions may differ, but they all work together for the welfare of all (1 Cor. 12:4–11). There is a difference between lay people and consecrated ministers, to be sure, but that ought not lead to a social rift or a class-mentality.

This basic vision led the participants to assert that lay ministers are in no way clerical. They are part of the community, exercising their services in their own right. They are not mere helpmates of priests, though of course they must cooperate with consecrated ministers. Community and co-responsibility apply here too.

The following types of lay ministers were proposed. Evangelists would carry the good news to others. Catechists were to be leaders of one or more Christian communities; in the cities they would take charge of catechetics for children, teenagers, and adults. Prayer leaders would be in charge of prayer in groups and communities. There would be ministers to promote the liturgy and help create a new liturgy. There would be ministers to the family apostolate, helping people to solve their problems in the light of the gospel. There would be healing ministers to care for the sick and the handicapped. There would be ministers for social tasks, helping to carry on the work of development and fighting for a more just society. There would be ministers for working people, particularly in large industrial centers. There would be ministers for the mass communications media, who would help to call attention to people's various needs. There would be ministers to young people, training them for leadership and educating them as good citizens and Christians.

After lengthy discussion two types of deacons were agreed upon. One type would serve as the sacrament of the Church's concern for the betterment of the human condition. The other type would provide spiritual leadership in their own right for rural communities without priests. In either case, the term "deacon" here applied to both men and women, either married or unmarried, who would assume a full-time or part-time task in accordance with the needs of the Christian community. They had to be tested and found suitable by the community, and they also had to receive proper training in some pastoral center. This training would have to be in-service training so that they would not lose their ties with their group.

The priest had to ensure the unity of spiritual leadership. This, too, called for training, so that priests would be capable of building up a community. Attention had to be paid to the different demands of urban and rural environments. In rural situations the demand was for a married priest who knew the language and customs of the area and who could provide for his own support. Unless such a shift was made, it would never be possible to provide proper pastoral care for village areas. Guidelines for the training of such rural priests were laid down. Here again, as in the case of deacons, it was emphasized that rural priests were not to be estranged from their milieu during their training. In-service training combined with sessions in regional pastoral centers seemed to be the best approach. In parishes which encompassed many villages, the participants wanted to have an unmarried priest on the job on a full-time basis. The participants at the meeting also made it quite clear that lay ministers must be able to function as deacons. They also discussed admission of women to the priesthood.

Finally, the new Church in India would have to be a Church deeply associated with the needs and the joys of the people; co-responsibility and a team spirit should mark the exercise of offices and services. This is the ecclesial life that Vatican II wanted. It is quite possible that priests trained in a very different spirit might go through an identity crisis in this new Church; but that could be a healthy thing, provided that they found solid support from pastoral centers. The clock cannot be turned back! Structural changes must be implemented in order to make room for new services; otherwise any new services would simply reinforce the existing pyramidal setup.

The results of the Bangalore meeting, embodied in concrete proposals, were submitted to the Indian episcopal conference. They were also presented to the Asian Colloquium on services in the Church, which was held in Hong Kong from February 27 to March 6, 1977. I must say a few words about this Colloquium. It was initiated by the Asian Episcopal Conference, and there was a two-year period of preparation for it. Support seemed to come from the Holy See, which had already eliminated the subdiaconate and minor orders and introduced the two new services of lector and acolyte. Moreover, the Holy See had asked bishops, through their episcopal conferences around the world, to approach it and request the establishment of new ministries. The recommendations of the Colloquium were meant as suggestions for the Churches involved, and for Churches on other continents; the hope was to bring into being the new image of the Church which Vatican II had delineated.

The Asian Churches are well aware of their exceptional situation. More than half the world's population lives in Asia, and more than half of the Asian population is under the age of twenty-one. Asia is a curious mixture of ancient, venerable cultures and modernization, as one can readily notice in any big city. There are solid Asian values and aspirations: e.g., close family ties, good interpersonal relations, and a strongly religious bent. There is a desire to come to grips with sharp economic differences, and to organize small communities that are person-oriented. Asia, however, still lacks its own stable political structures, which would enable it to offer effective resistance to foreign influence in all its forms. And even though Asia is the cradle of all the major religions, the glaring contrasts in living conditions and lifestyles are driving many young people towards agnosticism, secularism, and materialism. Other Asians—including poor people, students, and intellectuals—are turning to revolutionary ideologies.

This is the challenge posed by the signs of the time to the Roman Catholic Churches in Asia, which still constitute less than 3 percent of the population.

They are still regarded as foreign, particularly in terms of religious expression, symbolism, and organization. New tasks must be shouldered, therefore. The Church must be turned into a sacrament of salvation and a community of love. There must be dialogue with the great world religions about their identity. There must be cooperative efforts to work out religious and moral values, which are so needed for progress and development that is worthy of human beings. Raw poverty must be eliminated through real-life dialogue with the poor. Some way must be found to preserve the authentic values of personalism and family life in a world dominated by urbanization and technology. Asians must seek out a truly Asian form of participatory leadership at every level of government. Finally, national and Asian identity must be achieved by combining ancient and modern values and learning how to look towards the future as well.

There we have a missionary program for Asia, and once again the emphasis is clearly on the local Church. It is a new image of the Church, and it is theologically sound. The salvation brought by Jesus Christ must assume concrete forms through dialogue with one's own cultural community. And the same holds true for services and ministries within the Church. So courage, creativity, and originality are called for, even as they were in the early Church; one can no longer be satisfied with imported models.

The whole Church is missionary, hence service-oriented. Its mission is a community mission, though that mission takes many different forms. The Church is an in-service community. Though there are differences in function, office, and service, all in that community are equal, co-responsible, and mutually dependent. Services are taken up spontaneously as the occasion arises. Offices are assumed with a certain amount of stability entailed, and they are exercised on a broader scope. Those involved may be lay people, but not lay people who have been "clericalized." Those involved may also be consecrated people (bishops, priests, deacons), who represent the charism of unity and spiritual leadership. They may exercise their function at various levels of community: regional, diocesan, parochial Church; or basic ecclesial community, which is truly the local Church because it is closest to the people.

Taking inventory, the Colloquium noted that the following services were arising in the Churches of Asia. The evangelist is the lay person entrusted with the task of sharing the good news with our non-Christian brothers and sisters. The catechist—also known as preacher or religion teacher—educates the Christian community in the faith; specialists are needed to offer religious education to children, teenagers, adults, and workers in large urban areas. Liturgy specialists help to promote prayer and worship; they include acolytes, lectors, cantors, and others involved in the liturgy of the Word and sacrament. Specialists in the family apostolate concern themselves with child care, family planning, and population issues. The healing ministry would help to associate doctors, nurses, and others more closely with the community. Inter-religious dialogue would be another area of service, helping to promote mutual understanding and cooperation. Social leaders seek to combat social injustice and to offer aid to drug addicts, prostitutes, and unwed mothers; they might also be considered peacemakers. Also needed are youth leaders, advisers for different professions, and promoters of a more humane lifestyle. Particular emphasis was placed on the need for community leaders in many small Asian communities; they would seek to handle needs at every level. Other needed ministries were indicated, such as those dealing with the mass media, assistance for the parish priest, the visiting of the sick, and the organizing of community activities.

The training of all these lay ministers was discussed in great detail. The plea was for in-service training to avoid creating a gap between leadership-training and concrete tasks in a community. The need for pastoral centers was pointed out. A strong plea was also made for enrolling women in these lay services. The difficulties surrounding the permanent diaconate were acknowledged, but the use of women was urged to ensure a holistic community life. Women, it was felt, could also be leaders of basic communities.

In this context the priest is the one who embodies or stands for unifying spiritual leadership. He shares this office with the bishop. He instills courage and inspiration, encouraging initiatives and the growth of various charisms. All this reaches its culmination in the Eucharistic celebration. A plea was made for married, part-time priests in the many small communities. The vocation of the bishop stands out more sharply in the context of these needs and activities. The bishop has two basic tasks. First, he must keep the local Church in contact with other local Churches—a community which is presided over by the successor of Peter. Second, he must maintain community ties between basic communities and parishes on the one hand, and between both of them and larger entities on the other. He is the bridge-builder between two shores. He must serve as an inspiration, leading the way for all by listening to his people and engaging in dialogue with other human beings. He must also be relieved of his administrative functions.[35]

AFRICA

Again I will confine myself to a few examples. The first is the archdiocese of Kinshasa in Zaire, which is headed by Cardinal Joseph Malula. His considered view is that Africa must be turned over to Africans in the ecclesial sense as well. Now that would mean waiting a long time if one held to the ideal of having enough unmarried African priests. So the Cardinal decided to entrust parishes to lay people, launching his project in 1973. In 1975 we heard for the first time that it had reached the stage of actual implementation. During a ceremony held on Sunday, March 2, 1975, he installed a lay person to head several parishes in Kinshasa. This lay leader is known as a *mokambi* (pl. *bakambi*). In the next two months seven more *bakambi* were installed in their respective parishes.

These appointments were preceded by a year-and-a-half of intensive training. A special handbook was prepared for these lay leaders by the archdiocesan council. It spelled out their place in the pastoral structures of the archdiocese, and it also stipulated the conditions they had to meet in their own personal lives because of the function they were undertaking. Another section dealt with preparing the faithful for the reception of the sacraments. Finally, the handbook also dealt with bookkeeping matters: how to handle finances and keep parish records. The lay leaders attend clergy meetings of their deanery where pastoral problems are being studied. Priests from nearby parishes are available to perform those functions which are reserved to priests.

During the Eucharistic service held when a *mokambi* was installed, the Cardinal stressed the point that Africans must now concern themselves with the growth of the Church in Africa. It is up to them to see to it that a truly local Church comes into being, and that the local culture finds expression in it. That calls for dialogue with Africa. Before the *mokambi* was installed, the Cardinal asked for the consent of his wife and the Christian community. After the recitation of a prayer and then a blessing, the *mokambi* received the symbols of his office: a crucifix, a gospel book, and a copy of the handbook for such lay leaders. A further step was the installation of district lay leaders. These *bakambi* had charge of basic ecclesial communities within the parish over which the parish *mokambi* presided.

A parish *mokambi* cannot handle everything. He has a job to do in society, and he is only partially paid by his parish. He exercises full responsibility in the latter, however, being accountable to his bishop rather than to a priest. Local priests constitute his chief advisers. The parish *mokambi* is the organizer and stimulator of all activities in his parish, including the activities of its basic ecclesial communities. He is not supposed to do everything himself but rather to stimulate and coordinate the work of others. Other people must be actively involved in the process of Africanization, which can only grow out of the grass-roots level. And to be authentic, it cannot be an armchair process.

Thus each district *mokambi* exercises some specific pastoral responsibility, and he is backed up by an advisory board. The district lay leaders hold prayer meetings, lead bible groups, and help the sick and the needy. They engage in social action, organizing social meetings and helping out with small developmental projects. Some try to raise people's awareness about spiritual and social matters, helping them to find solutions and implement them. Others preside over liturgical celebrations, supervise catechists, do youth work, and take charge of the family apostolate. Together they form the parish council, over which the parish *mokambi* presides. There the suggestions and reports of the district lay leaders and their advisers are discussed.

This enables the priest to get back to his own specific tasks: conducting the service of God's Word at specified times, administering the sacraments, and providing ongoing training for the *mokambi* and his aides through study sessions and retreats. Together with the lay leaders he must transform the local community into a missionary community.[36]

The South African Episcopal Conference has also concerned itself with the whole issue of services. An ad hoc commission was set up, and it was decided that there had to be a diversification of services—not because of a shortage of priests but because the whole people of God had to share responsibility for each other. Two things had to be fostered simultaneously. First, there was need of a more open and service-minded priesthood that put less emphasis on control. Second, in parishes and dioceses there had to be a more lively and active-minded community which knew how to engage in team work. Old attitudes and parochial structures had to be left behind. What was needed was a parochial community characterized by mutual service and shared responsibility for all tasks.

A survey revealed that the following forms of service were already in operation. Deacons and acolytes are already in training. Lectors are already on the job. There are leaders for Sunday services without priests, and they distribute Communion. Catechists take care of the religious instruction of children. There are leaders for funeral services, and catechists play a major role in the training of lay community leaders. There are training programs in many areas, and priests take part in them as well.

The survey noted that the new leaders were to be supported by their local areas. The importance of team work and cooperation among the various lay leaders was also stressed. Ways were also being sought to promote the role of women in the Church and to integrate nuns more fully into its work. The abolition of obligatory celibacy is strongly favored, but people are also convinced that the special charism of celibacy will endure in the Church.[37]

LATIN AMERICA

We have a lot of good information about the new forms of service in Latin America, but first I must set the whole issue in its broader context. From north to south the Latin American continent covers more than 10,000 kilometers and is divided into twenty-one countries. Its area is 21 million square kilometers, and in 1977 the population density was 320 people per square kilometer. Language (Spanish) and religion (Roman Catholicism) are almost the same everywhere, though Portuguese is the main language of Brazil.

Many different racial strains and mixtures can be found in Latin America. There are also marked differences in population density from place to place. Huge interior areas are still largely uninhabited, while millions of people are crowded into urban centers. In big cities some people live in modern luxury amid a mass of poor people. The rate of population growth is high: 7 million people per year. Forty percent of the population are under the age of 15. Land distribution is also very uneven: 1.5 percent of the people own 65 percent of the land. Agriculture predominates, but it is handled poorly. The average GNP per capita is $742; for nine countries it is still less than $300. Illiteracy is still high: 85 percent in some places such as Haiti, and 50 percent in places such as Brazil. Also noteworthy is the fact that democracy and respect for human rights have been steadily disappearing.

The Roman Catholic Church claims 295 million members, and the area is divided into 605 ecclesiastical jurisdictions; 140 of the latter are real mission territories. After the impetus of Vatican II and the 1968 Medellín Conference, there has been much activity within the Church. CELAM, the Latin American Episcopal Conference, seems to be one of the most solid and active episcopal conferences in the world. Pastoral work and evangelization pose an enormous task, with one pastoral agent available for every 1,600 people. As can be seen from my remarks above, that ratio is much too small. In 1977 there were 7,000 faithful per priest. Such a situation points towards the rise of new ministries and services in the Latin American Church. Reflection on the proper role and task of the priest is also going on.

The traditional role of the priest cannot be fully maintained. He was liturgist, theologian, adviser, catechist, confessor, community leader, missionary, preacher, builder, apologist, developer, teacher, exegete, and writer. These roles must now be parcelled out. Excessively large parishes make the old approach impossible, and the rise of basic ecclesial communities within parishes is helping to foster a new approach. Latin America is leading the way in this area. The chief need is for a grass-roots priest who will serve as community leader and evangelizer; he must come from the community itself and maintain contact with it. Such priests do not need a classical academic training; and it seems inevitable that in the short or long run they will be married men. Also needed is a priest who will serve as coordinator and inspirer, and who must be able to move around. Such priests would need better training, and they would help to maintain ties between the bishop and the basic ecclesial communities.

Things cannot stop there, however. In a real community the gifts and charisms of each member must be given their rightful place. This is all the more necessary in the light of the present situation in Latin America. Latin Americans, too, are finding inspiration in the example of the early Church. They, too, are moving towards greater community responsibility. Tasks must be shared, and four main categories seem to be involved. First, the service of the Word calls for preachers of the kerygma, catechists, groups of evangelists, interdisciplinary centers, and so forth. Second, cultic worship requires celebrants, animators, cantors, explainers, lectors, study groups, and other groups devoted to prayer, retreats, and shared living. Third, the service of unity requires advisers, mediators, comforters, helping hands, communication experts, and promoters of participation. Fourth, the service of mutual aid and assistance requires people who will promote neighborly love, engage in prophetic criticism, fight for social justice, and side with the oppressed and needy. Latin America can count itself fortunate that many women, including nuns, are already involved in these ecclesial tasks of service to the community.

Let me present one example of what is going on in Latin America. The place in question is the small state of Santa Catarina in southern Brazil. There are solid colonies of German, Italian, and Polish immigrants in the state. The economy centers around textiles and light machine industry, and the self-awareness of the workers is well developed. There are eight dioceses. The clergy is largely of German or Italian descent, and they have received solid training in Western universities. The bishops are open to sociopolitical problems, and they have good relations with their priests and communities. These communities regard ecclesial service as a response to a concrete, urgent need that is presented by the community in question. Once the need disappears, so does the service. The services are offered gratis, and they are received by the community with the utmost trust. The charism of authority is regarded as normal. Here, then, we have an outstanding example of dialogue as a question-and-answer process.

There are community leaders, who usually preside over a chapel or a place of worship. They guide the spiritual life of the people and take care of the place of worship. Such a leader is assisted by a local advisory council; contact is maintained with a priest, who usually comes about once a month to celebrate the Eucharist. Thus Sunday services are held without a priest; prayers are said and the gospel message is read. Liturgical leaders spring up readily to prepare biblical readings and preside over spontaneous reflections and prayers. But the community leader is the real spiritual director of the community. The process has gone so far that these leaders have now been judged worthy to distribute Communion. They, and in some cases other people, are appointed as extraordinary ministers of the Eucharist for a year by the bishop.

Another service is catechetics. Teams take charge of religious instruction before such events as baptism, first Communion, confirmation, and matrimony. The surprising thing is that a wide variety of people can be found engaged in this work: doctors, chemists, teachers, businessmen, and civil servants. On certain days they also preach during a Eucharistic service. Another similar service is acting as leader of a bible study group.

Much of this development is spontaneous, particularly in rural areas covered by one huge parish. There are services dedicated to neighborly love and social concerns. A further development can be seen in the fact that the hierarchy is now consecrating some of the extraordinary ministers of the Eucharist as deacons. These deacons prepare parents and godparents for the baptism of children and perform the rite; they do the same for marriages. They also handle funeral services and preach the Word of God. Finally, they act as missionaries to those who have moved away from Christianity.

It is in this way that the Spirit is seen to be at work. Lifeless communities have become locales of active, thorough evangelization. The hierarchy is fully behind these spontaneous developments. It has organized courses in deaneries and at the diocesan level to offer further help to the new lay leaders. A truly new Church is coming to birth in Santa Catarina![38]

By way of conclusion let me point out once again what I regard as the most striking feature of the new ministries and services that can be found on different continents. It is the new sense of co-responsibility which the laity are feeling for the life of the Church. This new sense is the result of a dialogue between real life at every level and a renewed biblical vision of what ecclesial life really means.

17

Creative Forms of Liturgy

If there is anywhere that dialogue between the Judeo-Christian tradition and other religions should lead to real, concrete results, it is in the celebration of the liturgy. I will try to demonstrate that point by covering two specific examples, one in Zaire and the other in India.

THE ZAIRIAN EUCHARISTIC CELEBRATION

Visitors to Zaire are invariably offered the sound advice: Don't forget to attend a Zairian Mass. Before I describe that liturgy in detail, I should indicate how it all began. I will indicate some of the basic principles underlying the creation of it, and then I will show how they are embodied in concrete examples of the liturgy.

Back in 1974 the Zairian episcopal conference, and its general secretariat specifically, published a small brochure. The cover of it is green, the national color of Zaire. On the cover and in the booklet are eight photos of various moments in the Zairian liturgy, and they hint at a timid beginning. In one picture you see the joyous chant of the *Gloria*. The celebrant, preceded by two other ministers, is dancing around the altar while the congregation claps their hands and rocks along in front of their seats in the nave. A grey-haired reader in a loose *boubou*, a native dress, is asking the celebrant for a blessing. Another picture shows the celebrant, wearing a native garment and native headdress, in the act of enthroning the gospel. The gospel book is held high above his head in a veil or cloth; he is accompanied by other ministers, whose ritual lances can be seen standing behind the apse. Another photo suggests how much the people care for the penitential rite; they can be seen with their heads bowed slightly and their hands crossed on their breast. The last photo shows the congregation singing and clapping their hands as they proceed out of the church.

It is clear, then, that the liturgical experiment was already under way in 1974. There have been problems, to be sure, especially concerning the priest's dress and headdress. The change must have been enormous, but the enthusiasm evident in the photos makes it clear that this liturgy has won the hearts of the people.

In 1975 the episcopal conference's committee for evangelization issued a stenciled pamphlet of 35 pages in which the new rite was established. It has six parts: discreet arrival at the place of worship, be it a church, an open field in the savanna, or a small chapel built by the people themselves; the opening part of the liturgy; the liturgy of the Word; Eucharistic Prayer; Communion; and the concluding rite. That all may sound pretty typical, but in fact it is far from it. There are two appendices in the pamphlet: one contains two additional verses for the invocation of the saints; the other is an alternative formula for the penitential rite. The rite contained in the pamphlet was meant as an experiment; and the basic material in it was designed to help the Zairian Church, as a community, to seek further in search of its own liturgy.

After applying to the Roman Congregation for Worship, the national Zairian episcopal conference received permission to do what was necessary to integrate the new *Ordo Missae* into the local culture. This experimental stage is still in process, but the liturgy is well on its way already—as readers will soon see. The people have taken to heart Pope Paul VI's words when he spoke in Kampala: "You can and you must have an African Christianity." The greatest share of credit should go to the episcopal committee for evangelization. As far back as 1971 it began to keep bishops and priests abreast of its activities in the huge nation.

The Zairian rite did not drop ready-made from the sky; it was well prepared and presented. The episcopal committee also allowed complete freedom for experimentation along the basic lines set down. Efforts were made to keep the committee informed of difficulties encountered with the proposed rite, and also of further requests from the people. Thus the Zairian rite arose in a process of experimentation and dialogue.

Two points seemed to call for further clarification: the value and importance of the service of the Word; and the meaning and place of the penitential rite in the Eucharistic service. In 1975 the episcopal committee completed this task, after consulting a goodly number of theological works and the many books on African culture which it kept close at hand. The latter books were studied closely and digested. As a result, in 1977 the committee was able to issue an important paper which spelled out the basic anthropological vision underlying the structure of the Zairian Eucharistic rite.

In the paper we are told that the Eucharistic celebration, in accordance with native rites, should take five anthropological elements into account. These are the basic principles which I alluded to above, and which I want to illustrate with concrete examples.

The first element is mediation. In the traditional African worldview, the world of God is intimately linked up with the world of human beings. One striking feature is the fact that the dead, the living dead, are pictured as an integral part of the human family. For Africans the mediation of the dead is of the utmost importance when it comes to such events as birth, marriage, burial, and installation in some office. At such times the ancestors lead the way, and their will cedes only to the will of God. Every prayer, then, is really a community activity involving both the living and the dead. The ancestors carry the prayers to God and bring back his answer. So the Zairian Eucharistic service begins with an invocation of the saints in which the ancestors are included.

Mediation also finds expression in the fact that the faithful greet each other on the way to church, at the church door, and as they take their seats. And the celebrant points up the fact of mediation near the start of the service. Let me give you a few examples of how this works. The man or woman who is serving as the announcer for the parish group wears an expressive garment and calls for silence with a bell or a basket full of beads. He or she then offers a few extemporaneous words of welcome, to which the congregation replies "Amen." The announcer then gives the congregation the names of the celebrant, the lay leaders of the community, and all the concelebrants. People have to know each other, you see. If those responsible for the welcoming service discover strangers in the congregation, the latter are also introduced to the congregation. The strangers have been given choice seats. At the mention of their name they stand up and are loudly applauded. As the service starts, the celebrant and his assistants enter with a dance. When the altar has been venerated and the liturgical theme announced, the invocation of the saints takes place. The list includes the patriarchs and prophets (who are also fathers of the faithful), the ancestors, Mary, the apostles, the evangelists, the patron on the Church, the saint of the day, and the holy martyrs of Uganda. Here is the part of the invocation which is addressed to the ancestors:

Celebrant: Our ancestors,	*All*: Be with us.
People of worth who	
sought the gods,	Be with us.
see us pray.	Be with us.
Be with all those who are	
celebrating Mass at this hour.	Be with us.

A second basic element is universal participation. The whole plant, animal, and mineral kingdom is linked up with humanity, and humanity is linked up with the whole cosmos. God is the fullness of life, and he shares that life with everything that exists. The life force of God is discernible everywhere, and human beings must make it their own as much as possible. There is a great feeling of solidarity and shared destination. That is why worship includes such things as oil, bread, wine, flowers, water, fire, and perfume. One example of this feeling is an initial dialogue in the Eucharistic prayer, which contains a theological section and a christological section. Here is how the theological section goes:

Truly, Lord,
it is good that we give you thanks,
You our God,
You our Father,
You, the sun which one cannot gaze at,
You the almighty,
You, sight itself,
You the Master of human beings,
You the Master of life,
You the Master of all things,
We praise You,
We thank You,
through Your Son, Jesus Christ,
our mediator.

All: Yes, he is our mediator.

The christological section of the prayer links up nicely with the preceding:

Holy Father,
we praise you through Your Son,
Jesus Christ, our mediator.
He is Your word that confers life.
Through him You created heaven and earth.
Through him You created the stream, Zaire,
the rivers, brooks, and seas,
and all the fish living in them.
Through him You created the woods,
the plains, the savannas, the mountains,
and all the animals living in them.
Through him You created all the things we see,
as well as the things that we do not see.

All: Yes, through him You created all things.

The same basic line of thought finds expression in one of the alternative versions of the concluding rite. The celebrant and other ministers stretch out their hands over the congregation and pray:

May the Master of life,
Father,
Son,
and Holy Spirit,
preserve and keep you forever and ever.

All: Amen.

Only then is there a silent sign of the cross by the celebrant, the other ministers, and the congregation.

A third basic element is cultic expressiveness. All those who have taken part in a Zairian liturgy say that it is an indescribable experience. Dance and gesture make up one aspect of this distinctive approach, and I can offer only a few examples here.

The entrance of the celebrant has been described as follows. Accompanied by his male and female assistants, the celebrant enters the Church with a distinctive rhythmic movement. Dressed in multicolored garments, he moves left and right by turn. The basic professional dance pattern is: first one foot is put forward towards the left or right, then the other one moves up to join it; then one foot is put forward in the alternative direction, and the second foot moves up to join it. The result, it seems, is an elegant, serene cadence. Usually the celebrant wears the characteristic headdress of a chief and carries an elegantly crafted wooden staff in his right hand. He symbolizes and represents the great chief, Christ, leading all his followers to pay respects to God the Father.

The veneration of the altar is also a very expressive rite. The whole retinue stands around the altar with the celebrant in the middle. They face the people and venerate the altar by making a deep bow or prostrating themselves on the ground. The celebrant, however, stands erect after a low bow, his arms stretched out in the shape of a huge V. Then he proceeds to the brightly and richly decorated altar. He bows his forehead on one edge of the altar, stretching his arms out on the altar top. He then proceeds to the other three sides of the altar and does the same thing. This action performed on four sides has cosmic significance.

The *Gloria* is also beautiful. It is a great acclamation expressed by the celebrant, his assistants, and the congregation. Rhythm and voice are used to express all the feelings of their heart and soul. The celebrant and his concelebrants dance around the altar, just as David did long ago before the Ark of the Covenant. The congregation joins them by singing and dancing. While this is going on, fragrant materials are strewn on a small fire burning in an earthen pot. The pot is on a tripod which stands between the altar and the people. Another distinctive feature of the liturgy is the fact that each reading is followed by an extempore song which paraphrases the content and helps the congregation to assimilate its message.

The reading of the Gospel is also surrounded by a distinctive ceremony: the enthronement of the gospel book. A dialogue takes place between celebrant and congregation:

Celebrant: "My brothers and sisters, the Word of God became flesh."
All: "And dwelt among us."
Celebrant: "Let us listen to him."

When the procession reaches the place where the Gospel is to be read, the celebrant says: "Brothers and sisters, let us listen closely." After a few mo-

ments of silence, he says: "The Good News as written by St. _____."
The congregation replies: "Proclaim it, proclaim it, we are listening." The
people then sit down. When the reading is over, the celebrant says: "May the
person who has a heart to agree . . ." And immediately all reply: "May he
agree."

The homily which follows now reminds me of Augustine in his Church of
Hippo. The preacher makes use of Zairian proverbs, for in them the wisdom
of God as given to the ancestors speaks to the congregation today. The congregation offers a response as a group or as individuals. When the congregation feels moved enough, applause bursts out. A lively dialogue takes place.
An attempt is made to keep it down to fifteen minutes, but the Zairians are no
more successful at that than Augustine was. Clearly, then, cultic expressiveness is not restricted to dress and gesture among the Zairians; it is also embodied in words.

A fourth basic element typified in the Zairian liturgy is the need for community. There is community between human beings and God, between human beings themselves, between the living and their ancestors, between human beings and the universe, and between human beings and what lies
beyond the grave. Let me cite a few instances where this finds expression in
the liturgy.

The penitential rite comes after the reading of the Gospel and the homily,
not at the beginning of the Zairian liturgy. After all, people must first listen
and enter into communion with each other. Then the celebrant begins the
penitential rite:

> Brothers and sisters,
> God's Word has put us under obligation.
> It is living and forceful,
> and it can pass judgment on the feelings of the heart (Heb. 4:12–13).
> Everything is disclosed to God's sight.
> Together let us ask the Lord for strength
> to follow his ways.

After a moment of silence, the congregation assumes a penitential attitude.
The people stand up, heads slightly bowed, hands crossed on their breast with
the right palm on top of the left hand. The invocations have several alternative formulations, so I shall cite only one here:

> Lord, our God,
> just as an insect sticks fast on the skin
> and sucks the blood from a human being,
> so wickedness holds us in its grip.
> Who shall save us?
> Is it not You, O Father?
> Lord, have mercy.
>
> *All*: Lord, have mercy.

Celebrant:
Before the Virgin Mary,
all the saints,
our brothers and sisters,
we confess:
Our heart was far from You.
We honored You with our lips.
Lord, have mercy.

All: Lord, have mercy.

Celebrant:
Before You, O Father,
we confess:
If the world does not know Jesus Christ,
if injustice exists in many forms,
if there is hatred, the mother of hostility,
then perhaps it is because we are not
true witnesses to your kingdom.
Lord, have mercy.

All: Lord, have mercy.

Celebrant:
Most holy Father,
heed our prayer:
May our hearts not incline
to works of iniquity (Ps. 141:4);
Forgive our faults
for the sake of the sacrifice of Your Son, Jesus Christ;
may Your Spirit dwell in our hearts,
and may our sins be swallowed up
in the deep, still waters,
Through Jesus, the Christ, our Lord.

All: Amen.

The celebrant then proceeds around the area, sprinkling people liberally with water. The congregation strives energetically to get some. A baptismal chant recounts the beneficial and wholesome power of baptism.

The strong concept of community also finds expression in the offering of the gifts. Specially designated people approach with the gifts with a distinctive dance-step. These words are addressed to the celebrant:

O priest of God, see,
here are our gifts.

Accept them from us.
They make it clear
that we love one another.

The same feeling finds expression in another prayer of offering:

O priest of God,
see this bread and wine,
gifts from God,
they also come from the fields and from the labor
of human beings.
May they become nourishment for eternal life.

The feeling and need for community also finds expression in an alternative formulation for the concluding rite:

May the Lord almighty,
God, who created us,
God, who is in our midst,
God, who has given us the gift of his Spirit,
bless us.
From now on may we
enjoy the happiness
that we shall have in heaven.

A fifth and final basic element typified by the Zairian rite is originality. No culture is absolutely original, for human values are shared in common by the whole human family. The originality of the Zairian eucharistic liturgy lies in the effort to translate Christian worship into a specific African language and to ground its inspiration in a worldview that has grown out of the native tropical soil. The aim is to be both Christian and African.

The interesting thing is the very fact that the Zairian episcopal conference approached anthropologists with this request: Tell us whether this anthropological vision is of any real value or not. In the West such a request has never been made! It is as if we were experiencing once again the contact of the first Judeo-Christian communities with pagan communities. We are coming into contact with strange gifts of the Holy Spirit because we are hearing them speak in tongues and give praise to God.[39]

THE NEW INDIAN EUCHARISTIC RITUAL

To understand the present situation in India, we must again briefly consider how the new Order of the Mass came into being. It is an impressive history. When Vatican II issued its Constitution on the Liturgy in 1963, thus paving the way for liturgical renewal, there was no wild jubilation in India. People were satisfied with the three existing rites: the Latin, the Syro-

Malabar, and the Syro-Malankar. There was no big movement for liturgical renewal in India, which had other problems to deal with. So the initiative again came from the bishops. In 1963 they issued a letter stressing the need for liturgical renewal, and the 1964 Eucharistic Congress in Bombay helped greatly to instill a new outlook.

In 1966 the episcopal conference reached a number of decisions. They felt that their first and foremost duty was to promote the liturgical and catechetical apostolate. Why? Because all efforts to improve the social situation of the people and to foster dialogue with other Christians and non-Christians derive their inspiration and force from the mystery of Christ. A national liturgical commission was established under the leadership of the active Bishop Simon Lourdusamy, the auxiliary, and later the bishop, of Bangalore. There a National Liturgical and Catechetical Center was set up, to be headed by the extremely energetic Rev. D. S. Amalorpavadass.

The liturgical commission was given broad authority to proceed along several different lines. It was to inculcate profound respect for Christian worship and the Christian message. It was to further in-depth study of common elements in non-Christian forms of worship, particularly in Hindu and Muslim worship. And experiments were permissible with the express consent of local bishops.

A series of meetings have since taken place, but I can only mention the most important highlights here. In 1968 an All-India Liturgical Meeting was held, when the focus was still on adaptation to the program. The liturgy had to get rid of its foreign dress. But the participants went beyond any merely adaptational perspective confined to externals. Somehow the Church had to make itself at home in India, a land of age-old languages, cultures, and religions. Instead of treating others condescendingly, the Church had to preserve all that was good in them. The Church had to be Indianized in her way of thinking and feeling, in her way of praying to God and preaching the Christian message.

A second All-India Liturgical Meeting took place in 1969. Several striking observations were already in evidence. First, adaptation would be easier with regard to the sacraments and sacramentals than with regard to the Mass. Second, the vast size of India and the existing multiplicity of languages and cultures indicated that multiplicity would also have to be evidenced in the liturgy. Some elements could easily be integrated into existing liturgies, and the bishops were asked to do that quickly. Other elements, however, called for more radical and fundamental changes. There was a need for serious study and for the opportunity to experiment, so the bishops would have to designate certain centers where this process could be carried on.

Various data-sheets and questionnaires were sent out. For example, the Roman-rite bishops were approached about adaptations that might be made quickly and about the composition of an Indian Eucharistic liturgy. Two-thirds of the responding bishops approved, but objections were raised about the use of India's holy books in the liturgy. The complete dossier was then sent to the Vatican committee entrusted with the task of implementing Vatican II's Constitution on the Sacred Liturgy. Its response came within a month, and the points it made came to be known informally as the Twelve Points:

- It was permissible for people to sit on the ground and take off their shoes.

- A low bow with hands in front of the head could take the place of genuflection.

- Before the liturgy of the Word and at the end of the *anaphora* (i.e., the prayer of Eucharistic offering), the priest and congregation could prostrate themselves on the ground.

- Instead of kissing certain objects, one could touch them with the fingers or palms and then bring fingers or palms to the forehead or eyes.

- Instead of the kiss of peace, one person could place folded hands between the hands of the next person.

- It was permissible to use incense more.

- The vestments could be simplified.

- The square linen corporal used to hold the host could be replaced with a flat shell or some other suitable material.

- Oil lamps could take the place of candles.

- The opening rite could include the following elements: the presentation of the gifts, the celebrant's welcome in Indian form, the lighting of the lamps, and the giving of the kiss of peace by the congregation.

- A certain degree of spontaneity was permissible in the prayer of the faithful.

- Indian forms of veneration were permissible in the Offertory and at the conclusion of the *anaphora*.

The introduction of all these practices was left to the bishops and their episcopal conference. They would have to judge when the time and place was suitable and opportune, and solid catechesis would be a prerequisite. They could also proceed step by step, of course.

The proposal to put together a new Indian *anaphora* in collaboration with various scholars and experts was also welcomed. It was to be sent to the Vatican committee without a great deal of fanfare. The surprising thing about this prompt response from the Vatican was that it favored not only individual changes but also a new Indian *anaphora*.

There was some resistance to the introduction of the Twelve Points, and the controversy was fanned by a few Catholic weeklies. In general, however, they found acceptance when sound catechetical instruction preceded their introduction. The 1969 Pastoral Council of India brought a more Indianized liturgy closer, but continuing opposition required a meeting of the bishops in 1970. Careful investigation showed that it was not true that a small minority was trying to impose its will through the introduction of the Twelve Points. Father Amalorpavadass disproved one of the sharpest complaints: i.e., that people were trying to Hinduize the liturgy. He made it clear that they were simply trying to integrate into the liturgy various forms of worship and veneration which were proper to India's great religions and her sociocultural traditions. In the end all the bishops approved the Twelve Points.

Despite criticism the All-India Liturgical Meeting continued its work and held another meeting in 1971. The focus was now on an Indian *anaphora*. A suitable one was drawn up and submitted to the episcopal conference. It soon became obvious that this part of the Eucharistic prayer called for an overall Indian context. A subcommittee was appointed to work on a whole new Indian Order of the Mass, and to explore how religious texts from the sacred books of other religions might be included in the service.

There were objections and strong reservations. The farther north dioceses were situated in India, the greater their receptivity to the proposed changes. The Church had been in the south much longer, and there people were more attached to Western forms of worship. The Twelve Points were also more readily received in villages than in cities, the latter having been Westernized much more. The strongest negative reactions came from areas where the innovations were introduced too hastily or without sufficient preparation.

In addition, the bishops themselves were divided. Some encouraged the adaptations by their word and example, some rejected them, and some favored introducing them selectively. One cannot escape the impression that the opposition came from a small minority which had been educated in the forms of Western Christianity. They expressed their objections in open meetings, weeklies, pamphlets, and newspapers. I cannot list all the objections here, but they ranged from complaints that Indianization really meant Hinduization to suggestions that it was merely a trick to convert Hindus and the latter could easily see through it. Amalorpavadass was the great champion of the new liturgy, insisting that it embodied a much more important and profound process. It was an attempt to incarnate Christianity in India's culture, in its whole web of sociopolitical, economic, and religious relationships. To reject the new liturgy would really be to reject the whole process of turning to face the real India.

Several decisions were made at the 1972 episcopal conference. Several experimental centers were set up. There research and worship were to proceed hand in hand in order to arrive at complete liturgical adaptation and renewal. They had to get proper recognition from the liturgical commission and from the competent bishop. Evaluation and regular reports to the commission were also required.

In 1972 the liturgical commission had approved both a longer and a shorter version of a new Indian Eucharistic service.[40] The bishops now voted on it, and it was favored by 60 of the 81 bishops present. A dispute arose. The measure had to pass by a two-thirds majority, and some maintained that meant two-thirds of all the bishops whether they were present or not. Rome decided that this interpretation was wrong; the Indian bishops had approved the new Order by their vote. But so far Rome itself has not approved the text.

The text was worked out and formulated in committees. Two Orders of the Mass were formulated and put into use, but without the Indian *anaphora*. There was also opposition from some churchgoers, bishops, and officials in Rome. There were changes in the Congregation for the Liturgy in Rome, and in 1975 it forbade the use of nonbiblical texts and of the Indian *anaphora* even though it praised the hard work of the native liturgical commission. Rome also had reservations about creativity and experimentation. But the root reason for the slowing down of the whole process is to be found in the dissensions and divisions among the bishops, some of whom do not seem to appreciate their rights and obligations as leaders of a local Church.

Committees and liturgical congresses have continued. In 1975 the fifth liturgical congress asked the bishops to settle the matter with Rome: "Our opinion is that this is important, not just for India, but for all of Asia and for other culture areas which have not yet elaborated an indigenous liturgy."[41] It expressly pleaded for a theology of the local Church, which is still incomplete and, in some cases, wholly lacking.

Now I want to offer some sample passages from the Indian liturgy that was published in 1974. It was "a draft for private circulation and experimentation published pro manuscipto." In other words, these texts are actually being used in India, as I can attest from personal experience. And now and then the reading of Indian holy books is also included by way of experiment.

The welcome of the celebrant is completely Indian. Insofar as possible, the participants wash their hands and feet before entering. They and the priests get a colored mark on the forehead, and offerings are brought along. People exchange greetings in Indian fashion. The priest's greeting to the community is striking:

Fullness there, fullness here, from fullness comes fullness.
Once fullness has come from fullness, there is fullness.

This is followed by a purification ceremony. Water, placed on a low table, is blessed in Indian fashion. Various prayers can be said as the priest sprinkles the faithful. One beautiful prayer goes as follows:

> You, whose eyes nothing escapes,
> You, who rule over the whole world,
> You, who sustain the whole universe,
> Fill this place of worship with your presence.

The priest then washes his hands in the water and sips it three times from his hand. This is followed by a kind of penitential rite, and then by the lighting of a large oil lamp. In India light is one of the major symbols for God, and so prayers of praise for light take many different forms:

> Eternal light, shining far out in the heavens,
> Glittering sun, shedding light in all directions—above, below, and in between,
> True light, enlightening every human who comes into this world,
> drive out the darkness from our hearts
> and lighten us with the glow of Your glory.

Many typically Indian gestures are also evident during the readings. For example, the people place their hands on their knees, palms upward. After a reading from the sacred books of India, the well-known saying is uttered:

> From the unreal lead me to the real,
> From darkness lead me to the light,
> From death lead me to deathlessness.

This is followed by readings from the Old Testament, an apostolic letter, and the Gospels.

The preparation for the Eucharistic gifts begins with the presentation of symbolic gifts: e.g., flowers, gifts for the poor, bread and wine, and a plate with eight flowers on it. The celebrant places them on a low table and invites the faithful to formulate their intentions. Then he makes a ceremonial gesture with the plate and the eight flowers in eight directions, at the same time voicing various titles of Jesus.

The Eucharistic Prayer follows, and here I shall cite from the longer version of it. In a dialogue with the faithful, the celebrant praises God's work of creation as a revelation to human beings, God's word as spoken by the patriarchs and prophets, and God's arrival in our midst in the human being, Jesus of Nazareth. The ancient seers of India are also included, however:

> God of the nations,
> You are the longing and the hope
> of all who seek You with an upright heart.
> You are the almighty force
> revered as hidden in nature.
> You reveal Yourself

in the seers, who seek You through knowledge,
in the devout, who seek You through detachment and sacrifice,
in every human being who approaches You along the pathway of love.
You enlighten the hearts which look for redemption
by overcoming their desires and seeking universal goodness.
You show mercy to those who submit to Your inscrutable decrees.

Here we feel that we are in contact with the three pathways of holiness which have been revered in India for ages and ages: the way of insight and knowledge, the way of good deeds, and the way of devotion. At the end of the *anaphora* the faithful make this significant response:

Amen. You are the fullness of reality,
One without a second,
Being, Knowledge, and Bliss!
Om, Tat, Sat!

We find ourselves deeply immersed in the spirituality and mental outlook of India, and yet I think it harmonizes well with the Judeo-Christian tradition. I have only cited a couple of texts here, but my judgment is that the Indian liturgy embodies a solid synthesis of the two different traditions.

Another distinctive feature of the Indian liturgy shows up during the reception of the sacred gifts. The people keep repeating softly: "Jesu Om, Jesu Om . . . Iswara, Iswara." This is better left untranslated. Indeed anyone who has experienced the event will find it hard to translate. It is a meditative recollection of the great name of Jesus and his divinity. This leads to complete silence, then a dialogue between priest and congregation that ends with a blessing. The most Indian moment is the wish expressed by the priest: "May God, who dwells in the cavern of your heart, bring you to life with His own life."

My fragmentary description of the "Indian Mass" can hardly replace actual attendance at it. But I hope readers can now see a bit more clearly why it represents a valid step towards an authentic liturgy that is fully at home in the Indian cultural world. I am convinced that such forms of liturgy do have a future in India and that opposition to them will eventually fade away. This Indian Mass is a reality, and it will perdure. It is also clear, however, that India urgently needs a theology of the local Church if it is to keep moving along the pathway it has entered.

In this chapter I have offered only two examples of a truly incarnate liturgy. The Zairian liturgy seems to be proceeding smoothly whereas the Indian liturgy has encountered great obstacles. Couldn't contact between the Indian Church and the Zairian Church lead to some solution for the problems being encountered in India? They could offer each other mutual assistance, and the West could stay out of the picture. I look forward to such a relationship between the Churches!

18

The Necessary Pluriformity of Theology

In the foregoing chapters I have discussed the theology of the local Church, the reality of basic ecclesial communities, the multiplicity of ecclesial forms of service, and new forms of indigenous worship. Readers can readily conclude that all these things would not have been possible if native theological thinking had not been going on in the Churches of the Third World. Such happenings must be grounded in some form of indigenous religious thinking. The necessity for pluriformity in theology, then, need hardly be demonstrated.

At this point, however, I do need to offer my readers a few clear examples of what is going on in the area of indigenous theological thinking. Western theology remains all too unaware of what is going on in non-Western theology, and much ignorance of the latter is evident in Western theological literature. No one could now presume to cover the whole field, to be sure, but one can read a few compilations or anthologies to see the relativity of one's own point of view and to find enrichment in the thinking of others.[42]

In this chapter I want to offer a sketchy view of some of the new currents in theology from the Third World. Admittedly this treatment is incomplete and far from perfect. Moreover, I am going to focus on only one area of theology, christology, because it is such a basic and important matter. I will also restrict my presentation to the views of native theologians from the Third World, omitting other Western theologians who do their theological work in terms of a Third-World context.

We now have an Ecumenical Association of Third World Theologians (EATWOT). It was formed at the end of the August 1976 ecumenical conference among Third-World theologians, which took place in Dar es Salaam (Tanzania). Subsequent conferences by EATWOT have been held in Asia, Africa, Latin America, and India.[43] But here I shall focus on some christological developments in India, Japan, Sri Lanka, South Africa, and Latin America.

AN INDIAN CHRISTOLOGY

A long period of development lies behind this effort in India. Raja Ram Mohan Roy (1773-1833) started it all in the modern period, although he himself never became a Christian. Through his encounter with Western culture, and particularly with the Anglican Church, he came to feel that India needed an ethical revival if it was to have a future. Various age-old customs were no longer tenable. The best ethical precepts and recommendations for revivifying India, he thought, were to be found in the Sermon on the Mount (Matt. 5:1-7:29). From the very beginning, then, modern christology in India has been a theology of liberation.

Ram Mohan Roy did not reject other parts of the New Testament and the sacred books of India; he simply made a conscious choice of his own. He thus became the first advocate of Neo-Hinduism. He was a theist, who regarded God as the Father. Thus his position was contrary to what many Western missionaries and colonial authorities had to say about Hinduism. The Father stands above all things and all creatures. He also is above his Son, whose life was in full agreement with the Father's will. Christ expressed all this in his Sermon on the Mount. We might well call this an ethical christology.

Keshab Chandra Sen (1838-1884) went a step further, founding the Church of the New Dispensation in 1880. As he saw it, Christ was not a European but an Easterner; hence he was someone comprehensible to Indians. Whereas Roy regarded Christ as a human being, Sen was of the opinion that Christ possessed a divine nature in the sense that he is the Logos of the new creation and hence has cosmic, universal significance. Sen incorporated Christ into Hindu mysticism. Christ is truly the God-Human Being, a new creation, and the prince of all religious leaders.

Here, in the contrast between the views of Roy and Sen, we are already confronted with one of the enduring problematic issues in Indian christology. Is Christ merely a human being in whom God's will became visible, or is he the God-Human Being who has universal significance and in whom the world attained its acme? Does Christ reveal the will of the Father because he obeys the Father completely, or because he himself is the cosmic Word of God?

Another development within Hinduism can be found in the theology of Swami Vivekananda (1863-1902), who was a disciple of Ramakrishna. Vivekananda begins with the typical Indian notion of non-duality. Only the divine exists; the temporal world is merely a veil hiding this divine reality. One experiences liberation in realizing the identity of one's self with the Absolute. Hinduism must carry this message to the world, must become missionary.

Now Christ was one who realized this: "I and the Father are one." In other words, Christ realized God. Christ's lifestyle also made a deep impression on Vivekananda. He exemplified the lifestyle of the homeless Indian monk: "Foxes have holes and the birds of the air have nests, but the Son of Man has nowhere to lay his head" (Luke 9:57). Christ is also an example of kenosis, of one who sought inner reality and rejected the world. He realized the great Indian ideal of homelessness, hence God or the Absolute, thereby carrying the distinctive message of India to the world.

Mahatma Gandhi (1869–1948) also had a view of Christ. While he worked mightily to establish a new nation and a new national and social consciousness, his primary focus was the power of truth, nonviolence, and service to others. All of that he saw in the Sermon on the Mount. Truth is the Absolute Reality, about which various religions have different conceptions. This Absolute Reality is the inner ground out of which everything else unfolds. Human beings must focus on this inner reality rather than getting stuck in the temporal world. Nonviolence follows naturally from this as the virtue of interiority. Those who are seeking ultimate reality become lighter and lighter, ascend higher and higher; worldly human beings, by contrast, sink lower and lower. People must move beyond body, weight, and violence, emptying themselves of everything that blocks their access to inner reality.

Here Christ is the great model. He denied himself completely. Possessing nothing, he was still a great human being. Rather than seeking conquest and victory, he was able to accept self-effacement and self-abandonment. He was a truly inward human, yet his thoughts could suffuse and inspire others. He did right by his fellow humans, preaching love of neighbor; and he had a high regard for concrete human beings.

Gandhi sought to achieve the same thing through service to his fellow humans. This was to be the only weapon in the struggle to free India and to enable all Indians to live in the Truth. They had to be human beings of inwardness because only people seeking ultimate reality were in a position to serve their fellow humans. They also had to have a high regard for those deprived of caste-status. Like Christ, Gandhi did not choose to elaborate any social or political program. He wanted to convert human beings, to make it possible for them to feel at home in the cosmic order. Christ, then, is not the exclusive possession of Christians; he belongs to all humanity.

Two elements in Gandhi's view of Christ, already noticeable in his Indian predecessors, will recur later even among Christian thinkers: (1) its association with the liberation of India; (2) the notion of self-emptying, or kenosis.

The last non-Christian I shall mention here is the late philosopher and President of India, Sarvepalli Radakrishnan (1888–1975). He believed in an eternal religion, which had assumed a comprehensive form in Hinduism. All religions are forms of this eternal religion, stages in a larger process. One of the steps or stages is the veneration of the Buddha, Rama, Krishna, and Christ. They are descents of the highest, absolute Being into the world in order to lead the world to a higher stage. Hence they also are ascents to the Divine, but in a limited way. Christ, then, is a symbol, an aid in reaching the highest Being, the Absolute. It is good to honor and follow Christ so as to dam the flood of secularization. But Christ is one way, one truth, and one life marking the descent of God; he is not the only one, or unique. He can, however, pave the way to the highest stage of the eternal religion, where one is directly united with the Absolute.

For almost two hundred years, therefore, Hindus have been giving some thought to Christ. Questions and problems remain, of course. Christ is not unique. He may be admitted among the homeless seekers of the Absolute. He may be viewed as a model of how to establish an authentic world order. He may be viewed as a descent of the Absolute and as a doorway to true inwardness. But many others may be viewed in the same way, and there is no absolute surrender or abandonment to Christ.

Another basic issue is whether Christ can be separated or divorced from Jesus of Nazareth. Can we separate Christ and Christianity, or Christ and the Church? Aren't we leaving out something essential if we make such a separation? Attempts to answer these questions have been made by various Christians in India who have pondered their submission to Christ and tried to offer a reasoned explanation. Here I shall mention a few specific figures.

Two related converts from Hinduism were the theologians V. Chakkarai (1880–1958) and P. Chenchiah (1886–1959). They saw Jesus Christ as a unique, once-and-for-all descent of God. God and humanity are united in Jesus. The historical existence of Christ as Jesus of Nazareth takes first place. Dying on the cross and rising from the dead, he showed himself to be a divine force. He stands at the beginning of a new creation.

For Chakkarai this happening in Jesus, the new creation, is everything— not the proclamation of this happening, Christianity. Here he is dependent on Hindu thinkers and on Karl Barth. Chenchiah shares the same view of the new creation in Jesus Christ; but to him it represents the surmounting of all religions and all historical development. In his glorification Jesus Christ breathes spirit and life into this earthly life, thus bringing it to new life. This happening, Jesus of Nazareth, is the definitive impulse to a new cosmos; so we must constantly hearken back to it. Jesus dedicated himself whole-heartedly to the coming of God's kingdom, emptying himself out for it.

Here we again meet the notion of kenosis as well as the notion of God's avatars in human beings. In the thought of these Protestant Christians, however, the notions are used in a unique sense. Chakkarai maintained that Jesus was so egoless, so empty of selfhood and personality in the Western sense, that God could unite with him completely. For God, too, is no person and is totally selfless. Once again we see how difficult it is for Indians to accept the concepts of nature and person as used in Western theology. But their theology also is an Indian effort to explain how Jesus is both God and man, and for this they have recourse to the doctrine of kenosis.

Paul Devanandan (1901–1962) approached Jesus Christ from still another point of view. Starting off from Hinduism, he maintained that every faith elaborates a credo, a cult, and a culture. Culture defines the modes of human activity and human relationship. Cult is the whole complex of liturgical acts, rites, and myths that bind a community together. The credo is faith seeking to understand itself. Looking at modern Hinduism in those terms, one can see that it is facing great difficulties. Modernity is compelling us to think new thoughts about community, progress in history, and personhood. Hindu thought has great difficulty doing this, and so the progress of India has been disappointing. To develop a nation, one must simultaneously develop one's thinking and open up one's culture to new perspectives.

Now Jesus enables us to do that. He brought us the God of history. In him God becomes history and a dynamic force for development. Through proclamation we can carry that process on and enable the Word to become flesh. We thus find new social principles and a Christian ethic that must enter into dialogue with India. We can invite India to join in verifying the new creation in Jesus. We can draw Hindus out of their isolation and give them a feeling for community in the whole world order. But of course this assumes that we will remain Indian Christians, that we will continue to seek our own self-understanding and try to understand Jesus as Indians.

Finally, I will mention a current Indian theologian who is still active, S. Jesudason. He has founded a nondenominational community known as "The Family of Jesus Christ." Anyone who regards himself or herself as a follower of Jesus, even if only for a short time, can join. Jesudason begins with the historical Jesus. He sees the definitive revelation of God in Jesus' life, death, and resurrection. The key word here is kenosis once again: self-abnegation even unto death. It involves an ongoing effort to seek and carry out God's will, and we find it in Jesus' love for others. In him we find the two basic virtues associated with Indian religious homelessness: the quest for inner reality and nonviolence. Jesus' uniqueness lies in the fact that he realized these virtues completely and perfectly. In Jesus we see how God encounters human beings. Jesus' humble self-abnegation, manifested in his feeling for his fellow humans, reveals the basic human attitude that is right for us.

Looking back over the development of Indian christology, we can see that there are certain constant features that will have to be taken into account in any future developments. There is no consideration of the metaphysical aspects of Christ's divinity, or of the whole issue of nature and person. Hindu thought does not operate in such terms. To make Jesus Christ comprehensible to Hindus, we will have to stress his mystical and ethical oneness with the Father. Here the notion of kenosis will play a major role. Jesus empties himself so completely that an opening to the divine appears in him. He realizes this throughout his life, and it reaches its acme with his death. In his existence for others, which we call love of neighbor, Jesus opens himself to God. God gets a chance to show himself in Jesus. And since Jesus offers a model for the renewal of modern India, he also has national significance.[44]

A JAPANESE CHRISTOLOGY

Here I want to focus on the christology of Kazoh Kitamori (1916–   ). The publication of his *Theology of the Pain of God* just after World War II marked him as one of the leading Christian theologians in Japan. It met with objections too, but still it was a major effort to explore the Christ-happening more deeply; and it has remained influential.

To present Kitamori's thought properly, one must cover at least two basic questions: (1) What does he mean by the pain of God? (2) How do we move from this pain of God to the historical Jesus? All too many commentators on Kitamori's theology have focused solely on the first question, thus presenting a distorted picture of Kitamori's views.

What about the pain of God? Kitamori maintains that God loves human beings, but that this love is always operative "in spite of" something. Conflict and tension are at work because of human beings. God loves the individual and the world, but he cannot love us without reservation because we live our lives in opposition to him. God loves human beings only amid opposition and wrath, and this wrath is the source of pain. God's love, always operative in history, is dialectically accompanied by pain.

Kitamori then goes on to assert that only a Japanese person can truly suffer along with God and have compassion on him. This is evident from Japanese tragedy, for example, where interpersonal relations are always involved. A person of depth who truly understands the human condition knows what all this means. One who does not understand it is superficial and tiresome—and not Japanese! The Japanese person lives in an ongoing dialectics. For example, he may have to kill someone else or himself in order to save the life of still another person. Joy is born out of distress and suffering. (Here we might wonder to what extent the Buddhist experience of suffering has exercised an influence.)

In any case, God's love is grounded in God's pain. And God's love lies in the fact that this love overcomes his wrath and far surpasses it. Wrath is the alien work *(opus alienum)* of God, whereas love is his true and proper work *(opus proprium)*. Thus love becomes grace and mercifulness.

How do we get to christology from this starting point? Kitamori stresses the necessity of accepting the historical Jesus. All docetism is to be rejected because it would place us in an illusory world, a world of mere appearances. The pain of God means that God's love overcame God's wrath in the very midst of the historical world, a world that merited God's wrath. God's pain necessarily had to enter historical reality as a person: "For God has done what the Law, because of our unspiritual nature, was unable to do. God dealt with sin by sending his own Son in a body as physical as any sinful body, and in that body God condemned sin" (Rom. 8:3). The pain of God could not have existed unless the Redeemer, as the personification of God's pain, had been an historical person. The pain of God has to do with real sin, not with imaginary sin; and only the historical world is the world of real sin. Any and every imaginary world is a world of imaginary sin.

Jesus, the personification of God's pain, assumes the flesh of this historical world. Jesus in the flesh was a real human being, an historical person. God himself had to enter the world of sin in order to shoulder responsibility for real sin. Every form of docetism ends up denying the pain of God. It is the pain of God that is the endlessly deep backdrop for the historical Jesus. Any christology of the mediator which neglects that backdrop must be superficial.

Jesus is the real and true pain of God. And it begins not just with his death, but right at his birth. He agreed not only to die, but also to be born in the first place. This comes out clearly in John's Gospel. Jesus is constantly in danger of death because he calls himself the Son of God. He entered the history of sinfulness and thus became the pain of God. In Christ we see God turning to human beings, though they do not deserve it, and offering them forgiveness so that he can love them. He must give the same attention and forgiveness to his Son in his passion and death. And it is precisely in his act of forgiving that God suffers pain. In fact, the passion and death of Jesus are the reality of God's wrath.

The pain of God, then, has a twofold import. It has to do with human beings and with Jesus, and the two aspects are related. In his pain God loves human beings insofar as he overcomes his wrath. In the act of forgiving it looks as if God gives up being God. But in fact just the reverse is true. He shows and reveals what being God really means because his pain, now embodied as love in the forgiveness of the sinner, wins out; the sinner is converted into one totally obedient to him. This victory of the pain of God is really God's love, a love rooted in pain.

For human beings there remains the task of following the crucified one, of serving the pain of God by bearing their own personal pain. Thus did Abraham serve God by being willing to sacrifice his only son. Human pain is a re-presenting of God's wrath towards sin, a result of the break between God and humanity. Through pain we are united with God and driven to give witness. Christians must find non-Christians by sharing their pain, loving them as they love themselves. In this way they will draw non-Christians into the pain and pardon of God.[45]

A CHRISTOLOGY FROM SRI LANKA

There is a tough thinker in Sri Lanka named Tissa Balasuriya. He is one of the most outspoken champions of an authentic, native Asian form of theologizing. He has published many articles, mainly in the periodical *Logos*. But here I want to focus on his recent work in christology, which again shows up as a central issue in theology. Balasuriya's thought has been influenced by theologians from many other areas: Latin America, South Africa, Anglo-America, and Europe. And his own theological comments are preceded by biting sociological analysis.

Balasuriya's christology begins with strong criticism of the view of Christ which was brought to Asia, and specifically to Sri Lanka, during the colonial period. I can only summarize it briefly here. Balasuriya notes that both Protestants and Roman Catholics presented Christ as a liberator, but never as a liberator from social exploitation. For the past five or more centuries Christ was presented as he was viewed by the Spanish, Portuguese, French, Italians,

Belgians, Irish, and North Americans. Protestants brought the Anglo-Saxon view of Christ to Asia. Since Christianity came to Asia along with colonialism, it was impossible for the European and North American Churches to bring a christology that protested against the colonialist exploitation of Asia's peoples. On the contrary, their theology saw a divine plan for salvation in that exploitation. Redemption had nothing to do with the personal and social emancipation of Asians. In Catholicism, for example, emphasis was placed on establishing a Western Church, administering the sacraments, and venerating the saints.

The picture grew worse in the nineteenth century. The spirituality of both older and newer institutions stressed a personal relationship to our friend Jesus, his vicarious suffering, and his obedient servitude to the Father. The approach to Jesus was framed in extremely individualistic terms. Theology concerned itself with such questions as the following: Can Jesus suffer since he is both God and human being? Did he have full and perfect knowledge? Did he enjoy the beatific vision even while he was still here on earth? The personal life of the historical Jesus was viewed as a combination of evangelical zeal in converting people, active social work on behalf of the needy, and the practice of the more passive virtues such as obedience and self-abnegation. In this context the Churches and missionaries were viewed as institutions or people charged with forming baptized Christians, building schools, and rendering social services. All of these things were means of saving souls. The Church, however, was the only means of salvation; so other religious institutions and other religions had to be undermined. There was no dialogue. The Church was organized as a vertical pyramid, ranging from the pope at the top to lay people at the bottom. The Church was also strongly oriented to pious devotion; pious women and nuns in particular had a great role to play. Other characteristics were: a romanticized Jesus and Mary, a liturgy which highlighted such feasts as that of the Holy Family, a litany of the Sacred Heart, and an other-worldly imitation of Christ.

All these traits fitted in well with traditional, feudal, authoritarian, and superstitious strains in Asian communities themselves. The pull was so strong that even Vatican II could not change very much of it. The Church had little in common with thinkers and activists who wanted to propagate a liberating Christ. Human liberation and the Christian religion grew further and further apart. Modern studies of the real historical Jesus now make it possible for us to take a different tack. The past history sketched above was particularly noticeable in Sri Lanka because it was one of the few Asian lands that was really occupied until 1948 by the Portuguese, Dutch, and English.

However, the old pattern could not continue after independence came in 1948. Political leadership changed, the economy became more socialist, English control over economic matters diminished, the native languages of the people came back, and Hinduism and Buddhism emerged more forthrightly as social forces. A new struggle for liberation emerged, tending towards a more self-sufficient and egalitarian society. There were serious confrontations between social classes, political ideologies, and racial groups.

In the latter half of the 1970's a new outlook emerged in the Catholic Church: more attention to national cultures, respect for other religions, and changes in the liturgy. There was more talk about social options to be taken by the Church: development, liberation, welfare, involvement in political issues, human rights in society and the Church, the nature of the priesthood and ecclesial ministries, patterns of authority, decentralization and greater participation, family life, and so forth. Underlying all such questions was a different understanding of the nature of religion, God, the Spirit, and Jesus Christ. Young people and the oppressed, in particular, raised these questions; they were resisted by members of the elite. A better understanding of Jesus Christ, who was the founder of Christianity after all, could bring all these tendencies closer together.

It is good, then, to see Jesus as an historical person. He was a laborer who showed concern for all, but particularly for the poor. He did not stand on his privileges; he lived for others. He was firm and uncompromising in his opposition to injustice, and he lived in a situation much like ours. The human person was not respected as such, but rather in terms of social status. Exploitation was common. The poor, the weak, the uneducated, women, children, sinners, and others were exploited by the rich, the powerful, the social elite, and the foreign overlord. Illness was regarded as a punishment for previous sins.

In the face of that concrete situation Jesus proclaimed the reign or kingdom of God. He introduced new personal and social values. This was the "good news," the gospel, and it undermined the existing social order. Jesus saw God as love, and sin as a turning away from this loving God. He was more interested in values than in temporal institutions or forms of power, and this implied criticism of Roman imperial rule. The community which Jesus gathered around him was to realize his new set of values, and this called for a clear-cut choice. Jesus' message leads to personal liberation, to the discovery of a better self and the elimination of unnecessary social restrictions. His liberation also brings better interpersonal relations, eliminating the emphasis on individualism that is inherent in capitalism.

Neither the Roman nor the Jewish social order had given human persons their due. There was a great deal of exploitation. One need only think of the position of women and prostitutes, and Jesus' own attitude towards them. He liberated women. He prepared people to make a free, responsible decision, to follow him in walking the road to the Father. In this way he brought joy to people.

Another aspect of the liberation brought by Jesus was his reaction against formalism in the Jewish religion. He wanted to free people from such religion. The gospel message is full of strong statements by Jesus against the formalist-minded Jewish leaders of his day. Religion had become a form of oppression. In Jesus' eyes religion was a deeply inner relationship to his

Father and to one's own conscience. The Last Supper was not a formalistic prayer but a truly human event in a secular atmosphere. It was a meal, a communal meal in a private house, the table laden with meat and wine. Jesus was the priest, and indeed there is only one priesthood according to the New Testament. That priesthood is a sharing in the priesthood of Jesus, which is not some separate caste but rather loving service: e.g., washing other people's feet.

Jesus brought social liberation as well. Social justice and liberation in that very sense was his aim. In the course of time the teaching of Jesus came to be viewed and lived in excessively individualistic terms. This was particularly true in Asia, where religion came to be more pious devotion than service to and for God. It was stressed that Jesus loved rich and poor alike, that he gave Caesar his due, and that he was no revolutionary. Balasuriya sees this as a capitalist interpretation. In fact, we cannot love our neighbor as Jesus asked unless we are guided by a concern for justice. If we read the Gospels attentively, we will soon see that the rich do not come off too well; nor do the unjust. Reading the parables, we see that Jesus sharply challenged the social consciousness of his followers. He proposed new values which had to do with society and social relationships. So Asians must take a similarly critical look at problems around them.

What was Jesus' stand on political liberation? He saw power and authority in terms of service. He was essentially a spiritual and religious leader, but that does not mean that he had no outlook on politics or that Christianity is supposed to be apolitical. Jesus teaches us that all political power is meant to be a form of service to others, and particularly to the needy and distressed. He wanted to see a new humanity wherein authority exemplified love and service and honesty instead of being corrupt, self-seeking, and self-perpetuating. We must love our enemies; if we do, then it is impossible for us to entertain the idea of dominating others.

This was the revolution of Jesus, which no one had ever preached before, and he exemplified it magnificently in his own life. He was not an arms-wielding rebel. In fact, he stood for the absolute values of the Kingdom of God; so one cannot maintain that he favored feudalism, capitalism, socialism, or any other specific form of social organization. Every such system stands judged by the values of the Kingdom. The pedagogy of Jesus regarding how to arrive at social change involved the following elements:

- identification with the lives of the masses, with the plight of the poorest of the poor;
- a public, protest-oriented style of preaching in which he exposed and denounced unjust social structures, thereby trying to awaken people to the struggle for liberation;
- a willingness to risk everything for this cause, even death at the hands of the rulers of his day;

- the formation of a community to carry on his work, and the more intensive training of some followers so that they could be his special witnesses all over the world;
- the promise of deep inner peace to all who would follow him in seeking the values of the Kingdom of God.

Balasuriya then views the necessary revolutions in Asia from the standpoint of Jesus. In the historical Jesus, who also has a cosmic dimension as the Word of God, Balasuriya finds great inspiration for forthrightly tackling the great problems of Asia. Asia is a continent of poor people suffering under heavy and oppressive political structures. Land ownership is very poorly distributed and social conditions are a crying shame. There is famine, overpopulation, disease, and premature death. Some people lord it over the rest of the population. Balasuriya's christology is a dynamic approach to these major problems. Christians, in particular, must look to christology for their inspiration and ask themselves many questions. The Churches have built many schools, and they simply impart abstract knowledge. Are such schools the best way to serve the local community? Class conflict exists even in the churches. Is that not un-Christian? Many more such questions must be raised and answered.[46]

JESUS CHRIST, THE BLACK LIBERATOR

Professor David Bosch of South Africa distinguishes five kinds of black theology. I shall not discuss his classification here, nor shall I consider their relationship with North American black theology. After sketching in the background briefly, I shall focus on the voice of one African whose black theology offers a specific vision of Jesus Christ.

The theology of Christ as the black liberator arose against the peculiar and distinctive backdrop of South African life. In South Africa people are classified in terms of color and language. White human beings and their language are the measuring rod. The white man lays down the rules for social interaction and stands at the top. On every official form his name comes first. He is white, and that embodies everything worthwhile and worth striving for. All other human beings come after the white person, according to a clearly defined system of values: e.g., colored, Indians, Bantus. They are the non-whites. Even as human beings, they are defined in negative terms because they are not white. Their human dignity is not recognized because whiteness is the prerequisite for full humanness. Black human beings suffered the psychological effects of all this. They could not develop a normal and healthy self-awareness of their worth as human beings. Feelings of inferiority combined with an attitude of submissiveness so that blacks sometimes adopted the negative value-judgments of white society about blacks. It is against this backdrop that we must understand the rise of black theology and black christology in Africa.

The thinking of Manas Buthelezi is perhaps the most clear-cut and the most African. In his black theology we can also see an African theology which embodies a Christian view of what it means to be African. Buthelezi begins with the assertion that the category of humanness and the human being is increasingly becoming the major point of reference in contemporary discussions of social ethics. It cannot be overlooked in our talk about justice. Present-day interest in human rights and human dignity is part of the current human effort to gain greater self-understanding and self-fulfillment in the midst of dehumanizing elements within modern life. Every human being has an inalienable right to selfhood and self-development as he or she envisions it. Very often, however, people find that this is not permitted. Their life is a caricature of their humanness.

This situation prompts many questions in people: Who am I really? What form of existence is right for me, and where am I headed? How can I live in such a way as to overcome all the things which contradict my reality as a human being? For the African living in South Africa, these are urgent questions. He or she wonders whether being black is an insuperable barrier and a fated destiny, or a context in which God makes it possible for him or her to be a real human being to the fullest extent.

Where do we find the theological criteria of true humanness? Well, according to the Old Testament humanity is made in the image and likeness of God. That expresses humanity's exclusive relationship to God and the dignity of human beings. That is why humanity has dominion over other creatures, since it is God's representative in the world. It is really the Son who is the Image of God, but humanity was created after that image. In the fullness of time the Son came to show how like God the image is.

Great theologians, such as Thomas Aquinas and Martin Luther, elaborated this datum in their own different ways. It is certainly true that the Fall did not reduce the human being to a brute animal. Humanity remained the image of God, as it had been created. But it is no less true that in their dealings with others human beings often follow the law of the jungle. Still, even sinful humanity is redeemable because it has been created in God's image. Slavery and racial hatred exemplify the fall of humanity. But even as slaves and oppressed people, human beings are meant to be redeemed from the social consequences of sin. Even in such circumstances they remain the image of God.

According to 1 Corinthians 5:17, humanity can become a new creation in Christ. In Baptism a person becomes a member of a community of sinners to whom forgiveness has been granted. They can grow and renew themselves once again, finding nourishment in the Word and the sacraments. In baptism they participate in the death and resurrection of Christ, and only a living being can do that. The authentic humanity of *homo* is healed and made whole once again.

Now since God always dispenses his grace in and through earthly reality, human dignity and potential can be realized only in and through day-to-day life. Becoming a new human being is not something we look forward to in heaven; it is a process which is taking place here on earth. That raises a crucial question: Can human beings, as Christians, achieve their full flowering as humans when they are forced to live amid inhuman circumstances: poverty, slavery, and so forth?

In the thinking of Buthelezi we see that the anthropological and christ-ological data of the Old and New Testaments serve as the backdrop and foundation for the liberation brought by Christ, the full recovery of au-thentic humanness, and hence full human liberation.

As we have noted earlier, the African vision focuses on the totality of life. Religion is never something separate from everyday reality. There is commu-nity between the living and the dead, and death is not a finale. The active presence of the creator of life is pervasive. The more one participates in life, the more one experiences the presence of God. For the African, there is no separate sacral world alongside the profane world. Western culture, and even Western Christianity to some extent, has tried to encourage a separation be-tween the two. God supposedly would have power only over the spiritual realm; in the secular realm, human beings would be at the mercy of society.

Africa must resist this tendency and try to restore integrity to human life. Such an approach is also quite biblical, because the Bible asserts that God is and remains the creator of all things. Thus Africans cannot accept the aliena-tion now being imposed on them. They cannot remain objects of domination, colonized human beings who are not allowed to be themselves. Right now it is as if they were living under house arrest in their own land. Living on the margin of society, they are not given the chance to develop their human po-tential or to participate in life fully. As Africans and Christians, they cannot accept this situation. Nor can they accept the imported disjunction between ideal and reality. So long as such a disjunction is maintained, all talk about Christian fellowship remains mere theory.[47]

A LATIN AMERICAN CHRISTOLOGY

Liberation theology has never wholly overlooked christology, but it was well for Jon Sobrino to devote a whole book to the latter subject. Sobrino begins by describing some of the features of his Latin American christology.

First, such a christology is ecclesial. In the New Testament itself we find several different christologies, each of which developed out of the real-life situation of a particular ecclesial community. The first Christian communi-ties accepted the reality of Jesus in different forms and ways, but they all had recourse to Christ to justify themselves. You never have a christology without an ecclesiology. You can never detach doctrinal statements about Christ from the Churches, but neither is it permissible to regard them as exclusive. It is always the case that the way in which Christ is conceived by Christians is rooted in the concrete life and reality of the Christian community. By the same token, the meaningfulness and activity of a community is viewed in terms of Christ.

The same applies to Latin America. Latin American christology must reflect the life and practice of many ecclesial communities. By the same token, its teaching about Christ must give meaning to Latin American ecclesial communities, helping them to grow in their life and praxis. Here, then, we have the fundamental principles of any Latin American liberation theology regarding the nature of church theory and action. Dogmatic formulations about Christ guarantee the truth about him. However, that does not absolve ecclesial communities from the task of viewing Christ first from the standpoint of their own real-life situation. That is the only way to incorporate the truth about Christ into their own lives.

Second, Sobrino's christology is historical. This point must be properly and fully understood. Christ sets in motion a Christian reality and a Christian history. This process cannot be frozen at one point in history. Christ continues to unleash and monitor a new and renewed Christian history, otherwise he would not be the Christ at all. This means that we must now elaborate a christology on the basis of present-day history. The starting point is the affirmation that Christ is the Jesus of history. Logically this means that we cannot begin with direct reflection on christological dogmas. We must always follow the approach which made possible the formulation of those dogmas.

Thus Sobrino places great emphasis on the historical Jesus. The content of our profession of faith in Christ as the eternal Son of God must be derived from the content of Jesus' own history and fate. This also means that such a christology will show a preference for the praxis of Jesus over his teaching and what the New Testament authors concluded about it. The New Testament is viewed primarily as history, and only secondarily as a commentary on the real nature of history. The life of Jesus will not be viewed in idealistic terms, but rather in terms of sin and conflict. The person of Jesus grew in the course of his life and activity, amid the conflicts which that activity evoked. And so did his theological relationship to the Father.

From this historical look at Jesus, it is also obvious that he himself was not the central focus of his preaching and his activity. Jesus' nature was relational. At the center stood the coming kingdom or reign of God, Jesus' unreserved trust in his Father, and his work for the realization of the Father's kingdom. Since this is the case, and since the kingdom has not yet arrived, christology cannot tie us down hand and foot to the past. Christology must be oriented towards the future, towards the future of God and his kingdom.

Third, Sobrino's christology insists on being trinitarian. In the light of what has been said so far, that may seem illogical at first glance. But Sobrino is convinced that Latin American liberation theology is the very theology that poses this difficult doctrine as a serious theological subject. It is not that liberation theology is going to go in for abstract speculation on the Trinity. Instead it purports to show that the very process of theologizing itself is a trinitarian process. It cannot reflect on Jesus without reflecting on his relationship to the Father and his kingdom. Jesus poses the mystery of the Father and his kingdom as the ultimate mystery and horizon of human existence and history. Reflection on Jesus is likewise christological, since the claim is that in Jesus we have the revelation of the Son of God. The revelation of the Son in the history of Jesus shows us, in a full and definitive way, how human beings can respond to the ultimate mystery of God in the midst of their historical life and existence.

In this christology it is also clear that we can see Jesus as the Son and so get closer to the Father only if we try to live in accordance with the Spirit of Jesus: "We can come to know Jesus as the Christ only insofar as we start a new life, break with the past and undergo conversion, engage in Christian practice and fight for the justice of God's kingdom."[48] Thus christology is possible only when it is framed in terms of the Trinitarian reality of God:

> Christology is possible only if the Father continues to be the ultimate horizon of reality, the Son continues to be the definitive example of how human beings can correspond to the Father, and life according to the Spirit of Jesus continues to be the authentic Christian way of acting that makes us sons and daughters in and through the Son.[49]

Here the whole approach of liberation theology is extended to christology, thus providing that theology with a more solid basis. I cannot cover all the material in Sobrino's thick volume, but I will briefly mention some of the topics that he covers in some detail. Theology, he says, can only be carried on within the context of praxis. In other words, human beings can know and appreciate Jesus as Jesus, as the one who sends the Spirit, only if they lead a life that is in agreement with that Spirit. Moreover, this christology stresses the full realization of God's kingdom, thus indicating that the mysterious and utopian reality of the kingdom is the ultimate horizon of theology. Though it always lies ahead of us and we are not in a position to fully turn it into reality, it continues to be the deepest source of our being and life insofar as it points us towards the future.

This theology places full stress on the historical Jesus, indicating that his significance lies in the fact that he is the definitive model of divine filiation. This picture is fleshed out in concrete details. Jesus, the Son, proclaims the coming utopia and denounces injustice as the core of sinfulness. He favors the oppressed and he unmasks alienating religious mechanisms. He does this so that his Spirit will not remain vague; so that his God, the Father, will not remain abstract and open to human manipulation. What is involved here is mutual interaction between an active christological praxis based on the Spirit of Jesus and the firm hope in the utopia of God's kingdom.

Sobrino thus details a solid christological basis for liberation theology. The main point is that the historical Jesus of Nazareth and his work is placed in the foreground. The real-life history of Jesus becomes the point of reference for evaluating the real-life history of Latin America today. Christology again becomes relevant for community life in a concrete situation, though the import of age-old dogmas is not diminished or denigrated. There is much similarity between the christologies of Balasuriya and Sobrino.

Let me offer a few general conclusions from this brief sampling of Third World theology today. The theologians and Churches of the Third World want us to get more deeply involved with the historical Jesus. We must have the courage to go back to the situation of the first Christian communities. They comprehended Jesus of Nazareth in their own distinctive ways without contradicting each other, and we must recapture that same freedom. The Jesus-happening must be pondered anew on every continent and in every specific set of circumstances. Pluralism will be the result, but that is not un-Christian because it was already evident in the earliest Christian communities. We will get a theology and christology that is much closer to real life, that can offer saving benefits to human beings in concrete situations.

We have already set our foot on that road. Dialogue with other religions, cultures, and historical situations has opened our eyes to see what is essentially Christian. And we now realize that it does not have to be put together in exactly the same way for all times, places, and situations. There is room for freedom in oneness, for different formulations of one and the same faith. We are learning that anew from what is going on today in such places as Sri Lanka and Latin America.[50]

19

The Service of the Churches to the World

As the Churches carry on their life in the context of their milieu and enter into dialogue with the real situation, they discover completely new tasks to be carried out in the service of society. The localization of the Church is carried through on this level as well. Here I want to offer a few examples of the process in action.

A PROGRAM OF PASTORAL CONSCIENTIZATION IN NEW ZEALAND

Whenever one hears the word "conscientization," one cannot help but think of its great pioneer in Latin America, Paulo Freire.[51] It was he who did so much to introduce the process of consciousness-raising as a formal and significant pedagogy. But here I will simply focus on a consciousness-raising project undertaken by the Church in New Zealand. Its aim has been to eliminate various forms of ethnic prejudice.

Every society thinks that its own way of doing things is the right way. Other modes of living are written off as dumb, uncivilized, ridiculous, superstitious, or whatever. One group of people may go so far as to regard another group as less than human. More than one tribe has named itself "the people" or "humanity," and such a designation can imply that others are less than human and can be treated accordingly.

Ethnocentrism is widespread. It begins with a stereotype of the other party, a conception that some in-group has about some out-group. It is a preconception that is too generalized and unsubstantiated. But we must realize that such handy stereotypes and their widespread use are prompted and supported by strong impulses and emotional factors. People are tempted to see only what they really want to see. Comments about another group go from mouth to mouth, and what they have to say about the group grows worse in the process.

Ethnocentrism in many forms is likely to show up when some minority has to live in the midst of some majority. Such is the case in New Zealand, where

Maori and Polynesian minorities live among the white majority. The whites say that the Maoris are lazy, unambitious, apathetic, easy living, untrustworthy, and fit only for manual labor and other lowly jobs. The tragic thing is that some of the Maoris themselves may come to believe such accusations. Things had gone so far in New Zealand that the dominant group was unwilling to learn from the dominated group, and the latter group was isolating itself from the former. There were also attempts at assimilation which tended to overlook or suppress the distinctive features in the minority culture. People who nurture ethnic prejudices have little sympathy for multi-culturalism, for any suggestion that an encounter between two cultures can enrich both sides.

Multi-culturalism can never make headway without some tension being involved. Forceful programs are needed to get the process underway. Even before that, people must be motivated by education to do something positive to uproot their prejudices, which can be purely personal but which frequently are embodied in institutional forms. One need only think of the situation in South Africa, Australia, and Northern Ireland; or of the history of Anglo-Irish relations in Great Britain.

Interestingly enough, Jesus seems to have been quite aware of this problem. He himself was a Jew, but consider his attitude toward the Samaritans. In his parable he used the example of the Good Samaritan to denounce the evil of prejudice. His good Samaritan was far from a lazy good-for-nothing. He stepped in to help the assaulted Jew who had been bypassed by members of the Jewish elite. Jesus' pedagogical approach is also interesting. His parable must have been a shock to his Jewish audience, and yet it was also palatable. We see the same attitude in his dealings with the Samaritan woman at the well. He took water from her and conversed freely with her—an unheard-of way of acting for a Jew. By word and deed Jesus attacked Jewish ethnocentrism, and he broke through the passive front which the Samaritans had adopted in response.

The New Zealand Church has come to understand and appreciate Jesus' attitude and approach. Its episcopal conference elaborated the following program, which might well serve as a model for many Churches in different lands. There are four phases to the program. First, a questionnaire was sent out to as many priests and religious as possible. Personal visits were also made to those who responded. Responses came from 63 percent of the priests, 27 percent of the brothers, and 21 percent of the nuns. Then the questionnaire was sent to 16 representative parishes in four dioceses and to 25 Catholic high schools. Approximately 5,000 lay people responded to this mailing. Groups of Maoris and Polynesians were also asked about their feelings with regard to ethnic prejudice, and discussions were held with them.

Three months later, the results of the inquiry were compiled in a report. The main report ran to six hundred pages, and it was published as a textbook for teachers. It included up-to-date material on prejudice and inter-ethnic relations, as well as key elements of Christian doctrine on the matter. Previously there had been no such textbook on this particular subject. A thirty-page synopsis of the report was also prepared for those who could not read the full report.

In order to turn the findings into practice, it was first decided to tackle consciousness-raising at the leadership level. Seminars were held for bishops, religious superiors, priests, and diocesan lay leaders. They went over the material for three days and planned how to provide feedback to the rank and file. The mass media, both Catholic and secular, were mobilized. In each diocese a core group was assigned the task of getting the true situation across to the faithful. There were many meetings on the deanery level to alert priests, religious, and pastoral councils. Many seminars and workshops were held, with the focus on action. The ultimate goal was to reach parishioners and influence their concrete behavior. At the end of this campaign the leadership team met with the diocesan core groups to formulate ongoing programs. The first results of this conscientization process are already evident, and every bishop is on the alert to keep things moving along.

Investigations indicated that all these measures were necessary, since a high percentage of Catholics shared the national prejudices. They had adopted prejudicial attitudes uncritically and without much thought. Much patience is needed to change things, as everyone realizes. Changes in basic attitudes and behavior patterns never come quickly, and they make heavy demands on a person. It is also felt that the life of Jesus himself must be used as a source of ongoing motivation; otherwise the whole project will be nothing more than a sociological exercise.[52]

A NEW SYSTEM OF HEALTH CARE IN TANZANIA

As Dr. Lo Schröder reports, a whole new approach to health care is well under way in Tanzania and the Sudan; and it is in its initial stages in such places as Indonesia and the Philippines. Dr. Schröder has long been involved with health care in Tanzania, and the Churches have played an important role too. What exactly was the problem which led to the new approach?

All too long people thought that every problem could be solved simply by importing Western techniques and facilities. But the Tanzanian masses were not reached by the well-equipped hospitals, nor were the endemic diseases attacked at the source. Health care was too institutional; there was too much emphasis on buildings, hospitals, and clinics. People were not always willing to come to them, and often they could not reach them because of the long distances involved. Those most in need of health care were least likely to come in contact with it. The whole medical apparatus was also ill prepared for the native scene, since it focused on professionals and cures rather than on disease-prevention. Big campaigns against a certain disease did not solve the problem because they focused on effects rather than causes.

Some efforts were made to tackle the matter differently. For example, it was decided to focus on two of the most vulnerable groups, mothers and children. Pregnancy clinics and under-five clinics sprang up all over, and so did mobile clinics. Even the latter did not solve the overall problem, however. When the mobile clinic moved on, things went back to where they had been. These clinics were also more concerned with cure than prevention. An increase in native doctors did not solve the health-care problem either. They tended to stay in the big cities, where they could put their Western knowledge into practice; or else they remained in the Western country where they had received their training. (More than 35 percent of the doctors in England, for example, have come from former British colonies.) Moreover, the big hospitals remained the focal point of the health budget, absorbing 60 percent of it while caring for only 2 percent of the Tanzanian population.

It all seemed hopeless and senseless. Then the realization dawned that somehow the broad stratum of people at the grass-roots level had to be reached, and that health care alone could not do the job. It had to be combined with socio-economic progress and political consciousness-raising. The people themselves had to become the basis of integral development. Since the infant mortality rate was high, it made little sense to prattle on about birth control and family planning. Little was gained if people learned how to grow more crops but were not taught at the same time how to put together a well-balanced diet. Malnutrition would continue despite the increased food supply. If people earned more with the growth of industry and farming, they would also have to be taught to spend more on good nutrition and hygiene. Irrigation may be a good thing, but it can also breed infection. A tractor is a good thing; but if tractors mean that all the women are going to lose their farm jobs, then people must ask themselves exactly what they are accomplishing.

Carried out properly, health care can serve as the motor for socio-economic and political consciousness-raising on the grass-roots level. People learn to do things themselves. This point has been realized in Tanzania, and it has become the normal way of doing things. A whole new approach has come into being, thanks to the support of many different institutions and people. The Catholic University of Nijmegen is one of the collaborators, for example, and the health agencies of the Church are part of the national plan. Stress is placed on all sorts of simple health-care workers who have been trained to deal with local conditions. Instead of hospitals that are all too often elitist and remote, there are numerous local First Aid posts manned by local health workers. Those on the lowest levels are less trained than those on higher levels.

It is a carefully graded system of health care. Someone better trained is available to help at whatever level, but all are chosen by the people. Training is provided by government agencies, the Churches, and medical centers. Only here and there do you find large hospitals to care for people who cannot be helped by local facilities. Medical workers at the lower levels handle all sorts of things: health education, hygiene, lessons on diet and nutrition, lessons on water use and environmental pollution, etc. They themselves must set an example, since they are not bureaucrats who can live where they wish but members of the community.

For every 50,000 people there is a health center with a well-trained nurse and a certain number of beds. Half of its work is curative. An ambulance is available to transport patients who need more care to a large hospital. The people themselves must ask for such health centers and ponder their usefulness. All this has meant that the Catholic Church has been forced to do a great deal of rethinking. But the Church and Christian communities are now truly dedicated to the service of the people, who have benefited from the change in outlook and approach.[53]

SOCIALIST HUMANISM IN THE SERVICE OF INDIA

In Bangalore, India, the Churches run a very active Institute for Religion and Society. It has its own periodical and numerous other publications. Through its conferences and projects it also exerts a formative influence on the work that Christian communities are doing in and for Indian society. One important theologian involved in its activities is M. M. Thomas. Here I want to summarize his recent overview of the Indian situation.

In a recent publication Thomas examined some representative Indian advocates of secular ideologies. His aim was to explore the quest for a spiritual reality that underlay their ideological approach. In India there are many political and social ideologies which are secular in the sense that they start off from a scientific study of empirical reality rather than from the reality of religion or God. Yet all of these ideologies, according to Thomas, are looking for the meaning of human existence and for the ultimate underlying force behind it. Sometimes this quest is explicit, sometimes implicit, but in either case these ideologies must be confronted with the humanism of the gospel message. Thomas examines liberal nationalism, socialist humanism, Marxism-Leninism, anti-Brahmanism, and the three individual ideologies of Subhas Chandra Bose, M. N. Roy, and M. R. Masani. After reading Thomas's study, I would say that he thinks socialist humanism has the most to offer India, though of course he would subject it to further criticism and theological reflection. Here, then, I will offer a brief overview and evaluation of socialist humanism in India as presented by Thomas.

When the Congress Socialist Party was established in 1934, it already had formulated the goals of total independence from the British Empire and the establishment of a workers' society. The main figure in the party was its secretary general, Jayaprakash Narayan. Another important goal was equality in economic and political relationships through some democratic form of government and management. This was sometimes referred to as democratic socialism. After independence came, Nehru took over this program. He saw democratic socialism as the only possible way to achieve socio-economic and political equality for all; to banish poverty, unemployment, abject resignation, and the humiliating condition of the Indian people.

In economic life technological innovations were looked upon with favor, but they would have to be in the hands of the people. To keep technology human, as Gandhi had wished, it was not absolutely necessary for the national government to control everything. Local government and even local communities could play an important role. Small industries might be entrusted to individuals, with the proviso that profits went to benefit the community. In agriculture such an approach led to various forms of cooperatives. Much ground had to be made up, and the holdings of the big landowners had to be redistributed. The small farmer was considered the forgotten man in socialism.

The Congress Party wanted democratic socialism in the political sphere also. Otherwise, it was feared, British colonial rule would simply be replaced by other oppressive structures already present in Indian society. Some seemed to incline towards state totalitarianism, but most did not want to see democracy fail to arise as had happened in Russia. Most wanted constructive, parliamentary activities that would serve the interests of the people. Many forms of self-expression were open to the people, it was felt: e.g., trade unions, Churches, youth movements, community centers, literary clubs, and political parties. The state or government was merely one of these organizations. As the organ of society as a whole it had a certain priority, but it did not enjoy supremacy. Individual freedom and the quest for responsible self-fulfillment had to be promoted. So after a brief transition period it should be possible somehow to restrict the power of the state. Democracy itself had to rest on four pillars: the village, the district, the province, and the center. It was hoped that in the future a fifth pillar could be added: a world center. This approach, it was felt, would preclude the dictatorship of the proletariat as well as excessive concentration of power in the state as center.

India's democratic socialism also seeks to change society. Consciously shared community is to replace the old hierarchical structure based on caste, class, and their correlates. The task is an enormous one. Education and social mobility are among the prerequisites if greater economic justice is to be achieved. Otherwise the introduction of technology will only replace the old India with a lawless society of unfettered individualism. A social revolution is needed, and this calls for concerted efforts in many areas: education, religion, social management, political administration, and so forth.

Indian socialists talk about achieving human freedom and responsible self-fulfillment in a community of free persons. This is seen to be the goal and end result of a cosmic and historical evolutionary process. The future of humanity is viewed as the fulfillment of the personal destiny of each and every human being. This is a leap of faith, an a priori assumption, a hope for the future of humanity. Nehru and others admitted that there was no scientific justification for this a priori faith. Some call it a postrevolutionary utopia, but they maintain that it must be partially realized here and now if it is ever to be realized at all. The future postrevolutionary utopia must be preceded by a prerevolutionary utopia of some sort.

Why is this faith necessary? Because otherwise there is a danger that people will act unethically, turning the means to the end into absolutes and thereby shortchanging humanity; science will rule over human beings. From science itself we do not get any system or philosophy that can control science. That must come from some sort of spirituality, says Jayaprakash. Science and spirituality are mutually complementary.

There is another reason why this faith is needed. Power politics is necessary to achieve the peaceful socialist revolution. However, such politics can quickly degenerate into corruption and betray the real goals of the struggle. Ethical values are needed, otherwise people forget the true goals and get entangled in the means. Human beings must move beyond the material realm in order to find the inspiration they need to do good. It is only when materialism is surmounted that the individual achieves selfhood and becomes an end in itself. Matter is not the ultimate reality. The same basic line of thought is expressed somewhat differently by other Indian thinkers.

What about the relevance of Hindu spirituality in carrying out this task? What criticisms of Hindu spirituality are made by India's socialist leaders and thinkers? Nehru, for one, kept the problem at arm's length. He certainly was opposed to dualism in any form. He had no interest in people who espoused a practical life on the one hand and moments of inner solitude on the other, feeling that no real dedication to the community could come from such an outlook. Nehru did not believe in a personal God, nor was he concerned about personal immortality. After his death he wanted to be immersed in the ongoing current of the cosmos and India's history. That is why he asked that his ashes be scattered in the Ganges, so that they might be spread all over India. Nehru did acknowledge that there was a creative, life-giving force in matter which made self-movement and change possible. This is the spirit of Indian history, and Nehru called it India's spirituality. But he remained skeptical about all claims to absolute truth and virtue. Perhaps he was really more Western than Indian in his whole outlook.

Jayaprakash was more clear-eyed and explicitly Indian in his views, though he gave a different direction to Indian terminology and spirituality. He clearly saw the problem of religion and development, and indeed he was way ahead of his time in that respect. The ultimate goal of individuals is their integral human development as individuals. Social organizations must make it possible for the individual to achieve this goal. The Indian ideal of a full life is expressed in the four terms: artha, kama, dharma, and moksha. Human beings must earn their bread (artha), seek pleasure (kama), and carry out their societal responsibilities (dharma). By so doing, they can ascend to a stage of human life where their time-limited characteristics are surmounted, where oneness of spirit is discovered, and where they find themselves identified with others (moksha). Here we have a secular interpretation of Indian spirituality. The quest for oneness of spirit is extended to include the family, village community, state, nation, and ultimately the whole human community. Such values as love, cooperativeness, and responsibility for others are stressed in Jayaprakash's spirituality. Underlying his whole outlook is the conviction that all human beings, despite their differences, are basically good because they are fleeting clouds of God's glory; and God is our all.

Other thinkers have pondered these issues also. All of them tend to give a twist to Hinduism, advocating a spirituality that is more actively involved in the world. While I cannot cite all these thinkers here, it is clear that they tend to look forward to a time when organized religions will be replaced by certain moral and spiritual attitudes towards life. There is great admiration for such figures as Jesus, Mohammed, and the Buddha because they were spiritual rebels. Unfortunately their inspirations have been petrified in creeds, institutions, prescriptions, and customs. Vinoba Bhave feels this way, and he is not the only one. No religion is really necessary. What is needed is spirituality.

These socialist thinkers have a more dialectical view of Christianity. It gave spiritual sanction to Western humanism, but also to Western imperialism. Moreover, unlike Hinduism, it is missionary and proselytizing. But the person of Jesus Christ has exerted a profound influence on Indian socialists, both as a human being and as a symbol of humanity's future. Nehru, for example, was deeply impressed by the Sermon on the Mount. Others claim that Christianity gave rise to capitalism, and then to Marxism as a reaction. They feel that Western Christianity and socialism could go hand in hand, provided that Christianity goes back to the original spirit of Jesus himself.

It is a shame that these idealists have been dependent on liberal, Marxist, and Ghandian movements for their knowledge of Christianity. It seems that they have not been solidly or deeply influenced by Christianity, even though they may have been educated in Christian schools. That does not say much for the Indian and foreign institutes of higher learning. Moreover, in earlier days little interest or acquaintance with Indian socialist ideas and policies was evident in those schools.

The situation is changing now, and the Institute for Religion and Society in Bangalore is playing a major role. Socialist humanism is the prevailing line of thought in the Institute, so there can now be a real dialogue between the Churches and India. The dialogue is broadening out, but unfortunately the Christian Union of India has not yet joined it.

So we come to a brief evaluation. Socialist humanism is the strongest current in India. It is an ideology of social revolution based upon a conception of the human being in society. It takes in both the moral and spiritual nature of human beings as well as their rational and social character. It looks forward to building a cultural and political home for human beings where justice is done to all dimensions of their personality.

The comprehensive character of this ideology is both its weakness and its strength. It is a weakness insofar as history operates to a large extent on half-truths and thereby evokes the support of the masses. The one-dimensional aspect of this line of thought and action is its strength, but it is not a correct approach. It is the comprehensive features in this approach that will win out in the course of history. Human nature is multi-dimensional, but we need a better conception of it than the one we find in India's socialist humanism.

On the practical level its socialist ideology of democracy and humanism is ineffective to the extent that people do not see it as a real alternative. As an ideology it is assumed to set the new goals to be reached by a new India. But the common people and the leaders view it as the defender of the values and interests of the establishment. The mutual relationship of the various elements—of the half-truths contained in it—is too loosely put together for people to see it in the context of political realities. Moreover, the socialists have given up their desire to be a revolutionary force, concentrating too much on national unity, peace, and stability. As a result, many people now feel that only communism represents a real revolutionary force.

The socialists must make a more clear-cut choice in favor of the vast majority of the population living below the poverty line. Socialism must dare to expose itself to the danger of corruption, and hope for forgiveness when it haughtily sins. The Kingdom of God as an impossible possibility must always be kept in mind and realized in practice. Compromises are always necessary. Political democracy is always characterized by the law of love and by the fact of sinfulness. There is a great need for some sensible compromise between the two.

It should also be noted that socialist humanism in India tends to fluctuate between two possible alternatives. It may tend to think in terms of history and the future, or it may mystically focus directly on living together in unity. Both views are concerned with love and community, but to what extent will their advocates be willing to participate in power-politics? There is a recurrent tendency to go back to the ahistorical spirituality of India. One sees no radical reinterpretation of Indian spirituality, no formulation of India's concern to achieve its ultimate goal in and through national development, social liberation, and the fulfillment of an historical mission.

Here India might well learn from the reality of the cross of Christ. Human beings strive for spiritual self-realization and simultaneously experience constraints. In the light of the cross we see that the world is the realm of God's glorification, and that history is the hard core of evil which continually frustrates God's aim. But God finally overcomes evil through the redeeming act of Jesus Christ. This look at history could help socialist humanism in India to avoid extremes: the overly optimistic vision of self-redemption held by Western liberalism; and the overly pessimistic withdrawal from historical action as something unsatisfying, which is part of Indian spirituality. India could use the spirituality of the new humanity in Jesus Christ. Then the power structures of society could be incorporated into a faith in the new humanity: begun by God in the crucified and resurrected Christ, and firmly planted in world history when his Spirit was poured out over all humanity.

This teaching must be communicated to India's socialist humanism. That is precisely the task to be accomplished by dialogue between the Christian communities of India and Indian social movements advocating a society of greater justice.[54]

I have just offered several examples of new ways in which the Churches can get involved in service to the world. Many more examples could be cited. The point here, however, is simply that many new things can happen once Christian communities enter into real contact and dialogue with the religious, social, and political milieu around them. This also means that many things will have to be rethought.

Many other issues could be considered. For example, what about Black Africa's religious and cultural conceptions of illness and death? What could we learn from them? What about the cargo cults of Melanesia and their potential stimuli? What tasks face us if we wish to see an incarnate Christianity there? These examples are merely meant to indicate what is in the process of development right now. Undoubtedly we shall hear much more about these matters in the years to come. We have begun to move towards a whole new form of service to the world, and it will probably go much deeper than the traditional, age-old form of service.[55]

A MODEST LIFESTYLE AS A NEW SERVICE TO TODAY'S WORLD

The following thoughts were voiced by Pedro Arrupe, then superior general of the Jesuits, when he addressed an Inter-American Congress of Religious held in Montreal. I mention them here because they have significance for the world at large. With church support they are already being put into practice in such places as Tanzania and Sri Lanka, where people are trying to introduce a suitably adapted technology grounded in an indigenous spirituality. Even for us in the West a modest lifestyle is of the utmost importance because many people, and young people in particular, are looking for some alternative way of living.

Those chosen by Christ (John 15:16) are not called simply to preach Christ. They are also expected to win acceptance for the commands of the gospel message and the lifestyle embodied therein. This is done by bringing men and women to the mutual love wherewith Christ loved us. They must come to realize that this love was freely proffered to them by another. The latter chose to share his supreme love with them by dying for them, rising from the dead, and becoming their nourishment in the Eucharist. That is the way to attain the human measure of Christ. Thus the novelty of the gospel message entails loving and serving others as brothers and sisters, giving up egotism, and living a modest, selfless life. The task is incumbent on every Christian, of course. But consecrated religious make a qualitative leap by choosing to embody this gospel lifestyle in all its radicalness.

Christian service to today's world must encompass this task as well, for the world situation demands it. Much has been accomplished in many fields: science, technology, material progress, religious and humanitarian activity, and ethics. Yet our world continues to be haunted by the twin specters of poverty and war, which are not unrelated. War cannot be eliminated so long as hunger, malnutrition, and the absence of human dignity continue; and these things are caused to some extent by intolerable injustice and oppression. How are the six billion people over thirty to live, when five billion of them will be robbed of their natural rights if the nuclear powers get completely beyond our control? Unless there is a big change, the rich will continue to grow richer and the poor will continue to grow poorer. How long can that situation continue without leading to war?

It seems clear that we could make this a just world right now, but we really do not choose to do so. It is a mistake to lay all the blame on multinational corporations, or on unjust structures. These things exist and perdure because Christians and non-Christians have created them, fostered them, and abjectly served them. We can no longer let our lives be dominated by envy of what others have. We must curb our urge for possessions and choose a modest lifestyle if we want to decrease the poverty under which the vast majority of humanity lives. If we don't, then violence and guerrilla warfare will continue in the Third World; and it will rear its head in the First World too.

Homo sapiens has turned into *homo consumens.* Our whole milieu is teaching us how to create new needs. Ours is a consumption-oriented society where progress and development mean more possessions, industrialization, urbanization, and an ever-rising income. We want to open new markets everywhere. The focus is on myself; other people are regarded as brute things. But now young people are reacting against this sort of society and its misuse of nature. They are seeking alternatives, in the sphere of religion as well.

From all this it is clear that a modest and simple lifestyle is absolutely necessary for the material and social survival of humanity. This is obvious even to parties espousing Marxist materialism. How much more, then, is it incumbent on Christians to analyze our present society in terms of the gospel message and its criteria! But it seems that no one is willing to make the sacrifice; no one has the needed motivation. The poor say that the rich must start the process. The rich say that the poor must do the same thing; otherwise there is no point to it. The fact is that we must create a *homo serviens* (Phil. 2:7; Matt. 20:28). We must create human beings who understand what solidarity means, who are willing to become the brothers and sisters of all humanity. We must consciously choose to be satisfied with enough.

Here religious can play a leadership role. We need a conversion to simplicity and modesty, and this might be called poverty. We need effective deeds, not beautiful phrases and merely symbolic tokens of sympathy. Pope Paul VI repeatedly urged a prompt solution for the distressing situation of the present world. Latin America is one such critical area, as the pope himself noted. It is a kaleidoscope of cultures and clashing forces, of wealth and poverty; it is both the hope and the nightmare of the Church. Religious need to show real, effective solidarity with those who are truly poor. They must share the loneliness of the poor and embody that sharing in concrete deeds, even though they may have rich sources of revenue. Then they, like the poor, will find new experiences of God, discovering the face of Christ in the lowliest (Matt.

25:45). This ideal must be lived out concretely in basic ecclesial communities, of religious too. In this way they can approach young people and perhaps preclude their turning to other philosophies and worldviews; for the conversion to other worldviews does not always benefit the world or young people themselves.[56]

In this way service to the world, stemming from the local Churches, can be made truly real and concrete. It is of the utmost importance for peace and justice. And to carry through this program, we must proceed in dialogue with other Christians and other religions.

20

From Multiplicity to Oneness

My thesis in Part Three has been that the grass-roots Church—i.e., local Churches and basic ecclesial communities—is not a dead-end approach. It is well to point out that there is an alternative to a strongly centralized Church, particularly at a time when many Christians are having difficulty with *the* Church in that sense. This alternative was raised once again by Vatican II, then elaborated in theory by theologians and in practice by active Christians. In Part Three I have tried to let both have their say, though a selection had to be made. I hope my selection has not been purely arbitrary and subjective. I hope it has pointed readers towards a truly possible future.

One task remains. At the beginning of Part Three I said that church unity need not, and must not, be discarded in the process. It remains critical and valuable. I would like to discuss that issue now, showing that we shall have to rethink the matter of church unity in the process of preserving it.

THE CHURCH AS A CENTRALIZED, AUTHORITARIAN INSTITUTION IS HISTORICALLY CONDITIONED

At the start of Part Three I suggested that soon after the reign of Constantine the Great, hence fairly early, the Church took on the trappings of the Roman Empire. This thrust continued. There were reactions against it, of course, but sometimes even these reactions led to newly centralized Churches that imposed some system of thought and action. Here no distinction need be made between various Catholic and Reformation Churches.

The basic thrust was particularly evident in missionary activity. For all the good will in spreading the gospel message, the fact is that the Western pattern of ecclesial life was usually imposed on other areas of the world. This was true not only in the realm of church structures but also, and especially, in the refusal to let other local Churches freely find their own selfhood within Christianity. The problem was aggravated by the fact that the spread of the Church went hand in hand with colonial expansion. In such a setup freedom

228

was all but impossible. Only a few great spirits, such as Matteo Ricci and Robert de Nobili in the Catholic Church, managed to break with this system and make real overtures to the indigenous culture (e.g., in China and India). But as the rites controversy shows, they ran into serious difficulties with the central Church in trying to elaborate an indigenous form of ecclesial life in China and India.[57] At that point in time mission areas did not succeed in elaborating their own native liturgy, theology, church structure, etc. A monolithic Church prevailed. The watchword was that *the* Church—i.e., one historically conditioned form of the Church—had to be transported and planted in other places.[58]

History is now working against that older conception of ecclesiality, and we would do well to recognize the fact. Otherwise we will be travelling down a dead-end road. The tie-up between Church and colonialism has been unmasked by non-Western scholars, who are non-Christians in most cases; but even Christian communities around the world have seen through the problem, as the preceding chapters clearly indicate. The centralization of the Church and the older stress on one historically conditioned form of ecclesiality is also more obvious to us now. Vatican II itself offered us another vision of the Church, of a local Church deeply rooted at the grass-roots level. A very different ecclesiology has been elaborated. At their regular synods in Rome, the bishops of the world have tackled this issue and called for the incarnation of the Church among native peoples. Theologians have backed them up with careful research into the question, and scriptural exegetes have informed us that the early Church viewed the matter quite differently from the post-Constantinian Church.

These are facts, and I see no point in going over the whole issue here. Instead I should like to suggest what church unity might mean in our changed context.

A NEW PERSPECTIVE ON THE ONENESS OF THE CHURCH

Our approach here must be tentative. No one wants to do away with the oneness of the Church. By listening to some people who are trying to reformulate church unity in fresh terms, we might be able to establish a few points.

One important thing, I think, is to see how the New Testament viewed church unity. There is no doubt that there were many early church communities with their own particular views of Jesus Christ, church offices, and so forth. Yet we also find talk about unity among believers. Jesus himself prophesied that there would be one flock and one shepherd (John 10:16). The oneness of the believing community derives from the close relationship between the sheep and the shepherd. The community needs a shepherd who will lead the sheep to pasture. It is the shepherd that unites the flock. The unity of the believing community results from the care and concern of the shepherd for the individual sheep. They may stray away, but he will seek them out and bring them back (Matt. 18:10–14; Luke 15:3–6). The true shepherd assumes the task of taking individual care of the sheep, and he calls them by name (John 10:36). They, in turn, listen to his voice and heed it.

The voice of the shepherd is the principle of oneness or unity. The sheep will not heed the voice of a thief. It is the voice of the shepherd that forms the community. Those who come to Jesus have been given to him by the Father. They are the people sustained by God's word. Thus the oneness of the believing community is a God-given gift. Mutual knowledge and recognition between the shepherd and the sheep—i.e., the fact that they hear and heed his voice—finds its model in the mutual knowledge that exists between the Father and the Son. Listening to Jesus signifies oneness with him and oneness with those who know his voice. And this mutual knowledge implies humble obedience, trust, love, and mutual acceptance.

How does this unity on the local level give rise to unity on a worldwide or universal level? In the New Testament we see that Christian communities have their leaders. These leaders must provide for real Christian unity by creating a community of communities. Here the Pauline notion of *koinonia* enters the picture. Even though local communities display differences in their original Christian witness, in matters of faith they must spontaneously identify themselves with members of other communities when it comes to essential features; in this way they will form one community. Inspired by faith, the leader of the local community must make his group aware of the universal community. As Paul put it in Romans 12:3–8:

> In the light of the grace I have received I want to urge each not to exaggerate his real importance. Each of you must judge himself soberly by the standard of the faith God has given him. Just as each of our bodies has several parts and each part has a separate function, so all of us, in union with Christ, form one body, and as parts of it we belong to each other. Our gifts differ according to the grace given us. If your gift is prophecy, use it as faith suggests; if administration, then use it for administration, if teaching, then use it for teaching. Let the preacher deliver sermons, the almsgivers give freely, the officials be diligent, and those who do works of mercy, do them cheerfully.

In the New Testament we also read how Christian communities of Jews and Christian communities of pagans took pains to join together. This primordial example of church unity is a blueprint for future generations. Unity is a distinguishing feature of those who come to Christ; schism and divisiveness are indications of just the opposite. The oneness between the shepherd and his sheep has a spiritual dimension first and foremost: it is "unity of the Spirit in the bond of peace" (Eph. 4:3). This inner unity of the Church must also manifest itself outwardly. The outward manifestation is a visible sign and a guarantee of the dynamic inner unity.[59]

The leader of the Christian community guarantees its unity with other Christian communities. Besides discussing other functions in the Church, the Pauline texts also talk about the function of a leader. Here again we can detect a process of development in the New Testament, even though we cannot reconstruct it in complete detail. In the beginning the disciples of Jesus, with the twelve in the forefront, were the leaders. They had heard the message of Jesus, taken it to heart, and received from him the task of transmitting it: "Anyone who listens to you, listens to me" (Luke 10:16). That endowed them with authority in a visible way.

We can distinguish two trends as time went on. Election may take place in a clearly verifiable way, involving the laying-on of hands. Or election to an authoritative function may take place in a charismatic way without any visible sign being involved. Such was the case with prophets and teachers, who possessed authority in the whole Church. The tension between these two types of election has always been a fruitful element in the Church.

In the course of development the priest became the visible bond holding the community together; and the bishop became the one who confirmed the different local communities in faith, apostolic teaching, mutual love, participation in the sacraments, and the oneness of the apostolic office. In this apostolic office Peter assumed the role of Christ. He is the shepherd, and all the sheep must listen to him. But he in turn must heed what Christ said to him:

> After the meal Jesus said to Simon Peter, "Simon son of John, do you love me more than these others do?" He answered, "Yes, Lord, you know I love you." Jesus said to him, "Feed my lambs." A second time he said to him, "Simon son of John, do you love me?" He replied, "Yes, Lord, you know I love you." Jesus said to him, "Look after my sheep." Then he said to him a third time, "Simon son of John, do you love me?" Peter was upset that he asked him the third time, "Do you love me?" and said, "Lord, you know everything; you know I love you." Jesus said to him, "Feed my sheep" [John 21:15-17].

Here again, interestingly enough, we again encounter the images of lambs, sheep, and shepherd. The office of Peter is of necessity an ongoing office, but an office in the service of the faithful as a community. Peter, in fact, bore clear witness even during the earthly life of Jesus: "You are the Christ, the Son of the living God" (Matt. 16:13-20; Luke 9:18-21; Mark 8:27-30). This witness must continue to resound in all the Churches; it is what creates unity between them.[60]

Thus the unity or oneness of the Church is a basic theme in the New Testament. Since we are now learning to give local Churches and basic communities their true value once again, we must give form and shape to their unity as well. Here we must be creative both in our thinking and in our acting. We shall have to think of such things as willingness to serve each other, mutual assistance, coordinated activities radiating from a center, interchanges of our faith-experiences, and fidelity to the guiding norm—i.e., our faith in Jesus the Christ. These services are perduring ones in the Church. But do we need such a strongly centralized authority as is now operative in the Catholic Church in order to maintain these services? That is a very different question, and at this point I am only too happy to turn it over to ecclesiologists. I would simply point out that missiology is revealing a new reality in the praxis of local Churches and basic Christian communities. That reality offers much food for reflection to ecclesiologists and experts in Canon Law.[61]

Notes

PART ONE
CHRISTIANITY AND RELIGIONS OF THE WORLD:
NEW INSIGHTS AND NEW ACTIVITIES

1. See Walbert Bühlmann, *The Coming of the Third Church: An Analysis of the Present and the Future of the Church*, Eng. trans. (Maryknoll, N.Y.: Orbis Books, 1976), p. 151.

2. See Georg Schurhammer, *Franz Xaver, sein Leben und seine Zeit*, 4 vols. (Freiburg-Vienna-Basel, 1955–1963); Eng. trans., *Francis Xavier: His Life, His Times*, 3 volumes to date (Omaha: Jesuit Historical Institute [Creighton University], 1973, 1977, and 1980.

3. Vatican II, *Nostra aetate*, n. 1. Except for replacing "men" with "human beings," this is the translation to be found in Walter M. Abbott, S.J., ed. *The Documents of Vatican II* (New York: Guild-America-Association, 1966). Such terms as "man" and its cognates are replaced with "human being" and its cognates wherever possible, since this is more in line with the terms used in the original Latin documents. Reference to these documents are parenthetical and with abbreviations of their Latin letters *(Translator's Note).*

Chapter 1

4. See Paul Ricoeur, *Histoire et Vérité* (Paris, 1964); Eng., *History and Truth*, trans. Charles A. Kelbley (Evanston, Ill.: Northwestern University Press, 1965), pp. 271–284. See also E. F. Schumacher, *Small Is Beautiful: Economics as if People Mattered* (New York: Harper & Row, 1973).

5. See H. M. Enomiya Lasalle, *Zen Meditation for Christians*, Eng. trans. (LaSalle, Ill.: Open Court, 1974); *Zen: Way to Enlightenment* (New York: Taplinger, 1968). Yves Raguin, *Paths to Contemplation*, Eng. trans. (St. Meinrad, Ind.: Abbey Press, 1974). J. M. Dechanet, *Christian Yoga* (Westminster, Md.: Christian Classics, 1972). M. Maupilier, *Le yoga et l'homme de l'occident* (Paris, 1974).

6. See Khalid Saifullah Bruin, *15 jaar Islam in Nederland* (The Hague, 1962).

7. See Stanley J. Samartha, *The Hindu Response to the Unbound Christ*, Inter-religious Dialogue Series, No. 6 (Madras:, CLS-CISRS, 1974).

8. Bardwell L. Smith, ed. *The Two Wheels of Dhamma: Essays on Therevada Tradition in India and Ceylon* (Missoula, Mont.: Scholars Press, University of Montana, 1972). In general, the literature dealing with this topic goes back to the decade of the sixties and is now a bit dated. But see K. Hutten and S. von Kortzfleisch, eds.,

Asien missioniert im Abendland (Stuttgart, 1962); also Georg F. Vicedom, *Die Mission der Weltreligionen* (Munich, 1959).

9. See J. Freytag and H. J. Margull, *Junge Kirchen auf eigenen Wegen* (Neukirchen-Vluyen, 1972). *Christianity and the New China,* reprint of 1974 ed., Lutheran World Federation (South Pasadena: William Carey Library, 1976). Edward Pirijns, *Japan en het Christendom,* 2 vols. (Tielt-Utrecht: Lanoo, 1971), I, pp. 250-274.

10. H. Achterhuis, *Filosofen van de derde wereld* (Bilthoven, 1975).

11. Arnulf Camps, "Een bezinning voor 'doeners' op het gebied van de ontwikkelingshulp," in *Een lopende rekening, kerk en ontwikkeling in de derde wereld* (Tilburg, 1976), pp. 94-106; idem, "Le dialogue inter-religieux et la situation concrète de l'humanité," *Bulletin of the Secretariat for Non-Christians* 10 (Vatican City, 1975): 315-318. See also C. J. L. Bertholet, *Een terreinverkenning in de probleemgebieden der ontwikkelingssociologie* (Tilburg, 1971); and *De strijd om een adequaat ontwikkelingsparadigma voor de derde wereld* (Eindhoven, 1975). See also R. Friedli, "La mission des religions et les réalités sociales," *Freiburger Zeitschrift für Philosophie und Theologie* 23 (1976): 146-165.

12. Edward Schillebeeckx, "De kerk als sacrament van de dialoog," *Tijdschrift voor Theologie* 8 (Utrect-Brugge, 1975): 155-169. H. Fries, "Von Polemik zu Dialog," in *Oecumenica* (Minneapolis: Augsburg, 1969), pp. 28-52.

13. René Laurentin, *L'Evangélisation après le IV*ᵉ *Synode* (Paris, 1975); *Le nuove via del Vangelo, I vescovi africani parlono a tutta la chíiesa;* IV Synodo dei Vescovi, 1974 (Bologna, 1975).

Chapter 2

14. See J. van Lin, "Zending en Dialoog," *Wereld en Zending* 1 (Amsterdam, 1972): 19-23, where the publications are mentioned. Also see P. Rossano, *Il problema teologico delle religioni* (Rome, 1975); A. Camps, "Le dialogue inter-religieux et la situation concrète de l'humanité," *Bulletin of the Secretariat for Non-Christians* 10 (1975): 315-318.

15. J. van Lin, *Protestantse theologie der godsdiensten: van Edinburgh naar Tambaram (1910-1938)* (Assen, 1974); G. Vallée, *Mouvement oecuménique et religions non chrétiennes, de Tambaram à Uppsala (1938-1968)* (Tournai-Montreal, 1975).

16. See Stanley J. Samartha, ed., *Dialogue Between Men of Living Faiths,* Ajaltoun (Lebanon) Consultation (Geneva: WCC, 1971); idem, *Living Faiths and the Ecumenical Movement* (Geneva: WCC, 1971); idem, *Towards World Community, the Colombo Papers* (Geneva: WCC, 1974); idem, *Living Faiths and Ultimate Goals: Salvation and World Religions* (Geneva: WCC, 1974, and Maryknoll, N.Y.: Orbis Books, 1975); idem, *Courage for Dialogue: Ecumenical Issues in Inter-Religious Relationships* (Geneva: WCC, 1981, and Maryknoll, N.Y.: Orbis Books, 1982). S. J. Samartha and J. B. Taylor, eds., *Christian-Muslim Dialogue,* Broumana Consultation (Geneva: WCC, 1973); H. Krueger and W. Mueller-Roemheld, *Bericht aus Nairobi 75* (Frankfurt-am-Main, 1976); and *Archief van de Kerken* (Amersfoort, 1976), Nos. 7/8.

17. J. H. Barrows, ed., *The World's Parliament of Religions,* 2 vols. (London, 1893). Also see J. F. Cleary, "Catholic Participation in the World's Parliament of Religions, Chicago 1893," *Catholic Historical Review* 55 (January 1970): 585-609;

D. H. Bishop, "Religious Confrontation," in *Numen* (Leiden: Brill, 1964), pp. 63–76.

18. F. P. Dunne, Jr., ed., *The World Religions Speak on the Relevance of Religion in the Modern World* (Atlantic Highlands, N.J.: Humanities, 1970).

19. J. Masson, "La deuxième conférence du 'Temple of Understanding,' " *Bulletin of the Secretariat for Non-Christians* 7 (1972): 62–63.

20. H. A. Jack, ed., *World Religions and World Peace* (Boston: Beacon, 1968).

21. H. A. Jack, ed., *Religion for Peace* (New Delhi-Bombay, 1973); M. A. Luecker, ed., *Religionen, Frieden, Menschenrechte* (Wuppertal, 1971).

22. M. A. Luecker, ed., *Neue Perspektiven des Friedens* (Wuppertal, 1975). *Deuxième conférence mondiale pour la paix,* proceedings published by Justice and Peace, Belgium, 1976. *Religion and the Quality of Life* (Tokyo, 1975). See also J. van Goudoever, "WCRP," *Kosmos en Oekumene* 10 (Den Bosch, 1976): 14–17. See R. Friedli, *Fremdheit als Heimat: Auf der Suche nach einem Kriterium für den Dialog zwischen den Religionen* (Fribourg, Switzerland, 1974); in the final pages of his thesis this author concludes that for the moment at least dialogue about salvation coincides with efforts and inquiries relating to peace.

23. Marcus Braybrooke, *Faiths in Fellowship* (London, 1976). For the Netherlands see the anthology edited by Dr. R. Boeke, *Verder dan de Oekumene* (Rotterdam, 1973).

24. M. Jung, Swami Nikhilananda, and H. W. Schneider, *Relations among Religions Today* (Leiden: Brill, 1963), pp. 145–170. A. Camps, "Enige Case-Studies over de ontmoeting van de kerk en verscheidene godsdiensten nu," in *Kerk aan het werk* (Amsterdam-Brussels, 1973), pp. 88–111.

25. There are reports in many of the issues of the *Bulletin of the Secretariat for Non-Christians*. Also see A. Nambiaparambil, "Dialogue in India," *Vidyajyoti* 39 (Ranchi, 1975): 111–126 and in *Journal of Dharma* 1 (Bangalore, 1976): 267–283.

26. Nambiaparambil in *Journal of Dharma* 1 (1976): 267.

27. See O. L. Abeysekere, "The Congress of Religions—Ceylon," in F. P. Dunne, Jr., ed., *The World Religions Speak,* pp. 192–196; see above Note 18.

28. See P. Rossano, "Relation sur la Vie assemblée de la 'Conference for Peace and World Federation,' " *Bulletin of the Secretariat for Non-Christians* 10 (1975): 192–195.

Chapter 3

29. Eric J. Sharpe, *Not to Destroy But to Fulfil,* Studia Missionalia Upsaliensia, no. 5 (Lund: Gleerup, 1965). "Some Indian Interpretations on Revelation in Hinduism," in the anthology edited by G. Oberhammer, *Offenbarung, geistige Realität des Menschen* (Vienna, 1974), pp. 221–225.

30. P. Knitter, *Towards a Protestant Theology of Religions* (Marburg, 1974). For a fairly total overview see J. Verkuyl, *Contemporary Missiology* (Grand Rapids: Eerdmans, 1978), pp. 357–362.

31. Arend T. van Leeuwen, *Hendrik Kraemer, dienaar der Wereldkerk* (Amsterdam, 1959); German edition, *Hendrik Kraemer: Pionier der Oekumene* (Basel, 1962).

32. Hendrik Kraemer, *Godsdiensten en culturen* (The Hague, 1963); Eng. edition, *World Cultures and World Religions: The Coming Dialogue* (Philadelphia: Westminster, 1960).

33. Hendrik Kraemer, *Godsdienst, godsdiensten en het christelijk geloof* (Nijkerk,

1958), p. 264; English edition, *Religion and the Christian Faith* (Philadelphia: West-minster, 1957); idem, *The Christian Message in a Non-Christian World* (Grand Rapids: Kregel, 1961).

34. Kraemer, *Godsdiensten en culturen,* p. 332.

35. Ibid., p. 333.

36. Arend T. van Leeuwen, *Christianity in World History: The Meeting of Faiths East and West,* trans. H. H. Hookins (London: Edinburgh House, 1965, and New York: Scribner's, 1967). See also A. Camps, "Enkele kanttekeningen naar anleiding van dr. A. Th. van Leeuwens Boek: *Christianity in World History,*" *Het Missiewerk* 44 (Den Bosch, 1965): 46–49.

37. Van Leeuwen, *Christianity in World History,* p. 147.

38. Verkuyl, *Contemporary Missiology,* pp. 341–372.

39. Ibid., p. 479.

40. Josef Mueller, *Missionarische Anpassung als theologisches Prinzip* (Muenster i. Wf., 1973), pp. 1–64. See A. Camps, *In Christus verbonden met de godsdiensten der wereld,* 2nd ed. (Utrecht-Nijmegen, 1964).

41. L. Elders, "Christianisme et cultures," *Neue Zeitschrift für Missionswissens-chaft* 18 (Schöneck-Beckenried, 1962): 1–21; and "Can Christianity Adapt Itself to Different Cultures?" *The Japan Missionary Bulletin* 17 (Tokyo, 1963): 388–395 and 417–422.

42. H. Bruning, "Het straelt toch elders," *Roeping* 38 (Tilburg, 1962–1963): 429–469.

43. Henry van Straelin, *The Catholic Encounter with World Religions* (London, 1966). See also *Our Attitude towards Other Religions* (Tokyo, 1965).

44. See the anthology edited by Owen C. Thomas, *Attitudes towards Other Religions* (London: SCM, 1969).

45. A. Camps, *Jerome Xavier and the Muslims of the Mogul Empire: Controversial Works and Missionary Activity* (Schöneck-Beckenried, 1957), p. 55.

46. Maurus Heinrichs, *Katholische Theologie und asiatisches Denken* (Mainz: Matthias-Grünewald, 1963); French edition, *Théologie catholique et pensée asiatique* (Tournai: Casterman, 1965). Also see Ernst Benz, *Ideen zu einer Theologie der Religionsgeschichte* (Mainz, 1960), pp. 65–70.

47. William E. Hocking, *Living Religions and a World Faith* (New York: Macmillan, 1940, reprint, New York: AMS, 1976), pp. 190–208. Also see C. J. Bleeker, *Christ in Modern Athens,* 2nd ed. (London, 1966).

48. Ernst Troeltsch, *Christian Thought: Its History and Application* (New York and London: Meridian, 1957), pp. 35–63.

49. Hubert Halbfas, *Fundamentalkatechetik* (Düsseldorf and Stuttgart, 1968), pp. 240–242; Eng. trans., *Theory of Catechetics: Language and Experience in Religious Education* (New York: Seabury, 1971).

50. Arnold Toynbee, *Christianity among the Religions of the World* (New York: Scribner's, 1957).

51. Ibid., pp. 104–105.

52. H. van der Linde, *Rome en de Una Sancta* (Nijkerk, 1947), pp. 34–36.

53. P. Beyerhaus, *Allen Völkern zum Zeugnis: biblisch-theologische Besinnung zum Wesen der Mission* (Wuppertal, 1972). G. W. Peters, *A Biblical Theology of Mission,* 2nd ed. (Chicago: Moody, 1974).

54. Verkuyl, *Contemporary Missiology,* pp. 355–368.

55. My study here is based on the following works primarily: A. de Groot, *The*

Bible and the Salvation of the Nations, Eng. trans. (De Pere, Wis.: Norbert Abbey Press, 1966); J. Blauw, *The Missionary Nature of the Church* Grand Rapids: Eerdmans, 1974). Also important is Ferdinand Hahn, *Mission in the New Testament* (London, 1965), English edition. Also see Franz Mussner, "Die Religionen als Thema der Theologie—neutestamentlich gesehen," *Trierer Theologische Zeitschrift* 73 (1964): 247f; H. Waldenfels, "Zur Heilsbedeutung der nichtchristlichen Religionen in katholischer Sicht," *Zeitschrift für Missionswissenschaft und Religionswissenschaft* 53 (Muenster i. Wf., 1969): 257-278.

56. Jean Daniélou, *Les saints païens de l'ancien testament* (Paris, 1956); English edition, *The Pagan Saints of the Old Testament* (Baltimore: Helicon, 1958).

57. Ansfried Hulsbosch, *God in Creation and Evolution,* Eng. trans. (New York: Sheed and Ward, 1965).

58. Joachim Jeremias, *Jesus' Promise to the Nations,* Eng. trans. (Naperville, Ill.: Allenson, 1958).

59. N. A. Kehl, *Der Christushymnus im Kolosserbrief* (Stuttgart, 1967).

60. A. G. Honig, Jr., *De kosmische betekenis van Christus* (Kampen, 1968), p. 40. See Verkuyl, *Contemporary Missiology,* p. 358.

61. Richard H. Drummond, *Gautama the Buddha: An Essay in Religious Understanding* (Grand Rapids: Eerdmans, 1974). Also see A. Luneau, "Pour aider au dialogue: les Pères et les religions non chrétiennes," *Nouvelle Revue Théologique* 89 (Louvain, 1967): 821-841 and 914-939.

62. For Buddhism see Henri De Lubac, *La rencontre du bouddhisme et de l'occident* (Paris, 1952), and *Buddhism and Christianity,* ed. Claude Geffré and Mariasuai Dhavamony, Concilium 116 (New York: Seabury, 1979). For Hinduism see Thomas Mampra, "Encounter Between Hinduism and Christianity: An Historico-Theological Appraisal," *Dharma* 1 (Bangalore, 1976): 246-266. For Islam see Gaston Zaniri, *L'Eglise et l'Islam* (Paris, 1969); and R. W. Southern, *Western Views of Islam in the Middle Ages* (Cambridge: Harvard University Press, 1962, 1978). For Africa see E. Muga, *African Response to Western Christian Religion* (Kampala, Nairobi, Dar es Salaam, 1975).

63. J. Das, "D'une théologie des infidèles à une théologie des religions non-chrétiennes," *Revue du Clergé Africain* 25 (Mayidi, 1970): 20-52.

64. L. H. Cornelissen, *Geloof zonder prediking* (Roermond-Maaseik, 1946). H. Nys, *Le salut sans l'évangile* (Paris, 1966).

65. R. Klibansky and H. Bascour, eds., *Nicholas de Cusa, De pace fidei* (London, 1956), reproduced in the *Opera Omnia,* Vol. VII (Hamburg, 1959). See "Cusano e Galileo," *Archivio di filosofia,* no. 3 (Padua, 1964).

66. Klibansky and Bascour, *Nicholas de Cusa,* p. 7.

67. D. Cabanelas Rodriguez, *Juan de Segovia y el problema islámico* (Madrid, 1952).

68. Southern, *Western Views of Islam,* pp. 83-103; Cabanelos, *Juan de Segovia,* pp. 303-349.

69. Heinz R. Schlette, *Towards a Theology of Religions,* Eng. trans., Questiones Disputatae, 14 (New York: Herder and Herder, 1966). See also Erasmus, *Querela pacis.*

70. For Tempels' biography see Placide Tempels, *Notre rencontre* (Leopoldville, 1962), pp. 12-13 and 16. For his system see *Bantu Philosophy,* Eng. trans. (New York: Panther House, 1971). See also Willy De Craemer, *The Yamaa and the Church* (Oxford: Clarendon, 1977).

71. *Catéchèse Bantoue* (Brugge, n.d.).

72. Johannes Fabian, *Jamaa: A Charismatic Movement in Katanga* (Evanston, Ill.: Northwestern University Press, 1971).

73. Jacques A. Cuttat, *The Encounter of Religions,* Eng. trans. (New York: Desclée, 1960); idem, *The Spiritual Dialogue of East and West,* 2nd ed. (New Delhi, 1962); idem, *Expérience chrétienne et spiritualité orientale* (Paris, 1967); idem, *Asiatische Gottheit-Christliches Gott: Die spiritualität der beiden Hemisphären* (Einsiedeln: Johannes, 1970).

74. Robert C. Zaehner, *At Sundry Times: An Essay in the Comparison of Religions,* reprint of 1958 ed., (Westport, Conn.: Greenwood, 1977); idem, *The Convergent Spirit* (London, 1963); idem, *The Catholic Church and World Religions* (London, 1964); idem, *Concordant Discord: The Interdependence of Faiths* (New York: Oxford University Press, 1970); idem, *Evolution in Religion: A Study in Sri Aurobindo and Pierre Teilhard de Chardin* (New York: Oxford University Press, 1971); idem, *Dialectical Christianity and Christian Materialism* (New York: Oxford University Press, 1971).

75. See Drummond, *Gautama the Buddha,* pp. 172–174. H. De Vos, *Het christendom en de andere godsdiensten* (Nijkerk, 1962), pp. 30–39.

76. Robin Boyd, *An Introduction to Indian Christian Theology* (Madras: CLS, 1969). M. M. Thomas, *Man and the Universe of Faiths,* Inter-religious Dialogue Series, 7 (Bangalore: CISRS, 1975). See also the series still being published, Confessing the Faith in India (Bangalore and Madras), which often publishes the biographies and miscellaneous writings of Indian theologians.

77. J. Wietzke, *Theologie in modernen Indien—Paul David Devanandan* (Bern and Frankfurt a.M., 1975).

78. See the periodical *Jeevadhara* (Allepey), 1971 and following. See also the anthology edited by J. B. Chethimattam, *Unique and Universal: Fundamental Problems of an Indian Theology* (Bangalore: Centre for the Study of World Religions, Dharmaran College, 1972); idem, *Patterns of Indian Thought* (Maryknoll, N.Y.: Orbis Books, 1971).

79. See Karl Rahner, "Das Christentum und die nicht-christlichen Religionen," *Schriften zur Theologie,* vol. 5 (Einsiedeln: Benziger, 1962), pp. 136–158; Eng. trans., "Christianity and the Non-Christian Religions," *Theological Investigations,* vol. 5 (Baltimore: Helicon, and London: Darton, Longman and Todd, 1966), pp. 115–134. All *Theological Investigations,* now published by Seabury (New York) through vol. 16 (1979). Idem, *Hearers of the Word,* trans. Michael Richards (New York: Herder und Herder, 1969); "Kirche, Kirchen und Religionen," *Schriften zur Theologie,* vol. 8 (1967), pp. 355–373, and "Church, Churches and Religions," *Theological Investigations,* vol. 10, trans. David Bourke (New York: Herder and Herder, 1973), pp. 30–49; "Anonymes Christentum und Missionsauftrag der Kirche," *Schriften zur Theologie,* vol. 9 (1970), pp. 498–515, "Anonymous Christianity and the Missionary Task of the Church," *Theological Investigations,* vol. 12 (New York: Seabury, 1974), pp. 161–178. *Ueber die Heilsbedeutung der nicht-christlichen Religionen* (Rome, 1975). See also Anita Roper, Eng. trans. *The Anonymous Christian* (New York: Sheed and Ward, 1966); H. M. Kuitert, "De wereld valt mee," in *Kerk buiten de Kerk* (Utrecht: Baarn, 1969), pp. 55–91.

80. See Schlette, *Towards a Theology of Religions.*

81. Josef Heislbetz, *Theologische Gründe nicht-christlichen Religionen* (Freiburg i. Br., Basel, and Vienna, 1967).

82. Raymond Panikkar, *Die vielen Götter und der eine Herr* (Weilheim: Barth, 1963); idem, *The Unknown Christ of Hinduism* (New York: Humanities Press, 1968, and Maryknoll, N.Y.: Orbis Books, 1981); *Kultmysterium im Hinduismus und Christentum* (Freiburg i. Br. and Munich: Alber, 1964), French edition, *Le mystère du culte dans l'hindouisme et le christianisme* (Paris, 1970); *Religionen und die Religion* (Munich: Hueber, 1965), Italian edition, *Religione e religioni* (Brescia, 1964); idem, *Kerugma und Indien: Zur heilgeschictlichen Problematik der christlichen Begegnung mit Indien* (Hamburg: Reich-Enang, 1967); *The Trinity and the Religious Experience of Man* (Maryknoll, N.Y.: Orbis Books, 1974).

83. N. Klaes, *Stellvertretung und Mission* (Essen, 1968).

84. Piet Schoonenberg, *Het geloof van ons doopsel,* vol. 3 ('s-Hertogenbosch, 1958), pp. 175–230; idem, *Gods wordende wereld* (Limburg, 1965); Eng. edition, *God's World in the Making* (Pittsburgh: Duquesne, 1964); idem, *Covenant and Creation* (Notre Dame, Ind.: University of Notre Dame Press, 1969); "De kerk en de niet-christelijke godsdiensten," *Het Missiewerk* 44 ('s-Hertogenbosch, 1965): 157–166; German article, "Heilsgeschichte und Dialog," *Theologisch-praktische Quartalschrift* 115 (Linz, 1967): 132–138; "Versuch einer christlich-theologischen Sicht des Hinduismus," in the anthology edited by G. Pberhammer entitled *Offenbarung, geistige Realität des menschen* (Vienna, 1974), pp. 170–187; "Christologie en theologie der godsdiensten," *Wereld en Zending* 4 (Amsterdam, 1975): 26–37.

85. Rafael Esteban Verastegui, "Les religions non-chrétiennes n'ont-elles aucune valeur salvifique? Evaluation critique de la position du Cardinal Daniélou concernant les religions non-chrétiennes," *Euntes Docete* 27 (Rome, 1974): 25–64.

86. A. Camps, "Four Key Notions of an Empirical Missiology," *Neue Zeitschrift für Missionswissenschaft* 29 (Schöneck-Beckenried, 1973): 135–142.

87. Hendrik Berkhof, *Christelijk geloof,* 2nd ed. (Nijkerk, 1974), pp. 6–27; Eng., *Christian Faith,* trans. Sierd Woudstra (Grand Rapids, Mich.: Eerdmans, 1979).

88. Paul Tillich, *Systematic Theology,* vol. 3 (Chicago: University of Chicago Press, 1963); idem, *Christianity and the Encounter of World Religions* (New York: Columbia University Press, 1963); idem, *The Future of Religions,* ed. J. C. Brauer (New York: Harper & Row, 1976).

89. Georg Evers, *Mission, nicht-christliche Religionen, weltliche Welt* (Muenster i. Wf., 1974). Vladimir Boublik, *Teologia delle religioni* (Rome, 1973). Gustave Thils, *Propos et problèmes de la théologie des religions non chrétiennes* (Tournai, 1966).

90. Evers, *Mission,* pp. 125–128.

Chapter 4

91. Drummond, *Gautama the Buddha.*

92. C. F. Aiken, *Bouddhisme et Christianisme* (Paris, 1903).

93. Drummond, *Gautama the Buddha,* p. 183.

94. Ibid., p. 194.

95. Heinrich Dumoulin, *Christianity Meets Buddhism,* trans. John C. Maraldo (LaSalle, Ill.: Open Court, 1974). Also see A. Camps, "Two Recent Studies on Buddhism and Christianity," in the anthology edited by Nils E. Bloch-Hoell, *Misjonskall og forskerglede: Festskrift til professor Olav Guttorm Myklebust pa 70-arsdagen (July 24, 1975)* (Oslo-Bergen-Tromös, 1975), pp. 36–47.

96. M. Talbi, "Islam and Dialogue," *Encounter,* Nos. 11 and 12 (January-

February 1975); previously published in booklet form as *Islam et dialogue* (Tunis, 1972).

97. See *Encounter,* No. 15 (May 1975), pp. 2–4. See also the *Bulletin of the Secretariat for Non-Christians* 10 (1975): 199–205 (M. Borrmans, "Le congrès islamo-chrétien de Dordoue, 9–15 September 1974").

98. M. Lelong, "Colloque islamo-chrétien de Tunis (11–17 November 1974)," *Bulletin of the Secretariat for Non-Christians* 10 (1975): 196–198. Also see J. Gelot, "Islamic-Christian Meeting: Tunis, Hammamet, Kairouwan, 11–17 November 1974," *Encounter,* No. 15 (May 1975): 5–7.

99. *Osservatore Romano* (Vatican City), February 20, 1976, pp. 1–2 (French edition).

100. G. C. Oosthuizen, *Post-Christianity in Africa* (London, 1968); idem, *Theological Battleground in Asia and Africa: The Issues Facing the Churches and the Effort to Overcome Western Divisions* (New York: Humanities Press, 1972); see the best study: D. B. Barrett, Schism and Renewal in Africa (London: Oxford University Press, 1968).

101. See the anthology edited by D. B. Barrett, *African Initiatives in Religion* (New York: International Publication Service, 1971). See also Marie Louise Martin, *Kirche ohne Weisse* (Basel, 1971); Eng. edition, *Kimbangu: An African Prophet and His Church* (Grand Rapids: Eerdmans, 1976).

102. M. L. Daneel, *Old and New in Southern Shona Independent Churches,* 2 vols. (New York: Humanities Press, 1971 and 1975); idem, *Zionism and Faith-Healing in Rhodesia* (The Hague and Paris, 1970); idem, *The God of the Matopo Hills: An Essay on the Mwari Cult in Rhodesia* (New York: Humanities Press, 1970).

103. Daneel, *Old and New,* I, pp. 244–248.

104. A. Camps, "Indiase christologie," in *Wie zeggen de mensen dat ik ben?* (Baarn, 1975), pp. 125–137.

105. *Hindoeisme, Boeddhisme, Islam en de christelijke eredienst,* vol. 12, no. 2 of European *Concilium* (1976). D. Amalorpavadass, ed., *Research Seminar on Non-Biblical Scriptures* (Bangalore, 1975). Geoffrey Parrinder, *Worship in the World's Religions,* 2nd ed. (Totowa, N.J.: Littlefield, 1975). D. C. Mulder, *Heilig woord en heilige schrift in de religies* (Kampen, 1970).

106. Dhavamony, "De houding van de christelijke eredienst ten opzichte van hindoe geeschriften," in vol. 12, no. 2 of European *Concilium* (1976), pp. 5–17.

107. Ibid., p. 17.

Chapter 5

108. W. H. van de Pol, *The End of Conventional Christianity,* Eng. trans. (New York: Paulist Press, 1968).

109. Kenneth Cragg, *Christianity in World Perspective* (London: Oxford University Press, 1968).

110. Ibid., p. 193.

111. R. L. Slater, *World Religions and World Community* (New York: Columbia University Press, 1963).

112. M. M. Thomas, *Man and the Universe of Faiths,* Inter-religious Dialogue Series, 7 (Bangalore: CISRS, 1975).

113. John Hick, *God and the Universe of Faiths* (New York: St. Martin, 1974);

idem, ed., *Truth and Dialogue in World Religions: Conflicting Truth Claims* (Philadelphia: Westminster, 1974).

114. Henri Desroche, "Sociologie religieuse et sociologie du développement," *Développement et Civilisations,* No. 31 (Paris, 1967): 83–95; also in *Sociologies religieuses* (Paris, 1968), pp. 150–173; idem, *Jacob and the Angel: An Essay on the Sociologies of Religions,* trans. John K. Savacool (Amherst: University of Massachusetts Press, 1971). See also his book entitled *L'Homme et ses religions* (Paris, 1972).

115. A. Camps, "Missiologie en deze tijd," *Wereld en Zending* 1 (Amsterdam, 1972): 5–16. See also Bernard Lonergan, *Theologie im Pluralismus heutiger Kulturen* (Freiburg i. Br., Basel, and Vienna, 1975); idem, *Method in Theology* (New York: Seabury, 1972). See also the anthology edited by A. Bsteh, *Universales Christentum angesichts einer pluralen Welt* (Mödling, 1976); *Christian Faith in a Religiously Plural World,* ed. Donald G. Dawe and John B. Carman, an ecumenical symposium (Maryknoll, N.Y.: Orbis Books, 1978); Gerald H. Anderson and Thomas F. Stransky, eds., *Christ's Lordship and Religious Pluralism* (Maryknoll, N.Y.: Orbis Books, 1981); and Walbert Bühlmann, *The Search for God: An Encounter with the Peoples and Religions of Asia* (Maryknoll, N.Y.: Orbis Books, 1980), which reports on many different meetings and dialogues.

PART TWO
THE WAY, THE PATHS, AND THE WAYS:
CHRISTIAN THEOLOGY AND CONCRETE RELIGIONS

Chapter 6

1. I use the Dutch translation of the Koran by J. H. Kraemers for citations in this chapter. See J. H. Kraemers, *De Koran uit het Arabisch vertaald* (Amsterdam and Brussels, 1956); cited simply as Koran further on. On the Islamic view of Christ and Christianity see: Peter Antes, "Christus und Christentum in der Sicht der grossen Weltreligionen," *Theologie und Philosophie* 25 (Munich, 1976), 385–396; and "Christenen en Moslims," vol. 12, no. 6 of European *Concilium* (1976).

2. Koran, Sura 2, 136. (Verse numbers may vary in different translations.)

3. See Olaf H. Schumann, *Der Christus der Muslime* (Gütersloh, 1975).

4. Jean M. Gaudeul, "Bibel und Koran," in the anthology edited by M. Fitzgerald et al., *Moslems und Christen—Partner?* (Graz-Vienna-Cologne, 1976), pp. 179–195. See also the talk by J. Lanfry at the Dialogue Week in Tripoli, Libya (February 1–6, 1976). It is cited by M. Borremans, "Le séminaire du dialogue islamo-chrétien de Tripoli," *Islamo-Christiana* 2 (Rome, 1976): 151–152.

5. Koran, Sura 5, 48.

6. Koran, Sura 5, 82–83.

7. See Gaudeul, "Bibel und Koran," p. 184.

8. See "Das Christentum im Gespräch mit dem Islam," in the anthology edited by H. Boventer, *Muslime unter uns, Herausforderung an die Kirche* (Bensberg, 1976), pp. 81–86.

9. See Part One, Chapter 4, pp. 58–66 in this volume. See also J. Wansbeough, *Quranic Studies: Sources and Methods of Scriptural Interpretation* (New York: Oxford University Press, 1977).

10. Though I do not go along with this author on all matters, I want to mention the name and works of the Franciscan Giulio Basetti-Sani, who has been a trail-blazer in developing a new approach to Islam. See the following works by him: *Mohammed et Saint François* (Ottawa, 1959); *The Koran in the Light of Christ,* Eng. trans. (Chicago: Franciscan Herald Press, 1977); *Per un dialogo christiano-musulmano: Mohammed-Damietta e La Verna* (Milan, 1969); *Louis Massignon: Christian Ecumenist,* Eng. trans. (Chicago: Franciscan Herald Press, 1974); *L'Islam e Francesco d'Assisi* (Florence, 1975). Also see the critique by J. Henninger, "Zur 'christlichen Interpretation' des Korans," *Neue Zeitschrift für Missionswissenschaft* 30 (Immensee, 1974): 208–217.

11. R. Friedli, "Zur Weltverantwortung der Offenbarungsreligionen," in the anthology edited by A. Falaturi et al., *Drei Wege zu dem einen Gott* (Freiburg-Basel-Vienna, 1976), p. 218. R. Wielandt, *Offenbarung und Geschichte im Denken moderner Muslime* (Wiesbaden, 1971). Paul Khoury, *Islam et Christianisme: Dialogue religieux et défi de la modernité* (Beirut, 1973). Antonie Wessels, *De nieuwe Arabische mens: moslims en christenen in het Arabische oosten van vandaag* (Baarn, 1977).

12. See Friedli's article in the previous Note, wherein Islam gradually fades out of the picture in favor of Judeo-Christian revelation.

13. Koran, Sura 15, 19.

14. Koran, Sura 29, 20.

15. Koran, Sura 2, 30.

16. Bryan S. Turner, *Weber and Islam: A Critical Study* (Boston: Routledge & Kegan Paul, 1978).

Chapter 7

17. *Ways of Thinking of Eastern Peoples: India, China, Tibet, Japan,* Hajime Nakamura, rev. Eng. trans., ed. Philip P. Weiner (Honolulu: East-West Center Press, 1964), pp. 38–172. To Thi Anh, *Eastern and Western Cultural Values: Conflict or Harmony?* (Manila: East Asian Pastoral Institute, 1975).

18. R. Kranenborg, *Zelfverwerkelijking, oosterse religies binnen een westerse subcultuur,* 2nd ed. (Kampen, 1976). M. Maupilier, *Le Yoga et l'homme de l'Occident* (Paris, 1974).

19. N. K. Devaraja, *Hinduism and Christianity* (New York: Asia Publishing House, 1970).

20. See the German-language anthology edited by Heribert Bettscheider, *Das asiatische Gesicht Christi* (Sankt Augustin, 1976). This anthology contains a pertinent article on an Indian christology by L. F. M. van Bergen (pp. 35–47), and an extensive bibliography as well. For English-language readers, there is the anthology edited by Gerald H. Anderson, *Asian Voices in Christian Theology* (Maryknoll, N.Y.: Orbis Books, 1976); this also has an extensive annotated bibliography.

21. I shall return to this subject in Part Three of this book. See also the informative work by Friso Melzer, *Christliche Ashrams in Südindien* (Erlangen, 1976).

22. Otto Wolff, *Christus unter den Hindus* (Gütersloh, 1965). Otto Waack, *Verantwortung und Hoffnung, Jawaharlal Nehrus säkularer Humanismus und der christliche Glaube: Ein Problem korrelativer Relevanz* (Gütersloh, 1976). Nirmal Minz, *Mahatma Gandhi and Hindu-Christian Dialogue* (Bangalore-Madras: CLS, 1970).

23. Robin Boyd, *An Introduction to Indian Christian Theology* (Bangalore-Madras: CLS, 1969). Stanley J. Samartha, *The Hindu Response to the Unbound Christ* (Madras: CLS-CISR, 1974). John Britto Chethimattam, ed., *Unique and Universal: Fundamental Problems of an Indian Theology* (Bangalore: Centre for the Study of World Religions, Dharmaron College, 1972); idem, *Patterns of Indian Thought* (Maryknoll, N.Y.: Orbis Books, 1971). Eric J. Sharpe, *Faith Meets Faith: Some Christian Attitudes to Hinduism in the Nineteenth and Twentieth Centuries* (Naperville, Ill.: Allenson, 1977). M. M. Thomas, *The Acknowledged Christ of the Indian Renaissance* (Naperville, Ill.: Allenson, 1969).

24. Yves Raguin, *Chemins de la contemplation* (Paris: Desclée de Brouwer, 1968); Eng. *Paths to Christian Contemplation*, trans. Paul Barrett (St. Meinrad, Ind.: Abbey Press, 1974). Jacques A. Cuttat, *Expérience chrétienne et spiritualité orientale* (Tournai, 1967).

25. Werner Draguhn, *Entwicklungsbewusstsein und wirtschaftliche Entwicklung in Indien* (Wiesbaden, 1970). S. B. Naïdu, *La voie indienne du développement* (Paris, 1971). Hans Werner Gensichen, "Religion and Sozialethik im neueren Hinduismus," in the anthology edited by H. Ahrens and K. Gräffin Schwerin, *Aspekte sozialer Ungleichheit in Südasien* (Wiesbaden, 1975), pp. 181–192.

26. Paul D. Devanandan, *Christian Issues in Southern Asia,* 3rd ed. (New York: Friendship Press, 1963). Edward Schillebeeckx, *Gerechtigheid en liefde, genade en bevrijding* (Bloemendaal, 1977), Part IV.

27. Swami Abhishiktananda, *Hindu-Christian Meeting Point* (Bombay-Bangalore, 1969); idem, *Saccidananda: A Christian Approach to Advaitic Experience* (Delhi, 1974); idem, *Guru and Disciple* (Westminster, Md.: Christian Classics, 1974). Bede Griffiths, *Return to the Center* (Springfield, Ill.: Templegate, 1976); idem, *Christ in India: Essays Towards a Hindu-Christian Dialogue* (New York: Scribner's, 1966); idem, *Vedanta and Christian Faith* (Middletown, Calif.: Dawn Horse Press, 1973). See also J. Mattam, *Land of the Trinity: A Study of Modern Christian Approaches to Hinduism* (Bangalore, 1975); Ludger Franz Maria van Bergen, *Licht op het leven van religieuzen: sannyasa—dipika* (Nijmegen, 1975).

Chapter 8

28. Heinrich Dumoulin and John C. Maraldo, eds., *Buddhism in the Modern World* (New York: Macmillan, 1976). Heinz R. Schlette, *Toward a Theology of Religions,* Questiones Disputatae, 14 (New York: Herder and Herder, 1966), pp. 41–61. J. Lopez-Gay, *La mistica del Budismo* (Madrid, 1974). Heinz Bechert, *Weltflucht oder Weltveränderung: Antworten des buddhistischen Modernismus auf Fragen unserer Zeit* (Göttingen, 1976).

29. Hans Waldenfels, *Absolutes Nichts: Zur Grundlegung des Dialoges zwischen Buddhismus und Christentum* (Freiburg-Basel-Vienna, 1976). Yagi Seiichi and Ulrich Luz, eds., *Gott In Japan* (Munich, 1973). Ernest Pirijns, *Japan en het Christendom: Naar de overstijging van een dilemma,* 2 vols. (Tielt-Utrecht: Lanoo, 1971).

30. Waldenfels, *Absolutes Nichts,* pp. 87–121.

31. Maurus Heinrichs, *Der grosse Durchbruch: Franziskus von Assisi im Spiegel japanischer Literatur* (Werl, 1969).

32. Paul Tillich, *Christianity and the Encounter of the World Religions* (New York: Columbia University Press, 1963). Daitsetzu Teitaro Suzuki, *Mysticism: Christian and Buddhist* (Westport, Conn.: Greenwood Press, 1976), reprint of 1957 edition.

Patrick O'Connor, ed., *Buddhists Find Christ: The Spiritual Quest of Thirteen Men and Women in Burma, China, Japan, Korea, Sri Lanka, Thailand, Vietnam* (Rutland, Ver.: C. E. Tuttle, 1975). Elisabeth Ott, *Thomas Merton: Grenzgänger zwischen Christentum und Buddhismus* (Würzburg, 1977). Richard H. Drummond, *Gautama the Buddha: An Essay in Religious Understanding* (Grand Rapids: Eerdmans, 1974). Heinrich Dumoulin, *Christianity Meets Buddhism,* trans. John C. Maraldo (La Salle, Ill.: Open Court, 1974). Aelred Graham, *Zen Catholicism: A Suggestion* (New York: Harcourt Brace Jovanovich, 1967); idem, *Conversations: Christian and Buddhist Encounters in Japan* (London, 1969). Winston L. King, *Buddhism and Christianity: Some Bridges of Understanding* (Philadelphia: Westminster, 1962). Georg Siegmund, *Buddhismus und Christentum: Vorbereitung eines Dialoges* (Frankfurt am Main, 1968). H. M. Enomiya Lassalle, *Zen Meditation for Christians* (LaSalle, Ill.: Open Court, 1974); idem, *Zen unter Christen: oestliche Meditation und christliche Spiritualität* (Graz, 1974); idem, *Meditation als Weg zur Gotteserfahrung* (Cologne, n. d.). Masatoshi Doi, *Search for Meaning through Interfaith Dialogue* (Tokyo, 1976). J. van Bragt, "Inter-Faith Dialogue in Japan," *The Japan Missionary Bulletin* 30 (Tokyo, 1976): 583–594. Yves Raguin, *Bouddhisme–Christianisme* (Paris, 1973). *Buddhism and Christianity,* ed. Claude Geffré and Mariasuai Dhavamony, *Concilium* 116 (New York: Seabury, 1979). Paul Clasper, *Eastern Paths and the Christian Way* (Maryknoll, N.Y.: Orbis Books, 1980).

33. Tillich, *Christianity and the Encounter of the World Religions,* pp. 67–69.

34. See Vol. 12, no. 2 of European *Concilium* (1976), on Hinduism, Buddhism, Islam, and Christian worship.

Chapter 9

35. Gunther Stephenson, ed., *Der Religionswandel unserer Zeit im Spiegel der Religionswissenschaft* (Darmstadt, 1976). Haralds Biezais, ed., *New Religions* (Stockholm, 1975).

36. Nakamura, *Ways of Thinking,* pp. 350–576; Pirijns, *Japan en het Christendom,* II, pp. 266–272. Edwin O. Reischauer, *The Japanese* (Cambridge: Harvard University Press, 1977).

37. See Part One, Chapter 2, pp. 14–16 in this volume.

38. H. Neill McFarland, *The Rush Hour of the Gods: A Study of New Religious Movements in Japan* (New York: Macmillan, 1967). Werner Kohler, *Die Lotuslehre und die modernen Religionen in Japan* (Zurich, 1962). Harry Thomsen, *The New Religions of Japan* (Westport, Conn.: Greenwood Press, 1978), reprint of 1963 edition. Clark B. Offner and Henry van Straelen, *Modern Japanese Religions: With Special Emphasis upon Their Doctrines of Healing* (Leiden: Brill, 1963). Henry van Straelen, *The Religion of Divine Wisdom: Japan's Most Powerful Religious Movement* (Kyoto, 1957). Rolf Italiaander, ed., *Eine Religion für den Frieden: die Rissho Kosei-kai, japanische Buddhisten für die Okumene der Religionen* (Erlangen, 1973). Pirijns, *Japan en het Christendom,* I, pp. 254–274 and 188–189.

39. Dietrich Wiederkehr, *Glaube an Erlösung: Konzepte der Soteriologie vom Neuen Testament bis heute* (Freiburg-Basel-Vienna, 1976).

40. Kazoh Kitamori, *Theology of the Pain of God* (Tokyo, 1946; Eng. trans., Richmond, Vir.: John Knox Press, 1965). Jung Young Lee, *God Suffers for Us: A Systematic Inquiry into a Concept of Divine Passability* (The Hague, 1974). Kosuke Koyama, *Waterbuffalo Theology* (Maryknoll, N.Y.: Orbis Books, 1974); idem, *No*

Handle on the Cross (Orbis Books, 1977; idem, *Fifty Meditations* (Orbis Books, 1979).

41. Pirijns, *Japan en het Christendom,* II, pp. 306–336. See the following articles in the same issue of *The Japan Missionary Bulletin* 30 (Tokyo, 1976): J. J. Spae, "Not a Japanese Theology but a Theology for Japan," pp. 565–570; Ernest Pirijns, "Towards a Japanese Theology," pp. 571–576; and S. Takayanagi, "Towards a Japanese Christian Theology," pp. 577–582. See also James M. Phillips, *From the Rising of the Sun: Christians and Society in Contemporary Japan* (Maryknoll, N.Y.: Orbis Books in collaboration with the American Society of Missiology, 1981).

Chapter 10

42. Christian R. Gaba, ed. and trans., *Scriptures of an African People* (New York: NOK, 1974). Aylward Shorter, *Prayer in the Religious Traditions of Africa* (New York: Oxford University Press, 1975). John S. Mbiti, *The Prayers of African Religion* (Maryknoll, N.Y.: Orbis Books, 1976). *Studia Missionalia* 24 (Rome, 1975) on "Prayer." Other works anthologize proverbs and the like. See T. Theuws, *De Lubamens* (Tervuren, 1962); idem, *Textes Luba* (Kinshasa, 1954). J. M. Janzen and W. MacGaffey, eds., *An Anthropology of Kongo Religion: Primary Texts from Lower Zaire* (Lawrence, Kans.: Regents Press, 1974). See also *How the Other Third Lives: Third World Stories, Poems, Songs, Prayers, and Essays from Asia, Africa, and Latin America,* comp. and ed. Margaret B. White and Robert N. Quigley (Maryknoll, N.Y.: Orbis Books, 1977).

43. Aylward Shorter, *African Christian Theology: Adaptation or Incarnation?* (Maryknoll, N.Y.: Orbis Books, 1977), p. 39.

44. John V. Taylor, *The Primal Vision: Christian Presence Amid African Religion* (Naperville, Ill.: Allenson, 1963).

45. Shorter, *African Christian Theology,* pp. 38–60 and passim.

46. Ibid., p. 117.

47. Mulago gwa Cikala Musharhamina, *La religion traditionelle des Bantu et leur vision du monde* (Kinshasa, 1973). He incorporates earlier works, such as those of Placide Tempels and Janheinz Jahn. Note the pertinent references in this volume, Part One, Chapter 3, p. 40.

48. R. J. Zwi Werblowsky and C. Jouco Bleeker, eds., *Types of Redemption* (Leiden: Brill, 1970); contributions to the theme of the study-conference held at Jerusalem, July 14–19, 1968. John S. Mbiti has produced several works on these matters: *New Testament Eschatology in an African Background: A Study of the Encounter between New Testament Theology and African Traditional Concepts* (New York: Oxford University Press, 1971); *Concepts of God in Africa* (New York: Praeger, 1970); *African Religions and Philosophy* (New York: Doubleday Anchor, 1970); and the article on "Eschatology," in the anthology edited by Kwesi Dickson and Paul Ellingworth, *Biblical Revelation and African Beliefs* (Maryknoll, N.Y.: Orbis Books, 1971). See also Hans Häselbarth, *Die Auferstehung der Toten in Afrika: Eine theologische Deutung der Todesriten der Mamabolo in Nordtransvaal* (Gütersloh, 1972).

49. A comprehensive study is David B. Barrett, *Schism and Renewal in Africa: An Analysis of Six Thousand Contemporary Religious Movements* (New York: Oxford University Press, 1968); idem, *African Initiatives in Religion* (New York: International Publications Service, 1971).

There are numerous specific studies, so I will indicate only a handful. Marie-Louise

Martin, *Kimbangu: An African Prophet and His Church* (London: Oxford University Press, 1975 and Grand Rapids: Eerdmans, 1976). M. L. Daneel, *Old and New in Southern Shana Independent Churches,* 2 vols. (Hawthorne, N.Y.: Mouton, 1971 and 1975). Gerhardus Cornelis Oosthuizen, *The Theology of a South African Messiah: An Analysis of the Hymnal of the 'Church of the Nazarites'* (Leiden-Cologne, 1967); idem, *Post-Christianity in Africa: A Theological and Anthropological Study* (London: Hurst, 1968); idem, *Theological Battleground in Asia and Africa: The Issues Facing the Churches and the Efforts to Overcome Western Divisions* (London: Hurst, and Atlantic Highlands, N.J.: Humanities Press, 1972). Bengt Sundkler, *Bantu Prophets in South Africa* (New York: Oxford University Press, 1961); idem, *Zulu Zion and Some Swasi Zionists* (New York: Oxford University Press, 1976). Werner Ustorf, *Afrikanische Initiative: das Aktive Leiden des Propheten Simon Kimbangu* (Frankfurt am Main, 1975). Marie-France Perrin Jassy, *Basic Community in the African Churches* (Maryknoll, N.Y.: Orbis Books, 1973), on the Luo.

50. Helmut Aichelin, *Religion: Thema von morgen* (Stuttgart, 1976).

51. See Note 42.

52. On Black Theology in the United States and South Africa we now have several valuable anthologies which bring the subject up to date. James H. Cone and Gayraud S. Wilmore, *Black Theology: A Documentary History, 1966-1979* (Maryknoll, N.Y.: Orbis Books, 1979). Allan Aubrey Boesak, *Farewell to Innocence: A Socio-Ethical Study on Black Theology and Power* (Maryknoll, N.Y.: Orbis Books, 1979). For a recent view of what African theologians are thinking see Kofi Appiah-Kubi and Sergio Torres, eds., *African Theology En Route: Papers from the Pan-African Conference of Third World Theologians, December 17-23, 1977, Accra, Ghana* (Maryknoll, N.Y.: Orbis Books, 1979). For an important recent study in the comparative history of race relations see George M. Frederickson, *White Supremacy: A Comparative Study in American and South African History* (New York: Oxford University Press, 1980). See also Marjorie Hope and James Young, *South African Churches in a Revolutionary Situation* (Maryknoll, N.Y.: Orbis Books, 1981).

53. See above, Note 49.

54. Harry Sawyerr, *God, Ancestor or Creator? Aspects of Traditional Belief in Ghana, Nigeria and Sierra Leone* (Atlantic Highlands, N.J.: Humanities Press, 1970). Bernard Hwang, "Ancestor Cult Today," *Missiology* 5 (1977): 339-365; Hwang cites much of the recent literature on the subject.

55. Mbiti, *African Religions and Philosophy,* pp. 15-28.

56. Aylward Shorter, *African Culture and the Christian Church* (London and Dublin, 1974). Byang H. Kato, *Theological Pitfalls in Africa* (Kisumu, 1975). Adrian Hastings, *African Christianity* (New York: Seabury, 1977). D. J. Bosch, *Het Evangelie in afrikaans gewaad* (Kampen, 1974). V. Neckebrouck, *L'Afrique noire et la crise de l'occident* (Tabora, 1971).

Chapter 11

57. Martin Gerbert, *Religionen in Brasilien* (Berlin, 1970), pp. 47-50. Ernst Benz, "Gebet und Heilung im brasilianischen Spiritismus," in the anthology edited by Gunther Stephenson, *Der Religionswandel unserer Zeit im Spiegel der Religionswissenschaft* (Darmstadt, 1976), pp. 30-36. Ingo Lembke, *Christentum unter den Bedingungen Lateinamerikas* (Bern-Frankfurt am Main, 1975), pp. 61-62 and the bibliography cited there.

58. Rainer Flasche, *Geschichte und Typologie afrikanischer Religiosität in Brasilien* (Marburg an der Lahn, 1973). Gerbert, *Religionen in Brasilien,* pp. 50–60. Benz, "Gebet und Heilung," pp. 37–52. Lindolfo Weingartner, *Umbanda* (Erlangen, 1969). Ulrich Fischer, *Zur Liturgie des Umbandakultes* (Leiden: Brill, 1970). Lembke, *Christentum,* pp. 62–64.

59. Lembke, *Christentum,* pp. 29–32. Gerbert, *Religionen in Brasilien,* pp. 9–20. J. Specker, *Die Missionsmethode in Spanisch-Amerika* (Schöneck-Beckenried, 1953). Pierre Duviols, *La lutte contre les religions autochtones dans le Pérou colonial* (Lima, 1971). Robert Ricard, *The Spiritual Conquest of Mexico* (Los Angeles: University of California Press, 1974).

60. The bibliography on Latin American liberation theology has grown enormously. Two valuable recent anthologies are: Rosino Gibellini, ed., *Frontiers of Theology in Latin America* (Maryknoll, N.Y.: Orbis Books, 1979); Sergio Torres and John Eagleson, eds., *The Challenge of Basic Christian Communities* (Maryknoll, N.Y.: Orbis Books, 1981), major papers from the 1980 São Paulo meeting of the Ecumenical Association of Third World Theologians. See also Noel Leo Erskine, *Decolonizing Theology: A Caribbean Perspective* (Maryknoll, N.Y.: Orbis Books, 1981).

61. Rogier van Rossum and Jan van Engelen, *Kerk op zoek naar haar volk* (Baarn, 1976). In addition to the titles listed in Note 60, see also Joseph C. Healey, *A Fifth Gospel: The Experience of Black Christian Values* (Maryknoll, N.Y.: Orbis Books, 1981).

62. José Comblin, "Prolegômenos da catequese no Brasil," *Revista Eclesiastica Brasiliera* 27 (1967): 845–874. José Míguez Bonino, "De volksvroomheid in Latijns Amerika," in vol. 10, no. 10 of European *Concilium* (1974), pp. 147–157. Philippe Ariès et al., eds., *Religion populaire et réforme liturgique* (Paris, 1975).

63. Leonardo Boff, *Teología do cativeiro e da libertação* (Lisbon: Multanova, 1976; 2nd ed., Petropolis: Vozes, 1980); idem, *Way of the Cross—Way of Justice,* Eng. trans. (Maryknoll, N.Y.: Orbis Books, 1980).

Chapter 12

64. See various articles in the anthology edited by Wolfgang Franke, *China Handbuch* (Düsseldorf, 1974). On this point see E. Wilkensen, "Unterpriviligierte," *China Handbuch,* cols. 1439–1440.

65. R. P. Kramers, "Konfuzianismus," ibid., cols. 656–668.

66. R. Machetzki, "Exterritorialität," ibid., cols. 334–338.

67. R. Machetzki, "Konzessionen und Niederlassungen," ibid., cols. 676–682. Hyobom Pak, *China and the West: Myths and Realities in History* (Leiden: Brill, 1974).

68. R. Machetzki, "Pachtgebiete," *China Handbuch,* cols. 1005–1008.

69. Alphonse Favier, *Péking: histoire et description* (Tournai, 1900), p. 269.

70. Johannes Beckmann, *Die Katholische Missionsmethode in China in neuester Zeit (1842-1912): Geschichtliche Untersuchung über Arbeitsweisen, ihre Hindernisse und Erfolge* (Immensee, 1931). Johannes Schütte, *Die katholische Chinamission im Spiegel der Rotchinesischen Presse: Versuch einer missionarischen Deutung* (Münster in Westfalen, 1957). Donald W. Treadgold, *The West in Russia and China: Religious and Secular Thought in Modern Times*, 2 vols. Volume 2: *China: 1582-1949* (New York: Cambridge University Press, 1973). J. J. A. M. Kuepers, *China und die katholische Mission in Süd-Shantung, 1882-1900: Die Geschiehte einer Konfrontation* (Steyl, 1974). Fritz Bornemann, *Der selige P. J.*

Freinademetz, 1852–1908: Ein Steyler China-Missionar (Bozen, 1972). John K. Fairbank, ed., *The Missionary Enterprise in China and America* (Cambridge, Mass.: Harvard University Press, 1974). Kenneth Scott Latourette, *A History of the Expansion of Christianity* (Grand Rapids: Zondervan, 1971), 7 volumes: Volume 6: *The Great Century in Northern Africa and Asia, A.D. 1800–A.D. 1914,* pp. 253–269: Volume 7. *Advance Through Storm, A.D. 1914 and After,* pp. 328–378. John Eagleson and Thomas Fenton, eds., *China Pac* (Maryknoll, N.Y.: Orbis Books and New York: Friendship Press, 1971). Ralph R. Covell, "God's Providence or Fatalism in China?" *Missiology* 5 (1977): 321–337.

71. Wallace C. Mervin and Francis P. Jones, eds., *Documents of the Three-Self-Movement* (New York: Far Eastern Office, Division of Foreign Missions, National Council of Churches of Christ in the U.S.A., 1963). V. Hayward, *Christians and China* (Belfast, 1974). Richard C. Bush, Jr., *Religion in Communist China* (Nashville: Abingdon, 1970). Niels-Peter Moritzen and Bernward H. Willeke, eds., *China: Herausforderung an die Kirchen* (Erlangen, 1974). Jonathan T'ien-en Chao, "The Christian Mission to the Chinese People, As Viewed from the Development of the Chinese Church 1949–1976," *Missiology* 5 (1977): 367–385.

72. Han Suyin, *Wind in the Tower: Mao Tse-Tung and the Chinese Revolution, 1949–1975* (Boston: Little, Brown, 1976). Adrian Hsia, *The Chinese Cultural Revolution* (New York: Seabury, 1972). Bill Brugger, *Contemporary China: An Introductory History* (Scranton, Pa.: Barnes & Noble, 1977). Jürgen Domes, *The Internal Politics of China: 1949–1972,* Eng. trans. (New York: Praeger, 1973); idem, *China nach der Kulturrevolution* (Munich, 1975). D. van der Horst, *Geschiedenis van China* (Utrecht and Antwerp, 1977). Raymond Whitehead, *Love and Struggle in Mao's Thought* (Maryknoll, N.Y.: Orbis Books, 1977). Al Imfeld, *China as a Model of Development* (Maryknoll, N.Y.: Orbis Books, 1976).

73. Donald E. MacInnes, "New Man and New Society in People's China," in *Christianity and the New China,* 2 vols. (South Pasadena: Lutheran World Federation/Pro Mundi Vita, 1976), I, pp. 135–152. See below Note 83.

74. Mao Tse-Tung, *Gedichten,* Dutch translation by Roger Andries (Brugge and Utrecht, 1972), p. 41.

75. Ibid., p. 45.

76. Ibid., p. 51.

77. Ibid., p. 73.

78. Ibid., p. 87.

79. Ibid., p. 89. The "master" is Confucius.

80. Ibid., p. 97. For another translation see the work cited below, Note 81, p. 18.

81. Mao Tse-Tung, *De Dubbele Negen,* Dutch translation by Theun de Vries (Utrecht, 1977), p. 10. The Double Nine is an old holiday on the Chinese calendar.

82. Ibid., p. 16.

83. *Christianity and the New China* (South Pasadena: Lutheran World Federation/Pro Mundi Vita, 1976), 2 vols. These are papers and reports from two Ecumenical Colloquiums. Volume I: *Theological Implications of the New China,* papers from the ecumenical seminar held in Badstad, Sweden from January 29 to February 2, 1974. Volumé II: *Christian Faith and the Chinese Experience,* papers from the ecumenical colloquium held in Louvain, Belgium, from September 9 to 14, 1976. Michael Chu, ed., *The New China: A Catholic Response* (New York: Paulist Press, 1977). For up-to-date information one can read the LWF Information Letter on Marxism and China study that is published from Geneva several times a year. Claude Aubert et al., *Regards froids sur la China* (Paris, 1976). *China and the Churches in the Making of One*

World, Pro Mundi Vita, No. 55 (Brussels, 1955). Arne Sovik, ed., *China and Christian Mission* (Geneva, 1977). James Whitehead et al., eds., *China and Christianity: Historical and Future Encounters* (Notre Dame, Ind.: University of Notre Dame Press, 1979).

84. Werner Schilling, "Das Rätsel der ökumenischen Mao-Begeisterung," in the anthology edited by Walter Künneth and Peter Beyerhaus, *Reich Gottes oder Weltgemeinschaft?* (Bad Liebenzell, 1975), pp. 141-158. J. A. E. Vermaat, "Love China '75: Evangelische bezinning op China," *Wereld en Zending* 5 (Amsterdam, 1976): 204-213; Vermaat deals with the Love China Conference held in Manila from September 7 to 11, 1975, in which 420 Evangelical Christians from 19 countries participated. Also see Werner Schilling, *Das Heil in Rot-China? Der 'neue Mensch' im Maoismus und im Christentum* (Bad Liebenzell, 1975).

85. Julia Chang, "The New China: A Dialectical Response," in Michael Chu, ed., *The New China: A Catholic Response,* pp. 3-24. Various papers in *Christianity and the New China* (see above Note 83) also deal with this problem.

Chapter 13

86. Dietrich Wiederkehr, *Glaube an Erlösung,* pp. 123-135 (see above Note 39). Francis A. Sullivan, "Theological Implications of the 'New China,' " in Michael Chu, ed., *The New China,* pp. 146-164. Horst Rzepkowski, *Der Welt verpflichtet* (Sankt Augustin, 1976).

87. A. Camps, "Een bezinning voor 'doeners' op het gebied van de ontwikkelingshulp," in *Een lopende rekening: Kerk en Ontwikkeling in de derde wereld* (Tilburg, 1976), pp. 94-106.

88. A. Camps, "Dialog der Religionen und Entwicklung: die maieutische Methode," *Zeitschrift für Missionswissenschaft und Religionswissenschaft* 56 (Münster in Westfalen, 1972): 1-9. Idem., "Four Key-Notions for a More Empirical Missiology," *The Japan Missionary Bulletin* 27 (Tokyo, 1973): 583-592.

89. A. Camps, "De volgelingen van de weg en de wegen," *Tijdschrift voor Verkondiging* 49 (Maastricht, 1977): 312-315.

PART THREE
NO DEAD-END WAY:
LOCAL CHURCHES IN DIALOGUE
WITH THEIR SURROUNDINGS

Chapter 14

1. Leonardo Boff, *Eclesiogênese: as comunidades eclesiais de base reinventam a Igreja* (Petropolis: Vozes, 1977), p. 32: "A Igreja particular é a Igreja toda mas não toda a Igreja."

2. Boff, *Eclesiogênese,* pp. 21-37. Also see Paul VI, Exhortation entitled *Evangelii nuntiandi.* Choan-Seng Song, *Christian Mission in Reconstruction: An Asian Analysis* (Maryknoll, N.Y.: Orbis Books, 1977). Jürgen Moltmann, *The Passion for Life: A Messianic Lifestyle*, Eng. trans. (Philadelphia: Fortress, 1978).

3. Boff, *Eclesiogênese,* pp. 21-37.

4. "Kerkelijke basis-gemeenschappen," *Pro Mundi Vita*, Cahier 62 (Brussels, 1976), p. 4.

5. Roland Allen, *Missionary Methods: St. Paul's or Ours?* (Grand Rapids: Eerdmans, 1962). Hans Wolfgang Metzner, *Roland Allen: sein Leben und Werk* (Gütersloh, 1970). Walbert Bühlmann, *The Coming of the Third Church*, Eng. trans. (Maryknoll, N.Y.: Orbis Books, 1977). Karl Rahner, *Grundkurs des Glaubens* (Freiburg, 1976). Eng. *Foundations of Christian Faith: An Introduction to the Idea of Christianity*, trans. William A. Dych (New York: Seabury, 1978), pp. 326–33.

6. "Kerkelijke basis-gemeenschappen," p. 2.

7. Ibid., p. 3. See also *Pro Mundi Vita*, Cahier 41 (Brussels, 1972), pp. 8–16. J. Masson, "Problémes pastoraux des grandes villes africaines," *Nouvelle Revue Théologique* 110 (Louvain, 1978): 36–90.

8. Bühlmann, *The Coming of the Third Church*, Chapter 19. José Comblin, "De basis-gemeenschappen als plaats van nieuwe ervaringen," vol. 11, no. 4 of European *Concilium* (1975): 71–80.

9. "Kerkelijke basis-gemeenschappen," pp. 3–4.

10. Stephen B. Clark, *Building Christian Communities: Strategy for Renewing the Church* (Notre Dame, Ind.: Ave Maria Press, 1972), p. 19. For more recent developments in Latin America see the papers of the International Ecumenical Congress of Theology, held in São Paulo, Brazil, February 20 to March 2, 1980: Sergio Torres and John Eagleson, eds., *The Challenge of Basic Christian Communities* (Maryknoll, N.Y.: Orbis Books, 1981).

11. See Boff, *Eclesiogênese*, pp. 51–72. Hans Küng, *On Being a Christian*, Eng. trans. (New York: Doubleday, 1976). Karl Lehmann, "Perspectieven van de nieuwe theologie inzake kerkgemeenten," *Communio* 2 (Gentbrugge, 1977): 92–110. Dominique Barbé, *Demain, les communautés de base* (Paris, 1970).

Chapter 15

12. For example: Jesus Andres Vela, *Las comunidades de base y una iglesia nueva* (Buenos Aires, 1970), and Alvaro Barreiro, S.J., *Basic Ecclesial Communities and Evangelization of the Poor*, trans. Barbara Campbell (Maryknoll, N.Y.: Orbis Books, 1982).

13. "Kerkelijke basis-gemeenschappen," p. 7.

14. Ibid.

15. Vela, *Las comunidades de base*. José Marins, *La decada del 70* (Buenos Aires, 1970). For an informative historical overview of recent trends in Latin America see Phillip E. Berryman, "Latin American Liberation Theology," in Sergio Torres and John Eagleson, eds., *Theology in the Americas* (Maryknoll, N.Y.: Orbis Books, 1976), pp. 20–83.

16. Cyril W. Meijers, "Zending tot bevrijding," in *Naar een andere kerk?* (Amersfoort, 1974), pp. 52–55. The volume compiles testimony from Churches in the Third World.

17. "Kerkelijke basis-gemeenschappen," p. 13. José Marins, "Kerkelijke basis-gemeenschappen in Latijns Amerika," in vol. 11, no. 2, of European *Concilium* (1975), p. 26.

18. Barbé, *Demain, les communautés de base* (Paris, 1970).

19. See Part Two, Chapter 11, in this volume.

20. Marins, "Kerkelijke basis-gemeenschappen in Latijns Amerika," pp. 27–28.

21. Patrick Kalilombe, Pastoral Letter entitled *Christ's Church in Lilongwe: Today—Tomorrow* (Likuni, 1973).

22. Ibid., pp. 13–14.

23. Ibid., p. 16.

24. See Part One, Chapter 3, pp. 40–41 in this volume. Willy De Craemer, *The Jamaa and the Church: A Bantu Catholic Movement in Zaire* (New York: Oxford University Press, 1977). A. J. Smet, "Le père Placide Tempels et son oeuvre publiée," *Revue Africaine de Théologie* 1 (Kinshasa, 1977): 77–128.

25. Marie-France Perrin Jassy, *Forming Christian Communities: An Evaluation of Experiments in North Mara, Tanzania* (Kampala, n.d.); idem, *Basic Community in the African Churches* (Maryknoll, N.Y.: Orbis Books, 1973). For an overview of Ujamaa in Tanzania see John R. Civille and William R. Duggan, *Tanzania and Nyerere: A Study of Ujamaa and Nationalism* (Maryknoll, N.Y.: Orbis Books, 1978).

26. "De petites communautés chrétiennes à visage humain," *La Documentation Catholique* 59 (Paris, 1977): 919–920.

27. A. Camps, "New Ways of Realizing a Christian Togetherness in Non-Western Countries: A Missiologist's Contribution," *Internationales Jahrbuch für Religions-soziologie* 5 (Cologne-Opladen, 1969): 182–194.

28. Robin H. S. Boyd, *India and the Latin Captivity of the Church: The Cultural Context of the Gospel* (London: Cambridge University Press, 1974).

29. Justinian Cherupallikat, *Witness Potential of Evangelical Poverty in India* (Immensee, 1975), pp. 131–136. There is a growing literature on Mother Teresa of Calcutta. See, for example: Desmond Doig, *Mother Teresa: Her Work and Her People* (New York: Harper & Row, 1976); Malcolm Muggeridge, *Something Beautiful for God: Mother Teresa of Calcutta* (New York: Doubleday, 1977).

30. Cherupallikat, *Witness Potential*, pp. 136–137.

31. Abhishiktananda, *Saccidananda: A Christian Approach to Advaitic Experience* (Delhi, 1974), pp. 61–73.

32. Friso Melzer, *Christliche Ashrams in Südindien* (Erlangen, 1976). Ludger Franz Maria van Bergen, *Licht op het leven van religieuzen: sannya-sadipika* (Nijmegen, 1975), pp. 213–245. Richard W. Taylor, "From Khadi to Kavi: Toward A Typology of Christian Ashrams," *Religion and Society* (Bangalore, 1977), pp. 19–37. See also Bede Griffiths, *Christian Ashram* (London: Darton, Longman and Todd, 1966) and *Christ in India: Essays toward a Hindu-Christian Dialogue* (New York: Scribner's, 1966).

33. Camps, "New Ways of Realizing a Christian Togetherness."

Chapter 16

34. D. S. Amalorpavadass, ed., *Ministries in the Church in India: Research Seminar and Pastoral Consultation* (New Delhi, 1976). Also see the whole issue no. 9 of *Vidyajyoti* 40 (New Delhi, 1976).

35. FABC Papers, no. 3: *Conclusions of the Asian Colloquium on Ministries in the Church* (Hong Kong, 1977). Also see *The Japan Missionary Bulletin* 32 (Tokyo, 1978): 43–66. J. Dupuis, "Ministries in the Church: An Asian Colloquium," *Vidyajyoti* 41 (New Delhi, 1977): 242–260, and conclusions on pp. 279–289. For Japan see R. Renson, "Ministries in a Living Church," *The Japan Missionary Bulletin* 32 (Tokyo, 1978): 67–70, 130–133, and 196–200. Pro Mundi Vita, *Ministries and Communities,* no. 15 (Brussels, January 1978), pp. 2–8; "Nieuwe ambtsvormen in christelijke gemeenschappen," *Pro Mundi Vita,* Cahier 50 (Brussels, 1974).

36. Pro Mundi Vita, *Ministries and Communities,* no. 7 (January 1976), pp. 1–8; and no. 5 (June 1975), p. 15.

37. Pro Mundi Vita, *Ministries and Communities,* no. 5 (Brussels, June 1975), pp.

1-10. Oswald Hirmer, *Die Funktion des Laien in den katholischen Gemeinden: Untersuchungen in der afrikanischen Mission* (Münsterschwarzach, 1973). Adrian Hastings, *Mission and Ministry* (New York: Sheed & Ward, 1972); idem, *African Christianity* (New York: Seabury Press, 1977); idem, *The Faces of God: Reflections on Church and Society* (Maryknoll, N.Y.: Orbis Books, 1976). Paul M. Miller, *Equipping for Ministry in East Africa* (Scottdale, Pa.: Herald Press, 1969). Aylward Shorter and Eugene Kataza, eds., *Missionaries to Yourselves: African Catechists Today* (Maryknoll, N.Y.: Orbis Books, 1972). "La question des ministères en Afrique," *Spiritus* 18 (Paris, 1977): 339–350. Jean-Marc Ela, "Ecclesial Ministry and the Problems of the Young Churches," *The Churches of Africa: Future Prospects*, ed. Claude Geffré and Bertrand Luneau, *Concilium* 106 (New York: Seabury, 1977), pp. 45–52. H. Häring, *Anerkennen wir die Ämter* (Einsieden-Zurich-Cologne, 1974).

38. "Ministros y ministerios en America Latina," *Informes de Pro Mundi Vita America Latina* 1 (Brussels, 1977). For Brazil see Pro Mundi Vita, *Ministries and Communities*, no. 6 (Brussels, October 1975), pp. 11–15. José Comblin, *O futuro dos ministérios na igreja latino-americana* (Petropolis: Vozes, 1969); idem, *The Meaning of Mission*, Eng. trans. (Maryknoll, N.Y.: Orbis Books, 1977). William R. Burrows, *New Ministries: The Global Context* (Maryknoll, N.Y.: Orbis Books, 1980).

Chapter 17

39. S. DeSmet, "De Zaïrese liturgie: een jonge kerk in Afrika op zoek naar zijn eigen liturgische vormen," *Tijdschrift voor Liturgie* 60 (Maastricht, 1976): 285–307. DeSmet cites much of the pertinent literature.

40. *New Order of the Mass for India* (Bangalore, 1974).

41. J. A. G. van Leeuwen, "De lange weg van een liturgievernieuwing: een overzicht van de liturgische ontwikkelingen in India sinds Vaticanum II," *Communio* 2 (Gentbrugge, 1977): 475. J. van Lin, "Op zoek naar een eigen eredienst: Rooms-katholieke kerk in India," *Wereld en Zending* 6 (Amsterdam, 1977): 26–38. G. van Leeuwen, *Worship in Youth's Idiom* (Bangalore, 1971). J. Masson, "Problèmes pastoraux majeurs dans la chrétienté indienne aujourd'hui," *Nouvelle Revue Théologique* 110 (Louvain, 1978): 418–425.

Chapter 18

42. Douglas J. Elwood, ed., *What Asian Christians Are Thinking: A Theological Source Book* (Quezon City: New Day, 1976). Revised edition: *Asian Christian Theology, Emerging Themes* (Philadelphia: Westminster, 1980). "Third World Theologies," *Mission Trends No. 3*. ed. Gerald Anderson and Thomas Stransky (New York: Paulist Press, 1976). Gerald H. Anderson, ed., *Asian Voices in Christian Theology* (Maryknoll, N.Y.: Orbis Books, 1976). Sergio Torres and Virginia Fabella, eds., *The Emergent Gospel: Theology From the Underside of History* (Maryknoll, N.Y.: Orbis Books, 1978). Virginia Fabella, ed., *Asia's Struggle for Full Humanity* (Maryknoll, N.Y.: Orbis Books, 1980). Choan-Seng Song, *Third-Eye Theology: Theology in Formation in Asian Settings* (Maryknoll, N.Y.: Orbis Books, 1979). Noel Leo Erskine, *Decolonizing Theology: A Caribbean Perspective* (Maryknoll, N.Y.: Orbis Books, 1981).

43. The proceedings of these conferences have been edited by Sergio Torres and others, and published in English by Orbis Books (Maryknoll, New York 10545). See

Notes 10 and 42 for sample titles. The fifth conference, "The Irruption of the Third World: A Challenge to Theology," was held in New Delhi, August 17–19, 1981, the proceedings of which will also be published by Orbis Books.

44. L. F. M. van Bergen, "Eine Indische Christologie," in the anthology edited by Heribert Bettscheider, *Das asiatische Gesicht Christi* (Sankt Augustin, 1976), pp. 35–47; there is an extensive bibliography on pp. 90–94. Arnulf Camps, "The Person and Function of Christ in Hinduism and in Hindu-Christian Theology," *Bulletin of the Secretariat for Non-Christians* 6 (1971): 199–211. Eric Sharpe, *Faith Meets Faith: Some Christian Attitudes to Hinduism in the Nineteenth and Twentieth Centuries* (Naperville, Ill.: Allenson, 1977). Swami Satprakashananda, *Hinduism and Christianity: Jesus Christ and His Teachings in the Light of Vedanta* (St. Louis: Vedanta Society, 1975). George Rupp, *Christologies and Cultures: Toward a Typology of Religious Worldviews* (Hawthorne, N.Y.: Mouton, 1974). Wilfred Cantwell Smith, *Towards A World Theology* (London: Macmillan, 1981).

45. Kazoh Kitamori, *Theology of the Pain of God* (Tokyo, 1946, Atlanta: John Knox Press, 1965). For commentaries see: Horst Rzepkowski, "Zur 'Theologie des Schmerzens Gottes' von Kazoh Kitamori," *Theologia Mundi* (Munich, 1975), pp. 31–44, with much bibliographical data; Katsumi Takizawa, "Über 'die Theologie des Schmerzens Gottes' von Kazoh Kitamori," ibid., pp. 45–58. Werner Kohler, "Japanische christologische Versuche," in the anthology cited above in Note 44, *Das asiatische Gesicht Christi*, pp. 49–67. Yagi Seiichi and Ulrich Luz, eds., *Gott in Japan: Anstösse zum Gespräch mit japanischen Philosophen, Theologen, Schriftstellern* (Munich: Chr. Kaiser, 1973). Jung Young Lee, *God Suffers for Us: A Systematic Inquiry into a Concept of Divine Passibility* (The Hague, 1974). Kosuke Koyama, *No Handle on the Cross: An Asian Meditation on the Crucified Mind* (Maryknoll, N.Y.: Orbis Books, 1977). For another Asian perspective see Kim Chi Ha, *The Gold-Crowned Jesus and Other Writings* (Maryknoll, N.Y.: Orbis Books, 1978).

46. Tissa Balasuriya, *Jesus Christ and Human Liberation* (Colombo, 1976); idem, *The Eucharist and Human Liberation* (Maryknoll, N.Y.: Orbis Books, 1979).

47. See the article by Manas Buthelezi in Basil Moore, ed., *Black Theology: The South African Voice*, (London: Hurst, 1973), pp. 93–103; also under the title *The Challenge of Black Theology in South Africa* (Richmond, Va.: John Knox Press, 1974); Wilhelm Dantine, *Schwarze Theologie: eine Herausforderung der Theologie der Weissen?* (Vienna-Freiburg-Basel, 1976). Allan A. Boesak, *Farewell to Innocence: A Socio-Ethical Study on Black Theology and Power* (Maryknoll, N.Y.: Orbis Books, 1976). Hans-Jürgen Becken, "Schwarze Theologie in Afrika," *Theologia Mundi* (Munich, 1975), pp. 73–83, with an extensive bibliography. James H. Cone and Gayraud S. Wilmore, *Black Theology: A Documentary History, 1966-1979* (Maryknoll, N.Y.: Orbis Books, 1979). Marjorie Hope and James Young, *The South African Churches in a Revolutionary Situation* (Maryknoll, N.Y.: Orbis Books, 1981).

48. Jon Sobrino, *Christology at the Crossroads: A Latin-American Approach*, trans. John Drury (Maryknoll, N.Y.: Orbis Books, 1978), p. xxiv, in the Preface to the English edition.

49. Ibid., pp. xxiv–xxv.

50. Sobrino, *Christology at the Crossroads*. Ivo Lorscheider, "Die Theologie der Befreiung," *Theologia Mundi* (Munich, 1975), pp. 59–71. Rosino Gibellini, ed., *Frontiers of Theology in Latin America*, trans. John Drury (Maryknoll, N.Y.: Orbis Books, 1978). Hans Schöpfer, *Theologie der Gesellschaft: Interdisziplinäre Grundla-*

genbibliographie zur Einführung in die befreiungs-und polittheologische Problematik, 1960–1975 (Bern-Frankfurt am Main-Las Vegas, 1977). For two sympathetic but critical studies of liberation theology from different perspectives see: Alfredo Fierro, *The Militant Gospel: A Critical Introduction to Political Theologies* (Maryknoll, N.Y.: Orbis Books, 1977); Dennis P. McCann, *Christian Realism and Liberation Theology: Practical Theologies in Creative Conflict* (Maryknoll, N.Y.: Orbis Books, 1981).

Chapter 19

51. The most basic work by Paulo Freire is *La concientización* (Caracas, 1970); for an English translation see the May and August 1970 issues of the *Harvard Educational Review* (Cambridge, Massachusetts); idem, *Pedagogy of the Oppressed*, Eng. trans. (New York: Seabury, 1970); idem, *Education for Critical Consciousness*, Eng. trans. (London, 1974): this contains two earlier works from Brazil and Chile. INODEP, *El mensaje de Paulo Freire: teoría y practica de la liberación* (Madrid, 1972). Denis E. Collins, *Paulo Freire: His Life, Works and Thought* (New York: Paulist Press, 1977). Alistair Kee, ed., *A Reader in Political Theology* (Philadelphia: Westminster Press, 1975); idem, ed., *The Scope of Political Theology* (Naperville, Ill.: Allenson, 1978).

52. Gerald A. Arbuckle, "Inter-Ethnic Prejudice: A Programme for Pastoral Conscientization," *Teaching All Nations* 15 (Manila, 1978): 68–77.

53. Lo Schröder, "De gezondheidszorg heeft op het verkeerde paard gewed," *ID-Information Service* (Tilburg, June 1978, no. 6), pp. 1–4. Wolfgang Erk and Martin Scheel, eds., *Ärtzlicher Dienst weltweit* (Stuttgart, 1974). *Medicus Mundi*, Documentation of the General Assembly, Amsterdam, May 20–22, 1977 (Aachen, 1977). Kevin M. Cahill, ed., *Medicine and Diplomacy: The Untapped Resource* (Maryknoll, N.Y.: Orbis Books, 1977); idem, *Health and Development* (Maryknoll, N.Y.: Orbis Books, 1976).

54. M. M. Thomas, *The Secular Ideologies of India and the Secular Meaning of Christ* (Bangalore-Madras, 1976), pp. 35–84; idem, *Religion and Development in Asia: A Sociological Approach with Christian Reflection* (Baguio, 1976). Robert F. Spencer, ed., *Religion and Change in Contemporary Asia* (Minneapolis: University of Minnesota Press, 1971). Robert N. Bellah, *Religion and Progress in Modern Asia* (New York: Free Press, 1968). *Religion and Development in Asian Societies* (Colombo, 1974). *Journal of Dharma* 3 (Bangalore, 1978), no. 1.

55. Jan Heijke, "Ziekte in Afrika meer dan motorpech aan het lichaam," *ID-Information Service* (Tilburg, June 1978, no. 6), pp. 4–7. John G. Strelan, *Search for Salvation: Studies in the History and Theology of Cargo Cults* (Adelaide, 1977). "The Church and Adjustment Movements," *Point* 1 (Port Moresby, 1974): 1–216.

56. Pedro Arrupe, "A New Service to the World of Today," *Teaching All Nations* 15 (Manila, 1978): 91–100. L. Zinke, ed., *Religionen am Rande der Gesellschaft: Jugend in der Sog neuer Heilsversprechungen* (Munich, 1977). S. Senge and A. Wienand, *Ist der Heutige Jugend noch religiös ansprechbar?* (Cologne, 1977). Harvey Cox, *Turning East: The Promise and the Peril of the New Orientalism* (New York: Simon and Schuster, 1977). R. Kranenborg, *Zelfverwerkelijking: oosterse religies binnen een westerse subcultuur* (Kampen, 1978). E. F. Schumacher, *Small is Beautiful* (New York: Harper & Row, 1973); idem, *A Guide for the Perplexed* (New York: Harper & Row, 1977).

Chapter 20

57. The best studies of Robert de Nobili are S. Rajamanickam, *The First Oriental Scholar* (Tirunelveli, 1972); Peter R. Bachmann, *Roberto Nobili 1577-1656: Ein Missionsgeschichtlicher Beitrag zum christlichen Dialog mit Hinduismus* (Rome, 1972). Among other treatments of Matteo Ricci see: Johannes Bettray, *Die Akkommodationsmethode des P. Matteo Ricci S.I. in China* (Rome, 1955); Henri Bernard, *Matteo Ricci's Scientific Contribution to China*, Eng. trans. 1935, reprinted (Westport, Conn.: Hyperion Press, 1973).

58. André Seumois, *Théologie missionnaire*, 4 vols. (Rome, 1973-1978).

59. John Berchmans, "The New Testament Vision of Ecclesial Unity," *Jeevadhara* 7 (Kottayam, 1977): 277-292.

60. *Communio* 2 (Gentbrugge, 1977), no. 2.

61. E. Jansen Schoonhoven, *Wederkerige assistentie van kerken in missionair perspectief*, synopsis and evaluation of a study project undertaken by the Inter-University Institute for Missiology and the missiology department of Oecumenica from 1970 to 1976 (Leiden, 1977). F. J. Verstraelen, *An African Church in Transition: From Missionary Dependence to Mutuality in Mission*, 2 vols. (Tilburg and Leiden, 1975); it is a case study of the Roman Catholic Church in Zambia.

Index

Abbott, Walter M., S.J., 233
Abdul Hakim, Khalifa, 6
Abeysekere, O.L., 235
Abhishiktananda, Swami (Henri Le Saux), 97, 243, 251
Abraham, 31, 51, 85
Achaia, church in, 161
Achterhuis, H., 234
Adam, 31, 33, 88, 105
adaptation, 75, 97. *See also* theology of adaptation
Ad Gentes, 43, 160
African Apostolic Church, 67
African Congregational Church, 67
African independent churches, 122
African religions, 11, 77. *See also* Bantu
agnosticism, contemporary, 179
Ahrens, H., 243
Aichelin, Helmut, 246
Aiken, C. F., 239
alienation, 79, 212
Allen, Roland, 250
Althaus, Paul, 22
Amalorpavadass, D. S., 194, 196, 240, 251
Anabaptists, 43
ancestors: in African worldview and liturgy, 187-88; in Bantu religious life, 115-16, 117-24, 154; in Chinese culture, 147; in Latin American folk religion, 126, 127, 130, 132; in Shona culture, 68
Anderson, Gerald H., 241, 242, 252
Andries, Roger, 248
angelology, 122
anonymous Christianity. *See* Rahner, Karl, on anonymous Christianity
Antes, Peter, 241
Antioch, church in, 161
Appasamy, A. J., 44
Appiah-Kubi, Kofi, 246
Aquinas, Saint Thomas, 211
Arbuckle, Gerald A., 254
Argentina, 126
Ariés, Philippe, 247
Arkoun, Mohammed, 62
arms race, 14. *See also* war
Arrupe, Pedro, 225, 254
Asian Colloquium (1977), 179, 180
atheism, 49-50, 56, 79, 100
Athenagoras, 35
atom bomb, 20
Aubert, Claude, 248
Augustine, Saint, 36, 191
Aupiais, Father, 40
Aurobindo, Sri, 78
Australia, 174, 217
Austria, 137
authority, papal, 163
Bachmann, Peter R., 255
Bahaists, 14
Balasuriya, Tissa, 206, 209, 210, 215, 253
Balic, Smail, 88
Bantu, 40-41, 210; community among, 118-19; and dialogue with Christianity, 121-24; marriage

among, 116, 123; oral tradition of, 114-15; religious outlook of, 84, 114-24
baptism: of desire, 38; in liturgy of Zaire, 192; salvation through, 36-37, 207, 211
Barbé, Dominique, 169, 250
Barreiro, Alvaro, S.J., 250
Barrett, David B., 240, 245
Barrett, Paul, 243
Barrows, J. H., 243
Barth, Karl, 12, 24, 47, 51, 80, 81, 203
Bascour, H., 237
Basetti-Sani, Giulio, 242
basic ecclesial communities, 157-58, 160–76, 231-32; in Africa, 172-74, 182-83; in Asia, 174-76, 177-81; in Brazil, 169; catechesis among, 132; in Guatemala, 169; 169; in Honduras, 169; laity in, 170-74; in Latin America, 168-72, 183-85; of religious, 227; in Tanzania, 173; Vatican II and, 160, 228; in Zaire, 173
Bechert, Heinz, 243
Becken, Hans-Jürgen, 253
Beckmann, Johannes, 247
Belgium, 16, 137
Bellah, Robert N., 254
Bellarmine, Saint Robert, 37
Benz, Ernst, 236, 246, 247
Berchmans, John, 255
van Bergen, Ludger Franz Maria, 242, 243, 251, 253
Berkhof, Hendrik, 49, 51, 239
Berlin Declaration, 134, 148
Bernard, Henri, 255
Berryman, Phillip E., 250
Bertholet, C. J. L., 234
Bettray, Johannes, 255
Bettscheider, Heribert, 242, 253
Beyerhaus, Peter, 30, 134-35, 236, 249
Bhave, Vinoba, 223
birth control, 163-64, 180, 219
Bishop, D. H., 235
bishops. *See* hierarchy
blacks, 13, 210-12. *See also* theology, black
Blauw, J., 237
Bleeker, C. Jouco, 28, 236, 245
Bloch-Hoell, Nils E., 239
Boeke, R., 235
Boesak, Allan Aubrey, 246, 253
Boff, Leonardo, 159, 164, 166, 247, 249, 250
Bornemann, Fritz, 247
Borremans, M., 241
Bosch, David J., 210, 246
Bose, Subhas Chandra, 220
Boublik, Vladimer, 239
Bourke, David, 238
Boventer, H., 241
Boyd, Robin H. S., 238, 243, 251
van Bragt, J., 244
Brauer, J. C., 239
Braybrooke, Marcus, 235
Brazil, 127, 128, 132, 183, 184
Bread for the World, 7
British East India Company, 138. *See also* colonialism; England

257